On the Edge, above the Vale

Collection Management Facility, Science and Innovation Park
Swindon, Wiltshire: archaeological excavations 2018–2020

On the Edge, above the Vale

Collection Management Facility, Science and Innovation Park
Swindon, Wiltshire: archaeological excavations 2018–2020

by Jonathan Hart, Clare Randall and Alistair J. Barclay

with contributions by Pete Banks, Claire Collier-Jones, Dana Challinor
Sharon Clough, David Dungworth, Julie Dunne, Richard Evershed
Toby Gillard, Derek Hamilton, Matilda Holmes, E. R. McSloy, Ruth Shaffrey
Jacky Sommerville and Sarah F. Wyles

Illustrations by Ryan Wilson, Helena Munoz-Mojado, Krissy Moore
Aleksandra Osinska and Li Sou

Cotswold Archaeology Monograph No. 23
Cirencester 2024

Cotswold Archaeology Monograph No. 23

Published by Cotswold Archaeology
Copyright © Cotswold Archaeology 2024
Building 11, Kemble Enterprise Park, Cirencester, Gloucestershire, GL7 6BQ

ISBN 978-1-917215-02-2

British Library Cataloguing in Publication Data
A catalogue record of this book is available from the British Library

The mapping in Figures 1.1, 1.5, 6.1 and 6.2 contains OS data © Crown copyright 2024.

Front cover: Iron Age settlement and pit alignments © Aerial-Cam Ltd
Back cover: The site with Barbury Castle on the horizon; excavation of an Iron Age burial; and a Roman brooch

Cover design by Ryan Wilson
Typeset and design by Kenneth Lymer
Edited by Philippa Bradley

Contents

List of Figures

List of Tables

Acknowledgements

The archaeological fieldwork and subsequent post-excavation project was commissioned and funded by Science Museum Group for which we appreciate the support of Gilly Cross, Suzanne Gough, Matt Moore, Pete Rom and Sian Williams, as well as Daniel Holford and his colleagues of Feasibility Ltd. Melanie Pomeroy-Kellinger (Wiltshire Council) is thanked for her advice throughout the course of the fieldwork and post-excavation work along with Tim Havard (previously of CA), and Donald Sutherland (Pegasus Group) is thanked for his advice and comments on aspects of the overall project at an earlier stage.

The excavations were directed by Tim Havard and Joe Whelan (both formerly of CA) with the supervisory assistance of Marino Cardelli and Pete Busby, of Cotswold Archaeology. The assistance of the Cotswold Archaeology excavation team is gratefully acknowledged along with the many colleagues who processed the finds and environmental samples. The fieldwork was managed for CA initially by Ian Barnes and then by Richard Young, who also managed the watching brief. Aerial photographs of the site were taken on behalf of CA by Adam Stanford (Aerial-Cam Ltd).

The post-excavation work was managed by Alistair Barclay and Clare Randall and the production of the book was overseen by Philippa Bradley. Jonathan Hart undertook the stratigraphic analysis and Alice Foster provided editorial assistance in the compilation of the volume. The authors of the finds, environmental and osteological reports are acknowledged in the text. The illustrations are by Ryan Wilson (plans and sections), Li Sou (metalwork, fired clay and stone), Aleksandra Osinka (block tuyère), Li Sou and Helena Munoz-Mojado (pottery), Helena Munoz-Mojado (worked bone) and Krissy Moore (animal bone and human bone). The archive was prepared by Hazel O'Neill and her team and has since been deposited with Swindon Museum under accession number SWIM:2018.79 and will be deposited with the ADS in due course.

This volume was kindly reviewed by Tim Havard and Melanie Pomeroy-Kellinger (both Wiltshire Council) and by members of the Science Museum Group. We would also like to thank various colleagues at CA for their support during the various stages of the post-excavation work including Martin Watts, Richard Young, Hazel O'Neill, Sarah Wyles, Andy Clarke and Dan Bashford.

Summary

Archaeological investigations by Cotswold Archaeology on behalf of the Science Museum Group ahead of the construction of the Collection Management Facility, Science and Innovation Park at the former site of RAF Wroughton, a Royal Airforce airfield that opened in 1940, produced evidence for a double pit alignment, an open settlement of Iron Age date and a series of Roman enclosures. The site lies on a raised chalkland plateau, part of the North Wessex Downs, and overlooks Swindon, the Thames Valley and the Cotswolds to the north with the higher chalk downs, the Ridgeway and Barbury Castle just to the south.

The earliest evidence for human activity included an isolated Beaker pit and a small number of worked flints of Neolithic and Bronze Age date. Some flint objects may have been intentionally collected and buried in deposits of Iron Age date. However, the first substantial evidence for activity on the plateau was a pair of converging pit alignments that crossed the north western part of the site. This arrangement may have been designed to funnel people and animals up onto the chalk plateau. The more eastern alignment may have acted, at least initially, as a boundary to an otherwise extensive open settlement made up of roundhouses and pits that was only partially revealed by the excavation. The pit alignments are very poorly dated but their spatial location with the settlement of Iron Age date indicates they are certainly of pre-Iron Age or earliest Iron Age date. The Iron Age settlement was made up of at least 11 roundhouses, a C-shaped ditched enclosure, over 150 pits, and a series of inhumation burials some of which were made in flat graves and others that were made within pits and more rarely a ditch. All the prehistoric burials were radiocarbon dated, which indicated that burial took place during the Early to Middle Iron Age. Some of the earliest burials appeared to have been bound and therefore possibly stored prior to burial within the settlement – suggesting that they were already old and had died sometime before the foundation of the settlement. In addition, to the occurrence of the presence of human remains some of the pits contained more unusual deposits, combinations of material, charcoal or burned deposits, notable dumps of chalk or sarsen. Amongst the material from the pits were groups of associated animal bone, some articulated, animal skulls, various objects including some of more unusual type and more mundane settlement refuse. The open settlement was replaced by a system of ditches and enclosures in the Late Iron Age and Early Roman period and this reorganisation of the immediate landscape also saw the construction of a droveway where the much earlier pit alignments had once converged and re-established this area of the site as a routeway onto the plateau. In contrast, by the Late Roman period the site was mostly used for burial with the creation of a small Roman rural cemetery in an area between two large enclosures of earlier Roman date. The C-shaped enclosure of Iron Age date was also reused as a focus for more isolated burial and to house an oven. After the Roman period, the use of this site was abandoned as a place of settlement and burial and primarily only used for cultivation until the construction of the airfield during the Second World War.

The results of this project mostly chart the Iron Age and Roman periods, and provide important evidence for the development and character of rural settlement of a community, its use of burial, and landuse on the margins of two distinct geographical zones – the chalkland edge of Wessex, the ridgeway and its hillforts, and one of the vales that make up the Upper Thames Valley.

Chapter 1
Introduction

Introduction and background

The more recent history at Wroughton Airfield, to the south-west of Swindon, was self-evident, but the archaeology which it concealed was perhaps more of a surprise. Whilst barrows and Barbury Castle hillfort overlook the site from the Marlborough Downs to the south, the site itself had some indications that there was potential for Iron Age settlement in the vicinity and that informed the strategy of the investigation.

The excavation by Cotswold Archaeology, was carried out at the Collection Management Facility, Science and Innovation Park, Swindon in advance of the creation of a new storage facility for the Science Museum Group and took place between September 2018 and February 2019. The site lies within the former airfield of RAF Wroughton, on the downs 1km south-west of Wroughton village and 3.5km south of the outskirts of Swindon (centred on NGR: 413900 179100).

The airfield occupies part of the Lower Chalk Plain of the Wiltshire chalk downs, a broad plateau lying at around 200m aOD which overlooks the clay vale of the River Ray to the north (Fig. 1.1). The plateau is extensive, today open land used primarily for grazing and arable and providing a sense of open space and dramatic skyscapes (Fig. 1.2). The chalk here is part of the Cretaceous Zag Chalk formation and there are no superficial geological deposits (BGS 2020). The airfield lies on the northern edge of the plateau, above a steep and dramatic scarp where the chalk gives way to Upper Greensand which falls away to the clay vale of the River Ray. Numerous coombes along the scarp edge have formed where springs feed water courses descending to the valley below. Many of these steep, narrow coombes are wooded and include footpaths which provide relatively gentle routes between the downs and the vale (Fig. 1.3). The River Ray flows eastwards 1.6km north of the site and is itself a tributary of the River Thames. The chalk plateau on which the site is located is overlooked from the south by the higher ground of the Marlborough Downs,

some 2.6km distant, which reach some 260m aOD (Fig. 1.4).

The excavated area lies within the northern part of the former airfield, between the runways and a row of extant hangars and other buildings. A single area was excavated, but additional watching briefs were undertaken during the construction of services and car parking areas, the last of which took place in June 2020.

Archaeological background

The Marlborough Downs overlooking the site provide the setting for numerous barrows, many of which are Scheduled Monuments. The closest to the site include four bowl barrows (SM 1012165; Fig. 1.1) and a saucer barrow (SM 1010468; Fig. 1.1) 2.7km south of the site forming a cemetery near Barbury Castle hillfort, and two bowl barrows (SM 1016356; Fig. 1.1) east of Barbury Castle (McQueen 2009). Although modern investigations into these is lacking, such monuments are typically Bronze Age, although Late Neolithic examples are known, and some were re-used during the Roman and Anglo-Saxon periods. An archaeological trial trench evaluation within the airfield, undertaken in 2006 (Fig. 1.5) as part of a separate planning application, recovered Bronze Age pottery from a trench immediately east of the current site, although this was residual within an Iron Age or Roman feature (OA 2006).

Barbury Castle hillfort lies 2.7km south of the site and is also a Scheduled Monument (SM ref. 1014557; Fig. 1.1). This bivallate hillfort lies in a spectacular location on the northern edge of the Marlborough Downs, overlooking the plain on which the site is located. The site and the hillfort are intervisible with Barbury Castle an obvious landmark (Fig. 1.6). Barbury Castle is the most substantial of the Ridgeway hillforts; the hillforts at Liddington Castle and Uffington are intervisible with Barbury Castle. Other hillforts in the wider environs, not visible from Barbury Castle, include those at Binknoll, Ringsbury and Blunsdon

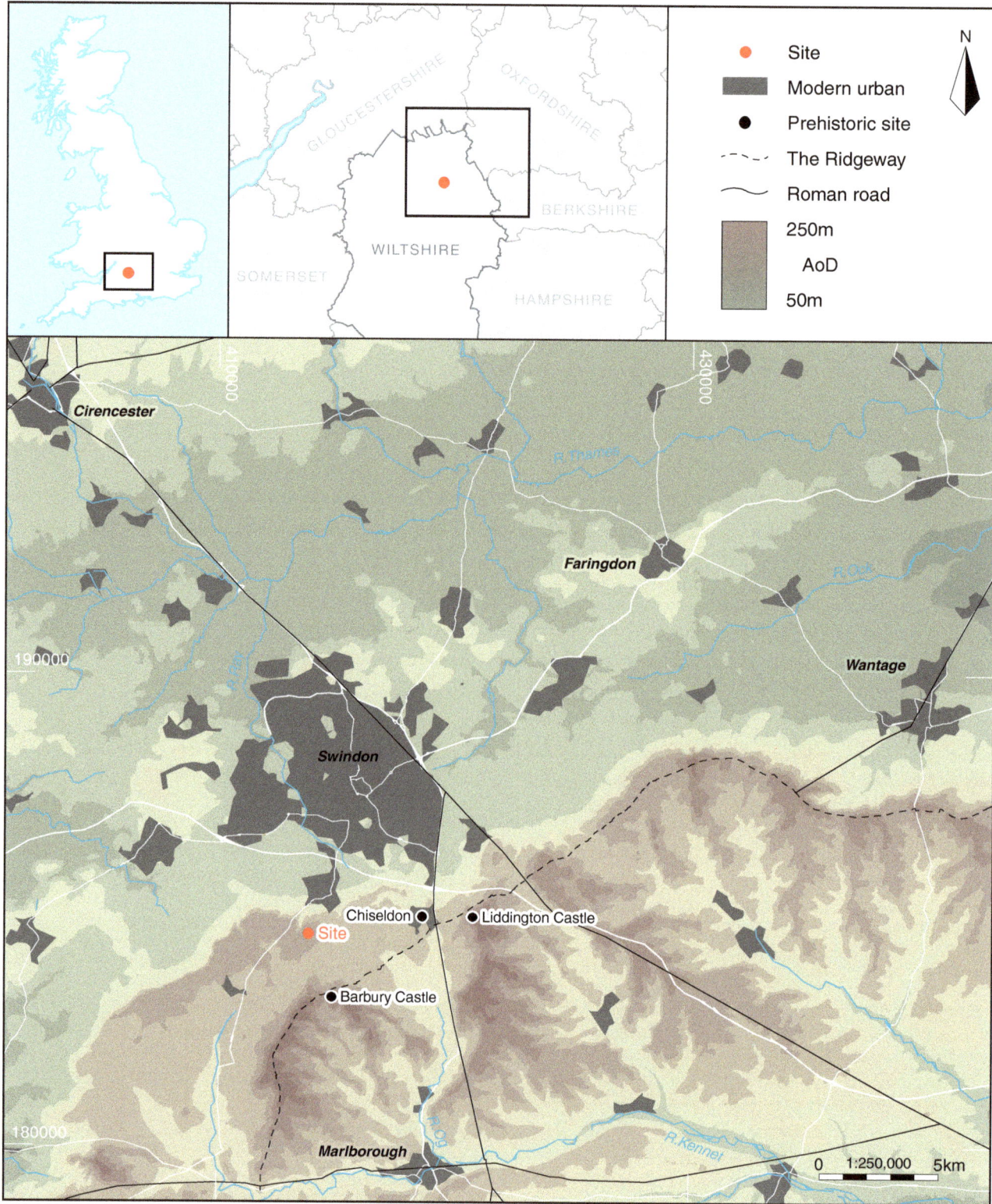

Figure 1.1 Site location showing selected archaeological sites

on the Lower Chalk scarp. All are located in prominent, visible locations.

A small excavation in 1875 at Barbury Castle discovered an Iron Age 'blacksmith's' hoard which included parts of a chariot and chariot harness furniture, sickles, spear heads and other metal work (SM ref. 1014557 list entry).

This and other small-scale investigations have recovered small quantities of pottery from the hillfort, mostly of Iron Age and Romano-British date. A geophysical survey undertaken by English Heritage (now Historic England) in 1998 revealed that the hillfort's interior contains dense concentrations of roundhouses and pits (McQueen 2009).

Figure 1.2 *The chalk plateau, looking south-east across the airfield*

Figure 1.3 *Aerial view of the north-western half of the site, looking north towards the scarp, with the adjacent coombe and clay vale beyond*

Figure 1.4 The site on the chalk plateau with the Marlborough Downs in the background

A second metalwork hoard has been recovered a few kilometres east of the airfield. The Chiseldon Cauldron hoard dating to the early Middle Iron Age (400–200 BC) and now in the British Museum comprises 12 cauldrons recovered from a single pit where they were accompanied by two cattle skulls (Baldwin and Joy 2017).

Closer to the site of the excavation, evaluation trenching in 2006 recorded indications of an Early Iron Age settlement immediately east (OA 2006; Fig. 1.5). The remains included roundhouses, postholes and pits and were found within several trenches over an area of some 1200m², suggesting that these represent an unenclosed, possibly shifting, Early Iron Age settlement. However, a previous evaluation, undertaken in 2005 to the north of the current site, again as part of an unrelated planning application, did not identify any Iron Age remains (OA 2005; Fig. 1.5). This suggests that the northern limits of Early Iron Age settlement may have been constrained by the position of the scarp. A geophysical (magnetometer) survey undertaken in 2013 in the southern half of the former airfield recorded no anomalies likely to pre-date the airfield, although it was noted that modern deposits may have masked any earlier remains (WYAS 2013; Fig. 1.5).

The 2006 evaluation also identified large features interpreted as ditches or quarry pits from which Roman pottery was recovered (OA 2006). A concentration of Romano-British finds has also been identified during field walking 760m north of the site (Fig. 1.5); the recovered assemblage included pottery, animal bone and fired clay, and may point to nearby settlement (CA 2017). Further afield, and just east of present-day Swindon, is the Roman settlement at Wanborough (*Durocornovium*), and the associated roads run a few kilometres to the east of Wroughton.

The site lies within the parish of Wroughton which, as 'Ellendune', is recorded in Anglo-Saxon charters of AD 844 and 956, and as an estate in the 1086 *Domesday* survey. During the medieval period it extended from the lowland Kimmeridge Clay vale to the Lower Chalk plateau, providing a balance of sheep husbandry and corn on the chalk and cattle pasture on the heavier clay soils, a practice widespread for parishes along the downs (Brown *et al.* 2005). The site probably lay within the arable fields and sheep-grazed land beyond the settled area. Possible furrows were recorded across parts of the site during the 2006 evaluation (OA 2006); none survive as earthworks, probably due to landscaping associated with the airfield.

The formerly open land at Wroughton was enclosed in 1796 (CA 2017). The site remained in agricultural use until 1939 when construction began to create Wroughton Airfield, built to house No. 15 Maintenance Unit (No. 15 MU) of the RAF, who were later joined by No. 76 MU. The first runway was completed in 1941, with two others by 1944, and the airfield operated throughout the Second World War, providing maintenance services, but also used for the assembly of aircraft, including for the Battle of Britain

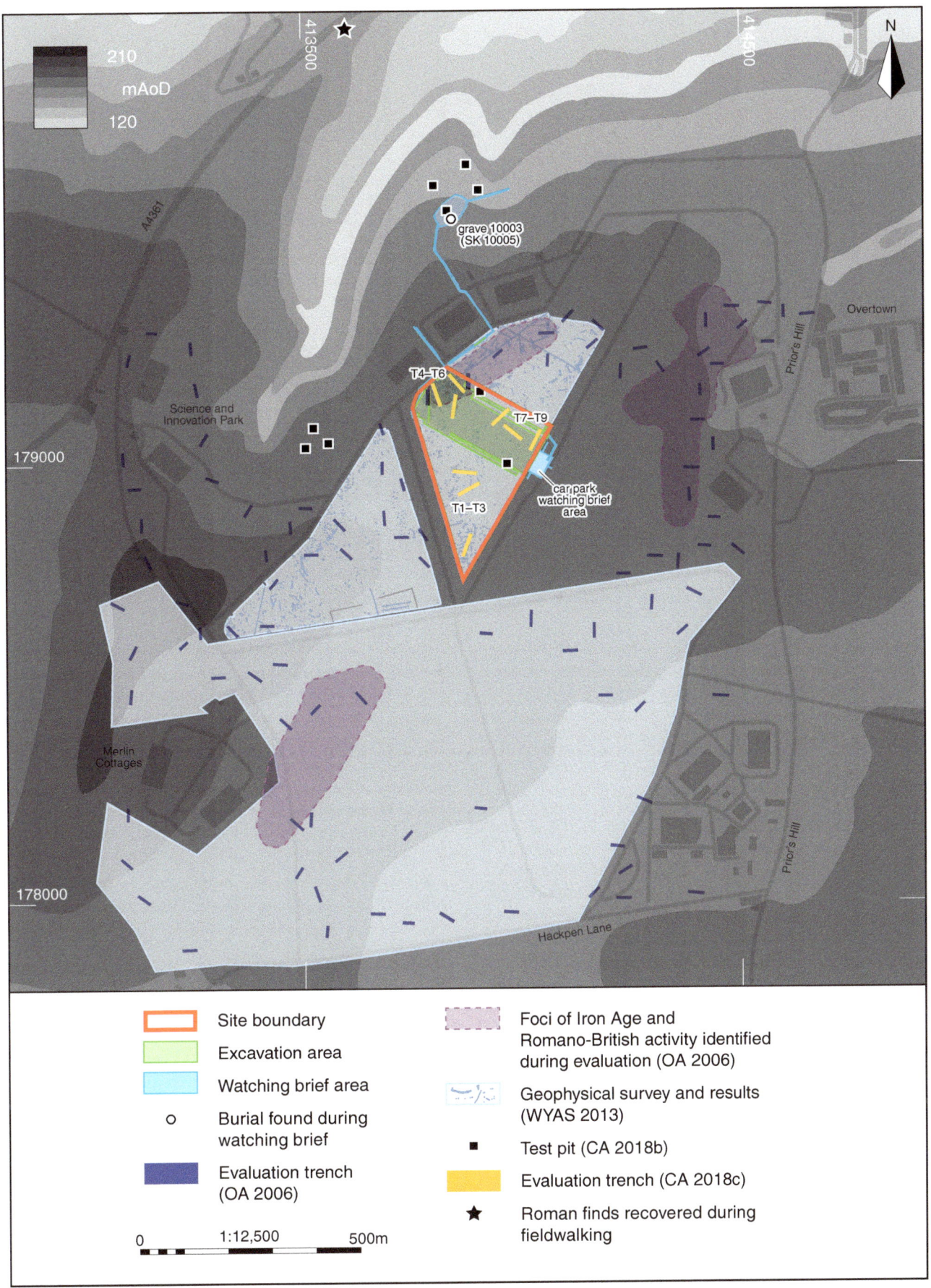

Figure 1.5 The site, showing location of groundworks and previous investigations

Barbury Castle Hillfort

Figure 1.6 Barbury Castle dominating the skyline above the site, looking south during the excavations

and the D-Day invasion, and their packaging for transport overseas (Gibbs 1982; HE 2020). The airfield continued to provide aircraft services, including aircraft maintenance and scrappage, until its closure in 1978, shortly after which it became a storage annex for the Science Museum.

Objectives, investigations and excavation methods

The archaeological indications outlined above were included in a heritage assessment (CA 2017). As the development area originally comprised an extensive part of the former airfield a geophysical survey was carried out across a significant area which revealed anomalies indicating the presence of ditches and pits (AS 2017; Fig. 1.5) in the area subsequently excavated. Archaeological monitoring was then carried out during the excavation of nine ground investigation test pits, each 2.5m long and 0.6m–0.9m wide (CA 2018a; Fig. 1.5). Seven of these were located along the scarp edge, whilst two were within the area which was later excavated; however, none contained archaeological remains (CA 2018b). Following these works, the area of investigations forming the current project was defined as a parcel of land in the apex between two of the runways (Fig. 1.5). This area was investigated by means of a trial trench evaluation, which comprised the excavation of nine trenches (Trenches 1–9), each measuring 50m by 1.8m (CA 2018c; Fig. 1.5). Of these, Trenches 1–3, located in the southern apex of the site, contained no archaeological remains. The remaining

trenches revealed Iron Age ditches as well as undated features, along with evidence for truncation relating to the airfield within the site's southern and central areas.

Based on the preceding investigations, open area excavation was carried out. Significantly more features were found than had been predicted by the geophysics and evaluation trenching, presumably due to the masking effects of the re-deposited chalk from construction of the runway. Additional areas were added as a watching brief, particularly in the south-eastern part of the site to ensure that everything within the footprint of the proposed new collections management facility building was examined.

Radiocarbon dating
Emma Aitken and Alistair J. Barclay

Radiocarbon dating was undertaken on selected human remains, animal bone and charred plant remains in order to confirm the date of graves, an oven, pits, a pit alignment and a ditched feature (see Table 5.10). The samples were analysed during August 2020, September 2021 and November 2021 at Scottish Universities Environmental Research Centre (SUERC), Rankine Avenue, Scottish Enterprise Technology Park, East Kilbride, Glasgow, G75 0QF, Scotland. The methodology employed by SUERC Radiocarbon Laboratory is outlined in Dunbar *et al.* (2016).

The uncalibrated dates are conventional radiocarbon ages. The radiocarbon ages were calibrated using the University of Oxford Radiocarbon Accelerator Unit calibration programme OxCal v4.4.4 (Bronk Ramsey 2020; Bronk Ramsey 2009) using the IntCal20 curve and a mix of the IntCal20 and Marine20 curves (Reimer *et al.* 2020; Heaton *et al.* 2020).

The results from the dating of the human remains are presented and discussed in Chapter 5. Radiocarbon dates in plain type are quoted throughout the text at the 95.4% probability level, unless otherwise indicated. Ranges quoted in italics are posterior density estimates and derive from Bayesian modelling using the OxCal program (Bronk Ramsey 2009; Bronk Ramsey 2020).

Location of archives

The finds and paper archive has been deposited with Swindon Museum and Art Gallery under accession number SWIMG:2018.79, whilst the digital archive will be deposited with the Archaeology Data Service (ADS) in due course.

Chapter 2
Excavation results

Introduction

The excavation was a rectangular area 290m by 110m that encompassed the earlier evaluation Trenches 4–9 (see Chapter 1). Outside this area, the groundworks associated with service trenches and a car park continued to be monitored during a watching brief.

Archaeological features occurred across the entire excavation area (Fig. 2.1), but with a higher density of pits and linear features in the north and west. The creation of the airfield might have been thought to have negatively affected the archaeological features and deposits, but the overburden which was dumped across the site during the construction of the airfield probably assisted in the site's preservation during more recent decades. Nevertheless, surfaces were absent and there were few postholes, which suggests that ridge and furrow cultivation in the medieval period had already truncated the site long before the airfield construction, resulting in the loss of smaller features and the upper parts of those that have survived.

The findings are described below in chronological order. Features and deposits have been assigned to periods of activity based on the dates of cultural material, mainly pottery, radiocarbon dates, and stratigraphic and spatial relationships.

Activity has been assigned to the following periods:

Period 1: Mesolithic–Early Neolithic
Period 2: Beaker–Early Bronze Age (2300–1600 BC)
Period 3: Late Bronze Age/Early Iron Age (1150–400 BC)
Period 4: Early/Middle Iron Age (400 BC–100 BC)
Period 5: Late Iron Age to Early Roman (100 BC–AD 200)
Period 6: Mid to Late Roman (AD 250–410)
Period 7: medieval to post-medieval (AD 1000–1800)
Period 8: Modern (AD 1800–present)

Period 1: Mesolithic–Early Neolithic

No features have been assigned to the earliest period of activity on the plateau, but it is attested by a small assemblage of flints. All were residual or from contexts with no independent datable material. The earliest is a Mesolithic truncation from an unphased pit (2737, Fig. 3.1, 2) and a core rejuvenation flake which dates to the Mesolithic or Early Neolithic period; these came from Middle to Late Roman ditch 13. A broken Early Neolithic leaf-shaped arrowhead (Ra. 1039; Fig. 3.1, 1) came from a Roman grave (2329), whilst a flake removed from a Neolithic polished flint axe came from a pit (1128, not illustrated) forming part of Late Bronze Age to Early Iron Age Pit alignment 2 (see Sommerville, Chapter 3).

Period 2: Beaker–Early Bronze Age

A Beaker/Early Bronze Age thumbnail scraper was recovered from Period 4 (Middle Iron Age, Fig. 3.1, 3) pit 8118 in which it was residual. However, a single feature, a shallow pit, could also be assigned to this period.

Pit 1245 near the north-western limit of excavation (Fig. 2.2) contained Beaker pottery. It comprised a circular, bowl-shaped cut 0.75m wide and 0.2m deep. A layer of grey-brown silty clay (1246) covered the base and may have been a natural silting suggesting the pit was left open for some time. Above this were two very dark silty clay fills. The lowest of these, 1247 contained some charcoal, and a few burnt stones, possibly debris from a hearth. It also produced 49 sherds of Beaker pottery and part of a roe deer antler which had been scorched. The uppermost dark fill 1248, which appears to represent a re-cut, was rich in charcoal. This produced nearly 1,000 hazelnut shell fragments along with a few charred barley grains and a charred sloe stone, as well as hazel charcoal (see Challinor, Chapter 4), also material which may have derived from a domestic hearth. This fill yielded a further 30 sherds of Beaker pottery. One of a group of the hazelnut shells provided a date range of 2338–2062 cal. BC (95.4% probability; SUERC-100004) (Table 5.10). Together, the sherds from the pit represent the remains of at least six vessels (Fig. 3.2, 1–6, see Banks, Chapter 3). In total, the two upper fills also contained 25 worked flints. Most had been broken and over half were

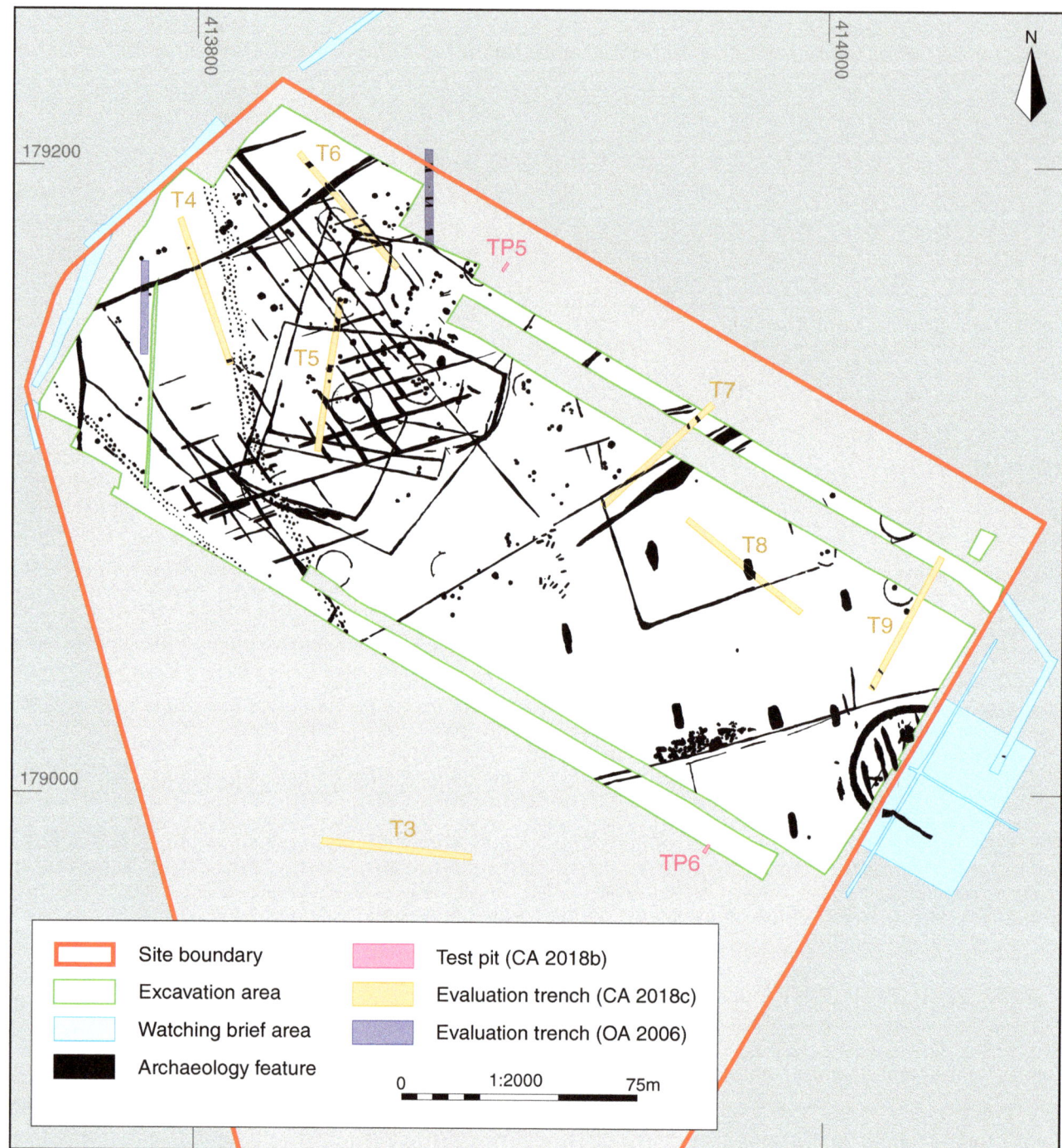

Figure 2.1 Plan of the excavation and watching brief areas

burnt. They include two blades, two retouched flakes, two scrapers and a spurred piece, but none are closely datable (see Sommerville, Chapter 3).

Period 3: Late Bronze Age/Early Iron Age

The first substantial activity represented comprised two pit alignments (Pit alignments 1 and 2; Figs 2.3–2.5) extending across the western corner of the site on diverging but broadly north-west/south-east alignments. Both

alignments are poorly dated as described below, but their form perhaps places them within the Late Bronze Age to Early Iron Age (see discussion in Chapter 6) and they were demonstrably earlier than some features of the Period 4 Iron Age settlement and those of the Late Iron Age/Roman period. It is possible that they were contemporary with at least part of the settlement during its lifetime.

Together the exposed lengths of the two pit alignments included almost 300 pits, and of these 137 were hand-excavated, generally in a half-section. Each alignment continued beyond the excavation limits at both ends. No corresponding anomalies were identified during the

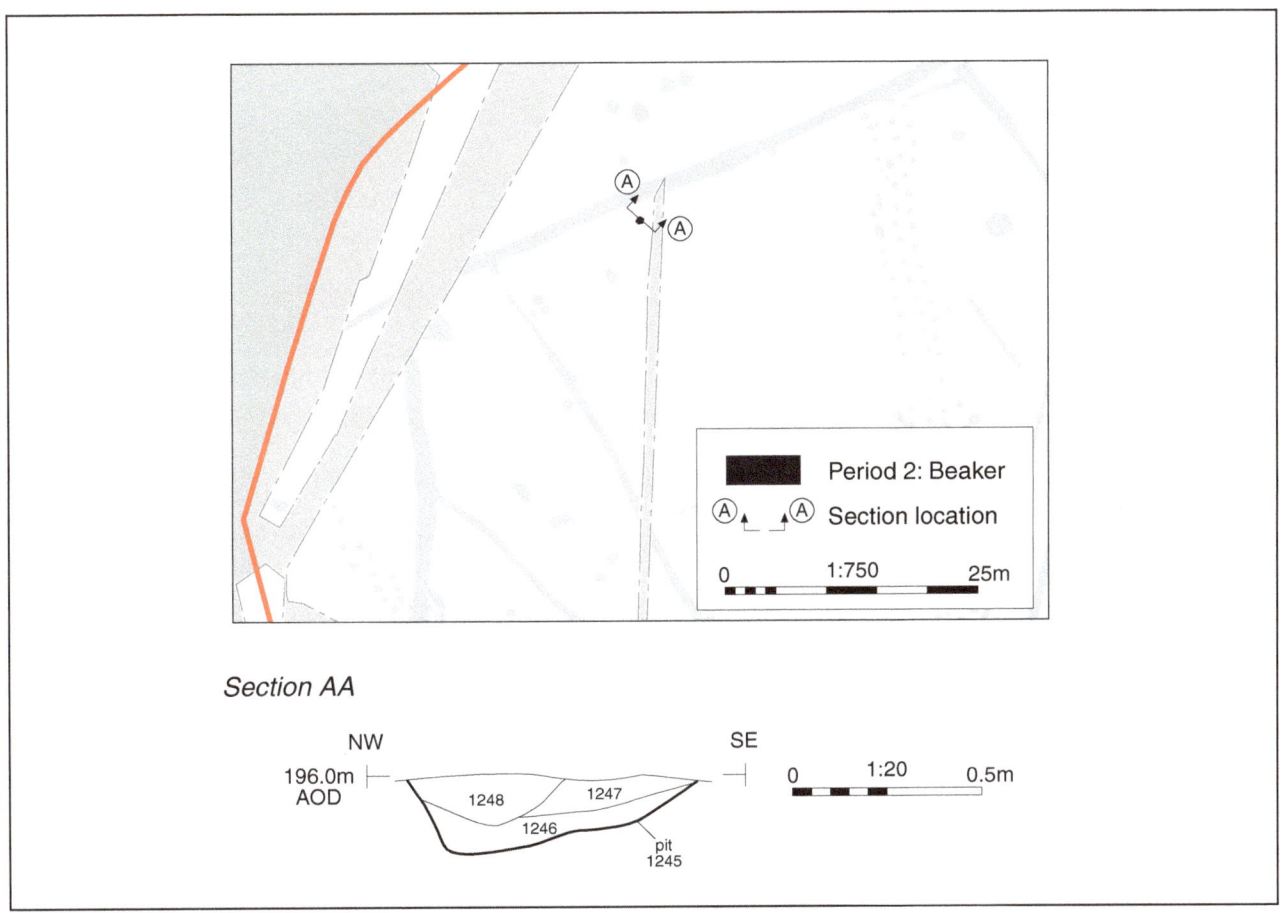

Section AA

Figure 2.2 Section drawing and photograph of Period 2 (Beaker) pit 1245

Figure 2.3 Pit alignment 1 at its north-westernmost exposed extent, looking north-east

Figure 2.4 Pit alignment 1, looking south from pit 1003

geophysical survey (probably because of the size of the features or lack of magnetic material within them), and the full extents of these alignments are therefore unknown. Despite the number of pits, collectively they produced very few finds and therefore are of uncertain date. The majority of the pits were circular, sub-circular or oval in plan and up to around 1m in diameter, often about half as deep as they

were wide (Fig. 2.4) with steep concave sides and generally a concave base. Whilst a few of the excavated examples contained postpipes and/or stone packing material indicating that they had held posts, most contained only single silty clay fills.

Pit alignment 1 comprised at least 95 pits, not all of which were excavated, paired regularly in a double row extending north-west/south-east for 85m across the western edge of the site and continuing beyond the limits of excavation in both directions. From the 30 excavated examples, pit 1043 produced an Iron Age-style fired clay triangular loomweight (Ra. 1020) but there were no other datable finds. The pits became smaller towards the south-eastern extent of the alignment; this may reflect truncation, although no corresponding pattern of truncation was noted along Pit alignment 2 (Fig. 2.5). Out of the entire row there were 14 pits which were less than 0.50m in length, 53 which were between 0.50m and 1m in length and 13 which were more than 1m. The smallest was 0.24m and the largest 1.64m long, but it is difficult to know the true original dimensions throughout the row due to effects of ploughing. The pits ranged in depth from 0.07–0.51m. The two rows were approximately 1–1.5m apart, with about 0.5–1m between pits. The pairs were slightly offset, almost staggered but no gaps were apparent along the length of the alignment. Several pits were identified in the field as having possible post-pipes and associated indications that they may have been extracted (postholes 1003, 1009, 1016 and 1024 which were located at various points along the alignment; Fig. 2.5). However, the evidence is not entirely clear, with the best evidence for post-packing which was disturbed or later slumped represented by 1003 where one of the fills was very chalk rich and the boundary between it and other fills. This is, however, not conclusive evidence of the presence of posts within the features of this alignment.

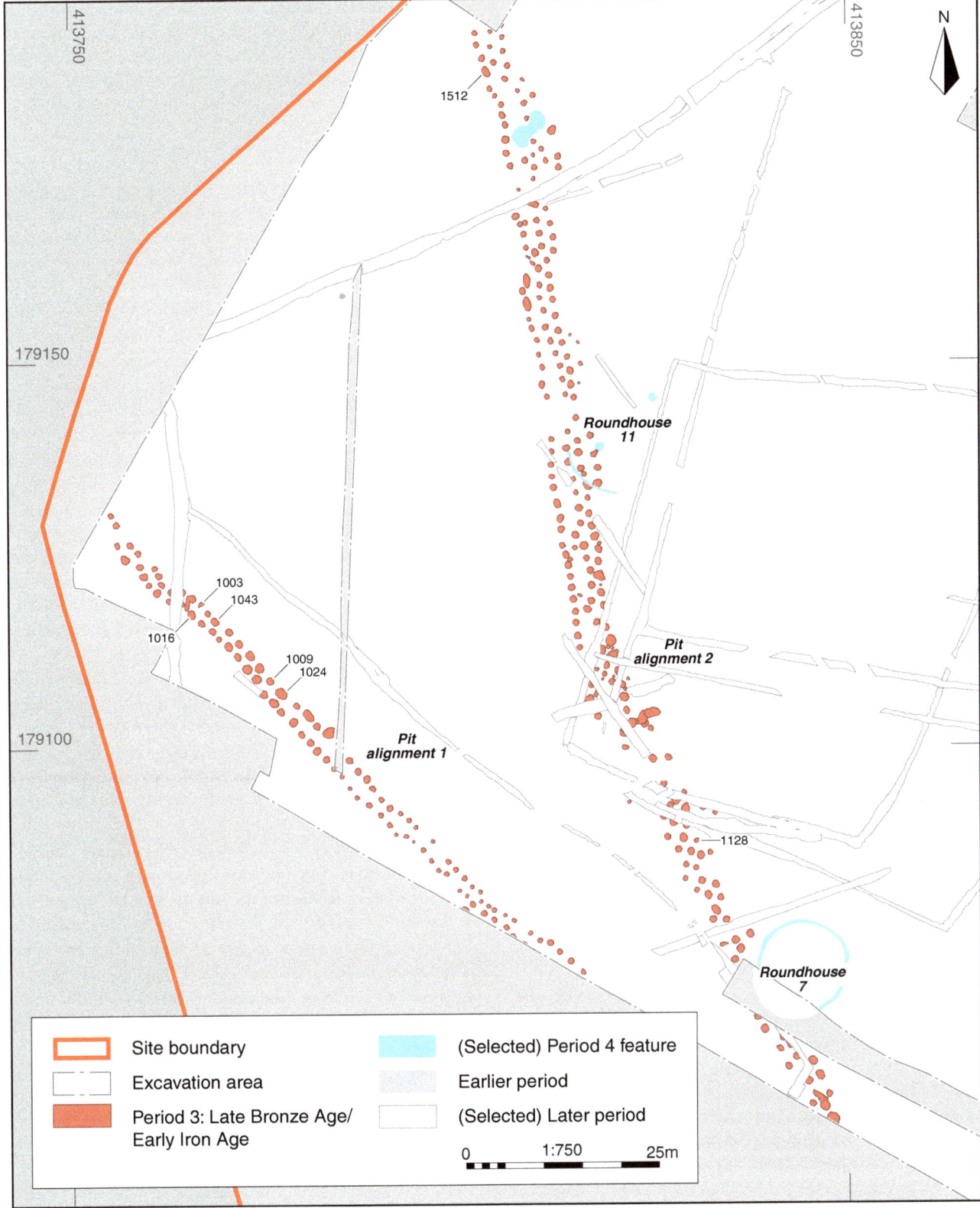

Figure 2.5 Plan of Late Bronze Age/Early Iron Age Pit alignments 1 and 2

Pit alignment 2, to the east of Pit alignment 1, comprised 201 pits (of which 108 were excavated). These were laid out over a distance of 150m generally in three rows, with a few outliers or possible replacements. This became increasingly irregular to the southern end. The alignment converged towards to alignment 1 as it progressed southwards, before turning to the south-east and on a more parallel course with Pit alignment 1. As with Pit alignment 1, Pit alignment 2 extended beyond the excavated area in both directions. In plan, gaps in the lines of the pits have been caused by their being cut through by later features in particular the ditches of the Period 5 field system (Fig. 2.5). One gap in the lines of posts is not clearly related to the position of these later features, so may represent an entrance, but it is on the alignment and spacing of the medieval plough trends, so it could also have been affected by truncation which was less discernible in the field. It is also difficult to discern the distances over which the multiple rows of post originally extended as the irregularity of the number or rows, the placement of the pits and their size, in comparison to the more regularly arranged alignment 1, has also probably been impinged on by later features associated with the edge of the Iron Age settlement and later fields. The pits within alignment 2 were of similar plan and profile as those in alignment 1, with circular–oval cuts and steep or concave sides and concave or flat bases. The occupied a similar range of sizes, perhaps averaging slightly larger, with the smallest being 0.25m long and the largest 1.82m, and where this could be ascertained, six pits being less than 0.5m in length, 95 between 0.50m and 1m in length, and 15 pits longer than 1m. The excavated pits ranged between 0.1–0.68m deep. There were a handful of features with possible post-pipes, in 1166, 1183, 3497, and 3371, but in other cuts where there was more than one fill present, the initial ones appeared to be more chalk rich, were spread across the pit base and may well represent erosion of the pit sides or more likely upcast from the digging of the features which had eroded back into the cut.

Almost no datable material was recovered from the pits within Pit alignment 2. A small sherd (3g) of Early Iron Age pottery from pit 1512 in the northern part of the alignment, broadly dated to 800–400 BC. In addition, the pits yielded small assemblages of flints and animal bone, the latter mainly cattle and horse, with a few sheep/goat and pig. Amongst the flints is a flake removed from a Neolithic polished flint axe (pit 1128 within the southern part of Pit alignment 2; Fig. 2.5).

Period 4: Early/Middle Iron Age

An Iron Age settlement was situated largely to the east of the pit alignments; a possible roundhouse or other structure belonging to this settlement truncated pits along Pit alignment 2, suggesting that they were earlier, or at least earlier than this part of the settlement (Fig. 2.6). The settlement accounted for the majority of individual features on the site. It was mainly concentrated in a broad north-west/south-east aligned swathe across the western part of the site and generally respected Pit alignment 2 which appeared to coincide with the westernmost spread of pits and buildings. This settlement included up to 11 roundhouses (RHs 2–4 and 6–13) which survived as penannular and crescent-shaped gullies (Figs 2.6, 2.9–2.11). There were, however, only two postholes possibly associated with one of the roundhouses, suggesting truncation of other structural features limiting interpretation of ground plans and construction methods.

Other features included graves, and numerous pits as well as a probably contemporary C-shaped enclosure type feature, with associated pits located to the south-east of what appeared to be the southernmost extent of the settlement.

Dating

The dating evidence for the Iron Age activity is provided by the ceramic assemblage and by 12 radiocarbon dates (Table 5.10; Fig. 5.27 and see Chapter 5). The radiocarbon determinations were made mostly on human and animal bone from articulated burials within pits and graves. In addition to the single sherd of Early Iron Age pottery from pit 1512 in Pit alignment 2, within the settlement area pit 2210 produced a sherd of Late Bronze Age/Early Iron Age date along with sherds which were only broadly datable to the Iron Age. Single Early Iron Age sherds came from pits 1260, 1384, 1724 (within the footprint of roundhouse 4), 2043, 2082, 2171 and 1426, and isolated pit 9009 located to the south-west of roundhouse 6, and three sherds from 1743 which have all been assigned to period 4, as well as a single sherd from period 5 pit 3275. Some of these appear to cluster in the north-eastern part of the excavated area, and possibly suggests that the earliest settlement was adjacent to the pit alignments. However, pit 9009 was located in the southern part of the site suggesting that Early Iron Age activity was as widespread as in later centuries.

The earliest of the radiocarbon dates (see Table 5.10 for details of the modelled ranges), provided a range that mostly falls within *759–462 cal. BC (93.0%)*(SUERC-94037) was from a human burial in cut 1204, Two other date ranges, both on human remains in pit 1207 and grave 10003 (an isolated burial to the north of the main excavation area), fall within the Early to Middle Iron Age (*514–366 cal. BC*, SUERC-100009; and *466–386 cal. BC*, SUERC-94043). It is possible that some of the earliest activity, contemporary with or closely following the use of the pit alignments occurred during the Early Iron Age. However, as discussed below the body positions suggests tight binding and there is potential for the remains to have been preserved for a considerable length of time prior to their deposition, which could have been contemporary with similar activity which produced later radiocarbon dates.

The majority of the late prehistoric pottery assemblage is datable to the Middle to Late Iron Age. Whilst the fabrics represented are long lived in this region, there are a number of deposits where more diagnostic forms, particularly upright straight-sided vessels ('saucepan pots') were present. Most of these also came from the northern settlement area, although consideration of the distribution of the material may have been affected by the limited number of diagnostic sherds in comparison to the density of excavated features in other areas.

Five radiocarbon date ranges fall within the Middle Iron Age, including three dates on human remains (SUERC-94041, SUERC-100011 and SUERC-100014: see Table 5.1), and two on dog skeletons (SUERC-100021

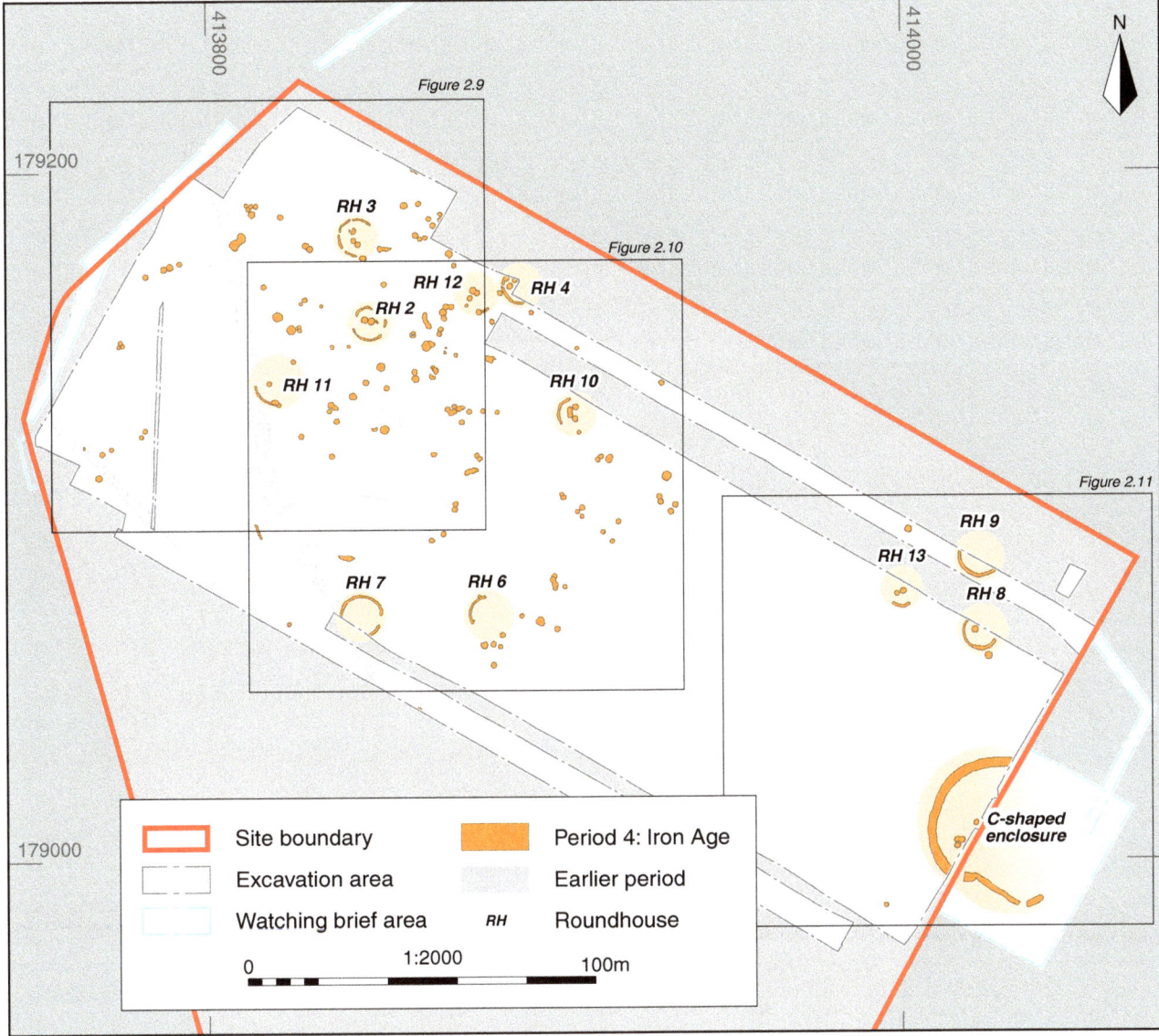

Figure 2.6 Plan of Period 4 (Iron Age) settlement

and SUERC-100020). The latest radiocarbon date ranges from the Period 4 settlement extend from the Middle to Late Iron Age, including two determinations made on human remains (SUERC-100015 and SUERC-100012) and one on a spelt wheat grain (SUERC-100005). A partial, articulated dog skeleton in the C-shaped enclosure, discussed below, produced a radiocarbon date range of *351–296 cal. BC (39.5%)* and *208–102 cal. BC (55.9%)* (SUERC-100660;), which can be seen alongside these dates.

The presence of some decorated (La Tène-style) ceramic vessels datable to the 2nd to 1st centuries BC and other diagnostically Late Iron Age forms, including bead rims confirms that activity continued into the Late Iron Age. Again, the distribution of the limited number of diagnostic sherds appears to be in the northern part of the site.

The degree of residuality and probability of intrusive later sherds, coupled with the low proportion of diagnostic forms in an assemblage which comprises of long-lived fabrics means that teasing out a more nuanced chronology is problematic. It seems from the distribution of what forms are available to provide greater chronological resolution are spread across the settlement area from the Early Iron Age to the Late Iron Age. A relative lack of intercutting and overlapping of ground plans between the roundhouses and the paucity of finds from their ditches, suggests that much of the settlement was contemporary. However, there are some indications of a shift over time. As mentioned above, Early Iron Age pottery came from the north-east part of the site whilst Early to Middle Iron Age pottery came from three adjacent roundhouses (RHs 4, 10 and 12), partly overlapping this, whilst Middle Iron pottery was associated with the rest of the structures and pits.

C-shaped enclosure

The curvilinear C-shaped ditch with a rather irregular southern extension was exposed at the eastern edge of the

Figure 2.7 Period 4 C-shaped enclosure ditch 1, looking north-east

excavation area, where it extended at both ends eastwards beyond the baulk (Figs 2.6–2.8). It initially appeared to be part of a ring ditch, albeit slightly flattened on the north-west side. A subsequent watching brief to the east carried out during the creation of a car park reduced an area to the top of the natural substrate which was the same as the level seen in the main excavation area. This revealed the remaining extent of the southern part of the ditch, which, rather than continuing, included a southern terminal (Fig. 2.8). A continuation of the northern part of the circuit was not seen extending into the stripped area, and it is assumed that any northern terminal lies beneath an unexcavated 3m-wide baulk between the excavation and watching brief areas. The feature therefore seems to have been generally C-shaped in plan, the enclosed area facing east and being 33m across and 15m deep. Extending from the southern terminal of the C-shaped ditch was a much slighter ditch. The relationship between the two was unclear, but the smaller ditch may have been a later addition/extension.

The C-shaped ditch was substantial, with steep sides that was cut into the chalk substrate and had a flat base. A step-like slot in part of the northeastern circuit (Fig. 2.8, Section BB) may be indicative of a cleaning slot although there is little indication of this from the fills. The initial fills commenced with a chalky deposit. This covered the ditch base but was deeper in the north-east (sections BB and CC) where it also covered the 'cleaning slot' where this was present. This may be indicative that this was actually

an original feature of the construction, given the lack of any remnant fill from an earlier phase of filling. No finds came from this lower fill and its chalky appearance, clean aside from pale grey clay, suggests it formed rapidly during the use of the ditch. It is probably upcast material which had slumped back into the ditch. Certainly, it lacked an organic component which might be expected if plants had had sufficient time to become established along the ditch sides and base. Tip lines were absent and there were no indications as to where any associated bank may have been positioned. There was no other indication of a bank, although one may have been originally present.

Above the lower fill was a sequence a grey-brown chalky silty clay deposits, often with up to around 40% chalk. Although the initial volume of chalk was different in the north-east part of the circuit, the subsequent fills were very similar in all interventions with multiple evenly distributed, and relatively thin, layers and lenses of material probably indicative of a slow and episodic process of filling. Along with small quantities of animal bone, they produced pottery which dates to the Iron Age. However, this amounted to only eight small sherds. A partial, articulated dog skeleton was present in fill 2436 (Fig. 2.8, Section BB), and produced a radiocarbon date range of *351–296 cal. BC (39.5% probability;* SUERC-100660) and *208–102 cal. BC (55.9% probability)* of broadly Middle Iron Age date, later 4th to 2nd cal. BC. In addition to the pottery from the ditch, there were also nine worked flints comprising

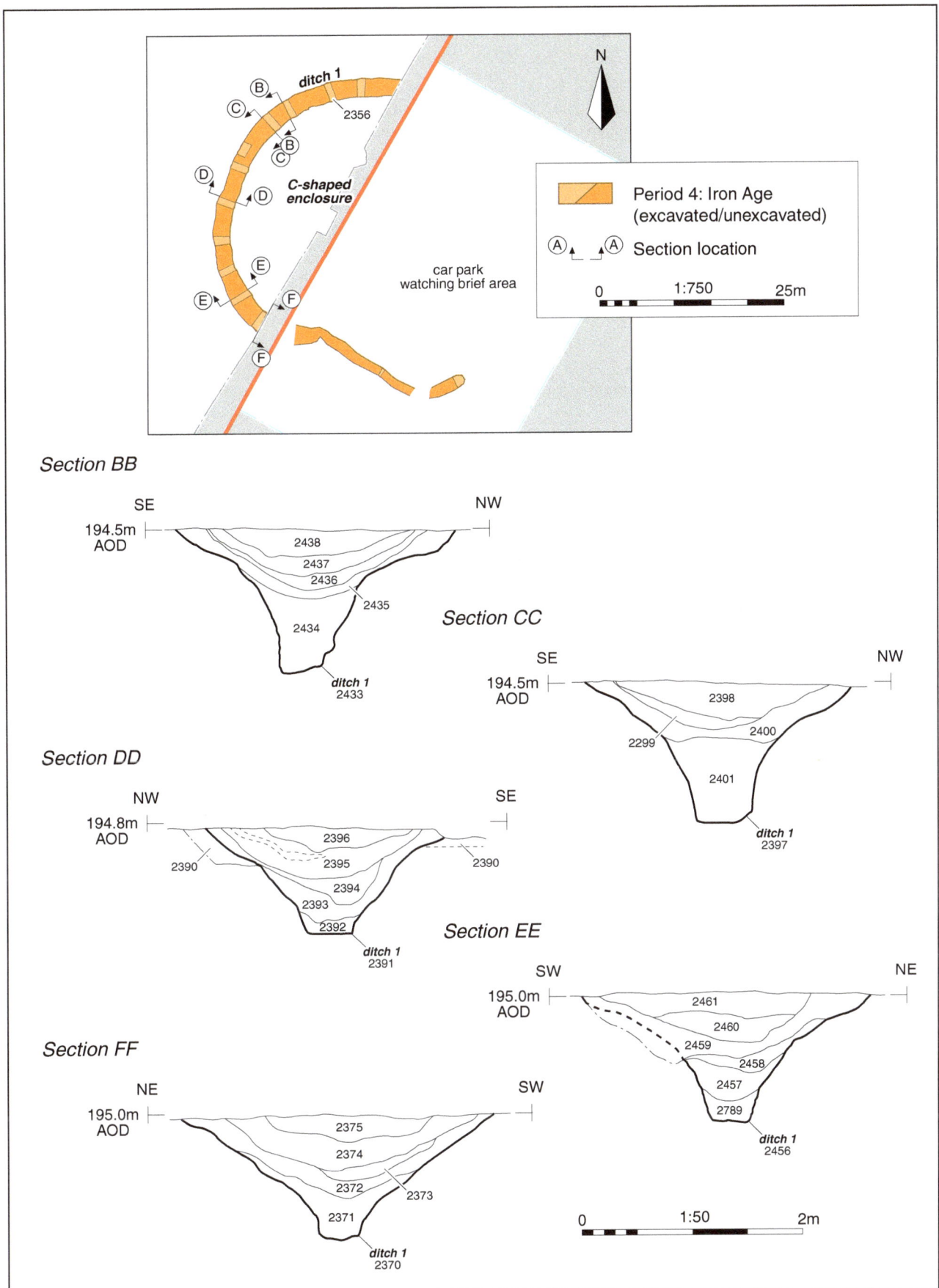

Figure 2.8 Plan and selected sections through Period 4 C-shaped enclosure ditch 1

six flakes, a core, a notch, and an end scraper, but none are closely datable, and they are likely to be residual. The modest assemblage of animal bones from the ditch fills comprised marginally more cattle than sheep/goat, as well as a few specimens from pig, horse and dog or fox as well as a butchered red deer tibia and an antler fragment. There were also two skulls, one of horse, the other a dog in contexts 2356 (in cut 2357) and 2398 (Fig. 2.8) respectively (see Holmes, Chapter 4). Some very limited amounts of charred plant remains came from the ditch, including cereals (see Wyles, Chapter 4). Whilst the construction date of the feature is unclear, it was certainly open and gradually filling with refuse, and possibly structured/deliberate deposits, during the Middle or Late Iron Age. However, the gradual accumulation of fills during the later Iron Age left the ditch visible as an earthwork at least 1m deep, evidently still open into the Roman period, which is discussed further below.

Roundhouses

At least nine, and up to 11, circular or sub-circular gullies were recorded across the excavated area, but most of which were clustered in the northern part of the site (Figs 2.6, 2.9–2.11). These were associated with clusters of pits and occasional postholes, and represent the remains of roundhouses, although the total number is unclear. None of the gullies comprised a complete circuit and only one had clearly associated postholes. However, most of the gullies overlapped with the distribution of pits. Given the apparent association of gullies with groups of pits within their circuit, some of the other pit clusters may indicate the location of additional buildings. It is probable that medieval and later ploughing is responsible for removing a large proportion of the features, leaving incomplete ground plans and meaning that it is difficult to associate features with each other or detect development of the settlement over time. Nevertheless, where more complete gullies were present, these could be extrapolated to represent an arc generally 10m–12m in diameter.

Roundhouse 3 was the most northerly of the possible structures and had one of the most complete gully circuits. It consisted of an incomplete penannular ditch enclosing an area 10m in diameter. The largest gap was east facing but as the gully was segmented it is difficult to know if this represented the genuine location of an entrance (Fig. 2.13) or had been caused by later truncation. The ditch itself was 0.45m wide and 0.15m deep with a U-shaped profile and contained two silty clay fills which generally lacked finds other than a single sherd of broadly Iron Age pottery. Within the circuit of the gully were three pits (including 2043 (Fig. 2.9) which contained a single sherd of Early Iron Age pottery, a small amount of later Iron Age pottery and a triangular fired clay loomweight, Ra. 1020, Fig. 3.9, 1).

Roundhouse 2 was 14m to the south and also had a relatively complete gully. It survived as an intermittent ditch enclosing an area 9m in diameter, with gaps along the north-west, north-east and eastern sides although it is not clear if any represented a genuine entrance. The ring gully was 0.5m wide and 0.2m deep with a U-shaped profile and contained a single chalky infill. The north-east end of gully section 1690 appears to have been cut by a small sub-circular pit or posthole (1706) which was 0.52m long by 0.42m wide and 0.19m deep and which produced two large sherds of Iron Age pottery.

Some 35m to the east, roundhouse 4 survived as a length of curvilinear gully describing about a third of the western side of a penannular construction or drip gully (Fig. 2.10). This continued beyond the excavated area at both ends, and most of the internal area was outside the area of excavation. The overall plan would have been of a similar diameter as roundhouse 2. The gully (1501, 1474, 1602) had steep sides to a flat/uneven base, 0.24–0.5m wide and 0.18–0.3m deep but produced no finds. Pits 1600, 1770 and 1724 were situated within the circuit. Broadly Iron Age pottery came from 1600, but the other two pits contained pottery of both Early and more broadly Iron Age date. A sheep/goat skull came from 1770, but with no other notable associated materials this may be an incidental discard.

A curvilinear gully (1698) and possibly pit 1718, defined roundhouse 12, immediately to the west of roundhouse 4. It only survived as a short (around 3m) length of shallow gully, 0.31– 0.34m wide and 0.1m deep, which appeared to describe the southern edge of another ring gully. This contained 26 sherds of pottery of broadly Iron Age date. Whilst it is difficult to estimate the exact position and diameter of a building from this, it would appear to be similar in scale to roundhouse 4. However, the building would have been so close as to have touched, or perhaps overlapped with, roundhouse 4. Within the arc of this putative building were pits 2032, 1389 and 1390, with 1389 containing broadly Iron Age pottery and 2032 and 1390 pottery including that of Middle Iron Age date, with the latter having a substantial amount and several clearly Middle Iron Age sherds.

Roundhouse 10, about 15m to the south-east of roundhouse 4 also survived as a crescent-shaped gully (2906), describing the north-western quadrant of another structure, probably 9m in diameter. The gully had moderately sloped sides and a concave base and was 0.46m wide and 0.15m deep but contained no finds. The area likely to have been covered by this building contained several pits including 2908 that included Iron Age pottery, although this also contained five Romano-British sherds, and tree-throw hole 3239 (not shown on plan) which contained no datable material.

Roundhouses 8, 9 and 13 which lay 120m south-east of roundhouse 10 were only partially exposed (Fig. 2.11). In each case they are represented by a curvilinear section of gully, which continued beyond, or could be extrapolated to continue beyond, the excavated area.

Roundhouse 9, the more northerly of the three, was possibly the largest estimated as having enclosed an area 11m in diameter. The gully (6008, 6066) comprised the south-western arc, continuous and almost half of the circuit, having moderate uneven sloping sides and a flat base and

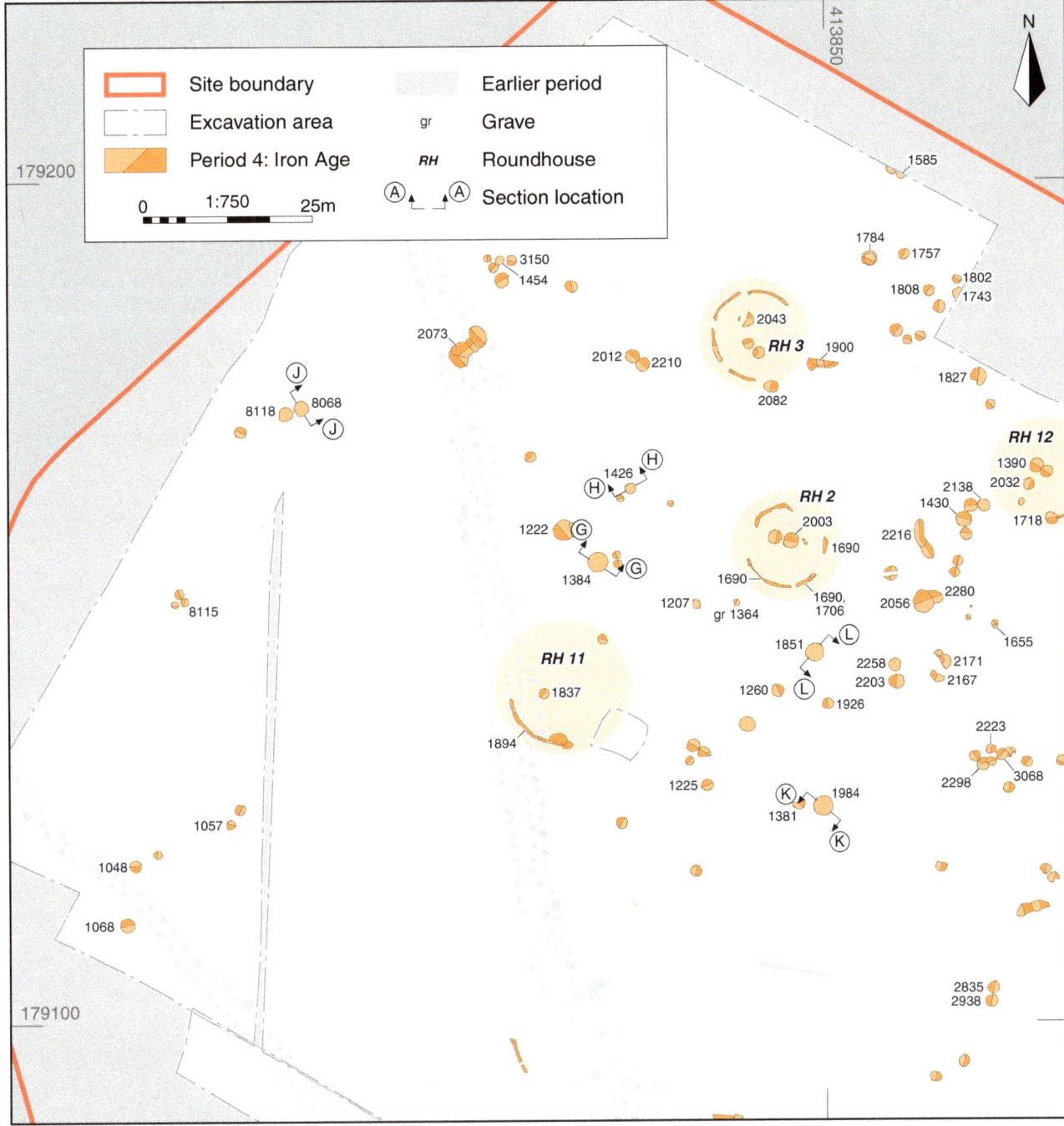

Figure 2.9 Detailed plan of the north-west part of the Period 4 (Iron Age) settlement

being 0.51–0.88m wide and 0.2–0.25m deep. It contained a single sherd of pottery of broadly Iron Age date. The gully continued beyond the edge of the excavation at both ends and did not seem to be immediately associated with any internal or adjacent features.

Roundhouse 8, 6m to the south, was probably about 9m in diameter; the gully (2602, 2604, 2728 and 2730) also comprised about half of the circuit around the south-western aspect of the building. It had both concave sides and base and was 0.32–1.1m wide and 0.07–0.18m deep. The single silty clay with chalk fill produced no datable finds. A single pit 2693 was located within the building footprint, only contained two sherds which could be

broadly dated to the Iron Age, with an additional pit 2689 outside of the circuit to the south-east. The latter contained pottery of broadly Iron Age date, and a probably intrusive sherd of Romano-British date. The terminal of the gully at the south-eastern extent cut an irregular feature 2733, but this may have been a tree-throw hole (not shown on plan) and contained no datable finds.

Roundhouse 13, about 5m to the north-west, was represented by a shorter length of curvilinear gully, approximately 4m long, but which is likely to have formed part of the southern circuit of a ring gully. If extrapolated it could have represented a building similar in size, or slightly smaller than roundhouse 8. The gully (3304, 3385, 3425)

Figure 2.10 Detailed plan of the central part of the Period 4 (Iron Age) settlement

had straight sides and a flat base and was 0.22–0.43m wide and 0.13–0.28m deep and contained no datable finds. Pits 2697 and 2852 were located in the centre of the area enclosed by the possible structure, the latter of which contained broadly Iron Age pottery.

Roundhouse 7 was located at the western extent of the excavation (Fig. 2.10). The ring gully was reasonably complete and it was one of the larger structures, enclosing

an area 11m in diameter. Part of the circuit lay outside the excavation, but the gully clearly continued into the unexcavated area. Due to the completeness of the gully, a break in the circuit on the east side may represent a genuine entrance. Part of the structure, if as extrapolated, would have overlaid Pit alignment 2 on its western side, although this area was not excavated, and no relationship was examined. The gully of roundhouse 7 (2613; 2615;

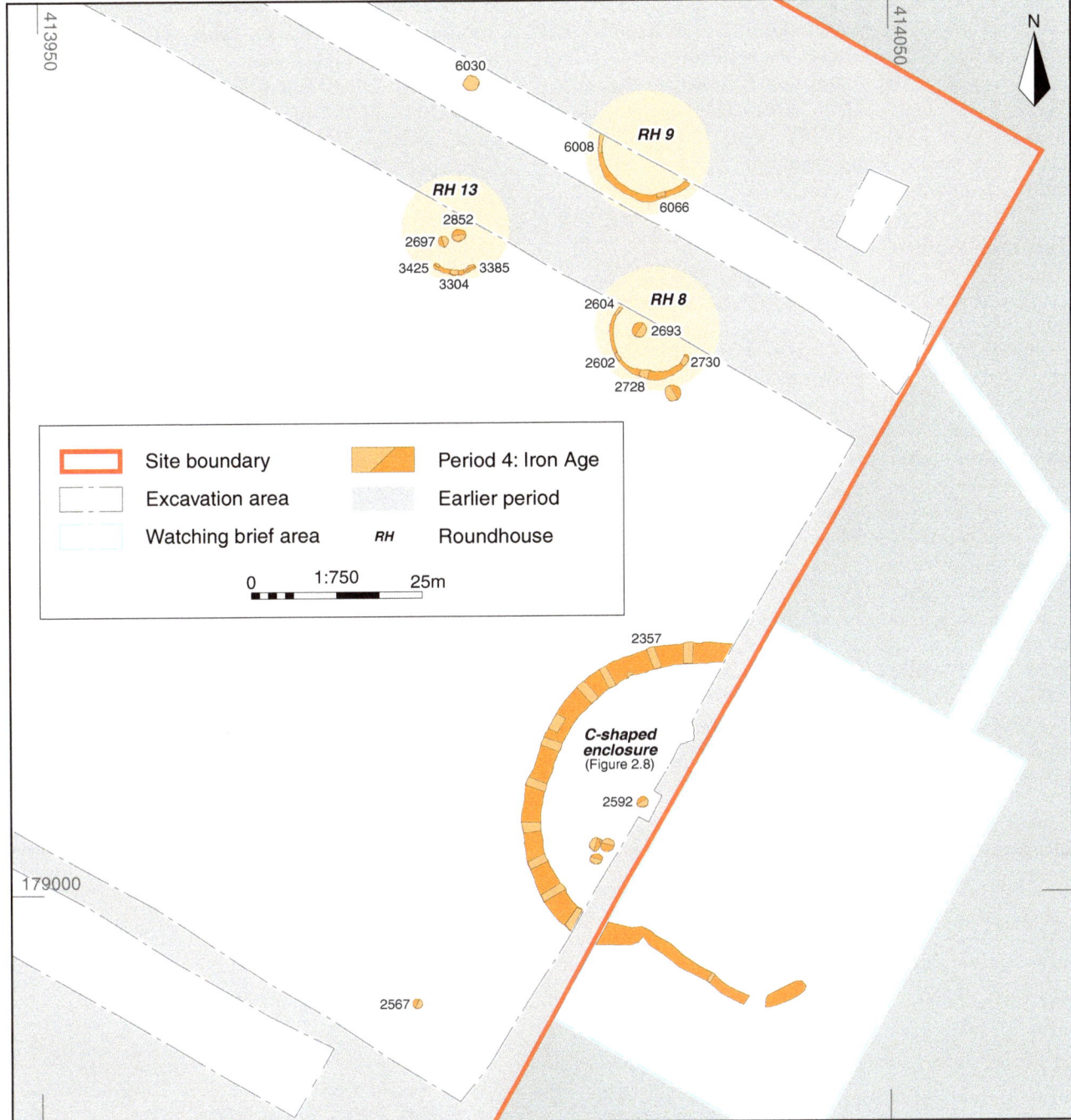

Figure 2.11 Detailed plan of the south-west part of the Period 4 (Iron Age) settlement

2617) had moderate concave sides and a concave base and 0.45–0.68m wide and 0.12–0.13m deep. The chalky fill of this ditch produced pottery of general Iron Age date. This roundhouse was not apparently associated with any contemporary features.

Some 25m to the east, roundhouse 6 only survived as a short crescent-shaped gully (2555; 2557; 2561; 2563) which defined the north-west quadrant of the circuit of a building similar in diameter to roundhouse 7. The gully had shallow concave sides and a concave base and was only 0.24–0.31m wide and extremely shallow at 0.03–0.8m deep. The gully produced a single sherd of broadly Iron Age

pottery. One posthole was found on the outer edge of the gully close to the northern end (2565), which had sloping sides and a concave base and was 0.56m in diameter and 0.15m deep. However, this lacked finds and it is uncertain whether it had a structural association with the ditch. A similar small posthole (2559) was located on the inner edge of the gully, and may have been associated with the structure.

Roundhouse 11 was located in the western part of the site, about 70m to the north of roundhouse 7 (Fig. 2.10). Its potential ground plan also overlapped Pit alignment 2 on its western side. A crescent-shaped gully (1894) with moderately steep concave sides and a concave base was

0.23m and 0.09m deep. It was slightly elongated which may cast doubt on its identification as a roundhouse but is comparable with other 'flattened' sections of gully associated with the other structures. It cut several pits along Period 3 Pit alignment 2 at its west end and two larger undated pits at its east end (1891 which in turn cut 1969) which were not part of the alignment. The single fill of the gully lacked finds.

Inhumation burials

A total of ten features within the main excavation area contained inhumation burials; a further burial was identified approximately 330m to the north of the main part of the site, during the excavation of an evaluation trench. These inhumation burials have produced dates throughout the Iron Age, but the possibility of curation of remains needs to be taken into account in the interpretation of these deposits, so they are described here together; they are further discussed in Chapter 5. The burials in the main excavation area were distributed across the north and north-western part, and the details of the features are included in Table 2.1 (see Fig. 2.12).

The burials fall into two categories, those which appear to have been interred in deliberately cut features, and those placed within pits, which may well have been pre-existing. The examples in apparently specific grave cuts have provided two of the earlier radiocarbon dates compared to those in pits, and this, along with the consideration that

the deposition of human remains in pits may be part of a continuum of depositional behaviour means that the 'graves' are dealt with here first.

Grave 10003 (SK 10005), which was seen in an evaluation trench 330m to the north of the excavation, was a shallow circular cut 1m wide and 0.2m deep (Fig. 1.5). It appeared to be an isolated feature. It contained, the poorly preserved remains of young-prime adult female. The body was in a crouched position on her left side/slightly supine (Fig. 2.16). The grave fill contained no finds but the left femur of the skeleton produced a radiocarbon date range of *466–386 cal. BC* (*95.4% probability;* SUERC-94043), Following excavation, further analysis identified the additional remains of a juvenile (SK 100005b) aged 11–12 years. The child's remains were only partially present and in poor condition but appears to have been in front of/beneath the woman's body. It is not possible to determine if the remains of the juvenile were partial when interred or due to taphonomic processes.

In the main excavation area, the earliest radiocarbon date was obtained from a grave cut into an earlier, wide but shallow pit (1222) located 20m west of roundhouse 2 in the north-west part of the site (Fig. 2.9). Two silty clay deposits had completely filled the pit, following which oval grave 1204 was cut into it. This shallow (0.17m deep) cut (1.65m long and 0.7m wide) contained an older adult female (SK 1206) who had been placed face down in very tightly flexed position (Fig. 2.14). The grave was orientated north/south, with the head to the north. The fills of the earlier pit, and

Table 2.1 Summary of Iron Age burials (see Chapter 5 for details of the radiocarbon dating results)

| Feature | Shape | Grave cut | | | Skeleton | Body position | Cultural material | Radiocarbon date |
		Length	Width	Depth				
10003	Circular	1m	1m	0.2m	SK 10005 & SK 10005b Adult female and juvenile	Flexed		SUERC-94043
1204 Cut into pit 1222	Oval	1.65m	0.7m	0.17m	SK 1206 Adult female	Very tightly flexed		SUERC-94037
1207	Oval	1.12m	0.73m	0.13m	SK 1209 Adult female	Very tightly flexed		SUERC-100009
1364	Sub-rectangular	0.76m	0.69m	0.19m	SK 1366 Neonate	Slightly flexed	Iron Age pottery	
1488 Cut into upper fills of pit 1384	Oval/sub-rectangular	0.90m	0.48m	0.24m	SK 1489 Juvenile		Early to Middle Iron Age pottery	
1658	Sub-circular	0.84m	0.53m	0.07m	SK 1659 Adult female	Flexed		SUERC-100014
1777 Cut into upper fills of pit 1781	Sub-circular	1.1m	0.90m	0.37	SK 1778 Adult female	Flexed	Middle Iron Age pottery	SUERC-100012
Pit 1426	NA	NA	NA	NA	SK 1845 Adult male	Tightly flexed	Middle Iron Age pottery, bone point	SUERC-94041
Pit 1947	NA	NA	NA	NA	SK 3235 Adult female	Flexed		SUERC-100015
Pit 8068	NA	NA	NA	NA	SK 8071 Adult female	Very tightly flexed	Charcoal, animal bone, bone pins and Iron Age pottery	SUERC-100011

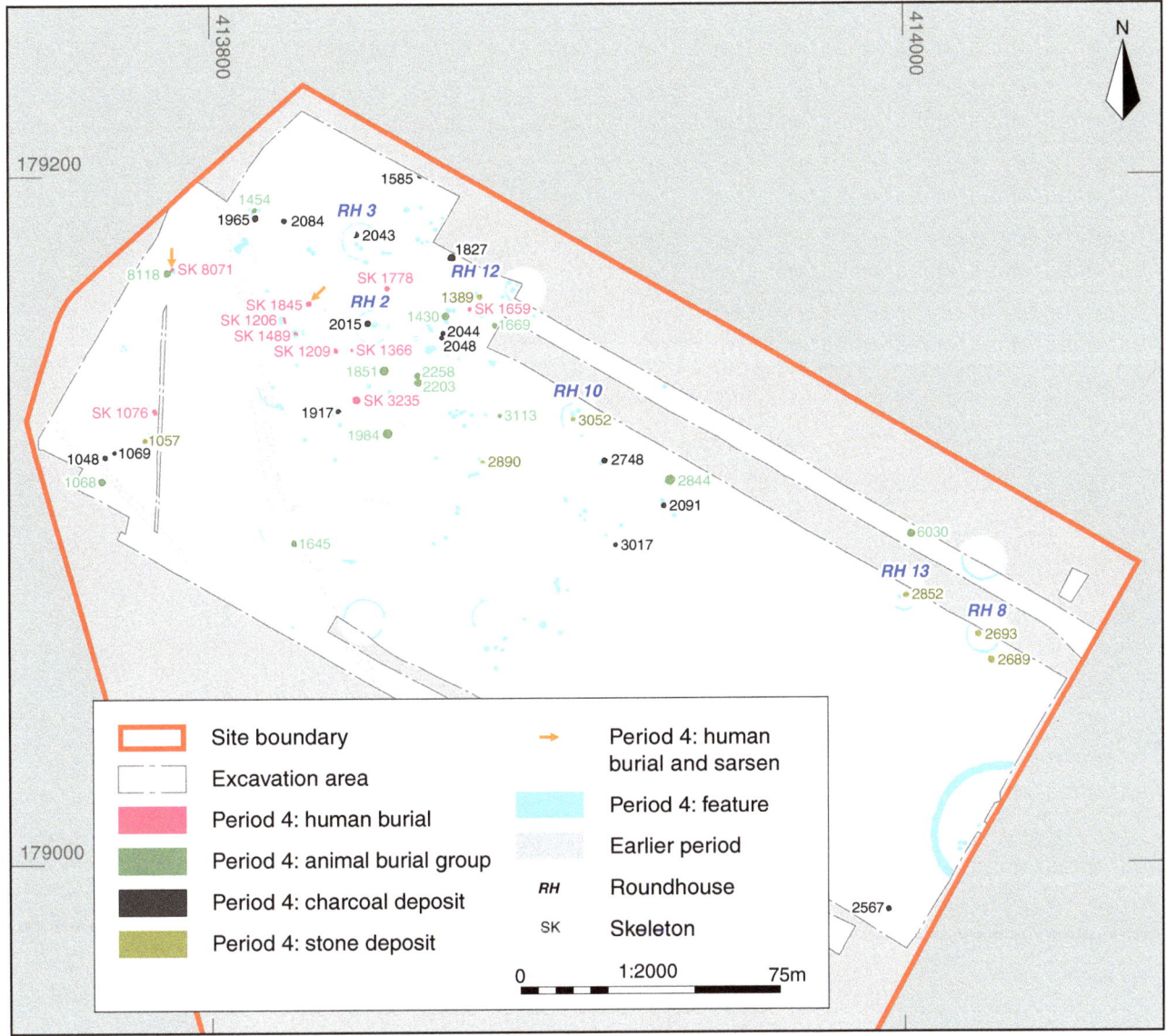

Figure 2.12 Plan showing the location within the Period 4 (Iron Age) settlement of human burials, animal ABGs, stone and charcoal deposits

that covering the burial contained no datable finds but a rib from the skeleton was radiocarbon dated and provided a range of *759–462 cal. BC (93.0%)* (SUERC-94037), providing the earliest date range from the settlement.

Grave 1207 was 16m south-east of pit 1222, cutting the natural substrate (Fig. 2.12). It too was a north/south aligned oval cut, at least 1.12m long, its southern extent cut through by a later ditch, and 0.73m wide and 0.13m deep. It contained a young adult female (SK 1209, Fig. 2.15) placed in a tightly folded supine position with her head to the north. There were no finds in the grave fill, but a rib from this woman produced a radiocarbon date range of *514–366 cal. BC (95.4% probability*; SUERC-100009). A further grave, 1364, also dug into the geology, was found 5m to the east (Fig. 2.12). The small sub-rectangular cut, 0.76m long by 0.69m wide and 0.19m deep contained a slightly flexed neonate (SK 1366). It was not possible to radiocarbon date this individual, but two sherds of pottery

were recovered, both of which were of Late Iron Age to Romano-British character. It may be that this neonatal burial dates from later than the settlement although the pottery may be intrusive. It has been included here as the latter seems more likely given the proximity of the other Iron Age burials.

Grave 1658 was badly truncated by ploughing leaving a shallow oval cut (0.84m long, 0.53m wide and only 0.07m deep) which contained the partial remains of a mature adult female (SK 1659, Figs 2.12 and 2.18) placed in a crouched position on her left side and on a north/south alignment. The skull was absent due to later ploughing but would have been at the north end of the grave. No finds were associated with the burial but a rib from this woman was radiocarbon dated, providing a range of *362–150 cal. BC (95% probability*; SUERC-100014).

Several graves (in addition to 1204 discussed above) appear to have been dug into the upper fills of pits – these

Figure 2.13 Aerial photograph of Period 4 (Iron Age) Roundhouse 3, north is to the bottom of the photograph

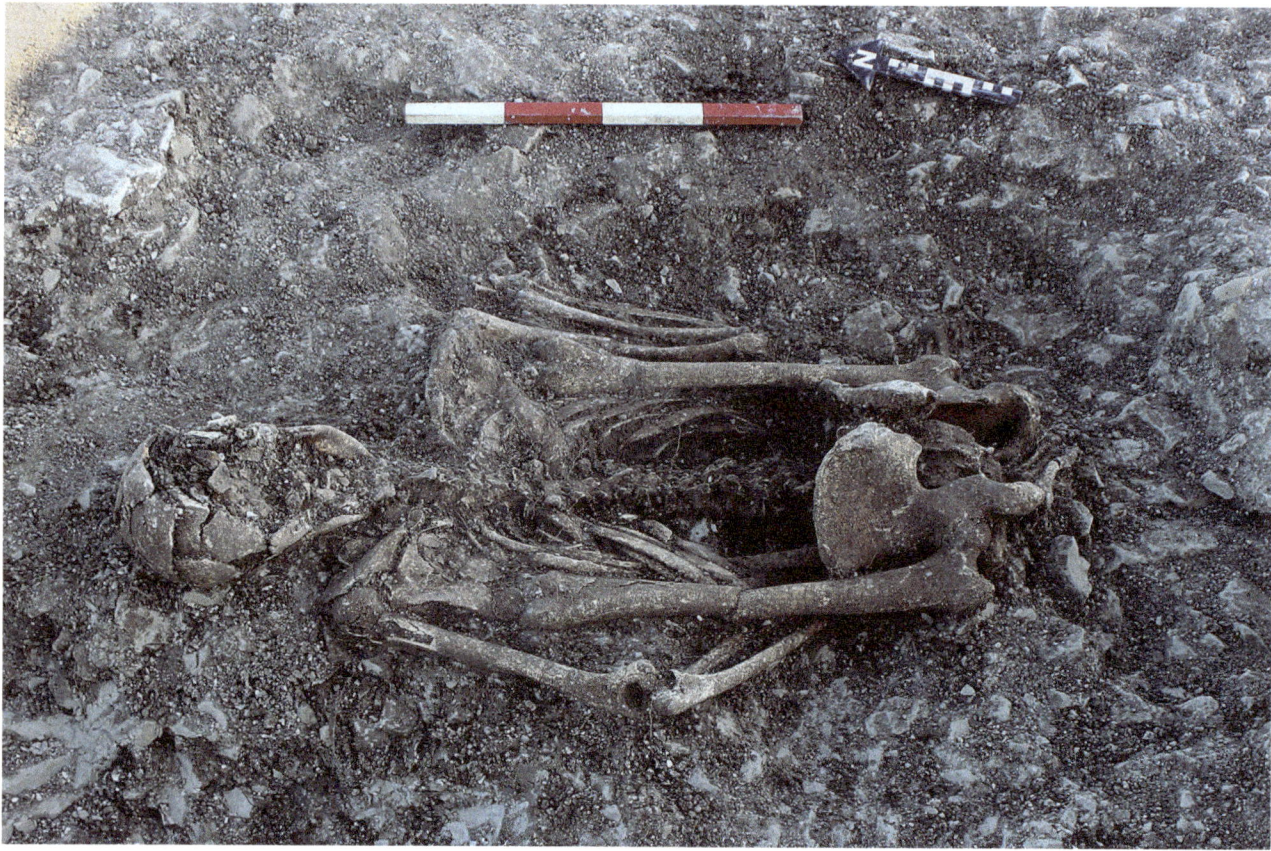

Figure 2.14 Period 4 (Iron Age) SK 1206 in grave 1204, looking north-east

Figure 2.15 Period 4 (Iron Age) SK 1209 in grave 1207, looking north

Figure 2.16 Period 4 (Iron Age) SK 10005 and SK 10005b in grave 10003, looking south-west

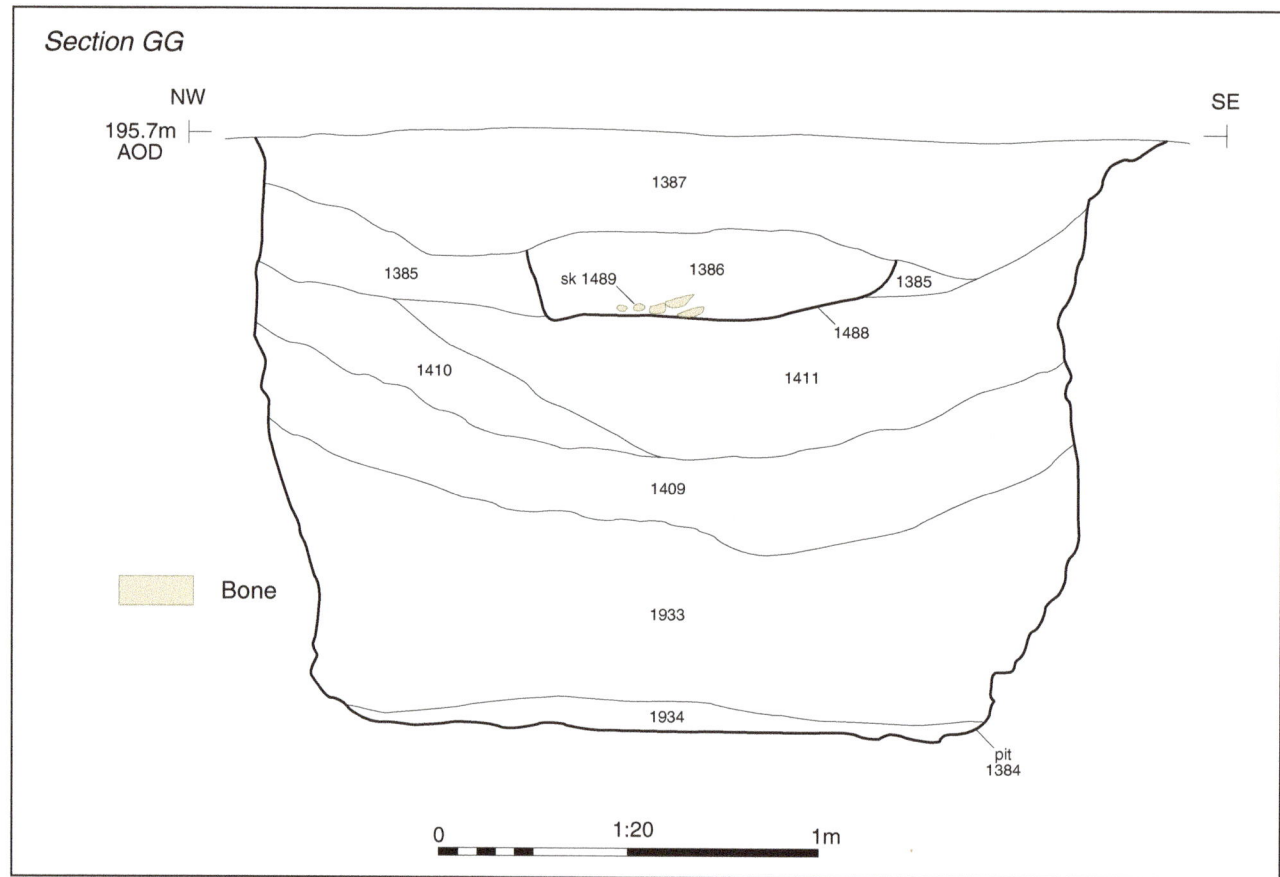

Figure 2.17 North-east-facing section through pit 1384

Figure 2.18 Period 4 (Iron Age) SK 1659 in grave 1658, looking north-east

were mainly long out of use and almost entirely backfilled when the remaining hollows appear to have been utilised. Grave 1488 was dug into the upper fills of pit 1384 (Figs 2.9, 2.12, 2.17), which included sherds spanning the Early to Middle Iron Age, but including some which can be more certainly assigned to the Early Iron Age. The pit was about three-quarters filled when an oval grave 0.90m long by 0.48m wide and 0.24m deep, was cut into the centre of it. Within this was a child aged 12–13 years (SK 1489) buried in a crouched position on its left side, the head to the north, facing eastwards. The covering deposits also contained pottery of Early to Middle Iron Age date, although this may have derived from the fills into which the grave had been dug.

Sub-circular grave 1777 had been cut into the upper fills of pit 1781 (Fig. 2.12). This sub-circular cut 1.1m long by 0.90m wide and 0.37m deep contained an older adult female (SK 1778) placed in a crouched position against the grave edge and on a north-east/south-west alignment with the head to the south-west (Fig. 2.19). The fills of the pit which had been cut by the burial contained a single sherd of broadly dated Iron Age pottery, with similarly broadly dated sherds in the fills over the burial. One of the ribs of the skeleton was radiocarbon dated, producing a calibrated range of *358–279 cal. BC (51.6%)* and *231–112 cal. BC (43.8%)*(SUERC-100012).

In contrast, several pits appear to have been utilised for burial early in their sequence of filling. Some 15m west of

Figure 2.19 Period 4 (Iron Age) SK 1778 in grave 1777, looking south-west

roundhouses 2 and 3 was a large pit, 1426 (Figs 2.9 and 2.12). This was 1.5m wide and 1.55m deep with vertical, slightly undercut, sides and a flat base (Figs 2.20–2.21). Across the base was a thin trample deposit (1846), which included diagnostic Middle Iron Age pottery and onto this had been placed SK 1845, the remains of a mature adult male placed face down in very tightly flexed position with his feet up against the north wall of the pit (Fig. 2.21). This individual had a range of pathologies, including a healed traumatic injury to his back, and an infection around the ankles which was active when he died. One of his ribs produced a radiocarbon determination with a calibrated range of *391–346 cal. BC (35.7%)* and *316–206 cal. BC (59.7%)* (SUERC-94041). Large chalk and sarsen fragments (1632) had been placed to cover the body, leaning against the pit wall. This deposit included further Iron Age pottery which included a single sherd of Early Iron Age date as well as fragments of structural daub which retained wattle impressions (see Collier-Jones and McSloy, Chapter 3). Above this deposit was backfill 1631, a chalky clay silt which included a few sarsen fragments, a significant amount of charcoal (largely oak and field maple, but also including substantial plant remains of cereals and weed seeds, see Wyles and Challinor, Chapter 4), animal bone, and Middle Iron Age pottery. This deposit also produced a complete sandstone saddle quern (Ra. 1014), a chalk weight (Ra. 1015; see Shaffrey, Chapter 3), a piece of slag (Ra. 1016) and a broken worked bone object, possibly a pin,

needle or textile awl (Ra. 1017; see Collier-Jones, Chapter 3). This deposit was sealed by further chalky clay fills which together produced animal bone and pottery, as well as an iron strip (Ra. 1007). This pit also contained mineralised seeds including flax. The uppermost fill, a grey silty clay, may represent natural infilling into a remnant hollow and produced broadly dated Iron Age pottery.

Pit 1947 also contained human remains (Fig. 2.12). It had slightly undercut sides and was 1.8m wide and 1m deep (Fig. 2.22). Onto its flat base had been placed SK 3235, the remains of a mature adult female, placed in a crouched position with the feet up against the southern pit wall (Fig. 2.23). Whilst the skeleton was in poor condition, it seemed to be in a generally north–south orientation. One of her ribs produced a radiocarbon date range of *359–277 cal. BC (54.4%), 258–248 cal. BC (1.1%)* and *233–120 cal. BC (40.0%)* (SUERC-100015). A thin layer of charcoal (unidentified) was also noted across the pit floor. She had been covered by two chalky silty clay backfills, themselves overlain by a dump of clean chalk. The uppermost pit fill, a further chalky silty clay, produced Iron Age pottery.

Pit 8068 was a cylindrical cut, 2m wide and 1.1m deep located to the west of Pit alignment 2 (Fig. 2.24). A layer of brownish clay silt (8098) on its base contained charcoal (containing a significant concentration of charred and mineralised cereals and weed seeds), animal bone and Iron Age pottery. Onto this had been placed the remains of a young adult female (SK 8071) with indications of metabolic

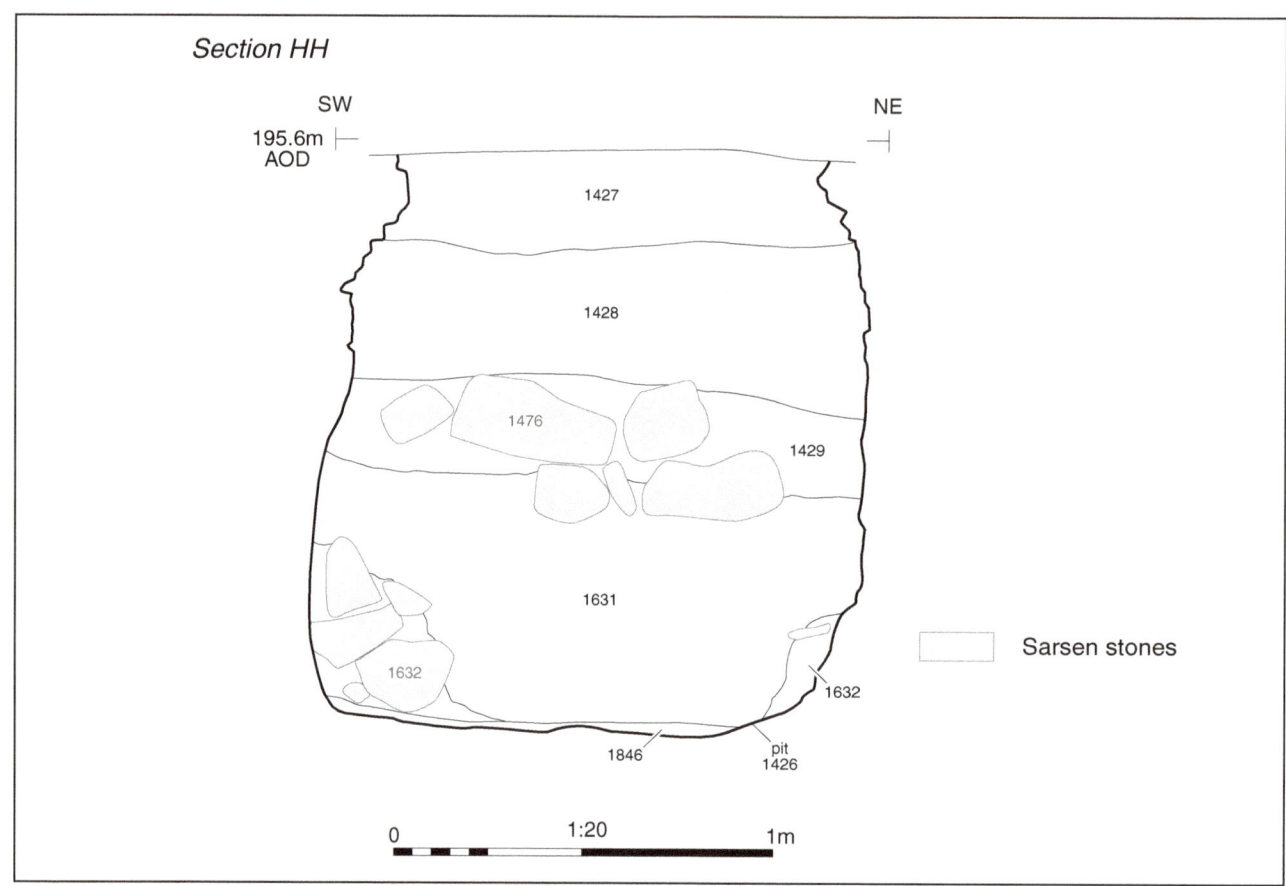

Figure 2.20 South-east-facing section through Period 4 (Iron Age) pit 1426

Figure 2.21 Period 4 (Iron Age) SK 1845 in pit 1426, looking north-west

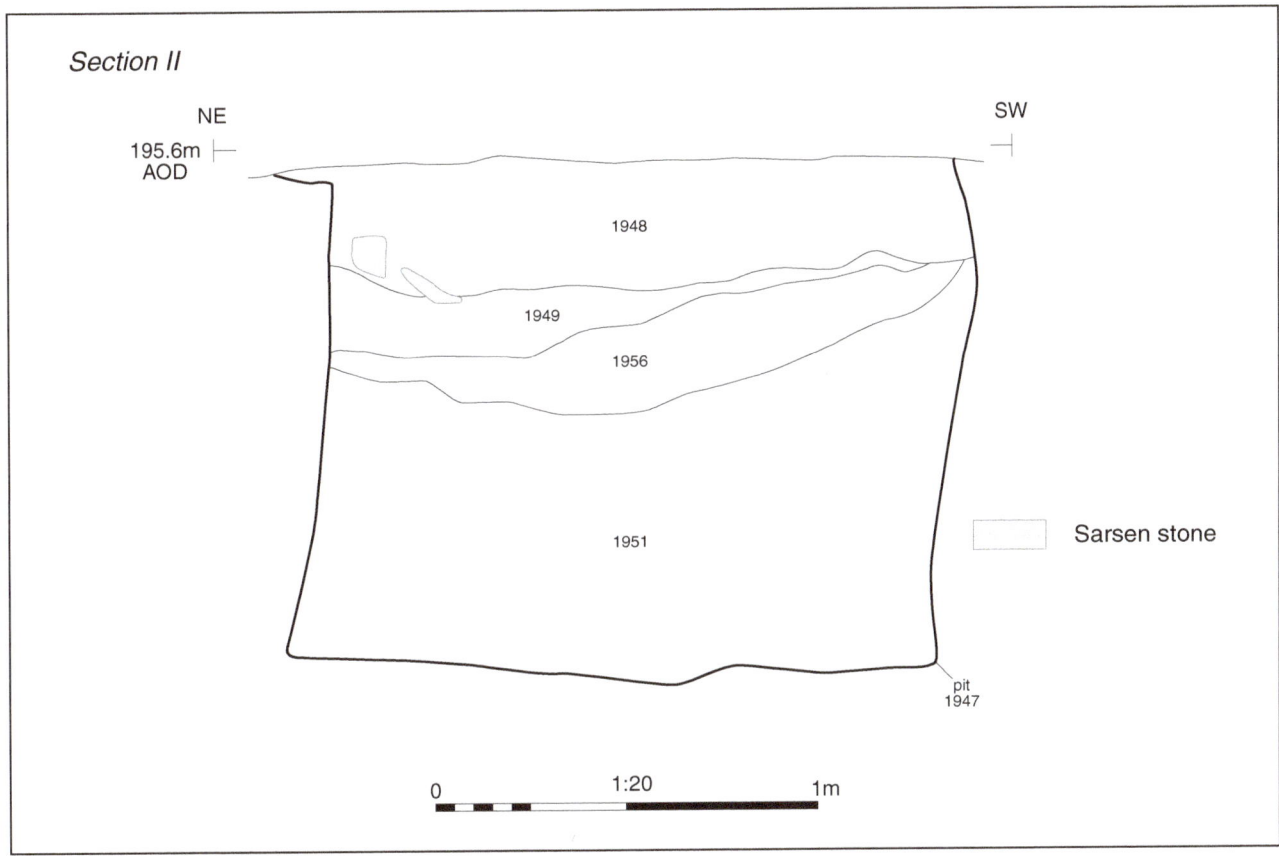

Figure 2.22 North-west-facing section through Period 4 (Iron Age) pit 1947

Figure 2.23 Period 4 (Iron Age) SK 3235 in pit 1947, looking south-east

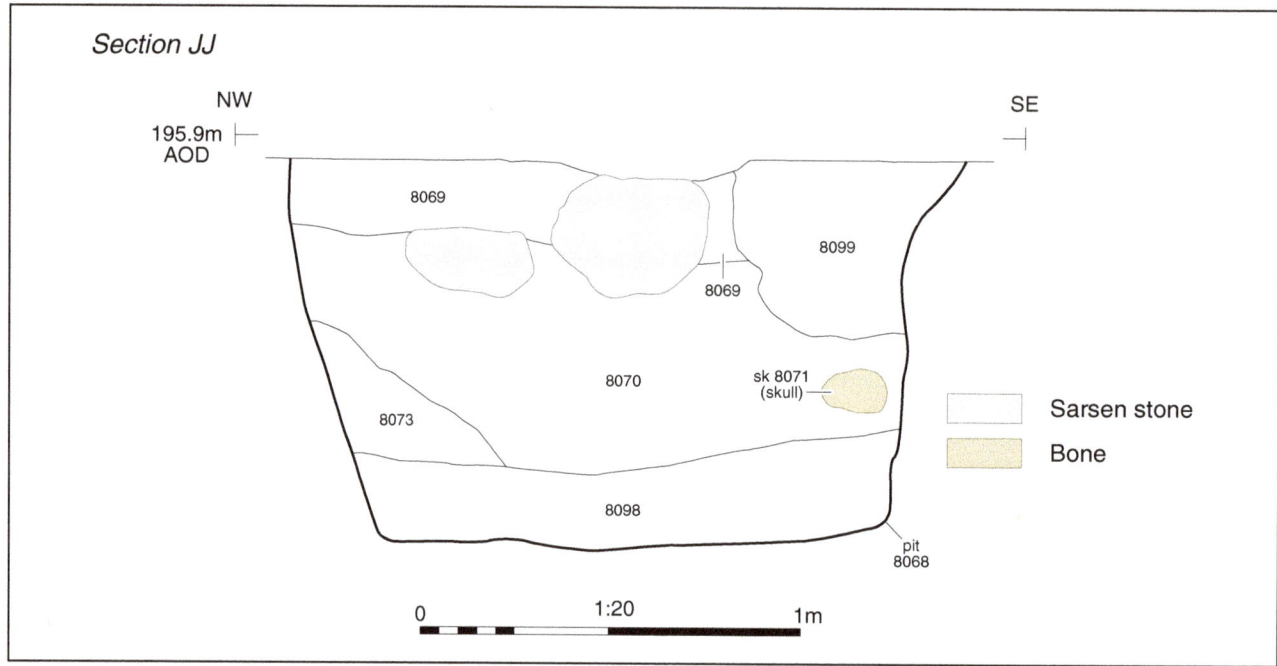

Figure 2.24 South-west-facing section through Period 4 (Iron Age) pit 8068

disease and a systemic infection active at the time of death, placed in a tightly folded position up against the pit wall and on a north–south alignment, with the head to the north, facing the pit wall (Fig. 2.25). A radiocarbon date range of *362–154 cal. BC* (SUERC-100011) was obtained from one of her ribs. Her body was sealed by layer 8070, a dump of chalk and sarsen blocks (up to 200mm across) and fragments, a deposit which included lenses of charcoal. The lenses perhaps suggest that this deposit occurred in several stages but could represent handfuls of charred material deliberately included amongst the stones and chalk during backfilling. This deposit also produced Iron Age pottery, a limestone weight (Ra. 1208; Fig. 3.17, 7), a stone loomweight or spindlewhorl (Ra. 1225; see Shaffrey, Chapter 3; Fig. 3.18, 9), and two bone pins (Ras 1204 and 1205; Fig. 3.15, 1 and 2) made from horse metapodials. Above was a capping deposit of two sarsen stones, each up to 300mm across, within grey-brown silty clay; this fill produced Middle to Late Iron Age pottery and a grain rubber made from a sarsen stone (Ra. 1200; Fig. 3.19, 11), an object type used in conjunction with a quernstone for processing cereals.

Pits

A total of 156 pits have been assigned to the Iron Age in the main part of the site. As mentioned above, some of these features occurred within the footprint of several of the gullies which probably indicate roundhouses and may be directly associated with their use. Others appear to be in parts of the settlement apparently without structures, although the degree of truncation by ploughing evident across this area should be taken into account.

The majority of these pits were circular or sub-circular cuts (176) with a smaller number of oval or elongated examples (25) and two irregular pits (Appendix 1). In most cases, the profile was of vertical sides with a flat or flat/uneven base, or vertical sides with varying degrees of undercutting. The form of the base seems likely to have been largely dictated by the underlying geology, whilst the under-cut sides seem to originate as straight, vertical sides which have eroded, either by aerial weathering or cleaning. The degree and location of the concavity or undercutting varies, in less deep features involving the entire side, elsewhere affecting one side more than another (e.g., pits 1770 and 2073) or being located near the upper part or the base of the pit (e.g., pits 1947, 2567, and 2583). There is no real similarity in the profile of these features, which suggests an individual origin of the form for each feature most likely related to localised variation in the substrate and the length of time it remained open to weathering or number of times it was cleaned out. This process is attested by the fills of some pits which appear to contain deposits related to the collapse of the sides.

There is a degree of uniformity in the dimensions of pits. Excluding some outlying examples (e.g., pits 3002 or 1706 which are small and shallow, and oval pits 2203 and 2216 which are in excess of 3m long), most pits were between about 0.65m and 2m diameter or greatest width with most between 0.75 and 1.25m. Depths varied, with some very shallow examples but also some examples well over a metre deep. Two thirds of the pits were no more than 0.75m deep. Unsurprisingly the number of fills increased with depth; some shallow features only contained a single context, whilst others contained up to 10, with a mean of three fills. Most fills were variations of clay/silty clay often with chalk

Figure 2.25 Period 4 (Iron Age) SK 8071 in pit 8068, looking south-east

inclusions, in some cases rare, and in others abundant. At the latter end of the spectrum are deposits which appear to relate to the erosion of the pit sides (e.g., 2003), but also includes noticeable layers or high-volume dumps of chalk material. Whilst rare or occasional charcoal occurred in many fills, and finds, largely of pottery or bone was found in at least one fill of these pits, many of the deposits in which chalk was abundant are lacking in indications of human derived material and suggest rapid covering or re-filling of some features. The number of fills which indicate deliberate filling from one side or another of a feature are rare, and many, particularly those in the middle or upper fills are more silty, mixed and suggestive of gradual filling.

Conversely, basal silts are rare, although there are a number of instances of deposition of animal bone, and sometimes pottery, on the pit base. This is also the case with discrete deposits of charcoal. Of 27 contexts regarded as likely to represent a concentrated charred deposit, 17 of these occurred on the base of the pit or formed the initial fill, and in three additional cases there was charred material in both the initial and a later fill. To this should perhaps be added pit 2748, the initial fill of which contained burnt chalk and pottery, and 2567 which had burnt flint and charcoal in its first fill. There was, however, no evidence of *in situ* burning within pits.

Along with the high-volume dumps of abundant broken chalk, there were several instances of inclusion of either large chalk blocks, or more specifically sarsen blocks, including some examples up to 450–500mm. This is suggestive of a deliberate practice which is less easy to explain in terms of practical availability of material to refill features. It should perhaps be seen in a similar light as a number of other deposits which stand out from the general distribution of pottery and bone, forming concentrations of finds, and more commonly, associated bone groups, and perhaps the small number of human interments (see above). There is, however, some variability in the nature of the features into which different materials are deposited. Whilst a small sample, all human remains occurred in circular pits, albeit with both vertical and undercut sides, which were 1.4–1.82m in diameter and 1–1.6m deep, containing between four and eight fills. In contrast eight Associated Bone Groups (ABGs) occurred in pits of various shapes, although these were larger features (1.3–3m in extent and 0.59–1.14m deep) with between three and seven fills. Charcoal also occurred in pits of all shapes, although these also tended to larger features (0.87–2.5m in extent and 0.43–1.19m deep) with three to ten fills. The ten dumps of stone, all occurred in circular or sub-circular features in excess of 1m wide (varying between 0.41–1.55m deep) with three to seven fills. Examples of some of the more complex pits, those with more interesting deposits, and those which contained more unusual items are described below, and the depositional practice is discussed in Chapter 6.

Pits with charcoal or burned deposits

Pit 1384 was one of those, the fills of which were cut into for the burial of human remains, but it also provides an example of another practice which was noted in a number of pits across the site. It had a relatively large number of fills and the earliest, 1934, was a thin deposit of dark silty clay which contained charcoal (unidentified), as well as Iron Age pottery and animal bone. This may have been the remains of stored material fired *in situ* and mixed with waste debris, or a deliberate deposit on the pit floor. This was overlain by five chalky silty clay fills which produced further pottery, including sherds datable to the Middle to Late Iron Age. These deposits left the pit largely but not completely infilled and once it was about three-quarters filled, an oval grave of a child (SK 1489) was cut into it (see above; Fig. 2.17). The grave backfill was sealed by a further deposit which also filled the remaining level of the pit and which produced Iron Age pottery. A final deposit then filled the pit.

Other pits had charcoal or burned deposits included in later fills. Pit 2210, 7m west of roundhouse 3 (Fig. 2.9) was sub-circular in plan with vertical sides and a flat base, and was 1.55m long, 1.46m wide and 0.75m deep. It contained three fills the lowest of which, 2211, was an apparently slow silting deposit (the chalk fragments occurred in thin lenses) across the base of the pit that produced the earliest closely datable pottery from the pits. This comprised a single Late Bronze Age to Early Iron Age sherd, which was probably residual, having been found alongside Iron Age pottery. Above was a dark, charcoal-rich (but unidentified) silty clay deposit up to 0.45m thick with scorched (red) stones which contained further Iron Age pottery along with animal bone. It was covered, by a chalk-rich deposit which probably formed over a period of time. This is one of a number of pits where a hiatus in filling is suggested, with a possibly deliberate dump of material left uncovered to gradually silt over.

A neighbouring pit, 2012, which slightly cut into 2210 along its western edge, displayed some similar characteristics, but perhaps a different cycle of filling. Pit 2012 was comparable in size and shape (1.55m by 1.42m wide and 0.7m deep) and contained four fills. The lowest fill, chalky silty clay 2214, was a substantial deposit which produced a sherd of Iron Age pottery, along with two broadly datable flint flakes and animal bone and probably resulted from gradual silting, displaying similar lensing of chalk and some charcoal as seen in pit 2210. The succeeding fill produced further animal bone and was chalk rich; it may have been a deliberate deposit or given its distribution may represent erosional collapse of the north-west side of the pit. Almost all of the remaining third of the pit was filled with 2014, a dark deposit with frequent charcoal (including cereals and weed seeds), only a small amount of chalk and some scorched (red) stones, animal bone (including a single bone of domestic fowl, see Holmes, Chapter 4) and Iron Age pottery. The final chalky silty clay fill was only a few

centimetres deep, however, and probably accumulated in a hollow left when the pit contents settled.

Pit 1048, one of the few pits in the north-western corner of the excavated area, and immediately adjacent to the east side of the earlier Pit alignment 1 (Fig. 2.9), was a vertical-sided cut 1.3m in diameter and 0.84m deep and contained five chalky silty clay fills, some of which produced animal bone and pottery. The initial fill, although not confined to the very base of the pit, was charcoal rich. This contained a lot of cereals, including chaff as well as weed seeds, as well as wood charcoal comprising blackthorn with a little oak, hazel-type and dogwood (see Wyles and Challinor, Chapter 4). The uppermost, fill 1049, produced animal bone, pottery and a shale bracelet fragment (Ra. 1002, see McSloy, Chapter 3, Fig. 3.14), which is compatible with a Middle Iron Age date.

Pit 1585, 20m north-east of roundhouse 3 (Fig. 2.9) was circular in plan, 0.87m in diameter and 0.43m deep with concave sides and a flat base. The lower silty clay fill which included Iron Age pottery. This was covered by an even layer of a very charcoal-rich fill 1587 (including blackthorn and hawthorn types along with charred and mineralised cereals and weed seeds), which also contained pottery and animal bone. This was covered by a fine silt layer with no finds; its orangey-yellow hue may suggest scorching. It was covered by a 0.09m thick layer largely consisting of broken chalk, but which also included some fire-cracked flints, as well as small amounts of animal bone and pottery. The silty uppermost fill appears to have accumulated into the remaining hollow (1590). A bone weaving tool or toggle came from this upper fill (see Collier-Jones, Chapter 3, Fig. 3.15, 9).

Pit 2748, 10m south-east of roundhouse 10, was another circular pit with vertical sides and a flat base 1.11m in diameter and 0.67m deep. The contents comprised five fills and were largely unremarkable other than the indications of burning. The initial fill contained burned chalk and clay; there was no indication that this had occurred *in situ*, more that it represented a dump of burned material. This was covered by a deposit which also contained some burned chalk and clay. Three further silty clay fills with some pottery overlay this, apparently the result of an extended period of gradual filling.

Pit 2258 was adjacent to pit 2203 (Figs 2.9 and 2.12, see below). It was 1.47m in diameter and 0.7m deep with undercut vertical sides and a flat base. An initial silty clay fill contained some animal bone. In the centre of the pit, resting on this initial deposit were three large sarsen stones, each up to 400mm by 600mm across. Covering this was a fill, 2260, which comprised the bulk of the pit contents It was dark grey, containing pieces of charcoal up to 30mm long (unidentified). A range of materials included Middle to Late Iron Age pottery and a significant amount of cattle and sheep/goat bone amongst which was a horse skull and a polished canid canine (not illustrated; see Collier-Jones, Chapter 3). With this were items associated with metal working comprising a fired clay block tuyère and a lump and droplets of copper alloy (Ras 1027 and 1029). The tuyère is a particularly rare object (see Dungworth, Chapter 3, Fig. 3.18). The uppermost deposit was an orange-brown silty clay.

Pits containing finds

A number of less usual finds came from a range of features which were in most respects unremarkable. Part of an iron knife came from pit 1837 (not illustrated, see McSloy, Chapter 3), located within the footprint of roundhouse 11 (Fig. 2.9). It was a typical sub-circular pit with straight sides and a flat base 1m wide and 1.27m long and 0.92m deep with four fills with little to differentiate them which contained some animal bone and pottery. Pit 2578, with similar form and dimensions contained a second fill which was charcoal-flecked and contained pottery, animal bone, a bone bead or toggle (Ra. 1106; Fig. 3.13, 4) and a cattle metacarpal with a polished shaft and proximal end.

Pit 2138 was sub-circular in plan (1.35m by 1.45) and 0.78m deep with vertical undercut sides and a flat base. It contained three fills, the initial one containing abundant chalk fragments with pottery and bone. This was covered by a large volume fill 2135 which filled most of the pit and also contained abundant chalk; down the south-east side of the pit a slump of similar material 2136 appears to represent the collapse of the pit wall. Within fill 2135 was a single very large sarsen stone, as well as Ra. 1022, an iron blade fragment (not illustrated). Amongst the pottery in this pit was a decorated sherd of probable 2nd–1st century BC date, in the upper fill, and there were further sherds of probable Late Iron Age date.

Two pits contained substantially complete pottery vessels (pits 1827 and 2669). Pit 1827, just north of roundhouse 12 (Figs 2.9 and 2.12), was a pit of typical size and shape (1.91m long 1.7m wide and at least 1.07m deep with vertical sides), which was largely unremarkable other than containing more fills than the average (six, although it was not fully excavated). A large portion of a Middle Iron Age jar occurred in lower fill 1833 (see Banks, Chapter 3, Fig. 3.4, 22).

Pit 2669, north-east of roundhouse 6, was another fairly typical pit, circular and just over a metre in diameter, 0.46m deep, with four fills and produced a near complete vessel in the Middle Iron Age saucepan pot tradition (Ra. 1077; Fig. 3.4, 25) from the upper fill. This was coated with a thick deposit of burnt food remains, and lipid analysis (WRO027; Dunne *et al.*, Chapter 3) indicated the pot had been used to contain dairy products. The only other characteristic which makes this pit stand out is that it was one with a substantial deposit of charred plant remains (see Wyles, Chapter 4). The combination of the two rather suggests a direct relationship to the discard of cooking waste.

A number of pits, some more broadly dated than others, contained stone and some ceramic objects which may be associated with textile production or food processing. Pit 2280 contained a large chalk weight (Ra. 1021; Fig. 3.14, 4) within one of its upper fills. This pit had a sub-circular plan, with undercut vertical sides and a flat base and was 1.61m long, 1.3m wide and 1.06m deep. It was one of the more complex as far as fills were concerned as it contained six deposits with differing amounts of chalk inclusions. The second fill 2277 included a charcoal lens, comparable with those described above. The animal bone in the central fills included the horn cores from at least four sheep/goats. One of the pottery sherds was the base from a saucepan pot, suggesting a Middle Iron Age date. Pit 8118 also contained nine weights, and this is discussed further below.

Pit 2908 was located within the footprint of roundhouse 10, one of several features (Fig. 2.10). It was a substantial circular pit (1.54m in diameter and 1.11m deep) with vertical sides and a flat base, and with seven fills one with a more complex filling process. Its initial fill was a dark silty clay with pottery and animal bone. This was covered by a silty clay with abundant chalk (2910). This was covered by a series of silty clays with varying indications of settlement debris and chalk inclusions, but also indicated that the sides of the pit had collapsed, suggesting that it was left open or reused.

A sub-circular pit 3083 (1.38m long by 0.99m wide and 0.58m deep) had vertical undercut sides and a flat base and contained four fills. The initial thin fill across the pit base was a silty clay which contained no finds. This was covered by a charcoal-rich silty clay which included pottery and bone. The charred material was dominated by a large proportion of cereal chaff. Over this across the width of the pit was 3086 charcoal-rich silty clay with chalk pieces, which produced pottery and a cylindrical fired clay spindlewhorl (Ra. 1096; Fig. 3.9, 2). This was covered by a similar silty clay with pottery and bone. In this case the process of filling appears to have been one of slow accumulation. Pit 1802 was circular in plan 1.16m in diameter and 0.56m deep with vertical slightly undercut sides and an irregular base. Two pieces of a bone comb (Ra. 1012; Fig. 3.13, 5) were recovered from each of two silty clay fills.

Pit 9009 was only partially exposed along the south-western edge of the site (Fig. 2.10). It was apparently circular and at least 1.53m in diameter, making it one of the larger pits. It had vertical sides and a flat base. Although it contained an Early Iron Age sherd most of the pottery was of Middle to Late Iron Age pottery, including a possible beaded rim, suggesting a date in the Late Iron Age. The base of the pit was covered by a silty clay which appears to be the result of weathering. Above this was a deposit with abundant (unidentified) charcoal, 9010, which included flint, animal bone and a clipped pottery vessel base with a central perforation indicating use as a spindlewhorl (Ra. 1206, not illustrated; see Banks, Chapter 3). This deposit also contained and two small chalk objects (Ras 1202 and 1203; Fig. 3.16, 8) which were either loomweights or further spindlewhorls (see Shaffrey, Chapter 3). Both were scorched and, for object Ra. 1203, this seems to have occurred after it was broken. The ceramic spindlewhorl had sooting from its use as a pottery vessel but was not otherwise scorched. This was covered by a silty clay with chalk which appeared to have accumulated gradually and contained no finds and completed the filling of the pit.

Pit 1757, 15m north-east of roundhouse 3, was approximately 1.3m in diameter and 0.61m deep, with only two fills. The lowest was a chalky silty clay with some animal bone and Middle Iron Age pottery (but including part of a decorated bowl which may date into the 2nd or 1st century BC, used for dairy products; see Banks and Dunne *et al.*, Chapter 3). The upper, similar, deposit included further pottery and animal bone but also the iron tip from an Iron Age ploughshare (Ra. 1010; Fig. 3.10, 2, see McSloy, Chapter 3). Another metal object came from pit 2265, 16m south-east of roundhouse 2. This was circular in plan 1.3m in diameter, 0.88m deep and contained four fills, the second of which was chalk rich dump containing pottery and bone. Over this was a silty clay with chalk and some charcoal (blackthorn and hawthorn-type with some field maple) and which included an iron strip with a rivet hole (Ra. 1026). The pit also produced two smithing hearth cakes (Dungworth, Chapter 3). Pit 2938 was cylindrical in profile and was 1.35m wide and 0.75m deep (Fig. 2.9). Its lower silty clay fill contained as well as animal bone and Middle Iron Age pottery. Above was a dark fill 2940 which included charcoal (cereal chaff with a few grains and weed seeds) and a few larger (up to 150mm) chalk blocks and a varied assemblage of finds comprising animal bone, pottery, flint, burnt stone and two small sandstone fragments, possibly a hone or grinding stone (Shaffrey, Chapter 3). A spelt wheat grain from this fill produced a radiocarbon date range of *354–286 cal. BC (39.8%)* and *210–96 cal. BC (55.7%)* (SUERC-100005), and two further silty clay fills completed the contents of the pit.

Another pit with a quernstone fragment (Ra. 1001, made from sarsen), was pit 1057, located towards the western corner of the site (Fig. 2.9). This pit was sub-circular with vertical sides and uneven base (1.1m by 1.2m) and 0.2m deep with a single fill; its shallowness, however, suggests it is a feature of a different character and function than most of those described here.

Pits with associated bone groups and animal skulls

Other pits contained animal skulls or associated groups of animal bone, some in articulation. Pit 2258 which contained a horse skull has been mentioned above. Whilst the presence of animal skulls should not be necessarily be regarded as 'unusual' in their own right, the presence of more complete examples is interesting taphonomically and can suggest more careful placement. Several features contained deposits which included largely complete or substantial proportions of the skulls of livestock and other domesticates.

Pit 3068 (Fig. 2.10) was cylindrical 1.51m in diameter and 0.97m deep but with undercut sides. It contained a series of six fills, which make it one of the more complex, although it is likely from the location that two of these were the result of the collapse of the pit sides. It produced Iron Age pottery. The earliest fill, 3066, contained a cattle skull/head placed on the pit floor and then covered by a clean chalk deposit. This formed the base onto which further animal bone, some charcoal and pottery sherds had been placed. This deposit was sealed by a dump of chalk above which was a blackish silty clay which included some charcoal, animal bone and pottery. This middle fill (3064) also contained an unworked piece of mineral, probably marcasite (Shaffrey, Chapter 3). This was sealed by a further clean chalk dump, whilst the final pit fill was a chalky silty clay which contained a worked bone awl (see Collier-Jones, Chapter 3; Fig. 3.15, 8).

Around 15m east of roundhouse 2 were several pits including 1430 (Figs 2.9 and 2.12). In this case the animal skull seems to be very deliberately placed. This was slightly sub-circular pit around 1.86m in diameter and 0.65m deep with vertical sides and a flat base. With seven fills it was one of the pits with a more complex sequence of filling. A cattle skull had been placed on the pit floor, up against the western side, within a silt containing some chalk gravels (fill 1435), in which there was Iron Age pottery, and there were several large stones placed against this towards the centre of the pit. This was covered by a dump of chalk, above which were a series of chalky silty clay deposits that contained very few finds, with the latest fill likely representing silting into a slight hollow left by the partially infilled pit. The only dog skull noted came from pit 3113, an isolated sub-circular pit in the centre of the settlement (Fig. 2.10), 1.05m in diameter, 0.36m deep with steep sides and a flat base. The almost entire skull came from the upper fill and does not appear to have been associated with any other materials.

Multiple animal skulls were also found in pit 1851, 7m south of roundhouse 2 (Figs 2.10 and 2.12). This was a very large (2.11m in diameter and 1.22m deep) circular pit with steep irregular sides and flat base and had one of the most complex filling sequences (Fig. 2.28, Section LL). It appears to have undergone a largely unremarkable initial process of filling until it was about half full. The pit floor was covered evenly to a depth of 0.18m by a chalky silty clay (1890) which appears to represent a gradual accumulation. It included a few fragments of cattle bone. Above this was silty clay with much more abundant chalk (1860) up to 0.64m thick, appearing to be a more rapid and deliberate act of backfilling and which included further animal bone, Middle Iron Age pottery and a sub-adult equid skull. This was capped by a layer of very chalky silt clay, 1861. From this level, it appears that the centre of the partially filled pit was dug out (cut 1869) creating a sub-circular pit 1.08m long and 1m wide and 0.63m deep with steep concave sides and a rounded base. Within this was deposit 1870, largely comprising broken chalk containing pottery and animal bone, and evidently rapidly backfilled. Within this deposit were two skulls of cattle and two of horse (1944) alongside further Middle Iron Age pottery sherds. Over this backfilled deposit, the filling of the main pit 1851 resumed with a silty clay with abundant chalk (1862) which was spread across the entire pit to a depth of around 0.19m. Over this, in the centre of the remaining depression in the pit, was a 0.04m-thick layer of charcoal-rich (unidentified) silty clay (1863). The filling of 1851 was completed by a series of apparently slow accumulations of chalky silty clay. Pit 2203 was adjacent to pit 2258 (see above; Fig. 2.9) also contained more than one animal skull. The pit was unusual being oval, 1.65m wide but around 3m long and 0.92m deep with steep but slightly undercut sides and a flat base. After the accumulation of a thin basal silt, suggesting that it had been open for at least a while, animal bone including a cattle skull was placed at the bottom of the cut near the north-east side of the pit. Another cattle skull was similarly located on near the south-west pit side. In both cases a silty clay fill with some chalk appeared to have been dumped from the pit side covering the animal remains. The rest of the pit filled up with a sequence of silty clays which appear to have accumulated over a period of time.

A number of pits also contained partial or largely complete remains of dogs, sheep/goat and cattle. Pit 1454 was oval, being 1.3m long, 0.9m wide and 0.61m deep, and had vertical, undercut sides and a flat base (Figs 2.9 and 2.11). The fills contained Middle–Late Iron Age pottery, although this did include a decorated sherd, which probably dates into the 2nd–1st century BC, and other Late Iron Age sherds. There were three fills, the first of which had a substantial amount of charcoal within it and contained the disarticulated remains of at least three perinatal lambs along with pottery and a piece of worked flint, the latter found towards the centre of the pit floor. The charred material was rich in cereal chaff, but also included a mixture of wood charcoal (Wyles and Challinor, Chapter 4). This was covered by two further deposits which also contained pottery and bone, but reduced amounts of charcoal and which appear to indicate general settlement waste.

Pit 1669, 8m south-west of roundhouse 4 (Figs 2.10 and 2.12), was sub-circular being 1.28 long and 1.14m wide and 0.59m deep, with vertical sides, overcut towards base, and a flat base. It contained four fills. The initial fill on the south-east side, and which may represent partial collapse of the side covered animal bone which lay on the base of the pit. This was covered with an orange brown silty clay with infrequent charcoal pieces (1671) which contained within it on the north side of the pit the partial remains of an adult dog (femur and pelvis) and the humerus and metacarpal of a sheep/goat. Above was a deposit 0.28m thick which included pottery and animal bone, and which seems to represent general settlement waste. The final fill contained frequent large stones, animal bone and Middle Iron Age pottery, probably a rapidly formed deposit, also containing general waste.

Pit 1984, was substantial and one of the pits with more complex fills, containing eight deposits. It was circular in plan, 2.4m in diameter and 1.85m deep and had vertical sides and a flat base (Figs 2.10, 2.12 and 2.26). It is one of the pits which contained a thin charcoal-rich deposit (1983) as the initial deposit (unidentified). On both sides of the pit were two chalk-rich deposits up against the pit wall which contained no finds. These appear to be deliberate deposits (1987 and 1988) as the profile of the pit does not suggest that they originated from collapse of the sides. Over this was a clay deposit with abundant chalk (2031) and no finds which filled the centre of the pit. On top of this, also in the centre of the pit was a silty clay with chalk (1962) which contained the ABG of a dog (Fig. 2.27). The dog was missing the skull and foot bones which suggests it may have been skinned prior to deposition, although no cut marks were noted (see Holmes, Chapter 4). A rib from this dog produced a radiocarbon date range of *364–164 cal. BC* (SUERC-100020). A piece of industrial waste (Ra. 1099) also came from this deposit. After this a deposit containing abundant chalk was placed across the width of the pit, and successive chalky silty clay deposits which produced Middle and Late Iron Age pottery completed the sequence of filling.

A dog skeleton was also found within pit 1068, located near the north-western corner of the site (Figs 2.9 and 2.12). This pit was circular in plan 1.6m in diameter and 1.14m deep with vertical sides and a round base. It only had three fills. Initially 1067 filled half the pit and was a chalky clay with occasional charcoal and burnt stone and contained the remains of the largely complete adult dog. This was covered by several further chalky clay silt deposits.

Another dog skeleton occurred in pit 6030. This was 15m west of roundhouse 9 where it was one of three intercutting large pits (Figs 2.11 and 2.12). It was 1.45m in diameter and 0.61m deep, with concave sides and a flat base, with three fills. The body of a dog aged 15–24 months had been placed in the centre of the pit base, on its right side with its head to the south. A rib from this animal was radiocarbon dated, providing a range of *379–176 cal. BC* (SUERC-100021). The remainder of the pit was filled with chalky silty clay backfills which included animal bone and some broadly datable Iron Age pottery. The penultimate fill (6028) also included an iron knife fragment (McSloy, Chapter 3).

A group of nine chalk weights came from pit 8118, located along the north-western edge of the site, and which had one of the more complex combinations of contents. Pit 8118 was sub-circular, 1.9 m long, 1.72m wide and up to 1.25m deep, making it one of the larger pits. It had undercut vertical sides and a flat base. The initial fill (8122) was apparently dumped into the pit, possibly from the eastern side and contained the weights, and co-mingled animal bone of cattle and sheep/goat, along with a thumbnail scraper datable to the Beaker/Early Bronze Age period (Fig. 3.1, 3); the latter may be residual, but in this context, but was readily identifiable as a worked object. This lowest context contained the remains of at least one frog and micromammal bone including a field vole skull, which probably represents pit falls whilst the pit was open. This pit also stood out as it contained one of the most complex combinations of associated bone groups, also

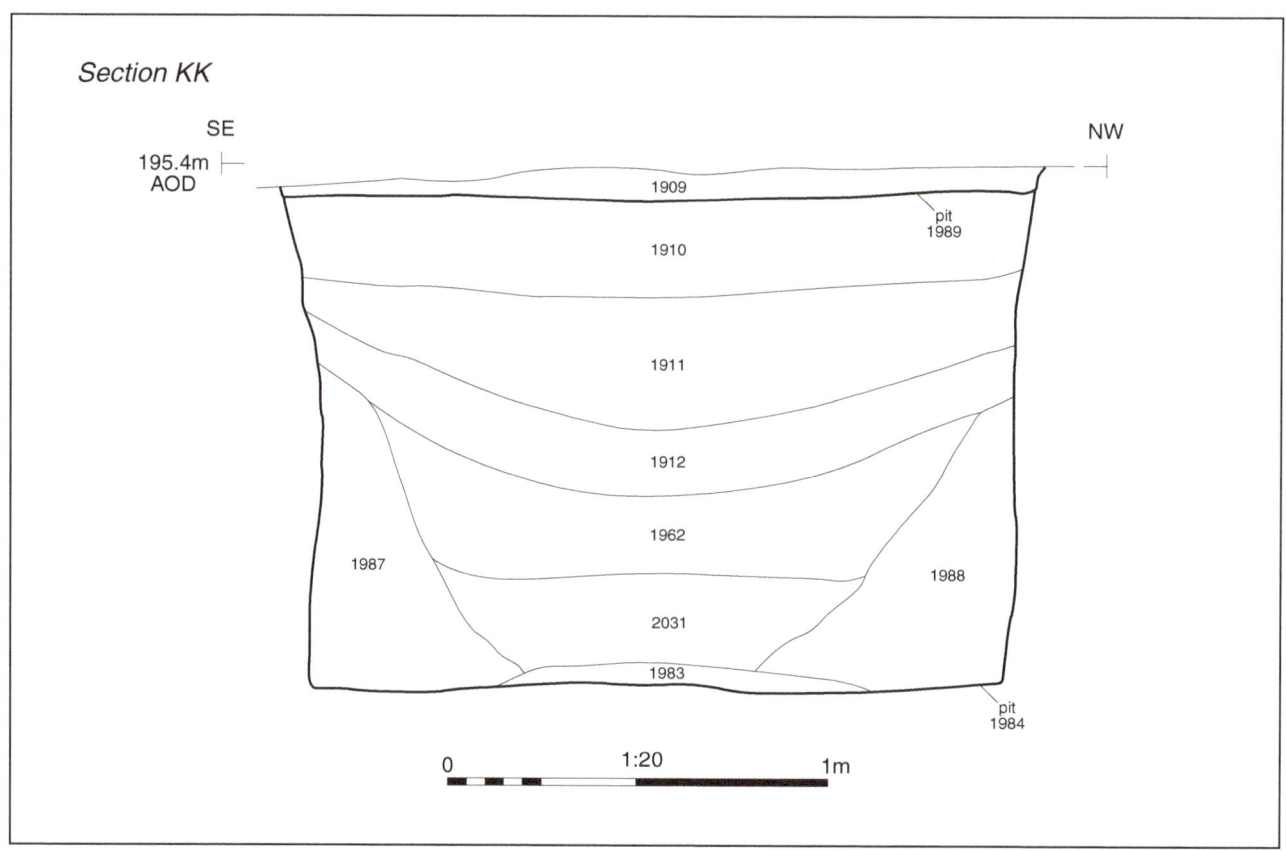

Figure 2.26 Section and photograph of pit 1984

Figure 2.27 Remains of dog in fill 1962, pit 1984

in this initial fill. These comprised the disarticulated but complete remains of four puppies (all aged 1–4 months) and a complete adult cattle skeleton. Also within the pit was a largely complete slack-shouldered jar (Ra. 1214, Fig. 3.5, 26), which lipid analysis demonstrated had contained ruminant dairy fats (WRO08; Dunne *et al.*, Chapter 4). The pottery includes a number of vessels which can be dated to the Middle Iron Age. On the north-east side, this was covered by a darker deposit with more charcoal (8121, containing scant charred plant remains), also including pottery and bone. After this, there appears to have been an episode of erosion of the pit walls which collapsed around the sides as a chalk-rich deposit 8120, although the spread of this across the centre of the pit may also imply a deliberate backfill of chalk. The rest of the pit then appears to have been left to silt up gradually, but this fill also contained part of a crucible (Dungworth, Chapter 3, Table 3.13).

Period 5: Late Iron Age to Early Roman

During the Late Iron Age to Early Roman period, a number of features were established on the plateau (Fig. 2.29). A few sherds in a coarse flint-tempered fabric may suggest a continuation of Late Iron Age potting traditions beyond the Roman conquest. The majority of pottery was transitional wares, mainly wheelthrown grog-tempered jars and bowls dating within the 1st century AD and probably not beyond AD 75 (see Banks, Chapter 3), although some Early Roman forms such as beaded rim jars and platters occur. This period is defined by the creation of linear boundaries and a series of rectilinear enclosures. Four sub-phases have been suggested (Periods 5.1–5.4; Figs 2.30–2.33), but these cannot be closely dated although they all appear to lie within the 1st centuries BC and AD. A single radiocarbon determination, from a human burial (assigned to sub-phase Period 5.2, Fig. 2.31), was in the range cal. AD 30–40 (1.8%) and cal. AD 60–212 (93.7%)(SUERC-94036).

The initial episode of activity (Period 5.1) saw the establishment of enclosure 1, two roundhouses and a smaller internal enclosure (enclosure 4) (Fig. 2.30). East of enclosure 1, a boundary ditch, re-cut at least twice, separated the settlement from the scarp, the edge of which lay just to the west.

Across the west part of the site, on a north-east/south-west alignment and parallel to the scarp was a substantial ditch (initially ditch 18). This was in places V-shaped, in others it had concave sides and a concave base and was up to 1.7m wide. It was relatively shallow, varying between 0.62m to as little as 0.16m deep, although it may have been truncated by ploughing. This was, however, a long-lived element of the landscape and was successively re-cut (ditches 13 and 19); it appears to represent the limit of this area of enclosed landscape. Ditch 13 contained a small slack shouldered jar datable to the Middle Iron Age (Ra. 1209; Fig. 3.3, 18); this was largely complete and may have been a curated object or heirloom. Analysis showed

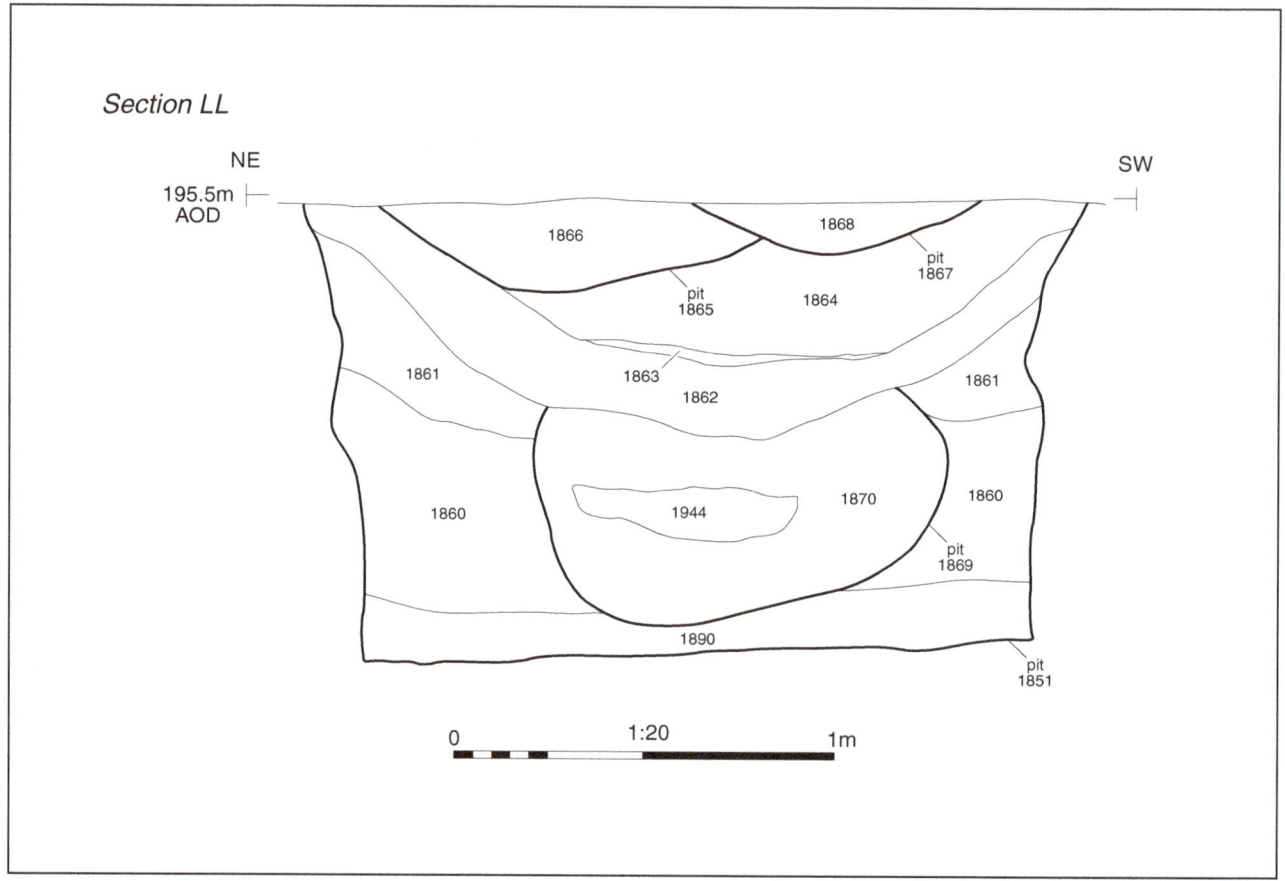

Figure 2.28 Section and photograph of pit 1851

Figure 2.29 Aerial view of the Period 5 (Late Iron Age to Early Roman) enclosures in the north-western part of the site, looking north-west and overlying earlier remains

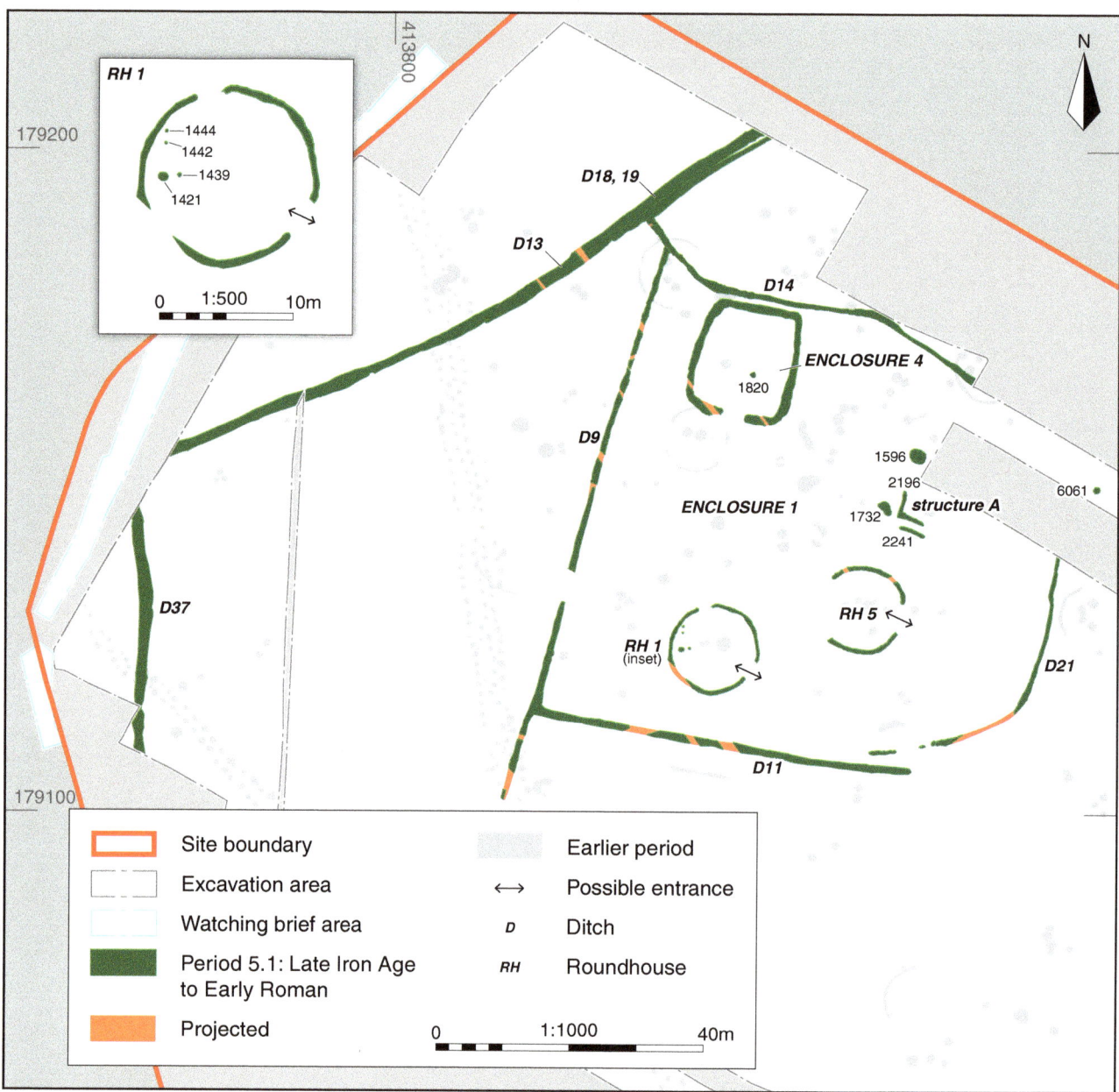

Figure 2.30 Period 5.1 (Late Iron Age to Early Roman) enclosed settlement plan

that it had been used for cooking dairy products (probably milk, cheese or butter) and leafy plant material (WRO032; Dunne *et al.*, Chapter 3). The fill also included a core rejuvenation flake datable to the Mesolithic or Early Neolithic period. A partial cattle skull may be the remnant of something deliberately deposited (although there was little in the same context) or incidental.

In the westernmost corner of the excavated area was ditch 37 (Fig. 2.30). This ditch was on a north-south alignment, almost perpendicular to ditch 18 (and its recuts 13 and 19). However, the junction between the two lay beyond the excavated area, so the exact relationship between the two is not known. More certainly attached to ditch 18 at its north-eastern end, was ditch 14. This was a slightly sinuous ditch with concave sides, and varying width up to 1.2m, again shallow, up to 0.4m deep. Ditch 14 was orientated

from west to east and formed the northern boundary of enclosure 1.

Along with ditch 14, ditches 9, 11 and 21 created enclosure 1 which was D-shaped, 65m by 70m in extent. It may be that ditch 21, a curvilinear length on the east side, and ditch 11 were continuous, and actually part of ditch 14, but there are various places in which the course of this boundary was truncated. It is therefore not possible to be certain as to where the entrance into this space lay. These ditches were relatively insubstantial, only being up to 0.86m wide and between about 0.2m and 0.4m deep, and having concave or irregular profiles. On the western side ditch 9 was aligned on a north-north-east to south-south-west, intersecting with ditch 14, about 5m from its intersection with ditch 18, and continuing across the excavated area in a straight line, meeting with the western

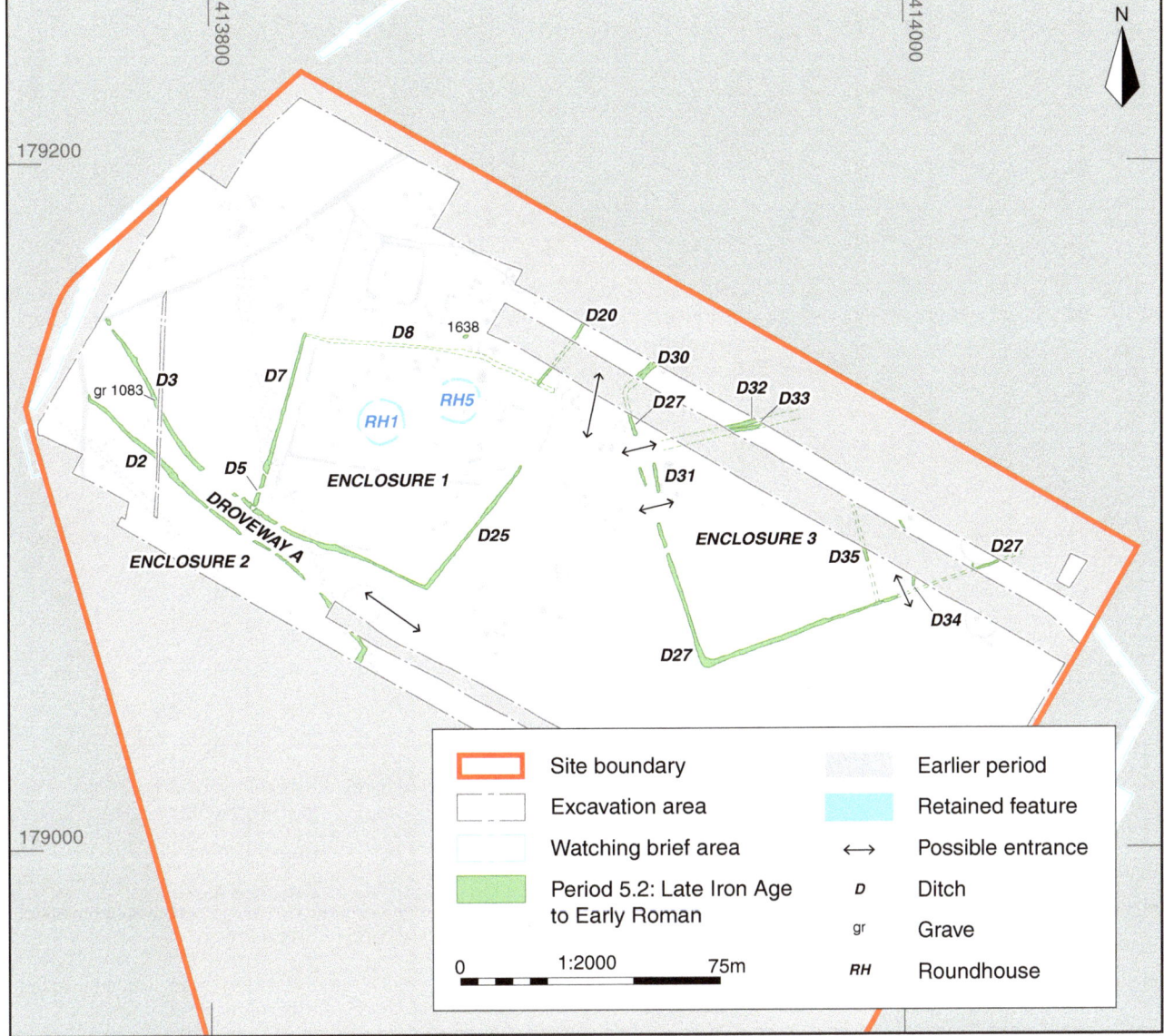

Figure 2.31 Period 5.2 (Late Iron Age to Early Roman) enclosed settlement plan

end of ditch 11, but continuing onwards. It may be that it performed a role not only as part of enclosure 1 but further sub-division of the wider landscape to the south and east. Ditch 11 contained an almost complete cattle skull which may have been a deliberate deposit, marking the space, although there was little else in the same context.

Roundhouses 1 and 5 were located within the southern half of enclosure 1. Roundhouse 1 survived as a penannular ditch, 0.4m wide and 0.15m deep with a U-shaped profile suggestive of this having been an eavesdrip gully. It was 12m in diameter and a break in the gully on the south-east side may represent an entrance. Postholes 1442 and 1444, located 0.75m–0.85m inside the line of the ditch may indicate the wall line, whilst posthole/pit 1421 and posthole 1439 may also have been internal features (Fig. 2.30), although none of these contained datable material. Roundhouse 5, situated 10m to the east, appears to have been similar in size, although the penannular gully was

interrupted and probably truncated. This may also have had a south-east facing entrance. However, no structural features survived.

In the north-western part of enclosure 1 was enclosure 4. This was an almost square ditched enclosure 15m by 13m, aligned north-south/east-west with a well-defined 3.5m-wide entrance in the centre of its south side, facing the roundhouses in the centre of enclosure 1. The ditch was more substantial than others with steep sides, often forming a V-shaped profile and generally 1–1.2m wide and 0.6–0.7m deep. The only possibly associated feature was small bowl-shaped pit 1820 which lacked dating evidence. The ditch of enclosure 4 produced small quantities of pottery, along with a vitrified hearth lining with traces of copper alloy.

Structure A was situated in the north-eastern part of enclosure 1. It consisted of L-shaped ditch 2196, with ditch 2241 parallel with one side to the south. Both

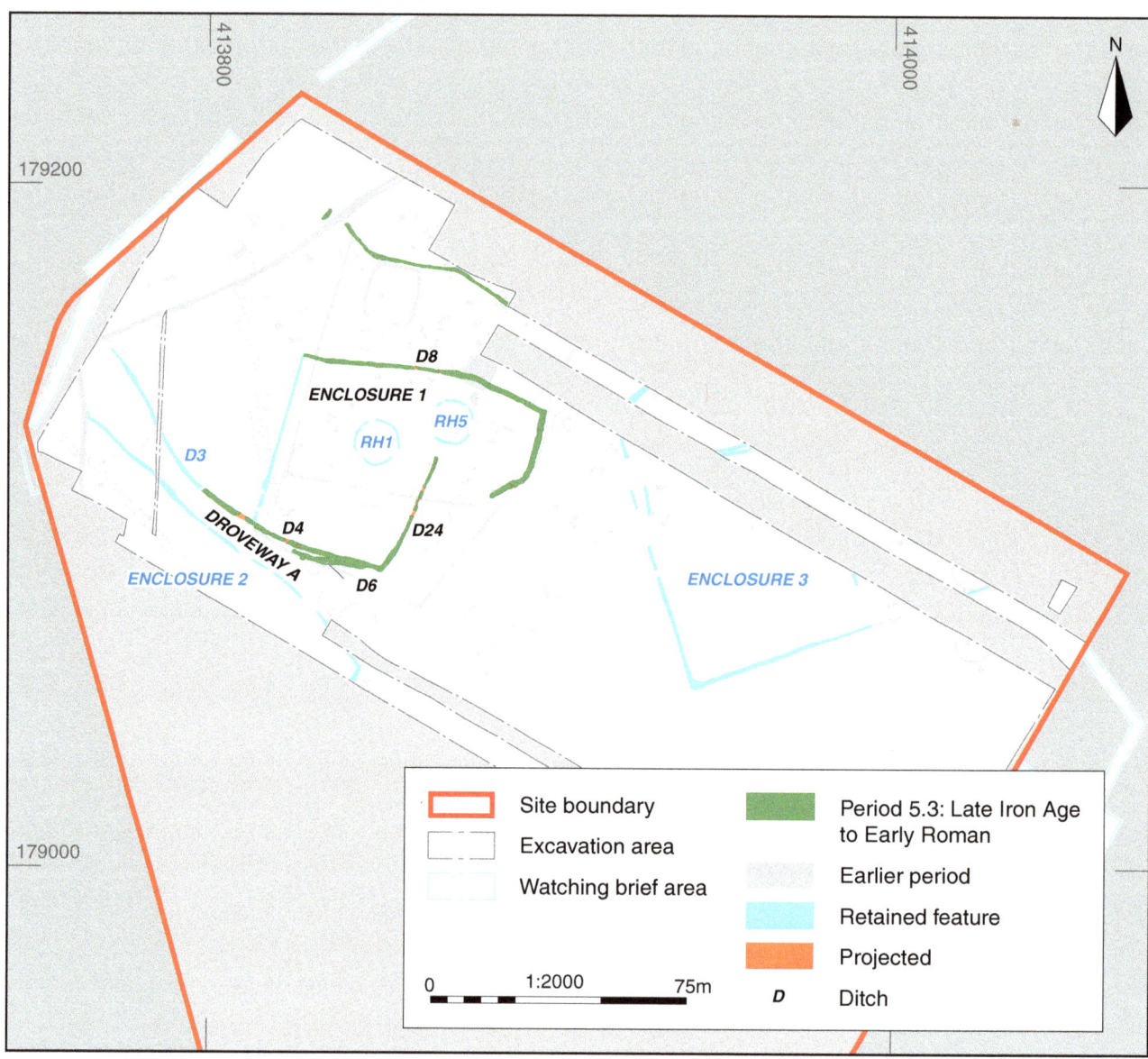

Figure 2.32 Period 5.3 (Late Iron Age to Early Roman) enclosed settlement plan

ditches had steep sides and flat bases being 0.29m wide and 0.08m deep and 0.41m wide and 0.28m deep respectively, although that of ditch 2241 was somewhat uneven. Their function is uncertain, but they may have been beamslots or other structural trenches for a small square or rectangular structure. They produced Early Roman pottery and probably represent a later development of the use of enclosure 1 during the Late Iron Age–Early Romano-British transition. Also within the terminal 2245 of structure A were a few elements of a neonate, probably the remains of a burial (see Clough, Chapter 5).

The development of the use of enclosure 1 can be seen in the next episode of use (Period 5.2; Fig. 2.31) with it shifting to the south and established as an enclosure which was unattached to other boundaries. The enclosed area was reduced being square in plan and measuring 65m by 65m, and it appears that the small enclosure (enclosure 4)

went out of use. As their exact dating is unclear, one or other of the roundhouses may have been in use for at least part of this phase, although it is possible that the enclosure functioned purely as a stock enclosure. This may relate to a droveway which was created on the south-west aspect. The droveway was defined by parallel ditches 2 and 3 and was traceable for about 90m; these diverged to create a funnel arrangement which was wider at both the north-west and south-east potentially opening out into open areas beyond the boundary which had been defined by ditch 13 on the edge of the scarp, probably leading to the natural coombe to access the valley floor, and to the south-east between the other enclosures, perhaps indicating that these were open grazing (see Chapter 6). Ditches 2 and 3 were variable in width along their length, but were up to 2m wide in places, despite being relatively shallow (0.06–0.6m deep) with variable profiles.

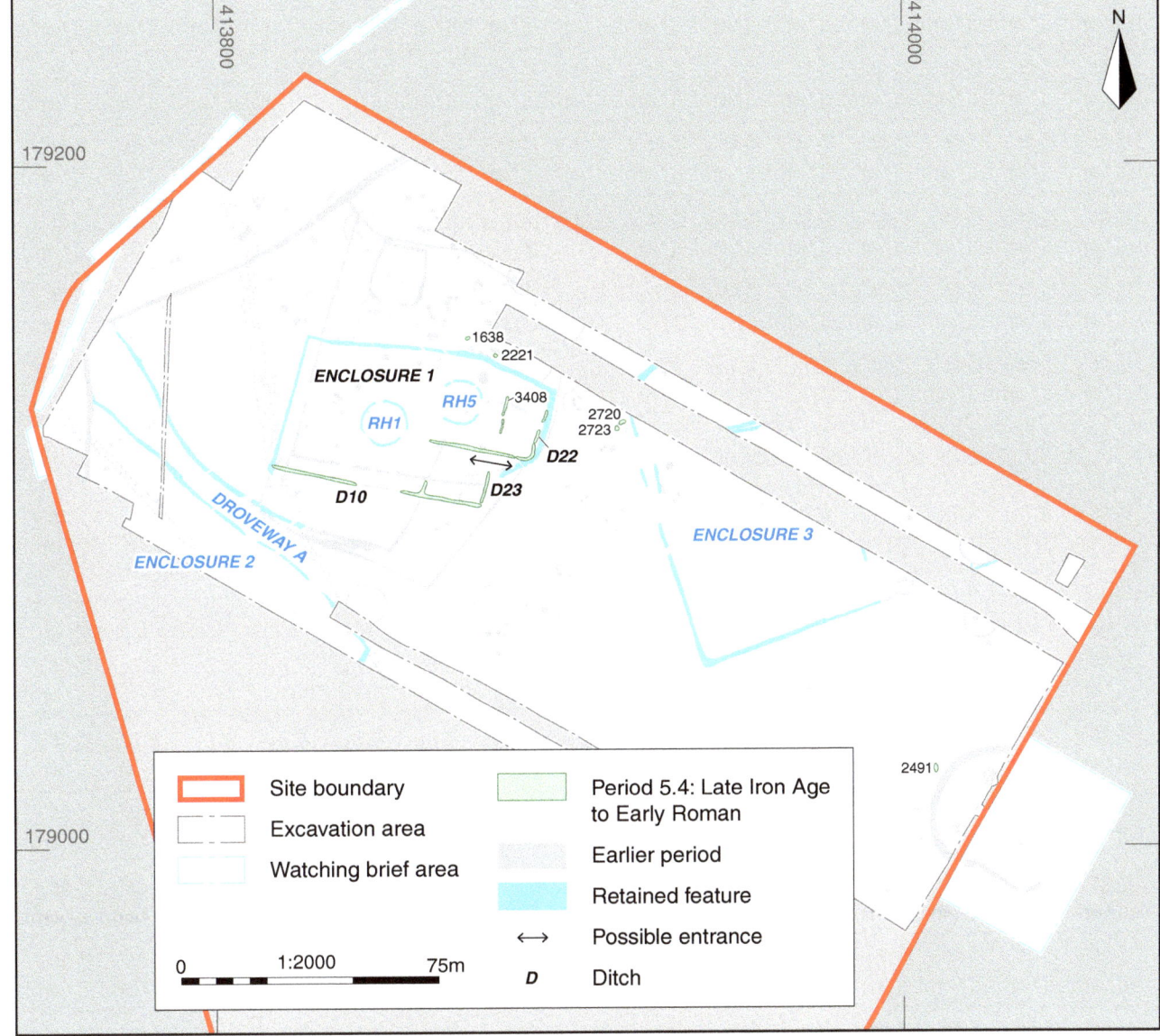

Figure 2.33 Period 5.4 (Late Iron Age to Early Roman) enclosed settlement plan

Cut into the base of ditch 3, was a single grave, 1083, which contained SK 1076, the partial remains of a mature adult female. This burial had perhaps been disturbed by ditch cleaning or re-cutting but seems to have been interred in an extended supine position along the ditch base, with the head to the south-east. A substantial number of chalk pieces were present in the fill, which may have been intentional but equally may have been incidental inclusions. A radiocarbon date was obtained with a range of cal. AD 30–40 (1.8%) and cal. AD 60–212 (93.7%)(SUERC-94036). Intervention 1030 of the same ditch (fill 1031) also produced a number of elements of human remains, which may represent a further disturbed burial (see Clough, Chapter 5).

In addition, enclosures 2 and 3 were created to the south-west and east of enclosure 1 (Fig. 2.31). The ditch which formed the south-western side of the droveway, ditch 2, turned through a right-angle at its south-eastern end,

suggesting that it not only bounded the droveway but created a land parcel which extended beyond the excavated area to the south-west. To the east of the re-modelled enclosure 1 was a complex of ditches (27, 30, 31, 32, 33, 34 and 35) created enclosure 3, which appears to have included sub-divisions. These ditches were generally V-shaped or concave and varied between about 0.5m and 1m wide and 0.07m and 0.68m deep. Enclosure 1 was rectilinear and extended on its northern side beyond the excavated area, although it was at least 90m by 85m in extent. Ditch 27 describes the majority of the main enclosure although it is segmented, probably as a result of truncation, although a genuine entrance or entrances cannot be ruled out. Paired internal ditches 32 and 33 were aligned north-east to south-west, subdividing the enclosure, although these were not seen at the south-western end, and the full arrangement cannot be interpreted. Ditches 34 and 35 at the south-eastern end of enclosure 3 were parallel with each other and perpendicular to ditch 27, creating additional sub-divisions. As well as small quantities of pottery from the enclosure ditches, ditch 32 produced a single *tegula* (roof tile) fragment. Indicating this complex was present, but going out of use during the Roman period. The arrangement of land parcels is suggestive of a series of paddocks, which should be seen in the context of the potential droveway and areas of open grazing.

There were further modifications to enclosure 1 (Period 5.3), whilst the enclosures and the droveway probably continued in use (Fig. 2.32). Ditches 4, 6, and 24 re-framed the southern extent of the enclosure, whilst ditch 8 re-established the original northern boundary of enclosure 1. It is likely that the roundhouses had fallen out of use, and the use of this enclosure was likely to be agricultural, albeit now of an isolated type. The latest pottery from the enclosure ditches spans the mid 1st to 2nd centuries, whilst other finds, all from ditch 8, comprised a shard of blue-green Roman window glass datable to the 1st–2nd/early 3rd centuries AD (see McSloy, Chapter 3); two Roman tile fragments, one a *tegula* roof tile; part of a lower rotary quern made using Lodsworth Greensand (Ra. 1088); a sandstone hone (see Shaffrey, Chapter 3); two Colchester derivative-style copper alloy brooches datable to AD 50–100/150 (Ras 1011 and 1078; see McSloy, Chapter 3; Fig. 3.13, 4 and 5). The Greensand quern was an Iron Age object but may have been curated since it had been re-used as a mortar. The probable date of the glass and brooches would suggest that these ditches were going out of use in the 2nd century.

A final re-modelling of enclosure 1 took place (Period 5.4) with the insertion of new ditches (10, 22 and 23) along its southern and eastern edges, which reduced its footprint (Fig. 2.33), to an area of about 60m by 40m. The ditches were variable in profile and width, ranging from about 0.5m to 1m, and generally shallow 0.07–0.5m. Finds from these latest ditches of enclosure 1 include pottery of the mid 1st to 2nd centuries, as well as a second Colchester derivative-style copper alloy brooch (Ra. 1081; Fig. 3.11, 3), datable to AD 50–100/150; the absence of later finds suggests that the ditch was probably open no later than the 2nd century, and together with the material from the Period 5.3 features suggests that the entire arrangement of land division was falling out of use at this point.

Pit 6061, 20m south-east of roundhouse 4 (Fig. 2.30), was circular in plan 0.92m in diameter and 0.65m deep with vertical sides and a flat base. It contained three fills, an initial one of silty clay with some animal bone and pottery, covered by a similar charcoal-flecked fill, and the uppermost very similar again, within a dip in the centre of the pit and from which came a partial ceramic disc, burnt on one side and possibly a lid or an item of oven 'furniture' (see Collier-Jones and McSloy, Chapter 3). However, the contents of this pit appear to have accumulated through gradual silting processes.

There were a few other features associated with this period, such as pit 1900 (an oval pit 2m in diameter and 0.73m deep with concave sides), which contained a Savernake ware base which had been perforated (see Banks, Chapter 3). Other pits were generally circular or oval, wide and shallow, being 1–2m across and about 0.25m deep. This included pits 2221, 2720, and 1638 (Figs 2.31 and 2.33) which contained examples of Early Roman beaded rim jar sherds, and 2723 which included an example of an Early Roman platter.

Period 6: Mid to Late Roman

Later Roman remains comprised an isolated oven and a cemetery (Figs 2.34 and 2.39).

Oven 2827

The Iron Age C-shaped enclosure, as mentioned above, clearly remained visible into the Roman period. It is during this period that its upper reaches gradually filled. Where datable, the pottery from the later deposits is consistent with the debris from the Late Iron Age–Roman enclosures, comprising Late Iron Age to Early Roman grog-tempered sherds, and Early Roman sherds, such as those of the Savernake industry. Molluscan evidence from these later deposits seem to indicate that the ditch had stabilised and from Period 5 onward existed in an open landscape in which there may have been some arable.

A substantial Roman oven was present within the northern part of the C-shaped enclosure (Figs 2.34–2.36), and if there was an associated bank which persisted into this period, it may have provided some shelter in an exposed location. A construction cut (2828) contained a deep bowl-shaped fire pit (2532) 2.8m by 2.2m in extent at the north end which was linked via a short flue to a square oven (2m by 2m) at the southern end that was 2m by 2m (Fig. 2.35). The overall length of the oven was 4.85m and the cut was 1.2m deep (Fig. 2.36). The flue, which survived to two courses high had been lined with chalk blocks (3315), the inner surfaces of which were scorched. Further chalk blocks lined the square oven end, where they survived to a total of seven courses. Behind the walling, the construction cut was infilled with sterile chalky clay. Fired clay with wattle impressions came from the pit 2532, and there was further fired clay in other deposits associated with the oven, presumably originating from its super-structure.

Evidence for the oven's use came from a charcoal and ash deposit (2826) found along the flue (here numbered as 3181–3183) and oven base (numbered as 3184–3186; see Wyles and Challinor, Chapter 4). These had accumulated to a thickness of 0.11m. A charred spelt wheat grain from fill 3184 produced a calibrated range of cal. AD 256–284 (16.0%) and cal. AD 326–422 (79.4%) (SUERC-100003). Four iron carpentry nails also came from these deposits. There were in total 26 nails from the

Figure 2.34 Plan of Period 6 (Mid to Late Roman) cemetery, isolated graves, oven and other features

oven as a whole (McSloy, Chapter 3), although whether these were part of the oven superstructure, secured oven furniture or were attached originally to structural timbers re-used as fuel is not known. Further ash and charcoal deposits (2530 and 2529) survived within the fire pit, to a depth of 0.6m. The uppermost of these, fill 2529, produced a small sherd of 2nd-century pottery, most likely residual.

Samples from various locations within the oven flue and chamber produced very large charred cereal assemblages, mainly chaff. Charred grains were mainly spelt, with some emmer and barley grains. This oven clearly was used for crop processing, The wood charcoal present suggested that the fuel used was largely oak with some poplar/willow, the latter containing beetle holes suggesting that it had been seasoned. Most or all seems to have come either from coppiced (managed) woodland, or from hedgerows, or a mix of the two.

The demolition deposits within the oven attest to its deliberate destruction, but also its upper structure. It is clear that there were additional upper courses of walling, but it seems that above this there was probably a clay superstructure. The lowest backfill within the fire pit, deposit 2528, included chalk and fired clay fragments, along with some chalk and sarsen blocks and a quernstone fragment from an upper stone (Ra. 1085). The quern fragment is in Old Red Sandstone/conglomerate and was probably part of an Iron Age quern. It seems most likely that it was re-used as part of the oven walls, since the quernstone had been scorched. Above this was a grey-brown clay silt infill (2527), which produced a sherd of mid 3rd to 4th-century pottery along with a lower rotary quern made from Old Red Sandstone (Ra. 1076), and which may have formed a pair with Ra. 1085 from layer 2528. The quern was worn from use and, also had been scorched. This may also have been re-used within the oven walling.

Figure 2.35 Period 6 (Mid to Late Roman) oven 2532, looking south from the fire pit towards the chalk-walled square oven end

A sequence of similar chalk with fired clay deposits mixed with silty clays filled the flue and oven base (fills 2825–2822; Fig. 2.36). The lowest of these, fill 2825, produced a small quantity of animal bone, as well as five iron carpentry nails, whilst a further nail came from the penultimate fill, 2823.

A short curvilinear ditch found parallel to the exterior of the western circuit of the C-shaped enclosure may have been of this period. This ditch, 2414, was 2.7m west of the C-shaped enclosure and consisted of a short cut 8m long, 0.85m wide and 0.25m deep with a U-shaped profile. It contained a grey-brown silty clay infill and had been re-cut twice. A small sherd of 2nd–4th-century pottery came from the lower fill of the first re-cut, whilst the upper fill of the same re-cut produced a small sherd more broadly datable as Roman.

There was also an isolated pit which may have dated to this period. Pit 1645 was located between the Period 5 droveway and enclosure 1 (Fig. 2.34). It was 1.6m long, 1.1m wide and 0.35m deep with vertical sides and a flat base. Onto the pit base had been placed articulated cattle ribs and vertebrae (1697). A rib was radiocarbon dated, providing a calibrated range of cal. AD 130–144 (1.9%), cal. AD 154–260 (60.2%) and cal. AD 278–335 (33.4%) SUERC-100019. This range allows for this deposit to have been contemporary with the Period 5 settlement, or with the Period 6 graves.

Inhumation burials

The main activity on the plateau during the Mid-Late Roman period was associated with burial. The majority of graves were found within a distinct cemetery, but also two graves were associated with the C-shaped enclosure.

Grave 2389 was situated within the area enclosed by the C-shaped enclosure (Fig. 2.34). The grave was located about 2m inside the encompassing ditch, and aligned north/south, which in this location was parallel with the arc of the ditch. It was a rectangular cut, 2.4m long, 1.1m wide and 0.55m deep; the grave sides sloped, so that at the base it was just large enough to inter the body. SK 2446 represents the remains of an older adult female, who was laid in an extended supine position with her head to the north (Fig. 2.37). Around the perimeter of the grave, surrounding the body were 22 carpentry nails which indicate the presence of a coffin, planked grave lining or some other wooden structure. A radiocarbon calibrated range of cal. AD 122–338 (SUERC-94042) was obtained from the right femur.

Grave 12052 was located in the watching brief area, 20m east of the C-shaped enclosure. This sub-rectangular grave was east/west aligned and was at least 1m long (the eastern end lying beyond the excavated area), 0.45m wide and 0.1m deep. Within, SK 12053, an older adult male, had been placed in an extended supine position, slightly

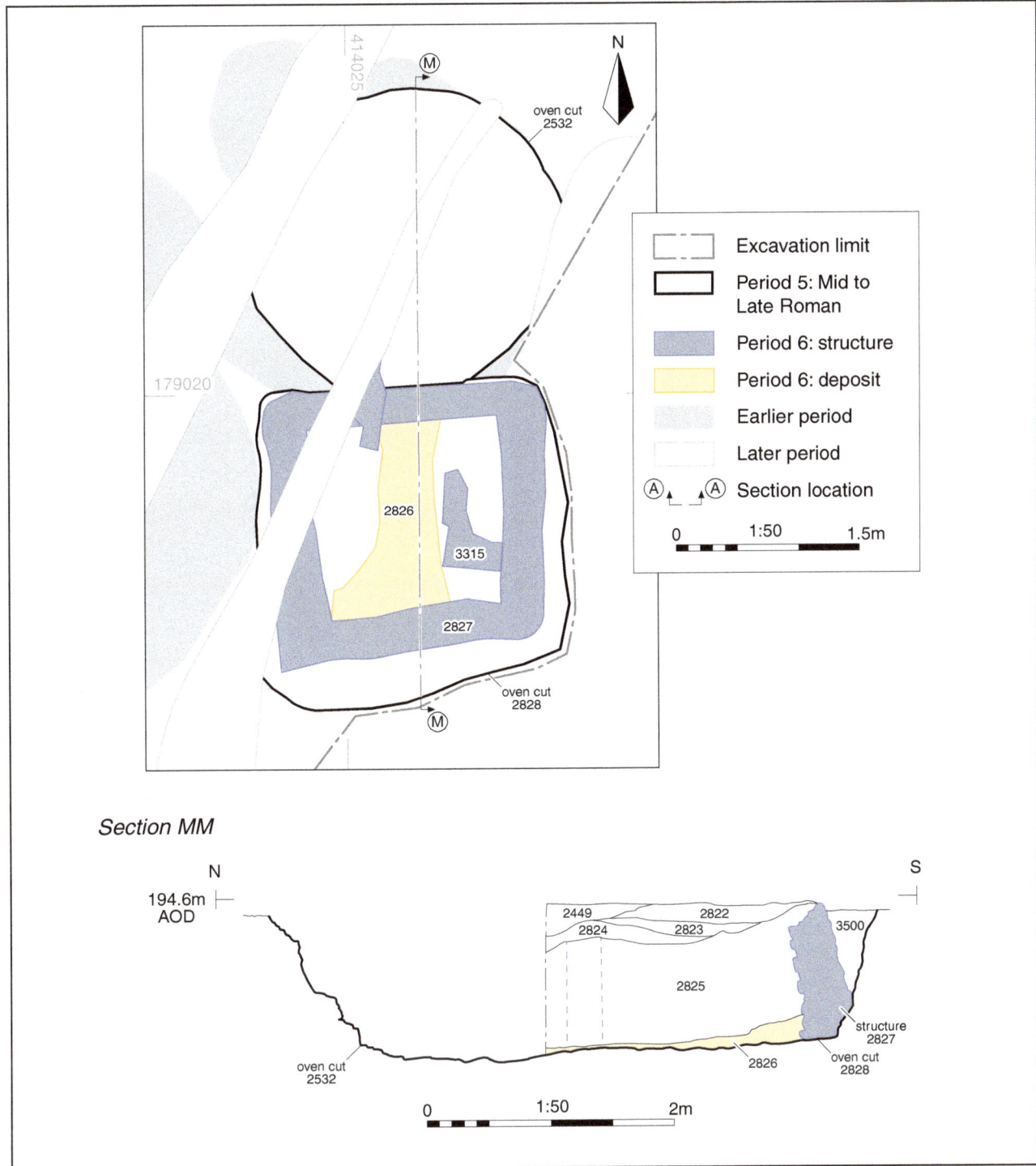

Figure 2.36 Plan and section of oven 2532

on his right side and with his head to the west. One of his ribs was radiocarbon dated, with a range of cal. AD 246–402 (SUERC-100010). As the burials have no direct relationship with each other, the C-shaped enclosure, or indeed oven, the sequence of events in this part of the site evidenced by finds and three radiocarbon dates is difficult to interpret with certainty. Both SK 12053 and oven 2827 produced dates covering the second half of the 3rd and the whole of the 4th centuries AD. In the case of the oven,

this could extend into the first couple of decades of the 5th century. SK 2446, however, produced a date range from the end of the 1st to the early 4th centuries. It is possible that the activity represented by the oven and both burials occurred within a short period, perhaps in the late 3rd or very early in the 4th century. Clearly the area encompassed by the C-shaped enclosure at some point became appropriate for burial. However, the contemporaneity with the grain drying activity represented by oven 2827 appears incongruous.

Figure 2.37 Period 6 (Mid to Late Roman) SK 2446 in grave 2389, looking west

This will be discussed further in Chapter 6. Nevertheless, it seems likely that the activity in the area attested to by the Roman period finds within the upper fills of the C-shaped enclosure ditch was associated either with the grain drying or burial activities. It also suggests that the presence of the ditch was gradually ceasing to have meaning at this time, excepting the deliberate deposition of a dog within the fills.

The majority of graves of this period, 17 in total, were found within the central part of the site, 100m north-west of the C-shaped enclosure (Figs 2.34 and 2.38). Each grave had been cut into the chalk substrate to a depth of up to 0.7m and contained the body of a single individual (Figs 2.39–2.41). The graves occurred within an area of approximately 20m by 10m and do not appear to have been enclosed in any way. In fact, it was located in an area which was outside all of the earlier land parcels. However, there does appear to have been some organisation, with two main clusters of graves, one to the north, and one to the south. Whilst there is some variation in the orientation and alignment of the graves, they are generally between north/south and north-east/south-west, albeit with the head at either end of the grave. The graves at the northern end of the distribution appear less organised, but from the centre of the group, spreading to the southernmost interments, an apparent arrangement of rows appears to have been used. This effectively created two loosely parallel lines of graves in the south of the cemetery.

The lack of intercutting of graves not only suggests a modest population burying individuals within living memory of previous interments, but perhaps the marking of graves, although this seems to have been in such a way that nothing has remained archaeologically visible. There is one posthole in the southern group, 2887, but this is not directly associated with a grave, being situated between graves 2315, 2309 and 2295 (Fig. 2.38). These are the most north-westerly of the southern group, and it is possible that it was some form of marker. It was oval, 0.33m by 0.25m and only 0.09m deep, with steep sides and a concave base and a single fill of silty clay with no finds. To the south-east of the posthole there were five other graves with another slightly to the north-east of this group (2344). In the northern group, several graves 2338, 2863, 2878, 2329, 2326 and 2320, were situated around tree-throw hole (2347). These graves show less adherence to a common orientation or rows, and their arrangement suggests that they may have been aligned on the tree. If it was in place at the time of the burials, they would probably have been within the overhang of the tree canopy. All but 2320 had their feet toward the probable location of the tree trunk.

Some of the graves were closer to each other and more clearly arranged in parallel, which might suggest some relationship between the interred. Males and females are distributed throughout the cemetery. Most of the individuals were over 45 years at death, with only one juvenile individual, a child aged 6–8 years (see Clough, Chapter 5).

The graves were all rectangular and between 1.5m and 2.16m long. Some were shallow, one being as little as 0.12m deep. Details are given in Table 2.2, and further

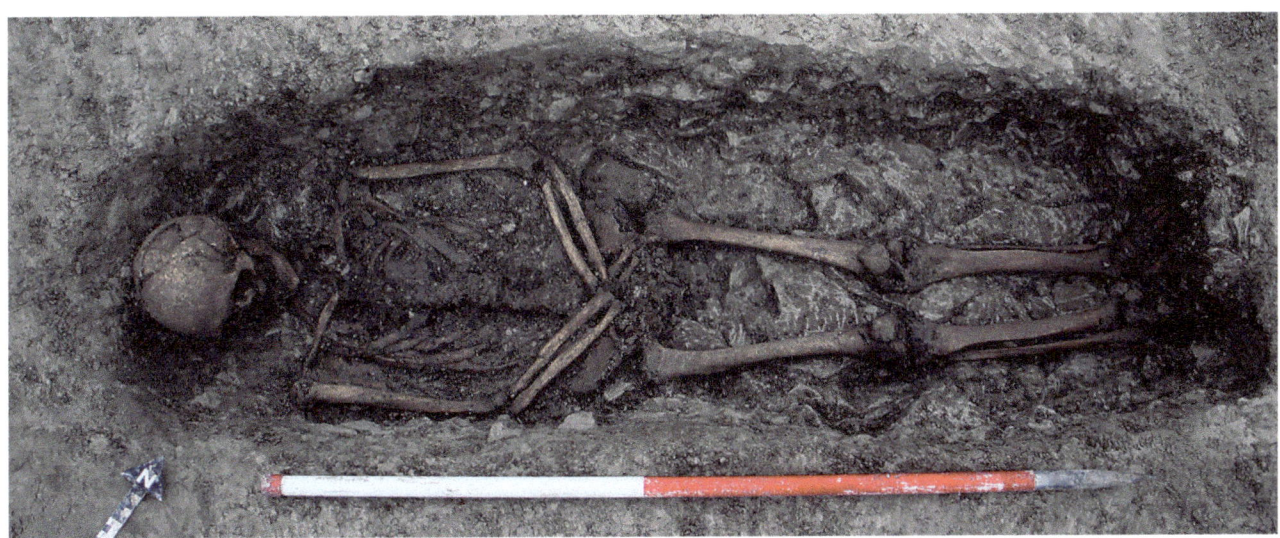

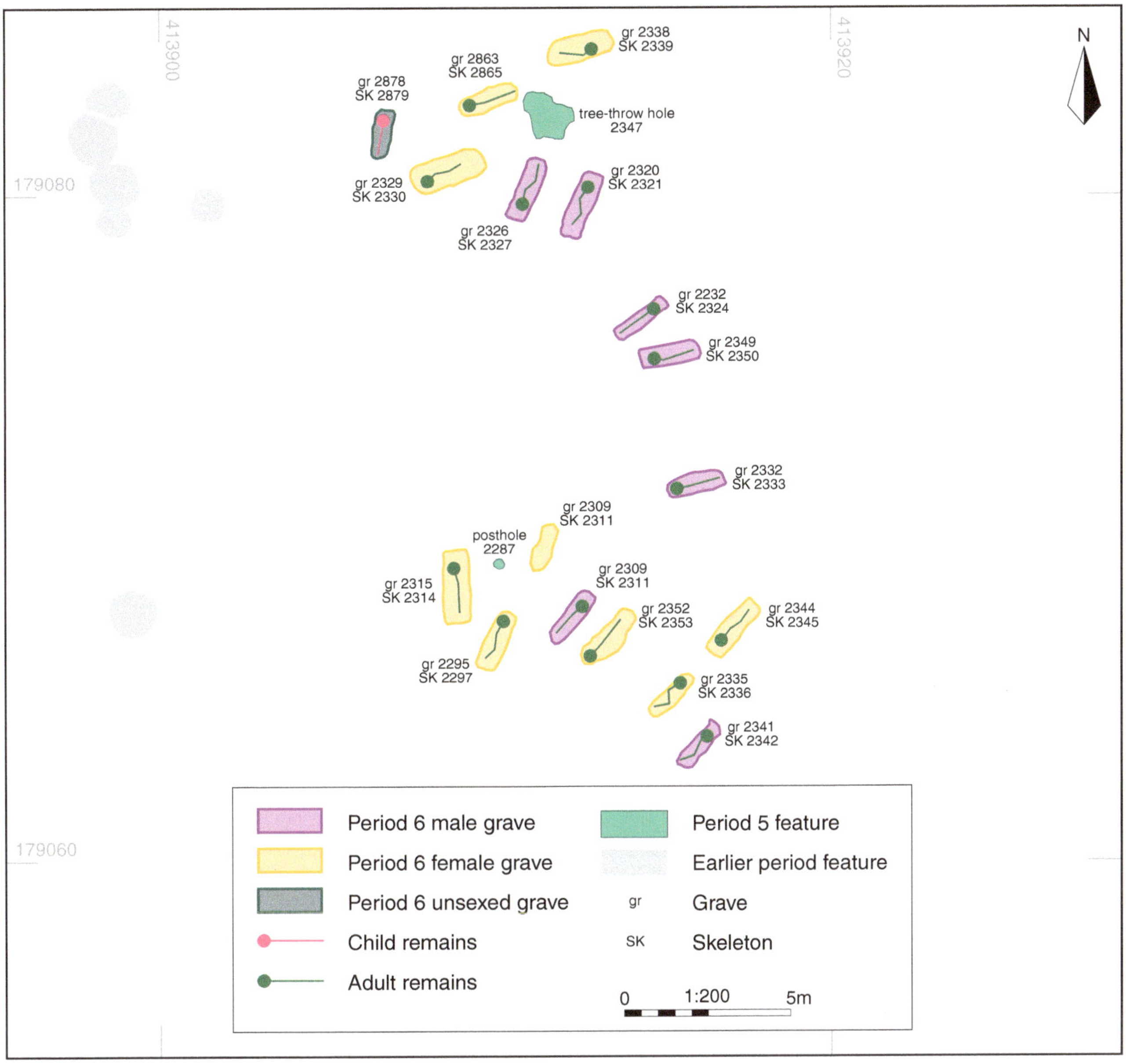
413900
413920
N
179080
179060
gr 2338
SK 2339
gr 2863
SK 2865
gr 2878
SK 2879
tree-throw hole
2347
gr 2329
SK 2330
gr 2320
SK 2321
gr 2326
SK 2327
gr 2232
SK 2324
gr 2349
SK 2350
gr 2332
SK 2333
gr 2309
SK 2311
posthole
2287
gr 2309
SK 2311
gr 2315
SK 2314
gr 2352
SK 2353
gr 2344
SK 2345
gr 2295
SK 2297
gr 2335
SK 2336
gr 2341
SK 2342
Period 6 male grave
Period 6 female grave
Period 6 unsexed grave
Child remains
Adult remains
Period 5 feature
Earlier period feature
gr Grave
SK Skeleton
0 1:200 5m

Figure 2.38 Plan of Period 6 (Late Roman) cemetery

Figure 2.39 Period 6 (Mid to Late Roman) SK 2333 in grave 2332, looking north-west

Table 2.2 The Late Roman cemetery

Grave	Length	Width	Depth	Skeleton	Sex/age	Alignment	Body position	?Cultural material/C[14]
Graves in the northern cluster								
2320	2.16m	0.72m	0.54m	SK 2321	Older male	NE/SW Head to NE	Slightly flexed	Hobnails around feet and in fill; Carpentry nail Flint flake by feet Broadly RB pottery within fill
2326	2.00m	0.75m	0.25m	SK 2327	Older male	NE/SW Head to SW	Slightly flexed, partly on right side	Hobnails around feet; Broadly RB pottery within fill
2329	2.09m	1.07m	0.39m	SK 2330	Older female	NE/SW Head to SW	Slightly flexed	Broken leaf-shaped Early Neolithic flint arrowhead (Ra. 1039) close to the waist. Broadly RB pottery within fill
2878	1.50m	0.60m	0.40m	SK 2879	Child 6–8 years	N/S Head to N	Extended Prone	Chalk slab capping layer
2863	1.82m	0.71m	0.23m	SK 2865	young adult female	NE/SW Head to SW	Extended Prone	No finds
2338	1.50m	0.50m	0.36m	SK 2339	Older female	NE/SW Head to NE	Slightly flexed Feet crossed at the ankles	Hobnails and cleats by feet. Pottery of late 3rd to 4th centuries in fill
Graves in the centre of the cemetery								
2323	1.70m	0.61m	0.44m	SK 2324	Older male	NE/SW Head to NE	Extended; feet against the end of the grave	No finds
2349	1.56m	0.42m	0.12m	SK 2350	Older male	NE/SW Head to SW	Extended	No finds
2332	1.66m	0.66m	0.30m	SK 2333	Older male	NE/SW Head to SW	Extended; hands crossed over stomach	Hobnails and cleats by feet. Pottery of late 3rd to 4th centuries in fill
Graves in the southern cluster								
2295	1.86m	0.64m	0.41m	SK 2297	Older female	NE/SW Head to NE	Slightly flexed, partly on left side	Hobnails by feet; two carpentry nails from diagonally opposite corners of the grave Pottery of 2nd to 4th centuries in fill
2315	2.09m	0.75m	0.55m	SK 2314	Mature ?female	N/S Head to N	Extended Prone with arms flexed	0.15m-thick lens of chalk over body SUERC-100013
2309	1.50m	0.55m	0.16m	SK 2311	Older female	NE/SW Head to NE	Slightly flexed	No finds
2352	1.60m	0.34m	0.14m	SK 2353	Older male	NE/SW Head to NE	Extended	Hobnails and shoe cleats in grave
2316	2.09m	0.83m	0.46m	SK 2318	Older female	NE/SW Head to SW	Extended	Hobnails in grave Broadly RB pottery within fill
2335	1.63m	0.56m	0.22m	SK 2336	Older female	NE/SW Head to NE	Slightly flexed, partly on left side	Hobnails by feet Broadly RB pottery within fill
2344	1.77m	0.62m	0.50m	SK 2345	Older ?female	NE/SW Head to SW	Extended	Hobnails and cleats by feet
2341	1.76m	0.59m	0.20m	SK 2342	Mature male	NE/SW Head to NE	Slightly flexed, partly on left side	Pottery of late 3rd to 4th centuries in fill

information on the individuals is given in Chapter 5. The body position was generally extended, in all but three cases supine, sometimes slightly flexed, and there is evidence for coffins or wooden structures in some graves. There were limited grave goods present, with the most common item being hobnails which were present in nine of the graves, and suggest a later Roman period date. Where datable cultural material was present it indicates a date in the late 3rd to 4th centuries AD, whilst one radiocarbon date was obtained on SK 2314, one of two prone burials in the cemetery, which provided a date range of cal. AD 247–405 (SUERC-100013). A broken Neolithic leaf-shaped arrowhead was recovered from grave 2329 (Fig. 3.1, 1); it is not clear if this was a deliberate inclusion or residual, although the latter is probable. A number of individuals, particularly older males, exhibited pathological changes including those associated with traumatic injury (see

Clough, Chapter 5). However, there does not appear to be any pattern in the distribution of these individuals within the cemetery.

Period 7: Medieval to Post-Medieval, and Period 8: Modern

Medieval or post-medieval remains comprised a series of furrows aligned north-east/south-west and others perpendicular to these, indicating at least two phases of ridge and furrow cultivation (Fig. 2.42, Period 7). These pre-date 1886, since the 1st Edition Ordnance Survey map depicts field boundaries which were recorded during the excavation as having cut across the furrows (see below). Most furrows were within the western two thirds of the site, although whether this reflects differential truncation, or the presence of a former medieval boundary such as a headland

Figure 2.40 Period 6 (Mid to Late Roman) graves 2295, 2309 and 2315 clustered around posthole 2887, looking north-east

to the east of the furrows of which no traces remain, is not known.

Several ditches (15, 26, 16, 17 and 29; Fig. 2.42, Period 8.1) corresponding to field boundaries depicted on the 1886 1st Edition Ordnance Survey map. These were, however, not shown on the 1796 Wroughton Inclosure map, at which time the site lay within land labelled as 'Great Tithes'; these therefore belong to an episode of land re-organisation which occurred during the first three-quarters of the 19th century. A number of large pits had been excavated alongside one of these boundaries towards the south-eastern end of the site. These are likely to represent modern chalk quarrying.

Later remains relate to the site's use as part of RAF Wroughton and included slit trenches, 7m to 10m long and up to 1.6m deep, excavated between the runways (Period 8.2 features, e.g., 2575; Figs 2.42–2.43). These may have been designed to provide emergency cover in the event of air raids for personnel too far away from structural shelters or dug as practice trenches for the Home Guard or US Army personnel stationed at RAF Wroughton during the Second World War; similar remains were recorded within Barbury Castle during English Heritage's 1998 geophysical survey (Listed Monument entry 221369). Disturbance to the site itself from the construction of the airfield was particularly prominent in the south-eastern third of the excavated area. In some areas chalk dug out from construction of the runway directly overlaid the natural chalk substrate. In other areas, it sealed a buried topsoil.

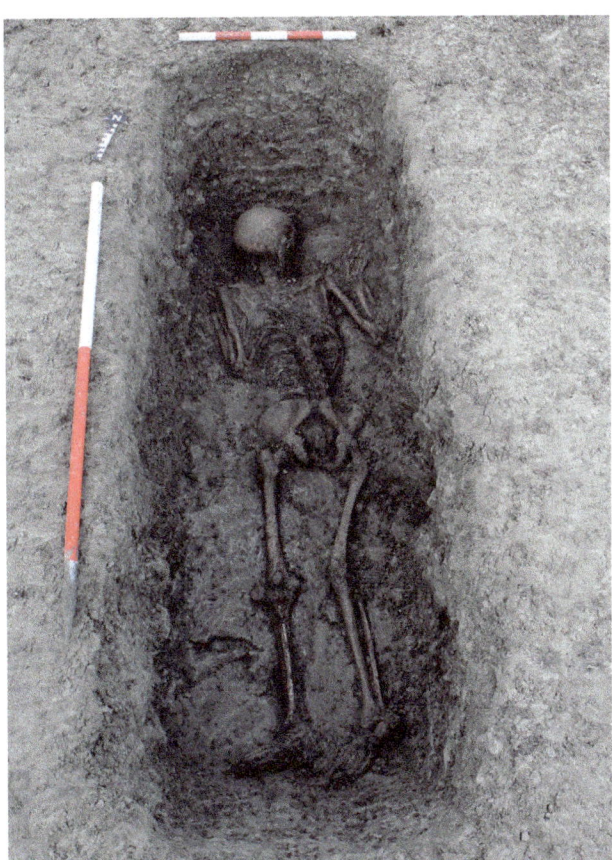

Figure 2.41 Period 6 (Mid to Late Roman) SK 2314 in grave 2315, looking north-west

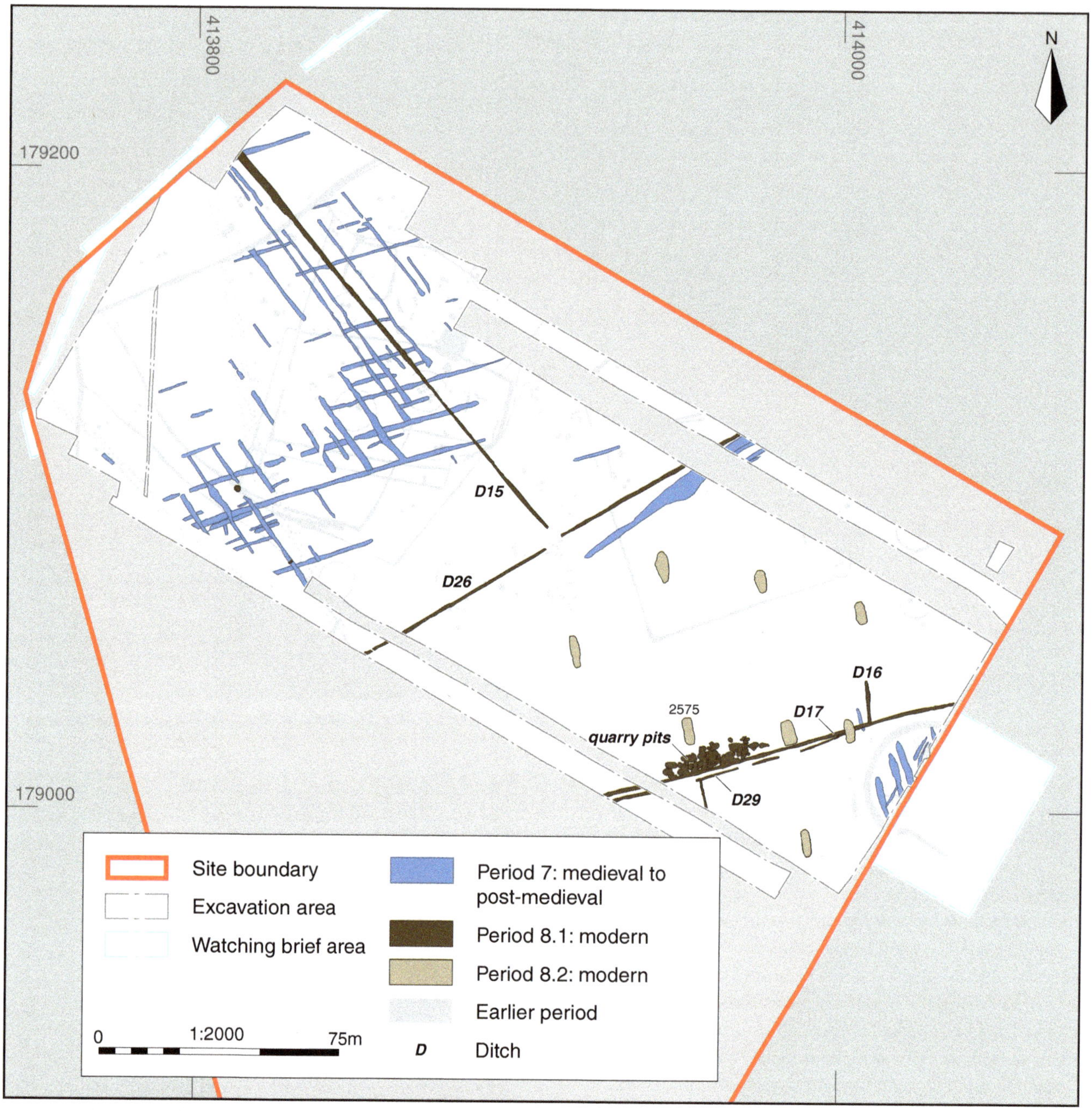

Figure 2.42 Plan of Period 7 (medieval to post-medieval) and Period 8 (modern) features

Figure 2.43 Second World War slit trench 2575, looking north-east

Chapter 3
Artefacts

The finds from the site reflect the chronological span and the differing nature of activity from later prehistory and throughout the Roman period. The amount and nature of finds related to each period therefore varies. The most significant material associated with the later prehistoric period is pottery, with a small assemblage dating to the Beaker period, and the bulk associated with the Late Bronze Age/Early Iron Age and Iron Age periods. There is a modest lithic assemblage, as well as worked stone and bone, industrial debris (including a fired clay block tuyère) and a few metal objects, amongst them an iron knife and a plough-share tip, associated with the settlement. Late Iron Age–Roman and Roman period pottery is also represented in lesser quantities with modest amounts of other materials (ceramic building material, glass, shale, industrial debris and metal) associated with the Roman land division. There were hobnails and a couple of carpentry nails from the Late Roman burials.

Lithics
Jacky Sommerville

Introduction and methodology

In total, 201 worked lithics (3551g) and 10 pieces of burnt, unworked flint (222.9g) were recovered via the hand excavation and bulk soil sampling of 124 deposits. The artefacts were recorded according to broad debitage/artefact type and catalogued directly onto a Microsoft Access database. Attributes recorded comprised raw material type and quality; weight; degree of edge damage (microflaking), rolling (abrasion) and re-cortication, the latter being a white or blueish surface discoloration resulting from soil conditions (Shepherd 1972, 109); colour; cortex description; and the presence of breakage and burning.

Raw material

One flake was made using Greensand chert and the remainder are flint. The main presence of Greensand chert is in the region of the Blackdown Hills on the Devon/Somerset border (Barton *et al.* 1995, 90) 120km to the south-east. However, there is also a band of Upper Greensand which stretches north-east of that area so the source may have been much closer to Swindon (Stewart 2012, 125, fig. 2).

The majority (69%) of the flints are fine-grained or very fine-grained and cortex is present on 140. It is chalky on 96 (68.6%) of these and abraded on 43 (31.4%). This indicates the exploitation of mainly primary sources, such as chalk, and a lesser use of secondary sources such as river gravels. The site is just within the North Wessex Downs and the bedrock is the Zag Chalk Formation of the Cretaceous Period with no recorded superficial deposits (BGS 2020), so chalk flint would have been readily available. The flint is mainly brown, grey or black in colour, with just one displaying a degree of blue discoloration due to re-cortication.

Provenance and condition

The bulk of the worked lithics were recorded from pits/postholes (115, 57%) and ditches (75, 37%). The remaining 11 items (6%) are mainly from graves, a spread deposit, and a tree-throw hole. Only a very small proportion of the flints were recovered from an early prehistoric feature: 25 flints (12%) came from Period 2 (Beaker/Early Bronze Age) pit 1245 (Fig. 2.2). The majority (165, 82%) were residual in deposits assigned to Period 3 (Late Bronze Age/Early Iron Age) to Period 8 (modern). The remaining 11 worked flints (5%) were recorded from unphased features. Eighty-four of the worked lithics (42%) are broken and 33 (17%) are burnt.

Range and variety

Primary technology
The debitage mostly comprises flakes, with just four blades present (Table 3.1). A residual core rejuvenation flake, from Period 6 (Mid to Late Roman) ditch 13, provides probable evidence of Mesolithic or Early Neolithic activity

Table 3.1 Breakdown of the lithic assemblage

Type	Number
Burnt unworked	10
Primary technology	
Blade	4
Core	25
Core rejuvenation flake	1
Flake	137
Flake from polished flint axe	1
Shatter	4
Secondary technology	
Arrowhead (leaf-shaped)	1
Knife	1
Notch	3
Retouched flake	6
Scraper (end)	8
Scraper (miscellaneous)	4
Scraper (side)	2
Scraper (thumbnail)	1
Spurred piece	2
Truncation	1
Total	**211**

Table 3.2 Lithics from Period 2 (Beaker) pit 1245

	Fill 1247 (middle)	Fill 1248 (upper)	Total
Primary technology			
Blade	1	1	2
Flake	8	10	18
Secondary technology			
Retouched flake	1	1	2
Scraper (end)	1		1
Scraper (miscellaneous)	1		1
Spurred piece	1		1
Total	**13**	**12**	**25**

since rejuvenation of the striking platform on the core was carried out during those periods. A flake removed from a polished flint axe, broadly datable to the Neolithic period, was redeposited in Period 3 (Late Bronze Age/Early Iron Age) pit 1128 from Pit alignment 2. The 25 cores comprise ten multi-platform, eight single-platform and five dual-platform types, in addition to two tested nodules. All were used for the production of flakes and none of the dual-platform cores feature opposed striking platforms.

Secondary technology

A total of 29 retouched tools were retrieved (Table 3.1). All were made using flake blanks and many are types in use throughout the prehistoric period, such as retouched flakes, notches and spurred pieces. A small number of items are chronologically distinctive. A truncation from unphased pit 2737 (Fig. 3.1, 2) is Mesolithic (Butler 2005, 109). A broken leaf-shaped arrowhead (Ra. 1039; Fig. 3.1, 1) was redeposited in Period 6 (Middle to Late Roman) grave 2329. It is a distal flake fragment with semi-invasive retouch on the dorsal face and retouch only on the edges on the ventral face. Leaf-shaped arrowheads were in use during the Early Neolithic period and this example most closely matches Green's Type 2B (Green 1980, 70). The site also produced 15 scrapers (Table 3.1). The only chronologically

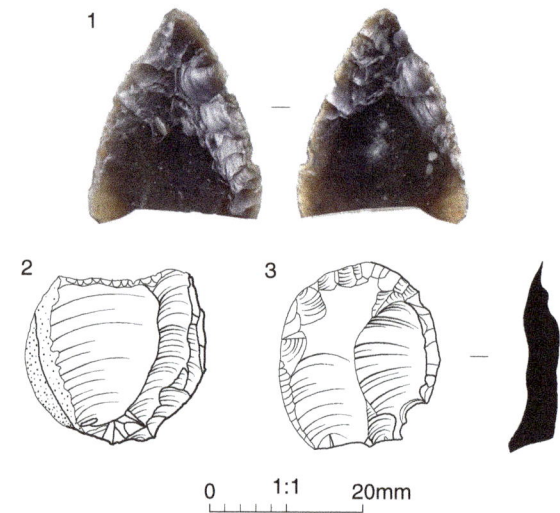

Figure 3.1 Lithics: 1–3

diagnostic example is a thumbnail scraper (Fig. 3.1, 3) residual in Period 4 (Middle Iron Age) pit 8118, which is retouched around 77% of the perimeter and dates to the Beaker/Early Bronze Age period.

Period 2 (Beaker/Early Bronze Age) pit 1245

This pit produced 25 worked flints from fills 1247 and 1248 (Table 3.2). The basal fill was devoid of artefacts and the flints from the two upper fills were associated with early Beaker pottery (see Banks, below). There are high degrees of breakage (90%, 20 items) and burning (60%, 15 items). The scrapers and spurred piece are fragmentary and burnt. The flints from this feature are otherwise in good condition, with moderate edge damage recorded on only one item (4%) and slight edge damage on seven (28%); only three items (12%) display a slight degree of rolling. This good condition suggests the flints are likely to be stratified in the pit. However, there are no closely datable types.

Discussion

Although the assemblage from the Collection Management Facility is small and has largely been redeposited, it includes residual items of Mesolithic, Early Neolithic, broad Neolithic and Beaker/Early Bronze Age date. The only material which appears to be stratified are the 25 flints from Period 2 pit 1245. However, these are mostly broken and burnt, and no typically Beaker/Early Bronze Age items (such as thumbnail scrapers or barbed and tanged arrowheads) are present. Other sites in the Swindon area which produced flints of Mesolithic and Early Bronze Age or Neolithic date include Swindon Gateway, Coate (Lamdin-Whymark 2006a; 2006b), 4km north-east of the site, and Marlborough Road, 5km north-east of the site (Anon. 2007, 237).

Beaker pottery
Pete Banks

Introduction and methodology

A small group (87 sherds, 588g) of early prehistoric pottery (Late Neolithic to Early Bronze Age) was recovered by hand from three deposits. The pottery assemblage was recorded directly into a Microsoft Access database. The pottery was examined by context, using a x10 binocular microscope and quantified according to sherd count and weight by period. The fabrics are described in accordance with the Historic England (Barclay *et al.* 2016) and the Prehistoric Ceramics Research Group guidelines (PCRG 2010). Vessel and rim forms have been recorded where the material has allowed for this; rim diameters have been measured (mm) and a minimum number of vessels (MNV) was recorded where possible. Decoration, surface treatments and residues have also been recorded when present.

Provenance and condition

Overall, the assemblage is in moderately good condition for an early prehistoric group. Although the highly fragmented nature is illustrated by the low mean sherd weight of 6.8g, most surfaces survived well, and fractures exhibited only minor signs of wear. The group was almost entirely derived from Period 2 (Beaker) pit 1245 (Fig. 2.2); a single sherd of prehistoric pottery was residual in ditch 2726 assigned to sub-phase Period 5.3 (mid-1st to 2nd centuries AD).

Assemblage range

Fabrics

BN Dark reddish-brown fabric throughout containing abundant finely crushed bone (≤2mm). (2 sherds, 10g).

GR1 Red to orange-buff exterior surface with light brown core and interior surface. Soft soapy texture with irregular fractures. Common sub-angular orange-buff grog (≤1.5mm). (77 sherds, 435g).

CGRC Dark brown to grey-brown fabric. Soft soapy texture with irregular fractures. Common orange-buff grog (≤1m) and sparse coarse calcareous grits (≤5mm). (8 sherds, 143g).

Ceramic Phase 1. Period 2 (Beaker) pit 1245

A minimum of six vessels were represented by the pottery recovered from pit 1245 (Fig. 3.2). The vessels belong to the Beaker tradition spanning the end of the Neolithic and Early Bronze Age periods (*c.* 2400–1900 BC). The full profile of Vessel 1 could not be reconstructed but it was represented by a slightly flaring rim and body sherds. The absence of the shoulder profile is perhaps suggestive of a low carinated vessel as the lower portion of the vessel was missing. The sherds were highly decorated with incised bands of cross hatching sandwiched between rows of combed dots, made with a square toothed comb. The use of this Maritime-Derived (MD) style of decoration is commonly associated with the earliest phase of Beaker use (*c.* 2400–2150 cal. BC), particularly in southern Britain (Needham 2005, 183). Similarly decorated vessels are known locally from Amesbury 51, Wiltshire (Clarke 1970, 301, fig. 162) and Bulford, Wiltshire (ibid., 302, fig.170), and regionally from Chilbolton, Hampshire (Needham 2005, 184, fig. 5, no. 4). Comb impressed low carinated Beakers were also found in the grave of the Amesbury Archer (Fitzpatrick 2011). Vessels 2, 4 and 5 are represented by rim sherds decorated with multiple rows of combed rectangular dots. The sherds from vessels 2 and 4 may be from the same vessel although refitting was not possible. The absence of full vessel profiles makes precise dating difficult; although an early date for vessels 2, 4 and 5 (*c.* 2400–2150 cal. BC) would not be inconsistent given the possible use of All-Over-Combed (AOComb) decoration and the presence of other early Beakers (vessel 1 and 3) from the same feature (ibid., 183). This style of decoration is relatively common and has been recorded on Beakers locally from sites at Dean Bottom, Wilts (Cleal 1992, 66, fig. 46, no. 6), Wilsford, Wilts (Case 2003, 185, fig. 9, no. 5) and Durrington Walls, Wilts (Clarke 1970, 309, no. 228). Although the profile of vessel 3 could not be fully reconstructed it is probably a S-Profile Beaker and the most complete vessel in this Beaker group. Several sherds decorated with All-Over Fingernail (AOFN) decoration represent a sinuous vessel with a slightly flaring rim and sagging lower body. This style of decoration is again fairly common amongst Beaker vessels in Wiltshire and comparanda are recorded from Dean Bottom, Wilts (Cleal 1992, 68, fig. 47, no. 2) and Eynsham, Oxon (Clarke 1970, 308, no. 220). A similar vessel from Chilbolton, Hampshire (Russel 1990), is associated with a radiocarbon date 2454–1937 cal. BC (OxA-1072) again suggesting a date sometime in the earliest phase of Beaker use (Needham 2005, 202, table 6). In addition, there are two sherds made in a crushed bone-tempered fabric (BN). One is decorated with a cordon and possible incised or impressed short diagonal lines. The use of bone-temper is uncommon but not unheard of. A vessel from Dean Bottom, Wilts, is decorated using a similar style (Cleal 1992, 68, fig. 47, no. 1). These dates earlier in the Beaker sequence are backed up by a radiocarbon date obtained from charred plant remains in the pit (2338–2062 cal. BC; SUERC 100004; Table 5.10).

Catalogue of illustrated sherds
(Fig. 3.2)

1 Beaker. Slightly flared rim and body sherds decorated with bands of combed dots and cross hatched decoration. Fabric GR1. Period 2 (Beaker) pit 1245 (fill 1247)

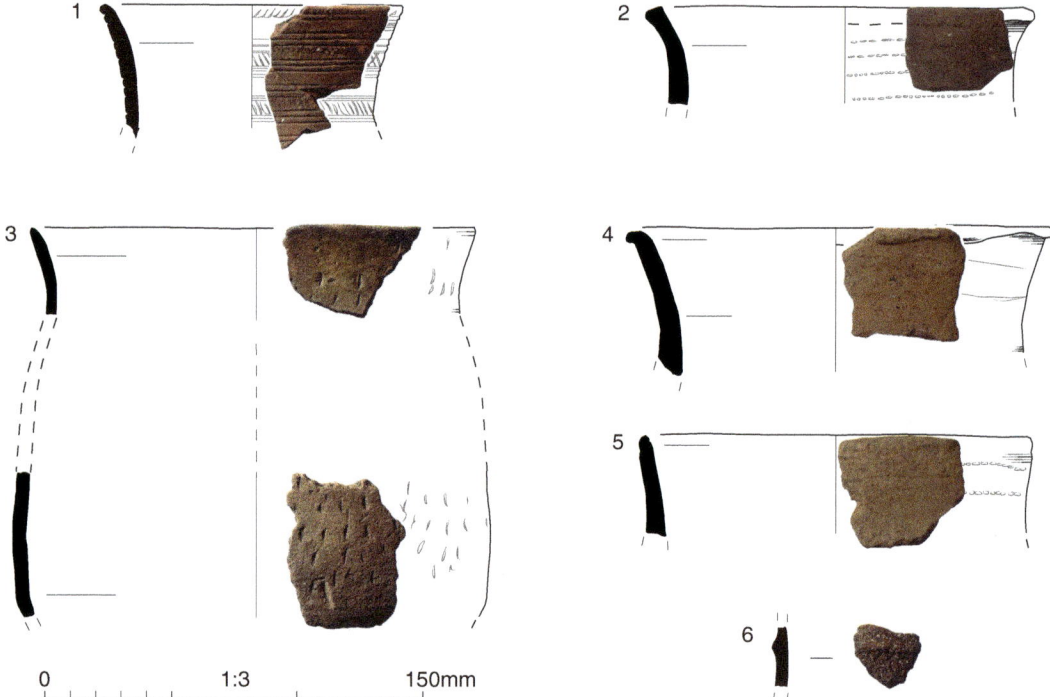

Figure 3.2 Beaker pottery: 1–6

2 Beaker. Everted rim with combed linear dots. Fabric GR1. Period 2 (Beaker) pit 1245 (fill 1247)
3 Beaker. Slightly flared rim and body sherds decorated fingernail impressions. Fabric GR1. Period 2 (Beaker) pit 1245 (fill 1248)
4 Beaker. Slightly everted rim with combed linear dots. Fabric GR1. Period 2 (Beaker) pit 1245 (fill 1248)
5 Beaker. Simple upright rim with combed linear dots. Fabric GR1. Period 2 (Beaker) pit 1245 (fill 1248)
6 Beaker? Two sherds made in fine crushed bone-tempered fabric BN. Decorated with an applied cordon and possible incised/impressed short diagonal lines. Period 2 (Beaker) pit 1245 (fill 1247)

Late prehistoric pottery
Pete Banks

Introduction
A total of 2848 sherds of late prehistoric (Iron Age) pottery weighing 43,777g was recorded. The methods used were those described in the preceding section. The condition is moderately good for a late prehistoric assemblage; most surfaces survive well, and fractures exhibit only moderate signs of wear. The mean sherd weight for the assemblage is also high at 15.4g.

Assemblage composition

Fabrics
The assemblage comprises handmade fabrics. Sandy fabrics (Q1, Q2, Q3) make up the largest proportion, accounting for 34% by count and 30% by weight. Many examples of sandy fabrics exhibit signs of iron-rich inclusions. Taken together, shell-tempered fabrics (SH1, SH2, SH3) account for 27% of the group by count and 34% by weight. A total of 16% of the late prehistoric material by count and 15% by weight are made in vesicular sandy fabrics (QV), the voids forming as a result of the carbonisation of organic material within the fabric during firing. Pottery made in sandy fabrics with calcareous inclusions (QC) accounts for 10% of the material by both count and weight. Sandy fabrics with inclusions of flint (QFL), limestone (QL) or mica (QM) account for 5% of the assemblage. Flint-tempered (FL1, FL2, FL3, FLGR), grog-tempered (GR2, GRC, GRV), vesicular (V, VC), calcareous (LI) and silty micaceous fabrics (M) are present but in very small quantities.

Fabric descriptions

Flint-tempered fabrics (80 Sherds; 834g; 0.39 EVEs (2.82% NOSH))

FL1   Common fine angular flint ≤0.5mm. Hard fabric. 6 Sherds; 6g.
FL2   Common medium angular flint ≤1mm. Hard fabric. 45 Sherds; 471g.
FL3   Common coarse angular flint 2mm+. Hard fabric. 22 Sherds; 314g.
FLGR Moderate coarse angular flint ≤2mm and coarse sub-rounded grog ≤2mm. Hard fabric. 7 Sherds; 43g.

Sandy fabrics (1940 Sherds; 27,162g; 8.97 EVEs (68.12% NOSH)):

M   Fine silty micaceous fabric. No visible inclusions. Soft fabric. 20 Sherds; 380g.

Q1 Common fine sub-rounded quartz sand ≤0.5mm. Soft fabric. 150 Sherds; 1260g.

Q2 Common to very common medium sub-rounded quartz sand ≤1mm. Soft fabric. 764 Sherds; 11,070g.

Q3 Common coarse sub-rounded quartz sand ≤3mm. Soft fabric. 74 Sherds; 1020g.

QC2 Moderate to common medium sub-rounded quartz sand ≤1mm and sparse to common medium subangular calcareous inclusions ≤1mm occ ≤5mm. Soft fabric. 286 Sherds, 4366g.

QC3 Moderate to common coarse sub-rounded quartz sand ≤3mm and sparse to common coarse round calcareous ≤5mm. Soft fabric. 21 Sherds; 540g.

QFL Common to very common medium sub-rounded quartz sand ≤1mm and sparse coarse angular flint ≤4mm. Hard fabric. 25 Sherds; 248g.

QL Common medium quartz sub-rounded quartz sand ≤1mm and medium oolitic limestone ≤1mm. Soft fabric. 3 Sherds; 26g.

QM Common to very common fine sub-rounded quartz sand ≤0.5mm and mica. Soft fabric. 123 Sherds; 1760g.

QV Common medium sub-rounded quartz sand ≤1mm and sparse to moderate coarse organic voids ≤9mm. Soft fabric. 474 Sherds; 6492g.

Calcareous fabrics (including shell) (803 Sherds; 15,621g; 5.60 EVEs (28.2% NOSH))

LI Common to very common medium oolitic limestone fabric ≤1mm. Soft fabric. 38 sherds; 426g.

SH1 Common to very common fine shell ≤1mm. Soft fabric. 86 Sherds; 465g.

SH2 Common to very common medium shell ≤2mm. Soft fabric. 185 Sherds; 6173g.

SH3 Common to very common coarse shell ≤6mm. Hard fabric. 494 Sherds; 8557g.

Organic-tempered fabrics (25 Sherds; 160g; 0.12 EVEs (<1% NOSH))

V   Sparse to moderate medium organic voids ≤2mm. Soft fabric. 8 Sherds; 45g.

VC Sparse to moderate medium organic voids ≤2mm and medium sub-angular calcareous inclusions ≤1mm occ ≤6mm. Soft fabric. 17 Sherds; 115g.

Vessel forms

Based on the number of rims, the minimum number of vessels (MNV) recorded is 155 with an EVE value of 15.08. Where vessel forms can be determined, the assemblage consists predominantly of jars and bowls (Table 3.3). Where it is not possible to assign a vessel form, a generic

Table 3.3 Late prehistoric pottery. Summary of vessel form by minimum number of vessels (MNV) and EVEs

Vessel Code	MNV	% of MNV	EVEs	% of EVEs
V1	5	3.2	0.77	5.1
V2	1	0.6	0.08	0.5
V3	11	7.1	1.41	9.4
V4	17	11.0	3.32	22.0
V5	15	9.7	2.04	13.5
V6	10	6.5	0.98	6.5
V7	9	5.8	1	6.6
V8	12	7.7	1.19	7.9
V9	9	5.8	1.31	8.7
V10	2	1.3	0.1	0.7
V11	1	0.6	0.05	0.3
Indeterminate	63	40.6	2.83	18.8
Total	**155**	**100**	**15.08**	**100**

jar/bowl category was attributed. The jars outnumber bowl forms by a ratio of approximately 3:1. Tall necked jars or jar/bowls, with simple upright or flaring rims (V1), two examples decorated with fingertip impressed shoulders, are a minor component of the group (Fig. 3.3, nos 7–10). A single sharp-shouldered jar with an upright rim was also recorded (V2) (Fig. 3.3, no. 14). Jar forms include slack-shouldered (V5) (Fig. 3.3, nos 15–18), rounded profile (V3) (Fig. 3.3, no. 13), globular (V6) and straight-sided jars (V4), including some in the saucepan pot tradition (Fig. 3.3 nos 19–20, Fig. 3.4, nos 21–25, Fig. 3.5, no. 26). Bowl varieties are slightly more restricted; those with round bodies (V8) (Fig. 3.3, no. 12 and Fig. 3.4, nos 27–30) accounting for most forms, although plain bowls with simple upright rims are moderately common (V9). Bowls with inverted (V10) or beaded (V11) rim are present only in small quantities.

Jars

V1 Tall-necked jars with flaring or upright rims: 5 MNV (0.77 EVEs).

V2 Sharp shouldered jars with upright rims: 1 MNV (0.08 EVEs).

V3 Round bodied/ovoid jars with beaded, everted or simple upright rims: 11 MNV (1.41 EVEs).

V4 Straight-sided jars with everted, expanded or simple upright rims: 17 MNV (3.32 EVEs).

V5 Weak/slack-shouldered jars with simple upright rims: 15 MNV (2.04 EVEs).

V6 Globular jars with simple upright rims: 10 MNV (0.98 EVEs).

V7 Indeterminate jars with everted, expanded or simple upright rims: 9 MNV (1.00 EVEs).

Bowls

V8 Round bodied bowls with simple upright rims: 12 MNV (1.19 EVEs).

V9 Bowls with simple rims: 9 MNV (1.31 EVEs).

Table 3.4 Late prehistoric pottery. Burnished sherds by fabric type

Fabric Codes	Sherd count	% of count	No of burnished sherds	% of burnished sherdsp
FL1	6	0.2		0.0
FL2	45	1.6	9	8.7
FL3	22	0.8	2	1.9
FLGR	7	0.2		0.0
LI	38	1.3	1	1.0
M	20	0.7	2	1.9
Q1	150	5.3	13	12.6
Q2	764	26.8	31	30.1
Q3	74	2.6	2	1.9
QC2	286	10.0	3	2.9
QC3	21	0.7		0.0
QFL	25	0.9	3	2.9
QL	3	0.1		0.0
QM	123	4.3	15	14.6
QV	474	16.6	17	16.5
SH1	86	3.0		0.0
SH2	185	6.5	2	1.9
SH3	494	17.3	3	2.9
V	8	0.3		0.0
VC	17	0.6		0.0
Total	**2848**	**100**	**103**	**100**

V10 Closed bowls with inverted rims: 2 MNV (0.1 EVEs).
V11 Bowls with beaded rims: 1 MNV (0.05 EVEs).

Rim morphology

R1 Flared rims: 5 MNV (0.61 EVEs).
R2 Squared/flat-topped upright rims: 39 MNV (4.44 EVEs).
R3 Simple upright rims: 88 MNV (8.12 EVEs).
R4 Everted rims: 8 MNV (0.86 EVEs).
R5 Externally expanded rims: 5 MNV (0.46 EVEs).
R6 Inverted rims: 3 MNV (0.17 EVEs).
R7 Beaded rims: 7 MNV (0.42 EVEs).

Deposition and vessel function

Lipid analysis of 34 late prehistoric vessels indicated that the majority contained lipids associated with the processing of dairy products (Dunne *et al.*, below). Although jars tended to be used for a variety of functions including the processing of dairy, ruminant and non-ruminant animal carcasses and plant material, there was a distinct tendency to use bowls for the processing (serving or cooking) of dairy products, most likely milk, butter or cheese. A vessel of particular interest was a La Tène jar (Period 4 pit 1757, fill 1756; Fig. 3.5, 32), which contained high concentrations of lipids derived from dairy products, suggesting extensive use (WRO02; Dunne *et al.*, below).

A number of substantially complete vessels were identified within the assemblage, including two saucepan or possible saucepan pots (Ra. 1077, Fig. 3.4, nos 22 and 25) and a small slack shouldered jar (Ra. 1209, Fig. 3.3, no. 18). It is

possible that these vessels represent special or placed deposits and they were found within Period 4 pits 1827 (fill 1833) and 2669 (fill 2672), and Period 4 ditch 13 (intervention 8076, fill 8078). These vessels exhibit signs of extensive use, and all contained burnt food residues. Organic residue analysis of the small jar-proportioned vessel with a slack-shoulder and a simple upright rim (Ra. 1209; Fig. 3.3, no. 18) from Period 5.1 Ditch 13 (fill 8078) indicated that this vessel was used for the processing of dairy products, probably cheese, milk or butter, together with leafy plant material (WRO32; Dunne *et al.*, see below).

Other vessels also provided specific evidence of use. Period 4 Pit 2669 (fill 2672) produced a substantially complete straight-sided vessel (Ra.1077) consistent with the saucepan pot tradition (Fig. 3.4, no. 25). Its interior is coated with a thick carbonaceous residue probably representing burnt food remains. Lipid analysis of this vessel suggested that it was used for the processing of dairy products (WRO27; Dunne *et al.*, see below).

A clipped pottery base with single central perforation (Ra. 1206), made in flint-tempered fabric FL2, had been adapted for use presumably as a spindlewhorl (Period 4 pit 9009).

Decoration and surface treatment

Examples of Early Iron Age styles of decoration and surface treatments are rare within the assemblage. Where present, they are represented by fingertip impressed shoulders (four sherds, Fig. 3.3, nos 7–8) or red surface finishes (two sherds). Decoration and surfaces treatments are also uncommon within the Middle and Late Iron Age assemblage. The most common type of decoration for those sherds comprises burnished or incised curvilinear La Tène style designs (12 sherds, Fig. 3.5, nos 33–34). A small number of sherds exhibit incised linear patterns (three sherds) including one with detailed horizontal or diagonal bands infilled with short horizontal or vertical lines (Fig. 3.3, no. 11). Burnished sherds are by far the most frequently recorded surface treatment (198 sherds; 7% NOSH) with smoothed or wiped surfaces noted on just two sherds. Burnishing tends to be associated with finer fabrics amongst the assemblage (M/Q1/Q2/QM/QV), although this is not exclusively the case (Table 3.4).

Stratigraphy/Dating

Ceramic Phase 2: Early Iron Age (800–400 BC)/ Periods 3–4

Evidence for activity during this ceramic phase is restricted to a small number of isolated sherds (Table 3.5). Most of the Early Iron Age material came from Period 4 pits and is most likely residual. One sherd came from pit 1512 (1 sherd, 3g) which has been assigned to Period 3 Pit alignment 2. Diagnostic features are limited to a small number of tall-necked jars or round bodied bowls, both with flaring rims. Red surface treatment was noted on a small number of sherds as were fingertip impressed shoulders (Fig. 3.3, nos 8–9).

Table 3.5 Late prehistoric pottery. Pottery quantification by stratigraphic period

Fabric codes	Unphased		Period 0		Period 2		Period 3		Period 4		Period 5		Period 5.1		Period 5.2		Period 5.3		Period 5.4		Period 6		Period 7		Period 8		Period 8.1		Period 8.2		Total	
	Ct	Wt (g)	Ct	Wt (g)	Ct	Wt (g)	Ct	Wt (g)	Ct	Wt (g)	Ct	Wt (g)	Ct	Wt (g)	Ct	Wt (g)	Ct	Wt (g)	Ct	Wt (g)	Ct	Wt (g)	Ct	Wt (g)	Ct	Wt (g)	Ct	Wt (g)	Ct	Wt (g)	Ct	Wt (g)
FL1															6	6															6	6
FL2	2	14							21	330	1	9	8	54			12	56	1	8											45	471
FL3			1	2			1	11	5	89	1	11	6	141	5	37	2	15									1	8			22	314
FLGR					3	19							3	18					1	6											7	43
LI			3	20					28	340	1	3	5	61							1	2									38	426
M									16	355	1	7	3	18																	20	380
Q1			2	34	3	108			134	990			6	72	1	1	4	55													150	1260
Q2	4	27	17	120	14	154	5	13	585	9546	4	52	81	613	23	230	7	52	4	23	9	42	2	5			9	193			764	11070
Q3			3	67	3	38	1	9	50	684			9	53	2	77					1	2					5	90			74	1020
QC2	1	10	2	62	2	40	10	17	238	3971	1	29	25	209	1	2	4	14							1	10			1	2	286	4366
QC3			1	118					17	355	1	6	1	50									1	11							21	540
QFL			2	4	3	55			11	126			2	13	1	15	6	35													25	248
QL									2	24											1	2									3	26
QM					11	90	2	14	98	1518	5	82	3	43			3	10									1	3			123	1760
QV	4	33	4	128			3	22	422	5615			34	572	4	47											1	53			474	6492
SH1			3	40					82	421			1	4																	86	465
SH2			2	96			1	2	171	6024	1	3	3	19	2	4					1	3									185	6173
SH3	1	8	28	399	1	34			444	7966			12	110			3	8	3	13	3	18									494	8557
V							1	3	5	18							1	17	1	7											8	45
VC			11	33	1	17			5	65					1	17															17	115
Grand Total	12	92	77	1027	43	651	24	91	2334	38437	16	202	202	2050	47	437	45	289	10	57	16	69	3	16	1	10	17	347	1	2	2848	43777

Ceramic Phase 3: Middle to Late Iron Age (400 BC–AD 43)/Periods 4–5

The majority of the late prehistoric assemblage (2358 sherds, 38,528g) derives from Period 3 or 4 features, with further material (358 sherds, 3479g) redeposited in later features. The bulk of the assemblage was recovered from Period 4 deposits with the majority suggesting Middle or Middle to Late Iron Age activity. Vessel types comprise slack-shouldered, globular and ovoid forms as well as some straight-sided jars, including a small number of saucepan pots. Surface treatments are largely restricted to burnishing with most vessels otherwise lacking decoration. The La Tène style decorated pottery (Period 4 pits 1454 (fills 1456, 1457), 2138 (fill 2137), 3048 (fill 3049) and 7012 (fill 7013)) can be dated to between the 2nd and 1st centuries BC (Cunliffe 2009). Overall, the group most likely dates within the 4th to 1st centuries BC.

Catalogue of illustrated sherds

(Figs 3.3–3.5)

7   Jar (V1). Fabric QV. Period 4 (Middle Iron Age) pit 1743 (fill 1740)

8   Jar (V1). Fabric Q2. Period 4 (Middle Iron Age) pit 2043 (fill 2041)

9   Jar (V1). Fabric QV. Period 4 (Middle Iron Age) pit 2210 (fill 2211)

10   Jar (V1). Fabric Q2. Period 4 (Middle Iron Age) pit 9009 (fill 9010)

11   Simple upright rim (R3). Fabric Q2. Period 4 (Middle Iron Age) pit 1512 (fill 1514)

12   Bowl (V9). Fabric SH3. Period 4 (Middle Iron Age) pit 1426 (fill 1428)

13   Jar (V3). Fabric SH3. Period 4 (Middle Iron Age) pit 1390 (fill 1391)

14   Jar (V2). Fabric Q2. Period 4 (Middle Iron Age) pit 1837 (fill 1838)

15   Jar (V5). Fabric SH2. Period 4 (Middle Iron Age) pit 2084 (fill 2085)

16   Jar (V5). Fabric Q2. Period 4 (Middle Iron Age) pit 2084 (fill 2085)

17   Jar (V5). Fabric QM. Period 4 (Middle Iron Age) pit 2615 (fill 2616)

18   Jar (V5). Fabric QV. Ra. 1209. Period 4 (Middle Iron Age) ditch 8078 (fill 8078)

19   Jar (V4). Fabric SH3. Period 4 (Middle Iron Age) pit 1390 (fill 1391)

20   Jar (V4). Fabric SH3. Period 4 (Middle Iron Age) pit 1426 (fill 1631)

21   Jar (V4). Fabric QV. Period 4 (Middle Iron Age) pit 1808 (fill 1810)

22   Jar (V4). Fabric Q2. Period 4 (Middle Iron Age) pit 1827 (fill 1833)

23   Jar (V4). Fabric SH3. Period 4 (Middle Iron Age) pit 1426 (fill 1846)

24   Jar (V4). Fabric Q2. Period 4 (Middle Iron Age) pit 2223 (fill 2224)

25   Jar (V4). Fabric Q2. Ra. 1077. Period 4 (Middle Iron Age) pit 2669 (fill 2672)

26   Jar (V4). Fabric SH2. Ra.1214. Period 4 (Middle Iron Age) pit 8118 (fill 8122)

27   Bowl (V8). Fabric QC2. Period 4 (Middle Iron Age) pit 2043 (fill 2041)

28   Bowl (V8). Fabric QV. Period 4 (Middle Iron Age) pit 2138 (fill 2135)

29   Bowl (V8). Fabric QV. Tree-throw hole 8079 (fill 8080)

30   Bowl (V9). Fabric Q2. Period 5 (Late Iron Age/Early Roman) ditch 8076 (fill 8078)

31   Bowl (10). Fabric SH2. Period 4 (Middle Iron Age) pit 8118 (fill 8122)

32   Jar (V4). Fabric Q2. Period 4 (Middle Iron Age) pit 1757 (fill 1756)

33   Burnished La Tène decoration. Period 4 (Middle Iron Age) pit 1454 (fill 1457)

34   Incised La Tène decoration. Period 4 (Middle Iron Age) pit 2138 (fill 2137)

Discussion

The small quantity of Early Iron Age material suggests activity began in the vicinity of the site during this period. The focus of the late prehistoric activity was, however, in the Middle and Late Iron Age. It is generally recognised that Early to Middle Iron Age sites in the Upper Thames Valley exhibit a chronological progression from the use of calcareous or shell-tempered fabrics to those containing sand (Allen and Robinson 1993, 42; Booth and Biddulph 2011, 353). The use of sandy fabrics, including those also with organic or calcareous inclusions, which dominate the late prehistoric assemblage, becomes increasingly common as the Middle Iron Age continued. This progression is in evidence elsewhere in the North Wiltshire region. At Groundwell West, Swindon, shell-tempered fabrics dominated in features associated with Early Iron Age activity (Timby 2001, 22), whilst at the adjacent primarily Middle Iron Age site of Groundwell Farm, sandy fabrics were more common (Gingell 1986, 62–3). The relative proportions of sandy wares (68% NOSH) to shell-tempered wares (28% NOSH) at Wroughton compares with those at Groundwell Farm and would tend to support a date commencing in the early Middle Iron Age and continuing into the Late Iron Age. Stylistically the slack-shouldered, straight-sided and globular jars and the round bodied jars and bowls are indicative of Middle to Late Iron Age activity in the Upper Thames Valley. Similar assemblage profiles can be seen elsewhere at sites like Watkins Farm (Allen 1990a) and Mingies Ditch (Wilson 1993) in Oxfordshire, Latton Lands, Wiltshire (Edwards 2009, 63) and Groundwell Farm (Gingell 1986, 60).

Wroughton's location on the northern edge of the Wessex Downs has also influenced elements of its assemblage. The saucepan pot tradition is more typical of the Wessex region than the Upper Thames Valley and their presence in the

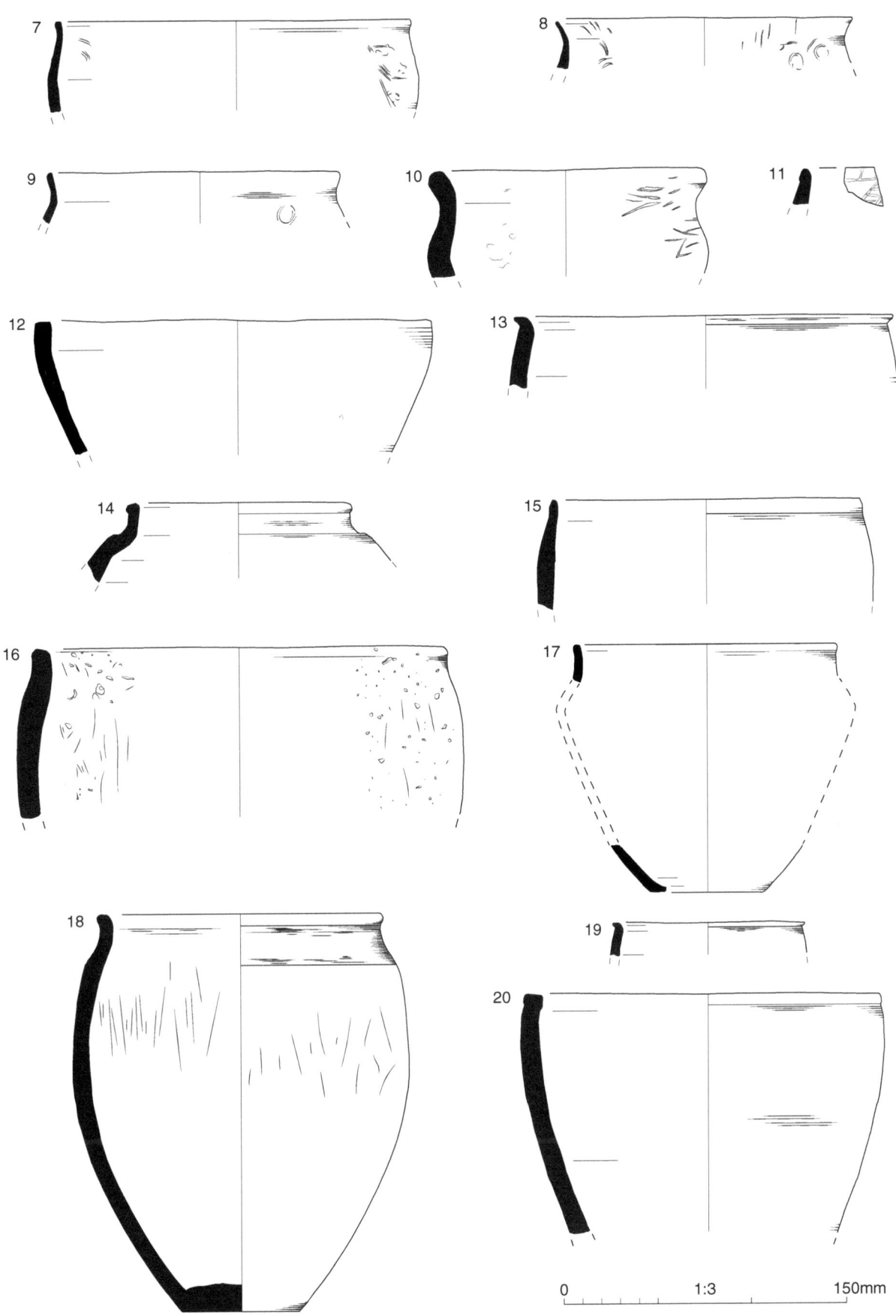

Figure 3.3 Iron Age pottery: 7–20

Figure 3.4 Iron Age pottery: 21–25, 27–30

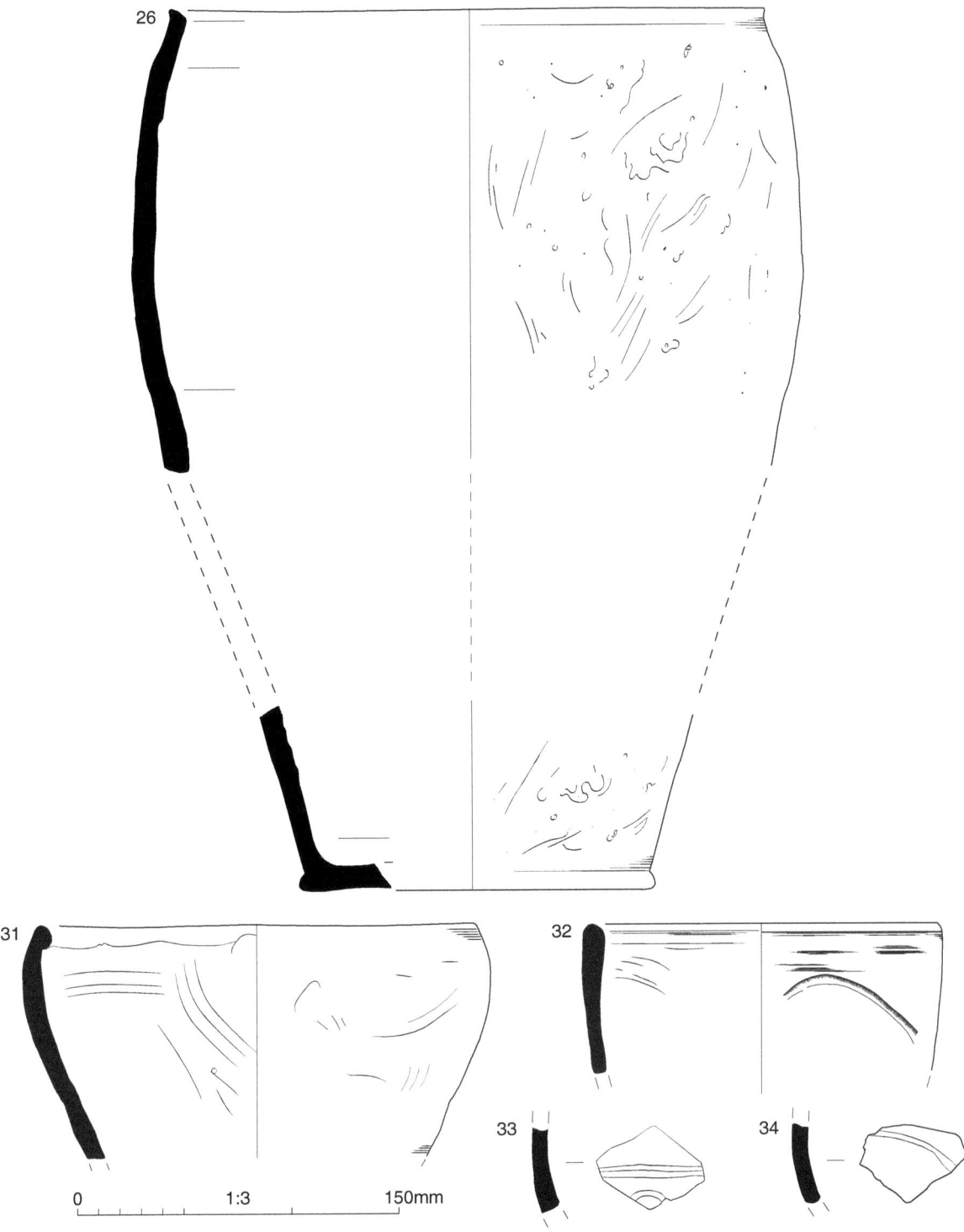

Figure 3.5 Iron Age pottery: 26, 31–34

Wroughton group would also support a Middle to Late Iron Age date. Comparable vessels dating to between the 4th–1st centuries BC were recorded at Brickley Lane, Devizes, Wiltshire (Timby 2002, 221) and Danebury Hillfort, Hampshire (Cunliffe 1984, 234). The scarcity of decorated sherds (<1%) together with the relative predominance of burnishing, is also indicative of Middle and Late Iron Age handmade traditions in the area which are commonly represented by highly burnished finewares and coarsewares with limited decoration. Just under 2% of the Middle Iron Age assemblage at Watkins Farm were decorated (Allen and Robinson 1993, 42) whilst the Middle Iron Age group from Latton Lands was entirely undecorated (Edwards 2009, 63).

That activity probably continued into the Late Iron Age is demonstrated by the presence of the La Tène style vessels which suggest a date between the 2nd and 1st centuries BC. The presence of handmade beaded rim jars in moderate quantities may suggest that activity continued into the 1st century AD, these were succeeded by 'transitional' Late Iron Age/Early Roman variants as discussed below.

Late Iron Age and Roman pottery

Pete Banks

Introduction and methodology

A total of 2222 sherds pottery, weighing 33,667g, were recorded with an EVEs value of 22.76. The methodology was the same as that employed for the prehistoric pottery, described above. The fabrics are described in accordance with the Historic England guidelines (Barclay *et al.* 2016) and, where appropriate, the National Roman Fabrics Reference Collection (Tomber and Dore 1998). The condition of the assemblage is moderately good; most surfaces survive well, and fractures exhibit only moderate signs of wear. The mean sherd weight for the assemblage is also moderately high at 15.2g.

Assemblage composition

Fabrics

A large proportion of the assemblage consists of Late Iron Age and Early Roman transitional grog-tempered fabrics (UNS GR, UNS GRC, UNS QGR, UNS SHGR, UNS FLGR). Grog-tempered fabric UNS GR accounts for the largest individual fabric group of the Late Iron Age to Roman assemblage. A coarse flint-tempered fabric (UNS CFL), represented by a small number of sherds, may be a continuance of Late Iron Age traditions into the Early Roman period, and comparable in dating to what Timby (2007) refers to as Silchester ware. A small number of sandy, vesicular sherds (UNS QV) are also likely to be of transitional date. The majority of sherds made in these fabrics were probably local products.

The majority of the Roman group consists of reduced and oxidised sandy coarse and fine wares (SGW, FSGW, SOX, FSOX, SBW, FSBW, SBUF, SRE, SWW, UNS Q, UNS QC, UNS ISW) made locally. Many (SGW, FSGW, SOX, FSOX) are probably from kilns at Toothill, Swindon, and Whitehill Farm, Wiltshire (Anderson 1979). Sandy grey wares make up the largest single fabric group within the Roman assemblage. Savernake grog-tempered wares (SAV GT) are also a common feature of the assemblage, and their production is known from kilns in the Marlborough area during the Early Roman period, between the mid 1st and mid 2nd centuries AD (Seager Smith 2001, 235, 240). Small quantities of North Wiltshire colour-coated wares (NOW CC, UNS WS) are also present, production of which may have been near the Roman small town at Wanborough from the 2nd century onwards (Anderson 1978).

Regionally produced fabrics are rare in the assemblage. Southeast Dorset Black burnished ware (DOR BB1) is the most frequent regional type (66 sherds, 837g). In production from before the conquest, this was distributed more widely across Britain from the 2nd to 4th centuries AD. Of a similar date (2nd to 4th centuries AD) are a small number of non-mortaria white ware sherds (OXF WW), most likely produced by the Oxfordshire pottery industries.

Fabric descriptions

'Transitional' wheelthrown fabrics (983 Sherds; 15,788g; 6.68 EVEs (44.24% NOSH)).

SAV GT	Savernake grog-tempered ware. 296 Sherds; 7053g. 2.85 EVEs.
UNS CFL	Coarse flint-tempered. 42 Sherds; 901g. 1.09 EVEs.
UNS GR	Fine-medium grog-tempered. 773 Sherds; 11,723g. 4.05 EVEs.
UNS GRC	Fine-medium grog-tempered with calcareous. Mainly wheelthrown. 5 Sherds; 245g.
UNS QGR	Fine-medium grog-tempered with common quartz sand. 139 Sherds; 2530g. 1.34 EVEs.
UNS SHGR	Fine-medium grog-tempered with common shell. Mainly wheelthrown. 2 Sherds; 47g. 0.02 EVEs.
UNS FLGR	Coarse flint-tempered with common fine-medium grog. Mainly wheelthrown. 12 Sherds; 276g. 0.18 EVEs.
UNS QV	Medium quartz sand with organic voids. 10 Sherds; 66g.

Reduced wares (local/unsourced) (978 Sherds; 15,455g; 11.82 EVEs (44.01% NOSH).

FSBW	Fine black-fired (sparse sand) ware. Dark grey/black throughout. 4 Sherds; 20g.
FSGW	Fine (sparse sand) grey ware. Grey throughout. 31 Sherds; 271g. 0.2 EVEs.
IMT BB	Coarse dark grey Black-burnished ware 'imitations.' 4 Sherds; 12g.
SBW	Black fired sandy ware. Dark grey/black throughout. 98 Sherds; 1208g. 1.42 EVEs.
SGW	Sandy grey ware. Grey throughout. 471 Sherds; 6185g. 6.06 EVEs.
SRE	Sandy reduced ware. Dark grey/black surface with buff/grey core. 14 Sherds; 150g. 0.29 EVEs.
UNS ISW	Reduced iron rich sandy fabric. Dark grey/black throughout. 6 Sherds; 84g.
UNS L	Reduced ware (sparse sand) with abundant limestone. Dark grey/black throughout. 6 Sherds; 41g. 0.07 EVEs.
UNS Q	Reduced sandy ware (Early Roman). Dark grey/black surface with buff/grey core. 33 Sherds; 170g. 0.23 EVEs.

UNS QC Reduced sandy ware with common calcareous inclusions. Dark grey/black throughout. 13 Sherds; 203g. 0.7 EVEs.

UNS V Reduced ware (sparse sand) with organic voids. Dark grey/black surface with buff/grey core. 2 Sherds; 58g.

Oxidised wares (local/unsourced) (116 Sherds; 930g; 1.63 EVEs (5.22% NOSH)).

FSOX Fine (sparse sand) oxidised ware. Reddish-yellow throughout. 20 Sherds; 144g. 0.55 EVEs.

SBUF Sandy buff-fired ware. Buff-light grey throughout. 7 Sherds; 126g.

SOX Sandy oxidised ware. Reddish-yellow throughout. 88 Sherds; 659g. 1.08 EVEs.

UNS MD Sandy oxidised ware with mica dust coated exterior. 1 Sherds; 1g.

Whiteware (28 Sherds; 187g. 0.65 EVEs (1.26% NOSH).

OXF WW Oxfordshire white ware. 3 Sherds; 6g. 0.1 EVEs.

SWW Sandy white ware. White/cream throughout. 25 Sherds; 181g. 0.65 EVEs.

Colour coated wares (local/unsourced) (31 Sherds; 319g; 0.32 EVEs (1.4% NOSH)).

NOW CC North Wiltshire colour-coated ware. 20 Sherds; 178g. 0.32 EVEs.

UNS WS Sandy oxidised ware with white colour-coated surface. 11 Sherds; 141g.

Regional 'imports' (66 Sherds; 837g. 1.21 EVEs. (2.97% NOSH)).

DOR BB1 South East Dorset Black-burnished ware. 66 Sherds; 837g. 1.21 EVEs.

Continental 'imports' (20 Sherds; 151g; 0.35 EVEs (<1% NOSH)).

LGF SA La Grafufesenque South Gaulish samian. 7 Sherds; 55g. 0.13 EVEs.

LEZ SA2 Lezoux Central Gaulish samian. 12 Sherds; 78g. 0.22 EVEs

RHZ SA Rheinzabern East Gaulish samian. 1 Sherd; 18g.

Samian

In total, 20 sherds (151g) of Gaulish samian are present, equivalent to 0.9% of the total assemblage. Products from the three Gaulish production centres are represented with Central Gaulish material being most common. Plain vessels, platters (Drag 18 and 18/31) and cups (Drag 33) are the only forms positively identified and these are largely Early

Table 3.6 Late Iron Age/Roman and Roman pottery. Summary of vessel form by minimum number of vessels (MNV) and EVEs

Vessel	Count	% of Count	EVEs	% of EVEs
Flagon	6	2.90	1.41	6.20
Beaker	6	2.90	1.06	4.66
Cup	1	0.48	0.1	0.44
Jar	114	55.07	13.88	60.98
Probable jar/bowl	45	21.74	3.44	15.11
Bowl	20	9.66	1.74	7.64
Platter	14	6.76	1.08	4.75
Lid	1	0.48	0.05	0.22
Total	**207**	**100**	**22.76**	**100**

Roman types, dating to the mid 1st to mid 2nd centuries AD (Webster 1996). A cordoned body sherd (RHZ SA) may represent a Drag 44 bowl dating to the mid 2nd to mid 3rd centuries; precise identification is uncertain, however, due to the lack of a rim or full profile.

Vessel forms and stylistic affinities

The range of vessel forms is set out in (Table 3.6). The assemblage contains a minimum of 207 vessels (22.76 EVEs). In some instances, the rim sherd does not allow for full identification of the vessel form and in these cases a probable jar/bowl category has been assigned (45 MNV; 3.44 EVEs). Jars dominate the assemblage (114 MNV; 13.88 EVEs), although a significant number (41 MNV; 6.11 EVEs) are undiagnostic, having out-curved rims that were common throughout the Roman period. Jars with beaded rims are also a frequent component of the group (55 MNV, 6.16 EVEs) and can be closely dated to the Early Roman period (1st to 2nd centuries AD). Bowls make up a relatively small component of the assemblage (20 MNV; 1.74 EVEs) as do platters (14 MNV; 1.08 EVEs). A small number of transitional necked/shouldered bowls are present, but most are open forms with plain, flanged or dropped flanged rims typical of the Mid to Late Roman period (2nd to 4th centuries AD). Platters, aside from the samian varieties already discussed, mostly exhibit either plain rims or at least one internal moulding. Drinking vessels (cups/beakers) and liquid serving vessels (flagons) are poorly represented. The base of a vessel made in Savernake grog-tempered fabric SAV GT (Period 5 pit 1900, not illustrated) has been perforated multiple times, presumably to allow for the drainage of liquids.

Some regional distinctiveness is evident in the assemblage with a significant proportion of round bodied beaded rim jars (Fig. 3.6, no. 35–40) made in Savernake grog-tempered wares (SAV GT). These are common in the North Wiltshire region in assemblages dating to the mid to late 1st century AD (Seager Smith 2001, 235).

The base of a grog-tempered vessel (GR2) has been clipped and perforated centrally, adapting it for use as a

Table 3.7 Late Iron Age/Roman and Roman pottery. Pottery quantification by stratigraphic period

Fabric codes	Unphased Ct	Unphased Wt (g)	Period 0 Ct	Period 0 Wt (g)	Period 2 Ct	Period 2 Wt (g)	Period 3 Ct	Period 3 Wt (g)	Period 4 Ct	Period 4 Wt (g)	Period 5 Ct	Period 5 Wt (g)	Period 5.1 Ct	Period 5.1 Wt (g)	Period 5.2 Ct	Period 5.2 Wt (g)	Period 5.3 Ct	Period 5.3 Wt (g)	Period 5.4 Ct	Period 5.4 Wt (g)	Period 6 Ct	Period 6 Wt (g)	Period 7 Ct	Period 7 Wt (g)	Period 8 Ct	Period 8 Wt (g)	Period 8.1 Ct	Period 8.1 Wt (g)	Period 8.2 Ct	Period 8.2 Wt (g)	Total Ct	Total Wt (g)
Handmade IA	12	92	77	1027	43	651	24	91	2334	38437	16	202	202	2050	47	437	45	289	10	57	16	69	3	16	10	17	1	347	1	2	2848	43777
SAV GT	15	231	9	148	13	315			7	85	104	2340	17	820	17	328	73	2105	9	352					17	329					296	7053
UNS CFL			2	117					1	4	2	44		532	4			204													42	901
UNS GR	20	345	13	114	195	2215	1	1	24	348	72	1459	154	2301	53	543	201	3664	17	221	8	329	5	24	9	140	1	19			773	11723
UNS GRC									1	123	4			122																	5	245
UNS QGR	1	69	4	94	6	92			11	125	27	608	20	677	20	311	7	403	7	123	1		1	25			1	3			139	2530
UNS SHGR									1	36	1																				2	47
UNS FLGR			6	227									1	11	1	20	1	7													12	276
UNS QV			3	35					4	18	1	1			2		2	12	1	10											10	66
FSBW															1	2		18													4	20
FSGW															30	269					1	2									31	271
IMT BB											1	4	3		3	8															4	12
SBW	10	59	3	63					7	93	10	122	16	225	16	72	49	606	1	3	1	20	1	6	1	7					98	1208
SGW	9	63	32	349					27	259	76	1002	58	916	58	536	139	2131	61	265	26	419	1	6	1	23	13	155	1	2	471	6185
SRE									1	5	4	28	1	38	6		1	64	3	3	1	12									14	150
UNS ISW									5	79	1	5																			6	84
UNS L											3	27			1		1	3											1	2	6	41
UNS Q		7	3						6	65	8	10	6	34	6	5	6	37			7	18									33	170
UNS QC	1	7	3	16					1	15					7		1	141		24											13	203
UNS V	1	46	1	12																											2	58
FSOX	1	4			3	5			1	6	3	41	1	9	6	2	6	53	1	9	1	5			2	19					20	144
SBUF				4					1	4			1		4	5	1	108													7	126
SOX	3	6	5	13		21			3	14	21	180	10	147	12	55	3	81	12		3	34	3	57	3	39					88	659
UNS MD															1		1	1													1	1
OXF WH													3			6															3	6
SWW									2	14	8	24	6	56	7	41		67			1		1	1			1	2			25	181
NOW CC				2					4	17	3		2	36	6	2		74			4	25									20	178
UNS WS	1	2											2	32	2			73			6	34									11	141
DOR BB1	3	52							12	100	20	226	3	32	3	51	3	35			24	370			1		1	3			66	837
LGF SA											1	6	1	32	2	2	1	6			1	9									7	55
LEZ SA2	1	1							2	11	1	2			2	7					2	15			4			42			12	78
RHZ SA									1	18																					1	18
Grand Total (LIA/RB)	50	764	43	490	275	3468	1	1	122	1439	351	6129	384	6009	231	2265	553	9893	57	1019	88	1292	11	113	1	23	52	739	3	23	2222	33667

spindlewhorl or gaming counter (Period 6 fill of Period 4 C-shaped enclosure ditch).

Stratigraphy/dating

Ceramic Phase 3: Late Iron Age (transitional) to Early Roman (AD 1–200)/Period 5 (Table 3.7)

The 'transitional' pottery consists mainly of wheel thrown grog-tempered wares comparable with Thompson's 'Belgic' forms common in south-east Britain (Thompson 1982). The abundance of round jars with beaded rims (C1-1/C1-2) and girth groove jars (B1-5) or bowls (D1-3) would suggest a date during the 1st century AD, probably no later than AD 75 (ibid., 217).

Transitional Late Iron Age and Early Roman fabrics from sub-phase Period 5.1 features consist largely of grog-tempered wares (UNS GR, UNS GRC, UNS SHGR, UNS QGR). Although the use of Roman sandy wares (FSGW/SBW/SGWSOX) became more common from sub-phase Period 5.2 onwards, grog-tempering remained a major component of the Early Roman assemblage. Despite a noticeable increase in fully Romanised fabrics (SGW, SAV GT) during sub-phase Period 5.3, grog-tempered pottery (UNS GR) still dominates the pottery from features assigned to Period 5.3.

Early Roman forms such as the beaded rim jar are very common in the assemblage as a whole, with 38 (MNV) examples from Early Roman features such as Period 5 pits 2221 (fill 2222) and 2720 (fill 2722), sub-phase Period 5.2 pit 1638 (fill 1639), Period 5.2 droveway A, ditch 3 (fill 1142) and enclosure 3, ditch 31 (fill 2815), and sub-phase Period 5.3 enclosure 1, ditch 8 (fill 2727).

Another form associated with the Early Roman period, the platter, was also mostly derived (7 MNV) from features belonging to the same period: Period 5 deposit 2449 (the upper fill of oven 2827), Period 5 pit 2723 (fill 2724) and sub-phase Period 5.3 enclosure 1, ditches 4 (fill 2821) and 8 (fills 2870, 2955 and 3286).

The small quantities of samian wares are also derived from earlier phased features from Period 5 although the scarcity of samian feature sherds prohibits more refined dating based on the samian wares alone. Overall, the main focus of activity at the site would appear to be in the 1st and 2nd centuries AD, probably petering out towards the end of the 2nd century. Moderately sized groups are also recorded from the later fills of Period 4 C-shaped ditch 1 and from the upper fills of other Period 4 (Middle Iron Age) features but these reflect some intrusion as well as late infilling of the upper parts of some early features.

Ceramic Phase 4: Mid to Late Roman (AD 200–410)/Period 6

Good evidence from the pottery for continued activity after *c.* AD 200 is scarce. Regional finewares suggestive of Late Roman activity, such as those from the Oxford and New Forest regions, are absent. Some among the regional types (DOR BB1; OXF WH), and indeed the local coarsewares from sub-phases Periods 5.1–5.3, may extend into this period, however, the few certainly 'late' elements occur from discrete features assigned to Period 6. All three examples of dropped flange bowls and a jar with a flaring rim (Type 3) are indicative of Late Roman activity between the mid 3rd to 4th centuries AD (Seager Smith and Davies 1993, 231, fig. 122, no. Type 3 and 234, fig. 124, no. Type 25; Holbrook and Bidwell 1991).

Catalogue of illustrated sherds
(Fig. 3.6)

35 Round jar with beaded rim. Fabric UNS GR. Period 5.1 (Late Iron Age/Early Roman) ditch 13 (fill 1555)

36 Round jar with beaded rim. Fabric SAV GT. Period 5 (Late Iron Age/Early Roman) pit 1655 (fill 1656)

37 Round jar with beaded rim. Fabric SAV GT. Period 5 (Late Iron Age/Early Roman) pit 1655 (fill 1656)

38 Round jar with beaded rim. Fabric SGW. Period 5.1 (Late Iron Age/Early Roman) ditch 13 (fill 2028)

39 Round jar with beaded rim. Fabric UNS GR. Period 4 (Middle Iron Age) C-shaped enclosure ditch (Period 6 fill 2460)

40 Round jar with beaded rim. Fabric UNS FLGR. Period 4 (Middle Iron Age) C-shaped enclosure ditch (Period 6 fill 2460)

41 Round jar with beaded rim. Fabric SAV GT. Period 5.3 (Early to Middle Roman) enclosure 1, ditch 8 (fill 2727)

42 Girth groove jar. Fabric SAV GT. Period 5 (Late Iron Age/Early Roman) ditch 2756 (fill 2757)

43 Girth groove jar. Fabric SAV GT. Period 5.3 (Early to Middle Roman) enclosure 1, ditch 4 (fill 3098)

44 Girth groove bowl. Fabric UNS QGR. Period 5 (Late Iron Age/Early Roman) pit 1655 (fill 1656)

45 Round bodied bowl with out-curved rim. Fabric UNS CFL. Period 4 (Middle Iron Age) C-shaped enclosure ditch (Period 6 fill 2395)

46 Carinated bowl with slightly beaded rim. Fabric SGW. Period 5.3 (Early to Middle Roman) enclosure 1, ditch 8 (fill 3353)

47 Carinated bowl with flattened rim and burnished lattice neck decoration. Fabric UNS GR. Period 5.3 (Early to Middle Roman) enclosure 1, ditch 8 (fill 2244)

48 Beaker. Probably local copy of Butt Beaker with incised horizontal and vertical linear decoration. Fabric SBUF. Period 5.3 (Early to Middle Roman) enclosure 1, ditch 8 (fill 2244)

49 Beaker with everted rim. Fabric SWW. Period 5.1 (Late Iron Age/Early Roman) pit 1596 (fill 1598)

50 Bag-shaped beaker with corniced rim. Fabric NOW CC. Period 5.1 (Late Iron Age/Early Roman) structure A (fill 2246)

51 Flagon with bevelled rim. Fabric SAV GT. Period 5.1 (Late Iron Age/Early Roman) structure A (fill 2242)

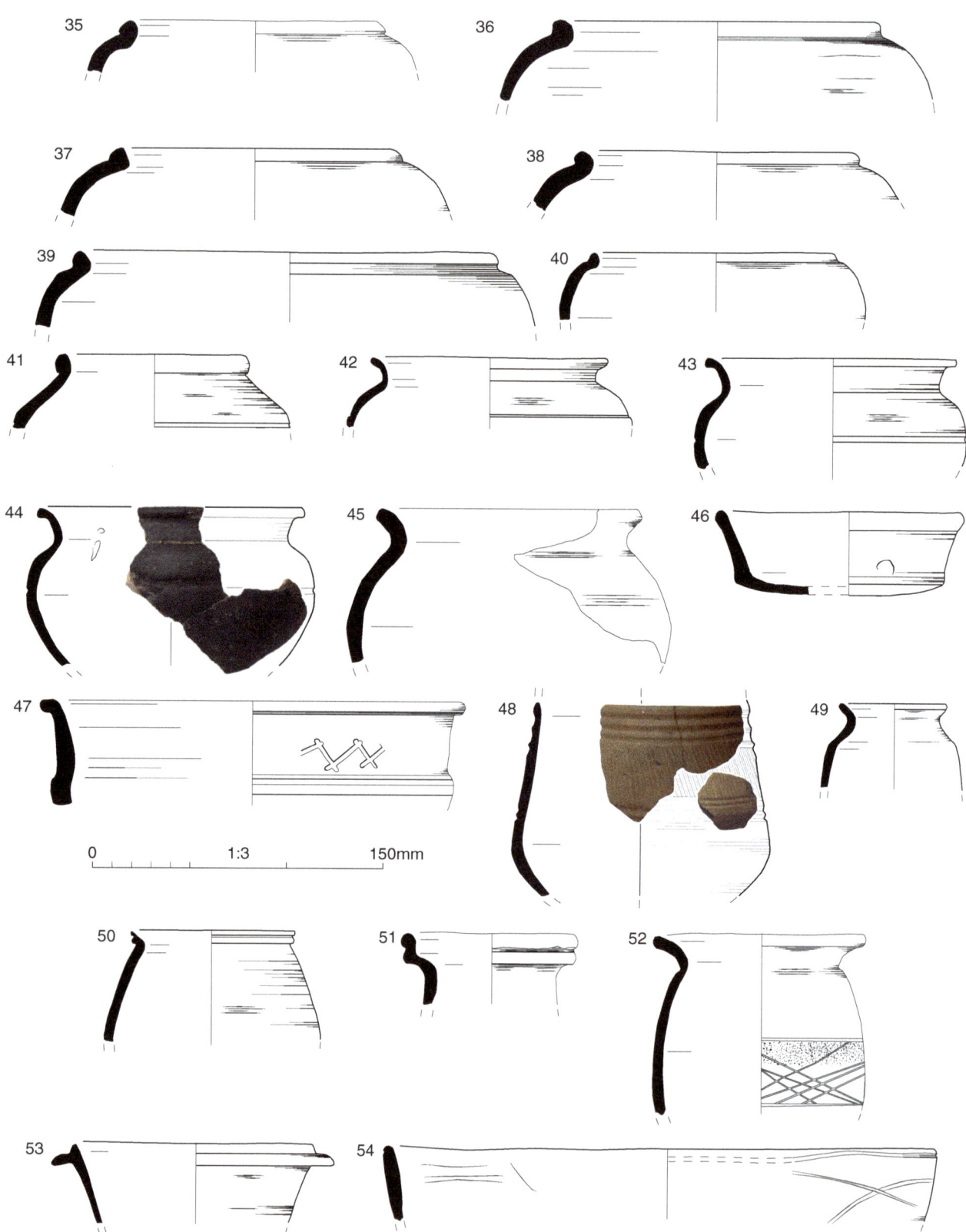

Figure 3.6 Late Iron Age/Early Roman pottery: 35–54

52 Jar with flaring rim and burnished lattice decoration. TYPE 3. Fabric DOR BB1. Period 6 (Middle to Late Roman) oven 2532 (fill 2527)

53 Dropped flange bowl. TYPE 25. Fabric DOR BB1. Period 6 (Middle to Late Roman) oven 2532 (fill 2527)

54 Plain rim dish. TYPE 20. Fabric DOR BB1. Period 6 (Middle to Late Roman) oven 2532 (fill 2527)

Discussion

Late Iron Age and Roman activity began on site in the 1st century AD, and evidence for Late Iron Age handmade traditions such as bead rim jars, already discussed in relation to the late prehistoric pottery, would suggest some continuity from the late prehistoric period (Period 4). The use of grog-tempered fabrics during the Late Iron Age and Early Roman periods can be seen elsewhere in the Upper Thames Valley region at sites such as Latton Lands, Wiltshire (Stansbie 2009, 70) and Thornhill Farm, Gloucestershire (Timby 2004, 90). Locally produced grog-tempered wares continued to be popular into the Early Roman period (mid 1st to 2nd centuries AD) in the form of Savernake wares. These were also a common feature of Early Roman phases at Wanborough where their use declined towards the end of the 2nd century AD (Seager Smith 2001, 235).

The scarcity of forms post-dating the 2nd century AD and of Late Roman fine and specialist wares would suggest activity peaked in the later 1st or early 2nd centuries, declining thereafter. The presence of small quantities of forms such as the Black-burnished ware dropped flange bowls indicates that activity continued in the vicinity of the site into the Late Roman period, but at a much-reduced level. The Late Roman (Period 6) cemetery may suggest that the focus of occupation in this period lay beyond the site.

Compositionally, the assemblage compares well with other Early Roman sites in the region. Early Roman phases at South Marston Park, Wiltshire (McSloy 2009, 121) and the A419 Blunsdon Bypass, Swindon (McSloy 2011, 106–7) are both dominated by grog-tempered wares including Savernake wares and locally produced Early Roman greywares. The dominance of coarseware jars at the current site and the relative dearth of fine tablewares or specialist wares, such as colour coated beakers and bowl/dishes, mortaria and amphorae, would tend to indicate domestic activity of relatively low status as is often evident at Roman rural sites away from urban centres (Stansbie 2009, 73), and is evident at rural sites such as Watkins Farm, Oxfordshire (Raven 1990, 47). Platters, beakers and bowls/dishes, generally associated with food preparation and service, were often made in coarseware fabrics and were not particularly high quality. The almost complete absence of regionally imported wares is also indicative of reliance on the local economy and with limited access to wider markets. This is a pattern reflected elsewhere in the Upper Thames Valley at sites such as Thornhill Farm, Gloucestershire (Timby 2004) and Gravelly Guy, Oxfordshire (Green *et al.* 2004).

Organic residue analysis of Iron Age and Roman pottery

Julie Dunne, Toby Gillard and Richard Evershed

Introduction

Lipids, the organic solvent soluble components of living organisms, in other words, the fats, waxes and resins of the natural world, are the most frequently recovered compounds from archaeological contexts. They are resistant to decay and are likely to endure at their site of deposition, often for thousands of years, because of their inherent hydrophobicity, making them excellent candidates for use as biomarkers in archaeological research (Evershed 1993). Pottery has become one of the most extensively studied materials for organic residue analysis (Mukherjee *et al.* 2005) as ceramics, once made, are virtually indestructible (Tite 2008). Survival of these residues occurs in three ways; rarely, actual contents are preserved *in situ* (Charrié-Duhaut *et al.* 2007) or, more commonly, as surface residues (Evershed 2008). The third and most frequent occurrence is that of absorbed residues preserved within the vessel wall, which have been found to survive in >80% of domestic cooking pottery assemblages worldwide (Evershed 2008).

The application of modern analytical techniques enables the identification and characterisation of these sometimes highly degraded remnants of natural commodities used in antiquity (Evershed 2008). Often, data obtained from the organic residue analysis of pottery or other organic material provide the only evidence for the processing of animal commodities, aquatic products or plant oils and waxes, particularly at sites exhibiting a paucity of environmental evidence. To date, the use of chemical analyses in the reconstruction of vessel use at sites worldwide has enabled the identification of terrestrial animal fats (Evershed *et al.* 1997a; Mottram *et al.* 1999), marine animal fats (Copley *et al.* 2004; Craig *et al.* 2007), plant waxes (Evershed *et al.* 1991), beeswax (Evershed *et al.* 1997b) and birch bark tar (Charters *et al.* 1993; Urem-Kotsou *et al.* 2002). This has increased our understanding of ancient diet and foodways and has provided insights into herding strategies and early agricultural practices. Organic residue analysis has also considerably enhanced our understanding of the technologies involved in the production, repair and use of ancient ceramics.

Preserved animal fats are by far the most commonly observed constituents of lipid residues recovered from archaeological ceramics. This demonstrates their considerable significance to past cultures, not just for their nutritional value but also for diverse uses such as binding media, illuminants, sealers, lubricants, varnish, adhesives and ritual, medical and cosmetic purposes (Mills and White 1977; Evershed *et al.* 1997a).

Today, the high sensitivities of instrumental methods such as gas chromatography and mass spectrometry allow very small amounts of compounds to be detected and identified. Furthermore, higher sensitivity can be achieved using selected ion monitoring (SIM) methods for the detection of specific marine biomarkers (Evershed *et al.* 2008; Cramp and Evershed 2013). The advent of gas chromatography-combustion-isotope ratio mass spectrometry in the 1990s introduced the possibility of accessing stable isotope information from individual biomarker structures, opening a range of new avenues for the application of organic residue analysis in archaeology (Evershed *et al.* 1994; 1997a).

This stable carbon isotope approach, using GC-C-IRMS, is employed to determine the $\delta^{13}C$ values of the principal fatty acids ($C_{16:0}$ and $C_{18:0}$), ubiquitous in archaeological ceramics. Differences occur in the $\delta^{13}C$ values of these major fatty acids due to the differential routing of dietary carbon and fatty acids during the synthesis of adipose and dairy fats in ruminant animals, thus allowing ruminant milk fatty acids to be distinguished from carcass fats by calculating $\Delta^{13}C$ values ($\delta^{13}C_{18:0}-\delta^{13}C_{16:0}$) and plotting that against the $\delta^{13}C$ value of the $C_{16:0}$ fatty acid. Previous research has shown that by plotting $\Delta^{13}C$ values, variations in $C_{3:0}$ versus $C_{4:0}$ plant consumption are removed, thereby emphasising biosynthetic and metabolic characteristics of the fat source (Dudd and Evershed 1998; Copley *et al.* 2003).

Materials and analytical methods

Lipid analysis and interpretations were performed using established protocols (Correa-Ascencio and Evershed 2014). Briefly, ~2g of potsherd were sampled and surfaces cleaned with a modelling drill to remove exogenous lipids. The cleaned sherd powder was crushed in a solvent-washed mortar and pestle and weighed into a furnaced culture tube (I). An internal standard was added (20µg *n*-tetratriacontane; Sigma Aldrich Company Ltd) together with 5mL of $H_2SO_4/MeOH$ 2–4% ($\delta^{13}C$ measured) and the culture tubes were placed on a heating block for 1 h at 70°C, mixing every 10 minutes. Once cooled, the methanolic acid was transferred to test tubes and centrifuged at 2500 rpm for 10 minutes. The supernatant was then decanted into another furnaced culture tube (II) and 2mL of DCM extracted and double distilled water was added. In order to recover any lipids not fully solubilised by the methanol solution, 2 x 3mL of *n*-hexane was added to the extracted potsherds contained in the original culture tubes, mixed well and transferred to culture tube II. The extraction was transferred to a clean, furnaced 3.5mL vial and blown down to dryness. Following this, 2 x 2mL *n*-hexane was added directly to the $H_2SO_4/MeOH$ solution in culture tube II and whirlimixed to extract the remaining residues, then transferred to the 3.5mL vials and blown down until a full vial of *n*-hexane remained. Aliquots of the TLEs were derivatised using 20µl BSTFA, excess BSTFA was removed under nitrogen and the derivatised TLE was dissolved in *n*-hexane prior to GC, GC-MS and GC-C-IRMS. Firstly, the samples underwent high-temperature

gas chromatography using a gas chromatograph (GC) fitted with a high temperature non-polar column (DB1-HT; 100% dimethylpolysiloxane, 15m x 0.32mm i.d., 0.1µm film thickness). The carrier gas was helium and the temperature programme comprised a 50°C isothermal followed by an increase to 350°C at a rate of 10°C min^{-1} followed by a 10 minute isothermal. A procedural blank (no sample) was prepared and analysed alongside every batch of samples. Further compound identification was accomplished using GC-MS.

FAMEs were then introduced by autosampler onto a GC-MS fitted with a non-polar column (100% dimethyl polysiloxane stationary phase; 60m x 0.25mm i.d., 0.1µm film thickness). The instrument was a ThermoFinnigan single quadrupole TraceMS run in EI mode (electron energy 70 eV, scan time of 0.6 s). Samples were run in full scan mode (*m/z* 50–650) and the temperature programme comprised an isothermal hold at 50°C for 2 minutes, ramping to 300°C at 10°C min^{-1}, followed by an isothermal hold at 300°C (15 minutes). The instrument was a ThermoFinnigan single quadrupole TraceMS run in EI mode (electron energy 70 eV, scan time of 0.6 s). Samples were run in full scan mode (*m/z* 50–650) and the temperature programme comprised an isothermal hold at 50°C for 2 minutes, ramping to 300°C at 10°C min^{-1}, followed by an isothermal hold at 300°C (15 minutes). Data acquisition and processing were carried out using the HP Chemstation software (Rev. C.01.07 (27), Agilent Technologies) and Xcalibur software (version 3.0). Peaks were identified on the basis of their mass spectra and GC retention times, by comparison with the NIST mass spectral library (version 2.0).

Carbon isotope analyses by GC-C-IRMS were also carried out using a GC Agilent Technologies 7890A coupled to an Isoprime 100 (EI, 70eV, three Faraday cup collectors *m/z* 44, 45 and 46) via an IsoprimeGC5 combustion interface with a CuO and silver wool reactor maintained at 850°C. Instrument accuracy was determined using an external FAME standard mixture ($C_{11:0}$, $C_{13:0}$, $C_{16:0}$, $C_{21:0}$ and $C_{23:0}$) of known isotopic composition. Samples were run in duplicate and an average taken. The $\delta^{13}C$ values are the ratios $^{13}C/^{12}C$ and expressed relative to the Vienna Pee Dee Belemnite, calibrated against a CO_2 reference gas of known isotopic composition. Instrument error was ±0.3‰. Data processing was carried out using Ion Vantage software (version 1.6.1.0, IsoPrime).

Results

Lipid analysis and interpretations were performed using established protocols described in detail in earlier publications (Dudd and Evershed 1998; Correa-Ascencio and Evershed 2014). Forty-eight potsherds were analysed, together with the burnt-on or surface residue from three of the sherds (WRO05, WRO06 and WRO21). Information on each sampled lipid-yielding sherd, with context information is included in Table 3.8.

The lipid recovery rate for the Collection Management Facility sherds was good at 63%, with 30 of the 48 sherds and all three burnt-on residues yielding interpretable lipid profiles, although it should be noted that whilst the burnt-on residue from vessel WRO21 yielded lipids, the vessel itself, a jar with a simple upright rim, did not. The mean lipid concentration from all lipid-yielding sherds (Table 3.8) was 1.6 mg g^{-1}, with a maximum lipid concentration of 22.9 mg g^{-1} (WRO22, globular jar with simple upright rim). A further seven potsherds contained high concentrations of lipids, at ≥ 2.0 mg g^{-1} (WRO02, 13.4 mg g^{-1}, WRO19, 9.9 mg g^{-1}, WRO28, 3.8 mg g^{-1}, WRO36, 3.9 mg g^{-1}, WRO37, 2.6 mg g^{-1}, WRO41, 3.8 mg g^{-1} and WRO52, 3.8 mg g^{-1}, Table 3.8), demonstrating excellent preservation. The surface or burnt-on residues also yielded high lipid concentrations at 3.1, 2.6 and 1.6 mg g^{-1} for extracts WRO05EXTRES (Fig. 3.7, D, round bodied bowl with simple upright rim), WRO06EXTRES (near straight-sided bowl with square rim) and WRO21EXTRES (straight sided/globular jar with simple upright rim), respectively. The presence of a burnt-on residue is known to represent the final foodstuffs cooked within vessels, whereas absorbed lipid residues are developed over a number of cooking events, providing information on the life use of a pot (Miller *et al.* 2020). The lipid extracts comprised lipid profiles dominated by free fatty acids, palmitic (C$_{16:0}$) and stearic (C$_{18:0}$), typical of a degraded animal fat (Fig. 3.7, A–C; Evershed *et al.* 1997a; Berstan *et al.* 2008).

Extracts from eight sherds (WRO02, WRO06, WRO07, WRO26, WRO27, WRO31, WRO37 and WRO52) include a series of long-chain fatty acids (in low abundance), containing C$_{20:0}$ to C$_{26:0}$ carbon atoms (Fig. 3.7, A and B). It is thought these LCFAs likely originate directly from animal fats, incorporated via routing from the ruminant animal's plant diet (Halmemies-Beauchet-Filleau *et al.* 2013; 2014).

Also present in potsherds WRO01, WRO15, WRO29, WRO30, WRO32, WRO35, and WRO38 (7 vessels) are a series of even-numbered long-chain fatty acids ranging from C$_{20:0}$ to C$_{28:0}$ carbon atoms (Fig. 3.7, D). These exhibit a different profile from those discussed above, maximising at C$_{24:0}$. These LCFAs are strongly indicative either of an origin in leaf or stem epicuticular waxes (Kolattukudy *et al.* 1976; Tulloch 1976; Bianchi 1995; Kunst and Samuels 2003) or, possibly, suberin (Kolattukudy 1980; 1981; Walton 1990; Pollard *et al.* 2008), an aliphatic polyester found in all plants. Although primarily found on the surface of plant leaves, sheaths, stems and fruits, epicuticular waxes are also found associated with other plant organs: seed oils and coats, flowers, bark and husks (Bianchi 1995). Long-chain fatty acids can also be found in plant oils, for example, groundnut oil comprises 4–7% of C$_{20:0}$, C$_{22:0}$ and C$_{24:0}$ saturated and monoene acids (Gunstone 2004). Also present in vessel WRO38 is the C$_{26:0}$ *n*-alkanol (Fig. 3.7, C). Long-chain *n*-alkanols are also often major components of plant leaf waxes, in the range C$_{20:0}$ to C$_{34:0}$, with even number

homologues predominating (Bianchi 1995). The alcohols commonly have three or four major homologues, although in numerous plants a single component dominates, such as C$_{28:0}$ in several *Triticum* species, C$_{32:0}$ in maize and C$_{26:0}$ in barley, rye and oats. The presence of even-numbered long-chain fatty acids and the *n*-alcohol strongly suggests the processing of leafy plants within these seven vessels (discussed further below). However, neither are diagnostic to families of plants, so cannot be used as anything other than a general indicator for plant processing.

GC-C-IRMS analyses were carried out on the sherds and burnt-on residues (*n*=33; Table 3.8) to determine the δ^{13}C values of the major fatty acids, C$_{16:0}$ and C$_{18:0}$, and ascertain the source of the lipids extracted, through the use of the Δ^{13}C proxy. The δ^{13}C values of the C$_{16:0}$ and C$_{18:0}$ fatty acids from the lipid profiles are plotted onto a scatter plot along with the reference animal fat ellipses (Fig. 3.8, A, blue circles for vessels and red circles for burnt-on residues). It has been established that when an extract from a vessel plots directly within an ellipse, for example, ruminant dairy, ruminant adipose or non-ruminant adipose, then it can be attributed to that particular source. If it plots just outside the ellipse, then it can be described as predominantly of that particular origin. However, it should be noted that extracts commonly plot between reference animal fat ellipses and along the theoretical mixing curves, suggesting either the mixing of animal fats contemporaneously or during the lifetime of use of the vessel (Mukherjee 2004; Mukherjee *et al.* 2005).

Fourteen of the lipid residues from the Collection Management Facility vessels and two burnt-on residues (WRO01, WRO02, WRO05, WRO06, WRO08, WRO15, WRO16, WRO26, WRO27, WRO29, WRO30, WRO31, WRO32, WRO42, WRO05EXTRES and WRO06EXTRES) plot within, or just on the border of, the dairy reference ellipse (Fig. 3.8, A), suggesting these vessels were solely used to process dairy products. Five vessels plot within or just on the border of the ruminant carcass products ellipse (WRO20, WRO39, WRO41, WRO44 and WRO51, Fig. 3.8, A), with four vessels plotting just outside the ellipse (WRO07, WRO12, WRO19 and WRO28), suggesting they were specialised for processing ruminant products (from cattle, sheep or goat). Two remaining vessels (WRO37 and WRO38) plot mostly between the ruminant dairy and carcass ellipses, although vessels WRO22, WRO35, WRO36, WRO40, WRO52 and the burnt-on residue WRO21EXTRES plot between these ellipses and the non-ruminant ellipse, albeit much closer either to the ruminant dairy or carcass ellipses, suggesting the possible addition of minor amounts of pig fats (Fig. 3.8, A), either contemporaneously or during the lifetime of use of the vessel.

Ruminant dairy fats are differentiated from ruminant adipose fats when they display Δ^{13}C values of ≥ -3.1 ‰, known as the universal proxy (Dunne *et al.* 2012; Salque 2012). Significantly, lipid residues from 17 of the 30 (57%) lipid-yielding vessels (WRO01, WRO02, WRO05,

Table 3.8 Sample number, period, context, vessel type, description, lipid concentration ($\mu g\ g^{-1}$), $\delta^{13}C$ and $\Delta^{13}C$ values, and attributions of pottery lipid residues

Sample name	Period	Context	Vessel type	Fabric codes	Description	Lipid concentration ($\mu g\ g^{-1}$)	$\delta^{13}C_{16:0}$ (‰)	$\delta^{13}C_{18:0}$ (‰)	$\Delta^{13}C$ (‰)	Attribution
WRO01	Late Prehistoric	1428	Bowl	SH3 – Coarse shell <6mm	Hemispherical bowl with square upright rim	561	-28.5	-32.8	-4.3	Ruminant dairy
WRO02	Late Prehistoric	1756	Bowl	Q2 – Medium quartz sand <1mm	'La Tène' style bowl	13377	-28.3	-34.4	-6.1	Ruminant dairy
WRO05	Late Prehistoric	2135	Bowl	QV – Medium quartz sand and organic voids	Round bodied bowl with simple upright rim	799	-27.3	-33.0	-5.7	Ruminant dairy
WRO05RES	Late Prehistoric					3117	-27.8	-33.3	-5.5	Ruminant dairy
WRO06	Late Prehistoric	2358	Bowl	Q1 – Fine quartz sand <0.5mm	Near straight-sided bowl with square rim	497	-28.9	-33.6	-4.7	Ruminant dairy
WRO06RES	Late Prehistoric					2585	-29.0	-33.6	-4.6	Ruminant dairy
WRO07	Late Prehistoric	8079	Bowl	QC3 – Coarse quartz sand ≤3mm and sparse to common coarse round calcareous ≤5mm	Slack shouldered jar with simple upright rim	1714	-28.2	-31.1	-2.9	Ruminant carcass
WRO08	Late Prehistoric	8119	Bowl	QC2 – Medium quartz sand <1mm and calcareous inclusions <5mm	Round bowl with square upright rim	79	-28.9	-33.1	-4.2	Ruminant dairy
WRO12	Late Prehistoric	1410	Jar	QV – Medium quartz sand and organic voids	Slack shouldered jar with simple upright rim	194	-29.2	-29.6	-0.5	Ruminant/non-ruminant carcass
WRO15	Late Prehistoric	1740	Jar	M – Fine silty micaceous fabric. No visible inclusions.	Globular jar w/simple upright rim (Near straight-sided vessel)	142	-28.3	-33.4	-5.1	Ruminant dairy
WRO16	Late Prehistoric	1810	Jar	QV – Medium quartz sand and organic voids	Saucepan pot with simple upright rim (Complete profile)	1261	-28.5	-33.6	-5.1	Ruminant dairy
WRO19	Late Prehistoric	1848	Jar	Fl2 – Medium flint <2mm	Globular jar w/simple upright rim	9919	-28.5	-31.5	-3.0	Ruminant carcass
WRO20	Late Prehistoric	1866	Jar	SH3 – Coarse shell <6mm	Straight-sided/globular jar with simple upright rim	1149	-30.3	-32.9	-2.7	Ruminant carcass
WRO21RES	Late Prehistoric					1575	-26.8	-31.7	-5.0	Ruminant dairy
WRO22	Late Prehistoric	1941	Jar	Fl2 – Medium flint <2mm	Globular jar with simple upright rim	22938	-27.6	-31.3	-3.7	Ruminant dairy
WRO26	Late Prehistoric	2544	Jar	SH3 – Coarse shell <6mm	Slack shouldered jar with simple upright rim	591	-28.2	-33.1	-4.9	Ruminant dairy
WRO27	Late Prehistoric	2672	Jar	SH3 – Coarse shell <6mm	Straight-sided jar with simple upright rim (poss saucepan pot)	512	-28.3	-33.3	-5.0	Ruminant dairy

Table 3.8 *continued*

Sample name	Period	Context	Vessel type	Fabric codes	Description	Lipid concentration (µg g⁻¹)	δ¹³C₁₆:₀ (‰)	δ¹³C₁₈:₀ (‰)	Δ¹³C (‰)	Attribution
WRO28	Late Prehistoric	3064	Jar	Q2 – Medium quartz sand <1mm	Jar with everted rim	3811	-29.1	-29.5	-0.4	Ruminant/non-ruminant carcass
WRO29	Late Prehistoric	3146	Jar	Q1 – Fine quartz sand <0.5mm	Round bodied jar with slight beaded rim	130	-28.6	-33.8	-5.2	Ruminant dairy
WRO30	Late Prehistoric	6040	Jar	QV – Medium quartz sand and organic voids	Globular jar with simple upright rim	908	-28.5	-33.3	-4.8	Ruminant dairy
WRO31	Late Prehistoric	8078	Jar	Q2 – Medium quartz sand <1mm	Round bodied jar with simple upright rim	804	-28.1	-32.9	-4.8	Ruminant dairy
WRO32	Late Prehistoric	8078	Jar	QV – Medium quartz sand and organic voids	Small slack shouldered jar w/simple upright rim (Complete profile)	277	-27.9	-33.1	-5.2	Ruminant dairy
WRO35	LIA-ERB	1656	Bowl	GR2 – Grog-tempered fabric	Girth groove bowl with everted rim	66	-28.0	-30.2	-2.2	Ruminant carcass
WRO36	LIA-ERB	1130	Jar	GR2 – Grog-tempered fabric	Beaded rim jar	3851	-28.0	-29.4	-1.4	Ruminant carcass
WRO37	LIA-ERB	1555	Jar	GR2 – Grog-tempered fabric	Beaded rim jar	2586	-28.6	-32.1	-3.5	Ruminant dairy
WRO38	LIA-ERB	1656	Jar	SAV GT – Savernake grog-tempered ware	Beaded rim jar	894	-28.2	-31.8	-3.5	Ruminant dairy
WRO39	LIA-ERB	1656	Jar	SAV GT – Savernake grog-tempered ware/GR2 – Grog-tempered fabric ?	Beaded rim jar	146	-29.5	-31.4	-1.9	Ruminant carcass
WRO40	LIA-ERB	2244	Jar	SBW – Sandy black fired ware	Beaded rim jar	1172	-28.0	-30.6	-2.6	Ruminant carcass
WRO41	LIA-ERB	2460	Jar	GR2 – Grog-tempered fabric	Beaded rim jar	3791	-29.5	-31.4	-1.9	Ruminant carcass
WRO42	LIA-ERB	2460	Jar	UNS FLGR – Unsourced flint and grog-tempered ware	Beaded rim jar	37	-28.3	-32.6	-4.3	Ruminant dairy
WRO44	LIA-ERB	2757	Jar	SAV GT – Savernake grog-tempered ware	Necked jar with out-curved rim	1891	-28.7	-31.5	-2.8	Ruminant carcass
WRO51	LIA-ERB	1656	Platter	QGR – Sandy grog-tempered fabric	Platter with high internal rim moulding	585	-28.4	-30.7	-2.3	Ruminant carcass
WRO52	LIA-ERB	3286	Platter	QGR – Sandy grog-tempered fabric	Platter with high internal rim moulding	3789	-27.6	-29.3	-1.7	Ruminant carcass

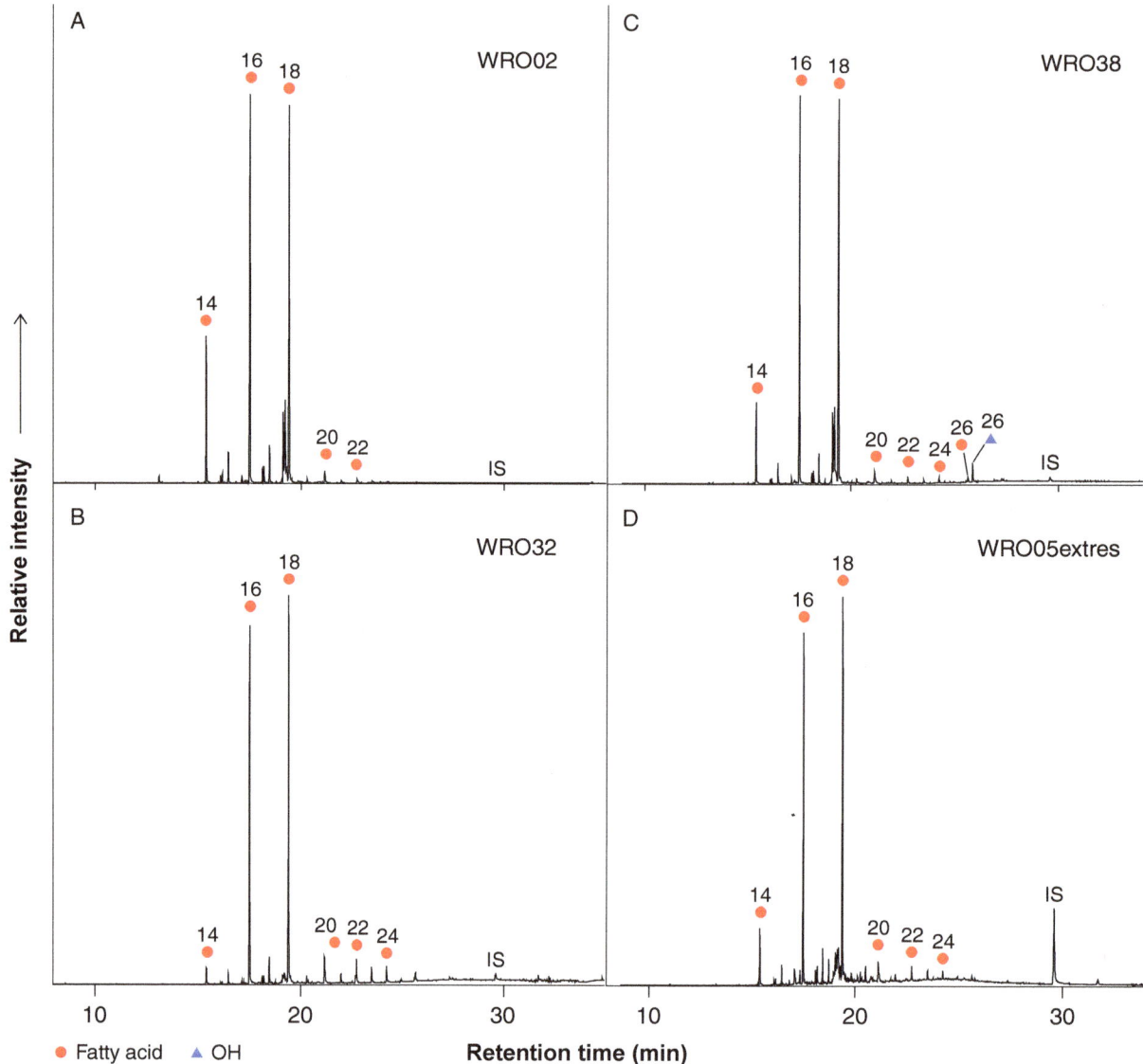

Figure 3.7 Partial gas chromatograms of acid-extracted FAMEs from Wroughton pottery extracts of A. WRO02, 'La Tène' style bowl, B. WRO32, small slack-shouldered jar with simple upright rim; C. WRO38, beaded rim jar and D. WRO05EXTRES, burnt-on residue from inside a round-bodied bowl with simple upright rim; red circles, n-alkanoic acids (fatty acids, FA); blue triangles, n-alkanols; IS, internal standard, C34:0 n-tetratriacontane. Numbers denote carbon chain-length

WRO06, WRO08, WRO15, WRO16, WRO22, WRO26, WRO27, WRO29, WRO30, WRO31, WRO32, WRO37, WRO38 and WRO42) plot within the ruminant dairy region (Fig. 3.8, B) with Δ^{13}C values of -4.3, -6.1, -5.7, -4.7, -4.2, -5.1, -5.1, -3.7, -4.9, -5.0, -5.2,-4.8, -4.8, -5.2, -3.5, -3.5 and -4.3 ‰ respectively, confirming that these vessels were used to process mainly secondary products, such as milk, butter and cheese. However, it should be noted that two of the vessels (WRO37 and WRO38) plot at the extent of the boundary (with Δ^{13}C values of -3.5 and -3.5 ‰ respectively), suggesting some mixing with ruminant carcass fats during the lifetime use of the vessel. The burnt-on residues (WRO05EXTRES, WRO06EXTRES and WRO21EXTRES) all plot within the ruminant dairy region with Δ^{13}C values of -5.5, -4.6 and -5.0 ‰ respectively

(Fig. 3.8, B, red circles). The Δ^{13}C values of the corresponding vessels are in good agreement, at -5.7 ‰ (WRO05) and -4.7 ‰ (WRO06), confirming these vessels were used to process dairy products throughout their life history (Miller *et al.* 2020).

Vessels WRO07, WRO19, WRO20, WRO35, WRO36, WRO39, WRO40, WRO41, WRO44, WRO51 and WRO52, with Δ^{13}C values of -2.9, -3.0, -2.7, -2.2, -1.4, -1.9, -2.6, -1.9, -2.8, -2.3 and -1.7 ‰ respectively (n=11, 37%), plot within the ruminant adipose region (Fig. 3.8, B) confirming these vessels were used to process ruminant (cattle, sheep and goat) carcass products. Two further vessels plot at the extent of the range (WRO12 and WRO28) with Δ^{13}C values of -0.5 and -0.4 ‰ respectively, suggesting these vessels were used to process ruminant

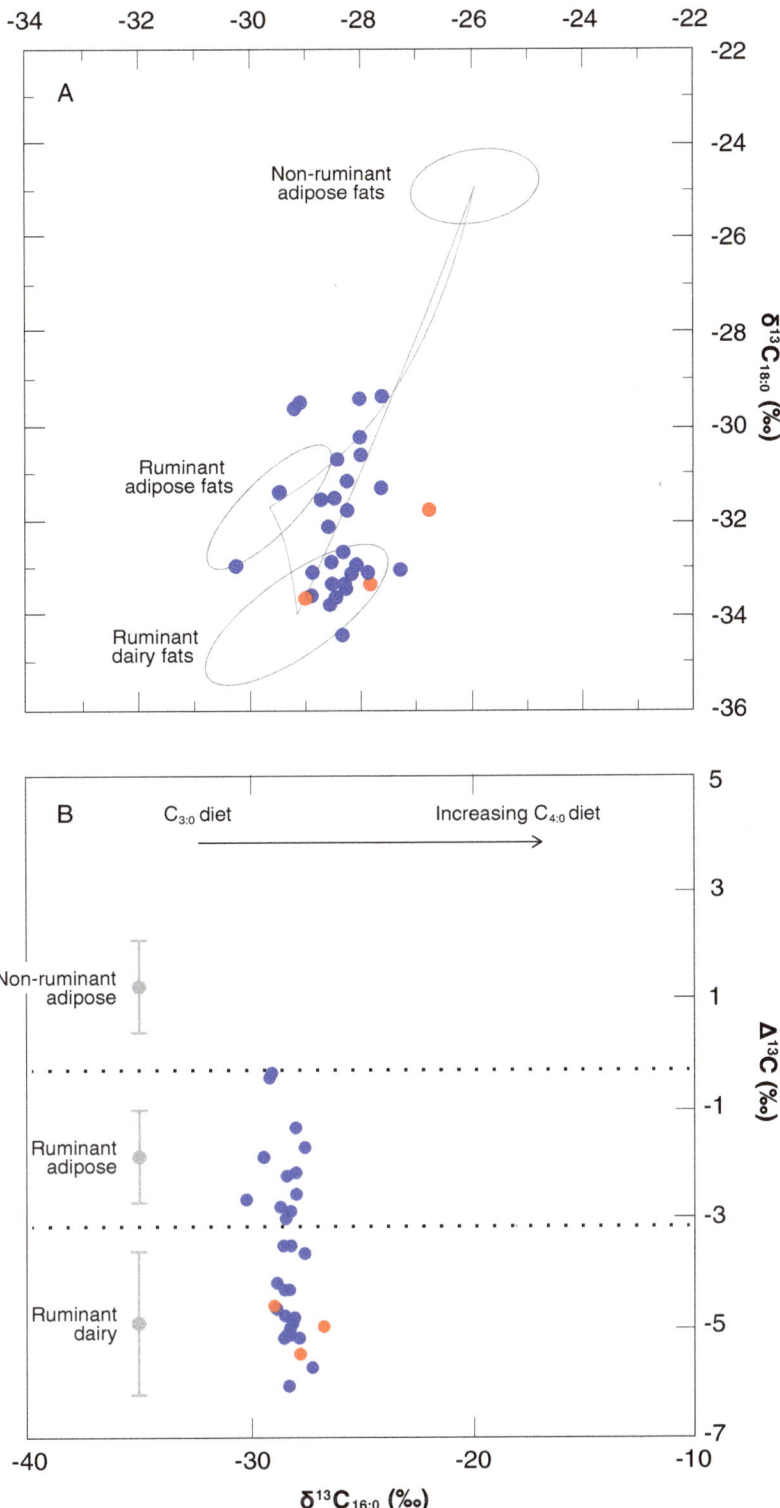

Figure 3.8 Graphs showing: A δ¹³C values for the $C_{16:0}$ and $C_{18:0}$ fatty acids for archaeological fats extracted from the Wroughton ceramics. Blue circles represent the vessels and red circles denote the burnt-on or surface residues. The three fields correspond to the P = 0.684 confidence ellipses for animals raised on a strict $C_{3:0}$ diet in Britain (Copley et al. 2003). Each data point represents an individual vessel. Figure B shows the Δ¹³C ($δ13C_{18:0} − δ13C_{16:0}$) values from the same potsherds and burnt-on residues. The ranges shown here represent the mean ± 1 s.d. of the Δ¹³C values for a global database comprising modern reference animal fats from Africa (Dunne et al. 2012), UK (animals raised on a pure $C_{3:0}$ diet) (Dudd and Evershed, 1998), Kazakhstan (Outram et al. 2009), Switzerland (Spangenberg et al. 2006) and the Near East (Gregg et al. 2009), published elsewhere

carcass products with the addition of some non-ruminant (pig) products.

Discussion

Lipid recovery from the site was good at 63% with 30 of the 48 sherds yielding interpretable lipid profiles, and with many vessels containing extremely high concentrations of lipids, suggesting they were subjected to sustained use in the processing of high lipid-yielding commodities. Lipid recovery was comparable to that of an Iron Age site at East Midlands Gateway (77%), Leicestershire, and higher than that at a Romano-British site at Highfields Farm, Derbyshire (53%; Dunne and Evershed unpublished data).

Meat and milk
Of the 19 lipid-yielding late prehistoric (Iron Age) vessels (Table 3.8), 14 (74%) were used to process ruminant dairy products, three (16%) to process ruminant carcass products, and two (10%) to process mixtures of ruminant and non-ruminant products. Previous research has demonstrated the importance of dairy products at the Iron Age sites of Maiden Castle, Danebury Hillfort, Yarnton Cresswell Field and Stanwick where up to 56% of the extracts (237 vessels, equivalent to 22% of all of the sherds), contained dairy products (Copley *et al.* 2005). Similarly, recent analysis of pottery from the East Midlands Gateway site showed that 71% of Iron Age vessels were used to process dairy products (Dunne and Evershed, unpublished data). These findings suggest a strong preference for dairy products by native Britons, as observed by Caesar (Book 5.14) and clearly indicate the importance of dairy products in Iron Age subsistence, as part of a mixed milk/meat economy, suggesting a heavy reliance on ruminant animals.

In contrast, of the 11 Late Iron Age to Early Roman vessels analysed, 8 (73%) were used to process ruminant carcass products, suggesting a reduction in the importance of processing dairy products in vessels in this later period. Although a small dataset, these data are similar to those obtained from analysis of Romano-British pottery from the East Midlands Gateway site where four of the Romano-British vessels were used for dairy processing (25%), similarly suggesting dairying was of greater importance at this site in the Iron Age, reducing in the Roman period (Dunne and Evershed, unpublished data).

The Late Iron Age to Early Roman lipid results from the Collection Management Facility and the Romano-British vessels from East Midlands Gateway suggest that the processing of animal carcass products was more important than dairying, somewhat in contrast to the analysis of cooking pots from the site of Stanwick, where dairying seems to have been an important component of the Romano-British economy (at 40% of vessels compared to 25% at East Midlands Gateway), at a level consistent with the preceding Iron Age population, although ruminant carcass product processing dominates at Faverdale (Copley *et al.* 2005;

Cramp *et al.* 2011; 2012). However, it should be noted that dairy products may have been processed in different types of vessels, such as wooden bowls or animal skins.

As noted, there is evidence for minor porcine product processing in vessels at the Collection Management Facility, in good agreement with the faunal assemblage which is dominated by sheep and lesser amounts of cattle, and a low incidence of pig bones. There is some mixing of ruminant and non-ruminant fats in two vessels, which correlates well with the results from East Midlands Gateway where only one vessel was used to process pig products. This is analogous to the low levels of absorbed pig fats found in pottery at the Iron Age sites of Maiden Castle, Danebury hillfort, Yarnton Cresswell Field and Stanwick (Copley *et al.* 2005). It also compares well with the low abundances of pig bones found at Iron Age sites in general (Cunliffe 1991; Hambleton 1999).

The absence of pork fats in Late Iron Age to Early Roman vessels is interesting as consumption of pork and bacon is known to be a distinctly Roman trait, both from literary sources and the bone assemblages of central Italy (King 1999), although it should be noted that this is a small dataset. There (central Italy), pig bones dominate over cattle, sheep and goat remains from the late Republic and into the early/middle Empire. This appears in part due to the agricultural conditions of the period, but mainly due to cultural preference, and it is thought that pork, particularly young pork and suckling pig, was considered to be a desirable and high-status dietary element (King 1999). However, in Roman Britain, pig bones are found at military and urban sites, but are less common in rural assemblages. For example, at Vindolanda, pork products (pork fat, young pig and ham) are mentioned in the accounts relating to the praetorium and the household of the commanding officer (Bowman and Thomas 1994) and pig neonate bones have been found in towns such as Lincoln, Dorchester and Silchester (Woodward *et al.* 1993; Dobney *et al.* 1995; Fulford *et al.* 1997), suggesting they were bred in towns.

Plant processing
The presence of even-numbered long-chain fatty acids and even-numbered *n*-alcohols, likely originating from plant epicuticular waxes, strongly suggests the processing of leafy plants within at least seven of the vessels analysed (23% of lipid-yielding vessels). Interestingly, plant-derived lipids were also detected in sherds originating from the Iron Age sites of Maiden Hill, Danebury Hillfort, Yarnton Cresswell Field and Stanwick and were often associated with vessels that had been used in the processing of dairy fats (Copley *et al.* 2005). At the Collection Management Facility, six of the seven vessels containing plant lipids were used to process dairy products, suggesting that plants may have been added to milk for consumption, for example, as a type of gruel or possibly in the heating of milk and herbs (or vegetables) to make more 'solid' dairy products, such as cheese, either to coagulate the curd or add to taste.

Vessel use and specialisation

Bowls

Ten bowls were analysed, nine Iron Age and one Late Iron Age to Early Roman, with all except three Iron Age bowls (WRO03 and WRO04, both round bodied bowls with simple upright rims and WRO09, a round bowl with upright rim) yielding lipids (Table 3.8). Notably, all Iron Age bowls were used to process dairy products, with the La Tène bowl containing a particularly high concentration of lipids (at 13.4mg g^{-1}), suggesting it saw significant use. The burnt-on residues, which represent the last use of a vessel (Miller *et al.* 2020), from two bowls (WRO05 and WRO06) also contained dairy products, suggesting that these bowls were dedicated to dairy processing throughout their life use. The Late Iron Age to Early Roman bowl, a girth groove bowl with everted rim (WRO35), was used to process or serve ruminant carcass products. Lipid concentration of this vessel was low at 65.6µg g^{-1}, suggesting the bowl may have been used for serving or did not see sustained use in processing ruminant carcass products.

Platters

Three platters with high internal rim moulding were analysed. Two were used to process ruminant carcass products, probably for serving or consuming meat from cattle, sheep or goat. The rim diameters of these were 260mm and 220mm for WRO51 and WRO52 respectively. The remaining platter did not yield a lipid profile. Notably, one of the platters contained a high concentration of lipids, WRO52 at 3.8mg g^{-1}, suggesting sustained use. As these platters are flat in shape, it must be assumed that they were used for serving joints of meat as opposed to more liquid dishes, such as stews.

Jars

There are 47 vessels that could be identified as jars in the Collection Management Facility assemblage, including 15 slack-shouldered jars, 15 straight-sided jars (of which at least three are saucepan pots), 11 round bodied jars and six globular jars. These outnumber bowls by a ratio of approximately 4:1. Thirty-six jars of various types, including saucepan pots, beaded rim jars, slack shouldered jars and globular jars (see Table 3.8 for full list), were analysed, with 22 (61%) yielding interpretable lipid profiles. The majority (*n*=13, 59%) were used to process ruminant dairy products, often displaying high lipid concentrations, for example, WRO22, a globular jar with simple upright rim, at 22.9 mg g^{-1}. Seven jars were used to process ruminant carcass products (WRO19, WRO20, WRO36, WRO39, WRO40, WRO41 and WRO44), often yielding high or very high lipid concentrations (9.9, 1.1, 3.9, 0.1, 1.2, 3.8, and 1.9 mg g^{-1}, respectively), suggesting that jars saw sustained use in the cooking of ruminant carcass products, probably in the form of stews. Two jars were used to process ruminant carcass products with the addition of some non-ruminant (pig) carcass products, one, a jar with everted rim (WRO28) comprises a high lipid concentration at 3.8 mg g^{-1}.

Notably, of the late prehistoric (Iron Age) jars (*n*=14), 10 (71%) were used to process ruminant dairy products, whereas of the Late Iron Age to Early Roman jars (*n*=8), five (62%) were used to process ruminant carcass products and three (38%) ruminant dairy products. These results from the Collection Management Facility Iron Age jars are in agreement with residue analysis of Iron Age pottery used to process dairy products, for example, at Mid to Late Iron Age Danebury hillfort (64% of extracts), Mid to Late Iron Age Maiden Castle (71% of extracts), Middle Iron Age pottery from Yarnton Cresswell Field (39% of extracts) and Early Iron Age pottery from Stanwick (46% of extracts) (Copley *et al.* 2005). This is also comparable to analysis of Late Iron Age potsherds from the Northern Isles, Scotland, which showed that 64% of lipid yielding sherds contained dairy products (Cramp *et al.* 2014) and Iron Age pottery recently excavated from Barn Elms, London (Dunne and Evershed, unpublished data), at 65%. Furthermore, recent analysis of pottery from the East Midlands Gateway (EMG) site, Leicestershire, showed that 71% of Iron Age vessels were used to process dairy products (Dunne and Evershed, unpublished data).

Interestingly, in a previous study on Iron Age vessels (Copley *et al.* 2005), vessel specialisation was clearly indicated in a comparison including 'saucepan pots', jars and bowls. The study revealed that milk products were processed in 'saucepan pots' at sites where these pots predominated, but at sites where jars dominated, then these instead were preferentially associated with milk products (Copley *et al.* 2005). At Collection Management Facility, as noted, saucepan pots were not common with only three having been found. Of these, only one (WRO16) yielded a lipid profile, with the Δ^{13}C value of -5.1 ‰ confirming it was used to process dairy products. There does not seem to be any relationship between vessel fabric, form and function.

Conclusions

Organic residue analysis was carried out on 48 late prehistoric (Iron Age) and Late Iron Age to Early Roman potsherds (and three burnt-on residues). Lipid recovery was good at 63% with 30 vessels (and three burnt-on residues) yielding interpretable lipid profiles, and with many vessels containing extremely high concentrations of lipids, suggesting they were subjected to sustained use in the processing of high lipid-yielding commodities. The results, determined from GC, GC-MS and GC-C-IRMS analyses, demonstrate that, overall, 57% of vessels were used to process ruminant dairy products, 37% to process ruminant carcass products, with minor evidence in two vessels for the exploitation of pig products, mixing ruminant and non-ruminant products (6%). Evidence for plant processing was

Table 3.9 Fired clay summary by form

Form	Loomweight		Spindle whorl		Ceramic plates		Ceramic disc		Daub		Amorphous		Total	
Fabric	Ct	Wt (g)	Ct	Wt (g)	Ct	Wt (g)	Ct	Wt (g)	Ct	Wt (g)	Ct	Wt (g)	**Ct**	**Wt (g)**
calc					1	47							**1**	**48**
cp					17	290					13	122	**30**	**412**
ccp					92	1796					4	17	**96**	**1813**
cp/fl					11	339							**11**	**339**
cp/org											1	12	**1**	**12**
cp/qz					3	103							**3**	**103**
ch									36	3644	14	125	**50**	**3769**
sandy											1	3	**1**	**3**
csandc					1	64							**1**	**64**
csand					3	221					1	11	**4**	**232**
fsand					1	122							**1**	**122**
fl					1	12							**1**	**12**
li/org					2	82							**2**	**82**
lic					1	33							**1**	**33**
org	1	348									4	16	**5**	**364**
silty			1	41	5	218	9	433	1	39	50	495	**66**	**1226**
ves									14	115	61	407	**75**	**522**
Total	**1**	**348**	**1**	**41**	**138**	**3327**	**9**	**433**	**51**	**3798**	**149**	**1208**	**349**	**9155**

found in just over one fifth of vessels (23%), predominantly in vessels used to process dairy products. Overall, the results provide valuable information on farming practices and animal management in central England, during late prehistory and are in good agreement with a previous study (Copley *et al.* 2005) which suggested the importance of dairying to Iron Age populations.

Some vessel specialisation is indicated, with Iron Age bowls being used to process dairy products and, conversely, the platters being used to process ruminant carcass products, suggesting these platters were used for serving or consuming meat, likely in the form of joints from cattle, sheep or goat. However, it should be noted that only three platters were available for analysis and a larger sample should be attempted, when possible, to confirm this. The jars do not seem to have been specialised in use, although the majority were used to process dairy products.

Table 3.10 Fired clay fabric summary

Fabric code	Fabric description	Ct	Wt (g)
calc	Calcareous inclusions	1	47
cp	Clay pellet inclusions	30	412
ccp	Coarse clay pellet inclusions	96	1813
cp/fl	Clay pellet and flint inclusions	11	339
cp/org	Clay pellet and organic inclusions	1	12
cp/qz	Clay pellet and quartz inclusions	3	103
ch	Chalky	50	3769
sandy	Sandy fabric	1	3
csandc	Coarse sandy fabric with sparse calcareous inclusions	1	64
csand	Coarse sandy fabric	4	232
fsand	Fine sandy fabric	1	122
fl	Flint tempered	1	12
li/org	Limestone and organic tempered	2	82
lic	Coarse limestone tempered	1	33
org	Organic tempered	5	364
silty	Silty fabric	66	1226
ves	Vesicular fabric	75	522
Total		**349**	**9155**

Fired clay
Claire Collier-Jones and E. R. McSloy

Introduction and methodology

A total of 349 fragments of fired/burnt clay, weighing 9155g, was recovered from the hand-excavation of 95 deposits. The fired clay was recorded directly onto an Ms Access database, which will form part of the site archive. The material was scanned by context and quantified according to fragment count and weight and according to category and broad fabric division. A range of fabric types were recorded (Tables 3.9 and 3.10).

The assemblage condition is poor, the majority of the fragments are soft-fired and susceptible to breakage and many pieces lack features indicative of original form or function. A total of 149 fragments (1208g) are fully amorphous, not preserving original surfaces or other features suggestive of use. Around half of the assemblage (50.98% by weight, Table 3.11) was recorded from Period 4 (Middle Iron Age) deposits, with much of the remainder from Period 5 (Late Iron Age–Early Roman) and Period 6 (Mid–Late Roman) deposits.

Some of the objects recovered provide evidence for craft activities (weaving and spinning) during the Iron Age. The remaining material is of lesser significance; the 'daub' is evidence for building materials which, although commonly assumed to have been used, is only rarely preserved. Quantities of 'daub' (17 fragments, 1068g) associated with drying oven 2827/2828 are likely to have come from the superstructure of this feature. The disc and plates are representative of poorly understood categories. Their presence in this location is noteworthy, although the fragmentary condition and occurrence in 'secondary' deposits, means that question of functionality cannot be addressed.

Table 3.11 Fired clay summary by period (quantities as weight in grams)

Fabric/Period>	2	3	4	5	6	7	8	0	Total
calc				47					47
cp	10		74	254	26		42	6	412
ccp	66		4	1740				3	1813
cp/fl				339					339
cp/org				12					12
cp/qz				103					103
ch			2464		1229			76	3769
sandy				26				3	29
csandc			64						64
csand			206						206
fsand			122						122
fl				12					12
li/org				82					82
lic				33					33
org			363	1					364
silty	3		985	157	39	2		40	1226
ves		96	385	32				9	522
Total	**79**	**96**	**4667**	**2838**	**1294**	**2**	**42**	**137**	**9155**

Assemblage range

Objects

Few portable fired clay objects were recorded. The triangular weight (Fig. 3.9, 1) is of common Iron Age type usually identified as for use with vertical, warp-weighted looms, though the typical arrangement of three corner perforations is yet to be satisfactorily explained. The significantly larger numbers of singularly perforated chalk weights, which are similarly identified as loomweights. are described elsewhere (Shaffrey, below). Weights in both materials, seemingly in use contemporaneously, is attested at Danebury, Hampshire and other sites of central southern England (Poole 1984, 401–6; Brown 1984, 419–22). There are no indications that use of individually heavier chalk weights reflects differing technology and the preference for these types at Wroughton probably reflects local availability and/or a greature durability.

The cylindrical form of spindlewhorl no. 2 compares to examples from among the large numbers of such objects from Danebury, Hampshire (Poole 1984, 402, fig. 7.46)

and Meare, Somerset (Coles 1987, 158, fig. 3.66, W1 and W4). Among both groups, discoid, biconical or globular forms are, however, more typical.

1 Loomweight. Fragment. Triangular, tri-perforated. Thickness 60mm. Period 4 pit 2043 (fill 2041). Ra. 1020. Fig. 3.9, 1
2 Spindlewhorl. Cylindrical. Diameter 32mm, height 31mm, internal diameter 10mm; weight 41g. Period 4 pit 3083 (fill 3086). Ra. 1096. Fig 3.9, 2

Ceramic plates and discs

A total of 147 fragments (3760g), recovered from 36 deposits, were attributable to this category, although for some smaller fragments, identification was uncertain. None of the ceramic plates were substantially complete, the few featured pieces with straight sides (Fig. 3.10, nos 3 and 4), suggest a square or rectangular form. Where measurable the plates range from 25–35mm in thickness, typically thickening towards the sides. The large majority occurred in a distinctively coarse fabric containing large argillaceous

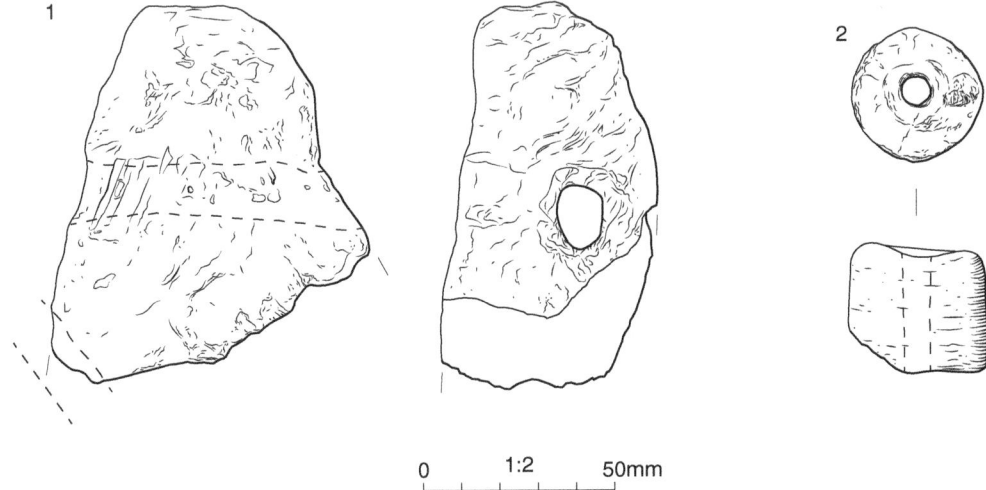

Figure 3.9 Fired clay objects: 1. triangular loomweight fragment; 2. spindlewhorl

Figure 3.10 Fired clay ceramic plate fragments: 3–4

(clay pellet or soft rock) inclusions. One surface featured the impressions of organic material (chopped straw or similar), possibly added to limit adhesion when drying prior to firing. Where datable material (pottery) was present in association it is clear that most material derives from deposits belonging to the transitional Late Iron Age/Roman or earlier Roman (*c.* mid 1st–2nd centuries) periods. The function of this class of material remains uncertain, although the sooting evident to some pieces suggests subjection to heat, and a form of oven furniture would seem most likely. Comparable material has been described from Romano-British sites in the wider area, including Watkins Farm, Northmoor, Oxon, where this material occurred in a coarse calcareous fabric (Allen 1990b, 53).

The single identified ceramic disc was from an Iron Age storage pit and appears to be approximately two-thirds complete. The function of such discs, which have been identified from a number of Iron Age sites in the wider area (Lambrick and Allen 2004, 384–5), is unclear although possible uses include lids or oven 'furniture'.

3   Plate fragment. Thickness 28mm. Period 5.2 ditch 2703 (fill 2705)
4   Plate fragment. Thickness 32mm. Period 5.3 ditch 3287 (fill 3285)
5   Ceramic disc. Fragment. Fine, silty fabric, one side heavily burnt. Diameter *c.* 150mm, thickness 23mm. Period 5 pit 6061 (fill 6058). Not illustrated

Burnt 'daub'

Some 50 fragments (3768g) were identified in this category. The majority is distinctively pale in colour with some material with large inclusions of chalk, suggesting locally derived clays or a chalk 'slurry' were used. Most material is well-fragmented and preserves only a smooth exterior surface and no other features. Wattle-impressions were, however, visible in some instances, most clearly among material from Period 4 pit 1426 (fill 1632) and Period 6 pit 2532, which was part of an oven (Fig. 3.11). Such material probably represents 'domestic' structural material, its preservation probably as the result of accidental 'firing.' Further material was recovered from the Roman-dated drying oven (Period 6 feature 2827/2828) and seems likely to have derived from the superstructure of this feature.

Ceramic building material
E. R. McSloy

Small quantities of ceramic brick and tile (14 fragments, 833g) were recorded from 12 deposits (Table 3.12). Where suggested by aspects of form, Roman dating is indicated. One small, unfeatured fragment from Period 8 ditch 2677 (fill 2678) probably dates to the post-medieval period. It is in a friable, red-firing fabric which is unlike that of the Roman material.

Only two fragments among the Roman group retain features indicative of form/class. Both are *tegulae* (flanged roof tile; recorded from sub-phase Period 5.2 enclosure 3, ditch 32 (fill 7011) and Period 5.3 enclosure 1, ditch 8 (fill 2727). That from deposit 7011 exhibits an arcing finger 'signature' to its upper surface, a feature commonly noted on Roman forms. Material identified only as (Roman) tile fragments are flat and measure 15–18mm in thickness. They probably represent further *tegula* fragments. Fragments described as miscellaneous in Table 3.12 lack measurable dimensions or other diagnostic features.

The few tile fragments are insufficient to indicate the presence of a Romanised structure in the immediate vicinity. As is common for many rural Roman sites, ceramic building material probably saw a variety of 'secondary' uses in hearths or similar and as hardcore.

Table 3.12 Ceramic building material

Context	Type	No.	Wt (g)	Comments
1336	tile	1	9	14mm thick
1578	tile	1	89	probably *tegula*
1656	misc	1	10	
2260	misc	1	35	fragment – ridged surface?
2527	tile	1	35	tile fragment 18mm thick
2554	misc	1	56	abraded; 18mm thick; large Fe inclusions
2678	misc	1	3	chip – red orange, friable – probably post-medieval
2687	misc	1	3	flake
2727	*tegula*	1	197	marks to flange
2727	tile	2	66	12mm thick
2823	misc	1	5	flake
6051	misc	1	6	small chip
7011	*tegula*	1	319	(probably *tegula*); flat fragment with finger signature

Metal finds

E. R. McSloy

Introduction

A total of 854 items of metal (3299g) were recorded from 54 separate deposits and with two unstratified objects. The majority are iron (845 items), including 697 hobnails and 79 carpentry nails. The assemblage includes 59 items (all iron) retrieved from bulk soil sample residues with the remainder recovered by hand. This report presents a selective catalogue, individually describing objects of individual interest and/or contributing to the understanding of the site and the activities undertaken, and a summary of the assemblage overall. Full description for all metal items is included in a Microsoft Access database within the project archive, onto which the assemblage was recorded directly.

Iron Age objects

A very small number of metal items were recorded from Iron Age (Period 4) deposits. Those of copper alloy were limited to small waste lump (Ra. 1027) and a droplet (Ra. 1029), both recorded from Period 4 pit 2258 (fill 2260). A fired clay block tuyère also from this feature is further evidence for its association with metalworking (see Dungworth, below).

Three very fragmentary bladed iron implements, all from Period 4 pits, are not individually described or illustrated. Those from pits 1837 (fill 1838) and 6030 (fill 6028) are from knives with centrally positioned tangs but retain little of the blade. That from pit 2138 (fill 2135, Ra. 1022) comprises the medial portion from a narrow-bladed implement.

Knife no. 1 appears to be of Iron Age type, although it was unstratified (Fig. 3.12, 1). The form of this fragmentary object (no. 2) is comparable to knives of Class 3 identified form Danebury and characterised by the form of the handle which features a tang with rivets to secure separate

0   1:2   50mm

Figure 3.11 Burnt daub fragments

handle plates (Sellwood 1984b, 349). In common with the Danebury examples, the edges of the tang on no. 2 form slightly raised 'flanges'.

1   Iron knife. Portion of blade and short, wide tang. There is one rivet *in situ* at the base of the blade and central to the tang and a second rivet hole seemingly off the centreline. The blade was probably triangular,

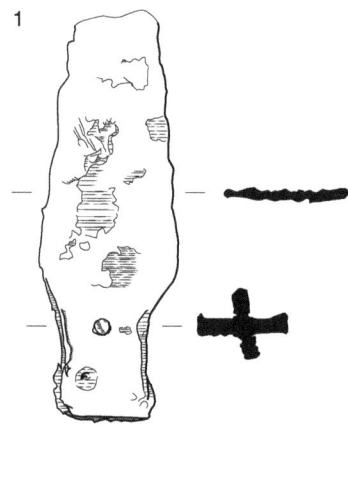

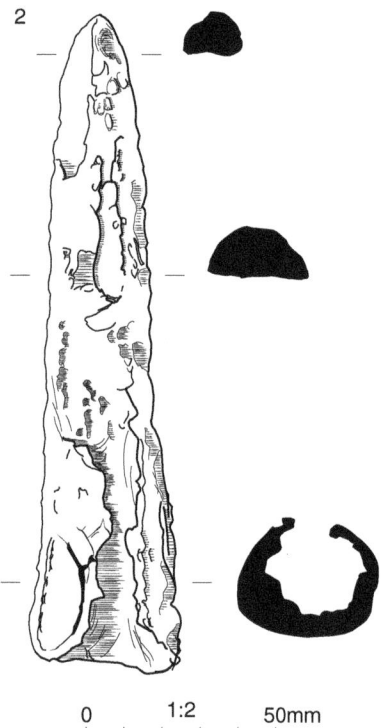

Figure 3.12 Iron objects: 1. knife fragment and 2. ploughshare tip

with straight or slightly curving back and edge. Surviving length 106mm; max. blade width 34.3mm. Unstratified. Ra. 1086

Ploughshare tip no. 2 was recorded from Period 4 pit 1757 in association with pottery dating to the Middle Iron Age (Fig. 3.12, 2). It compares with Iron Age examples from Danebury (Sellwood 1984b, 354–357; fig. 7.14, no. 2.70) and Hod Hill (Manning 1985, 43). As Manning describes, objects such as no. 2 formed the protective tip to a share bar of wood, with the socket fitted to a 'foreshare'. According to Rees's (1979) typology, object no. 2 belongs to group 1a, which describes shorter, socketed forms and is the most common of the approximately 40 ploughshare tips known from Britain.

The object appears to be complete and unworn, its serviceable condition a likely indication of intentional deposition. It is not known if no. 2 was deposited together with its wooden share, although no traces of mineralised wood (or iron coulter) were present. Its recovery as an isolated object in a storage pit would accord better with a 'special' deposit, rather than hoarding with the intention of recovery.

2   Iron ploughshare tip. The shaft is plano-convex in section, tapering to a rounded end. The terminal is flattened and formed to a sub-square socket. Length 173mm; max. width 26.3mm (shaft), 37.7mm (socket); max. thickness (shaft) 14.7mm. Period 4 pit 1757 (fill 1755). Ra. 1010

Roman objects

Iron

Roman Iron objects form the majority of the metalwork assemblage. Included are 697 iron hobnails and most of the 79 carpentry nails. Other items of iron from Roman deposits comprise mostly fragmentary items where function is unclear.

Some 62 nails (including fragments) were from Roman (Period 5 and 6) deposits. Where identifiable, they conform to common flat-headed Roman forms, corresponding to Manning's Type 1b (Manning 1985, 134), utilised for a variety of construction and other tasks. Some 25 were associated with (Period 6) inhumation burials, including 22 from grave 2389 (see Chapter 2). Nails numbering 1–2 fragments from graves 2295 and 2320 may be stray finds or might possibly represent coffins or other wooden structures. Such a structure was more certainly present in grave 2389 and the nails from this feature are of similar flat-headed form, and, where measurable (nine), are 50–62mm in length. Nails from Roman-phased non-funerary deposits number 37 examples. Most notable are the 26 examples from Period 6 oven 2827. Four nails from this oven are notably long, measuring 80–103mm.

The large majority of the hobnails and some 52 shoe cleats were derived from nine inhumation burials located in the Period 6 (Mid to Late Roman) cemetery. The hobnails/ cleats from the graves all occurred in the area of the feet in groups of 20–133 nails, and, although in a disordered state, indicate that footwear was worn. The cleats, which are of similar form to those described by Manning (1985, 131), were noted in groups of 8–19, occurring from (Period 6) graves 2332, 2338, 2344 and 2352, in all instances together with hobnails. The cleats almost certainly shared a similar function to the hobnails, providing strength and traction to the leather sole. Cleats appear to be a later Roman innovation (ibid., 131), dating which is supported here. The occurrence of the hobnails/cleats in graves accords with the commonly observed Roman practice of equipping the deceased with footwear, evidenced across the 2nd to 4th centuries and seemingly more common in rural cemeteries

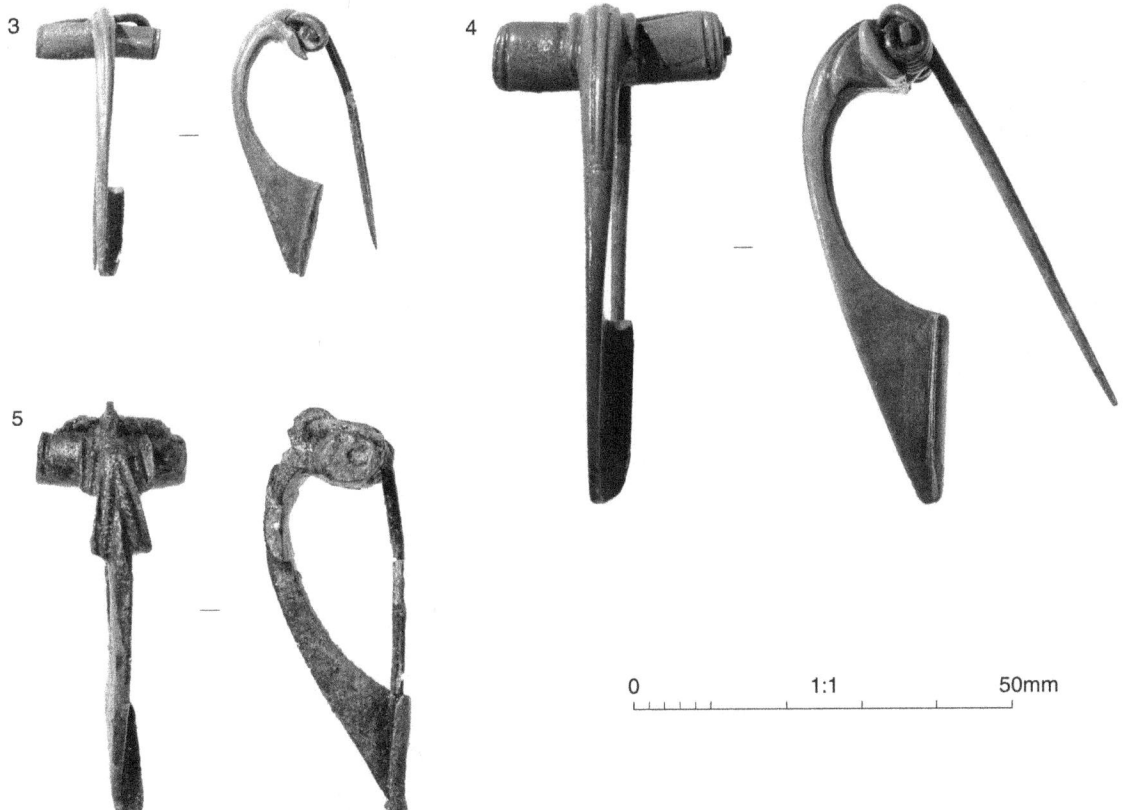

Figure 3.13 Copper alloy objects: 3–5 brooches

(Philpott 1991). Single hobnails from Period 5 occupation layer 2449 (the upper fill of oven 2827, Fig. 2.36) and pit 2491 (Fig. 2.33) probably represent casual losses.

Copper alloy

Five of the eight recorded copper alloy objects can be dated to this period morphologically or on the basis of context phasing/associated material. Fragmentary items from sub-phase Period 5.2 droveway A, ditch 3 (fill 2869) and Period 5.3 enclosure 1, ditch 8 (fill 2964) are of indeterminate function and not further described. The three brooches (nos 3–5; Fig. 3.13) belong to Roman types, all probably of the period AD 50–100/150. All the brooches are complete and survive in excellent condition, the preservation of surfaces probably due to an effect of the calcareous burial environment.

Although differing in size and the form and complexity of their decorative details, brooches nos 3 and 4 are both part of Mackreth's CD Ha3b grouping, which is known to have western British associations (Mackreth 2011, 58). Brooches of this type are of two-piece (Colchester Derivative) construction, with the bilateral spring secured in the Harlow manner, utilising an axis bar passing through the coils and a plate behind the brooch head. The Ha3b grouping is defined by stylistic traits, principally the presence of simple mouldings to the ends of the wings and a central ridge extending from the head. No. 4 is the more elaborate, with additional mouldings at the junction of the

head and wings, which is a feature of other western British brooch classes and with stylistic traits Mackreth saw as having 'West Country' origins (ibid.). Mackreth (ibid.) lists 42 examples of the type, with the biggest concentrations in Gloucestershire (23), Wiltshire (5) and Hampshire (5).

Brooch no. 5 is of a differing Colchester Derivative type, its spring held in the Polden Hill manner by an axis bar secured centrally and between the pierced plates at the ends of the wings. Stylistically, no. 5 belongs to Mackreth's type PH 5.c, distinguished by mouldings below the head in the form of an inverted V. The form of no. 5 is notably close to an example from Cirencester (Mackreth 2011, 53, plate 50, no. 1839) and the two may well have come from the same workshop. The type PH 5 grouping is again considered to denote Western British origins (ibid., 75) and for the PH 5.c, distribution is heavily biased to Gloucestershire with 12 of the 17 examples having come from this county, principally from the area of Cirencester and Lechlade.

3   Copper alloy brooch. Complete. Small brooch of Mackreth's CD Ha3b type. Narrow ridge central to bow, single grooves to wing ends and cross-cuts at foot. Length 34mm; width (wings), 15.9mm. Period 5.4 enclosure 1, ditch 22 terminal (fill 2817). Ra. 1081

4   Copper alloy brooch. Complete. Mackreth's CD Ha3b type. Narrow ridge central to bow, terminating in cross-cuts; double grooves to wing ends and cross-cuts at foot; mouldings either side of bow at join with wings. Length

63mm; width (wings), 27.2mm. Period 5.3 enclosure 1, ditch 8 (fill 1889). Ra.1011

5   Copper alloy brooch. Complete. Mackreth's CD PH 5.c type. Double inverted vee moulding to upper bow with cabled ridge details and notched 'pseudo hook' at head; double grooves to wing ends and up-turned foot. Length 55mm; width (wings), 19.5mm. Period 5.3 enclosure 1, ditch 8 (fill 2727). Ra.1078

Post-Roman objects

Two unstratified objects recorded as metal detector finds evidence low-intensity activity post-dating the Roman period. A tin or lead alloy button (Ra. 1080; not illustrated) is an example of a type known from as early as the 13th century, in use into the earlier post-medieval period to *c.* 1600 (Egan and Pritchard 1991, 272–280). The main part forms a hollow sphere, approximately 10mm in diameter and enclosing an iron loop which is largely missing.

An unstratified copper alloy buckle (Ra. 1079; not illustrated) probably dates to the earlier post-medieval period. It is of double-looped form, with trefoil type knops to each loop, features typical of buckles of the mid 16th to mid 17th centuries (Whitehead 1994, 64).

Shale
E. R. McSloy

Bracelets of shale are widely known from the Iron Age and Roman periods. The source for most such objects was the shale beds of Kimmeridge, Dorset and there is evidence that both finished objects and object roughouts were traded (Laws 1991, 368). The slight irregularity of no. 1 is an indication it was fashioned by hand, rather than on a lathe, and this would accord with its likely Middle Iron Age dating (Fig. 3.14). Similar examples occur from Danebury, Hampshire where they came from deposits spanning the Middle Iron Age (Cunliffe 1984, 396; Laws 1991, 368).

1   Fragment (approx. 20% surviving) from bracelet/armlet of plain, annular form. Oval in section, surfaces

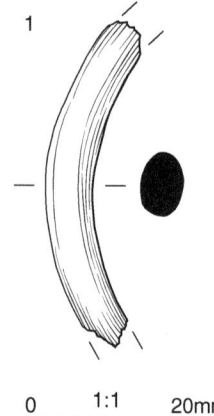

Figure 3.14 Shale bracelet fragment

well-smoothed, but slightly irregular. Internal diam. approx. 60mm; width 4mm; thickness 6mm in. Period 4 (Middle Iron Age) pit 1048 (fill 1049). Ra. 1002

Glass
E. R. McSloy

A single piece of Roman glass was recovered. No. 1 is identified as cast window glass of earlier Roman type. This suggested by its apparent manufacture in a wooden mould (indicated by it having one matt and slightly opaque surface). A further possibility that it comes from a mould-blown prismatic bottle is thought less likely due to its thickness (2.9mm). 'Cast' window glass, typically of 'natural' blue/green coloured glass, typically dates to the 1st to 2nd/earlier 3rd centuries AD.

1   Window glass. Blue/green-coloured glass. Flat fragment; all edges broken and abraded. Period 5.3 enclosure 1, ditch 8 (fill 2948). Thickness 2.9mm; weight 12g. Not illustrated

Worked bone
Claire Collier-Jones

Eleven items of worked bone were recovered from nine Period 4 (Middle Iron Age) pit fills. The preservation and condition of the bone items is good, although five items are broken. The worked bone catalogue is organised according to Crummy's functional categories (Crummy 1983, 5–6). The assemblage is small but includes objects which contribute to the understanding of Iron Age deposits and which provide evidence of textile working and dress habits.

Objects of personal adornment or dress

Object nos 1 and 2 have been manufactured from a horse metatarsal and metacarpal and are interpreted as clothes pins, secured by their shouldered shaft and a cord through the circular eye. They were discovered in Period 4 pit 8068 which also contained SK 8071, a young adult female. Similar pin-like objects with bone joint heads are common from Iron Age sites, including examples from Potterne, Wiltshire (Seager Smith 2000, 225), Meare, Somerset (Coles 1987, 55–6) and Danebury, Hampshire (Sellwood 1984a, 387–9). These, however, lack the eye and shouldered shaft of objects 1–2 and are identified as awls.

1   Pin. Probable 2nd horse metatarsal. Shaft is flat in section and has a gently sloping shoulder. Circular eye close to the head which is formed from the bone joint. Surface shows polish from use. Length 94mm, width 16mm, depth 10mm. Period 4 pit 8068 (fill 8070) Ra. 1204. (Fig. 3.15, 1)

2   Pin. Probable 2nd horse metacarpal. Shaft is round in section and has a steeply angled shoulder. Circular eye

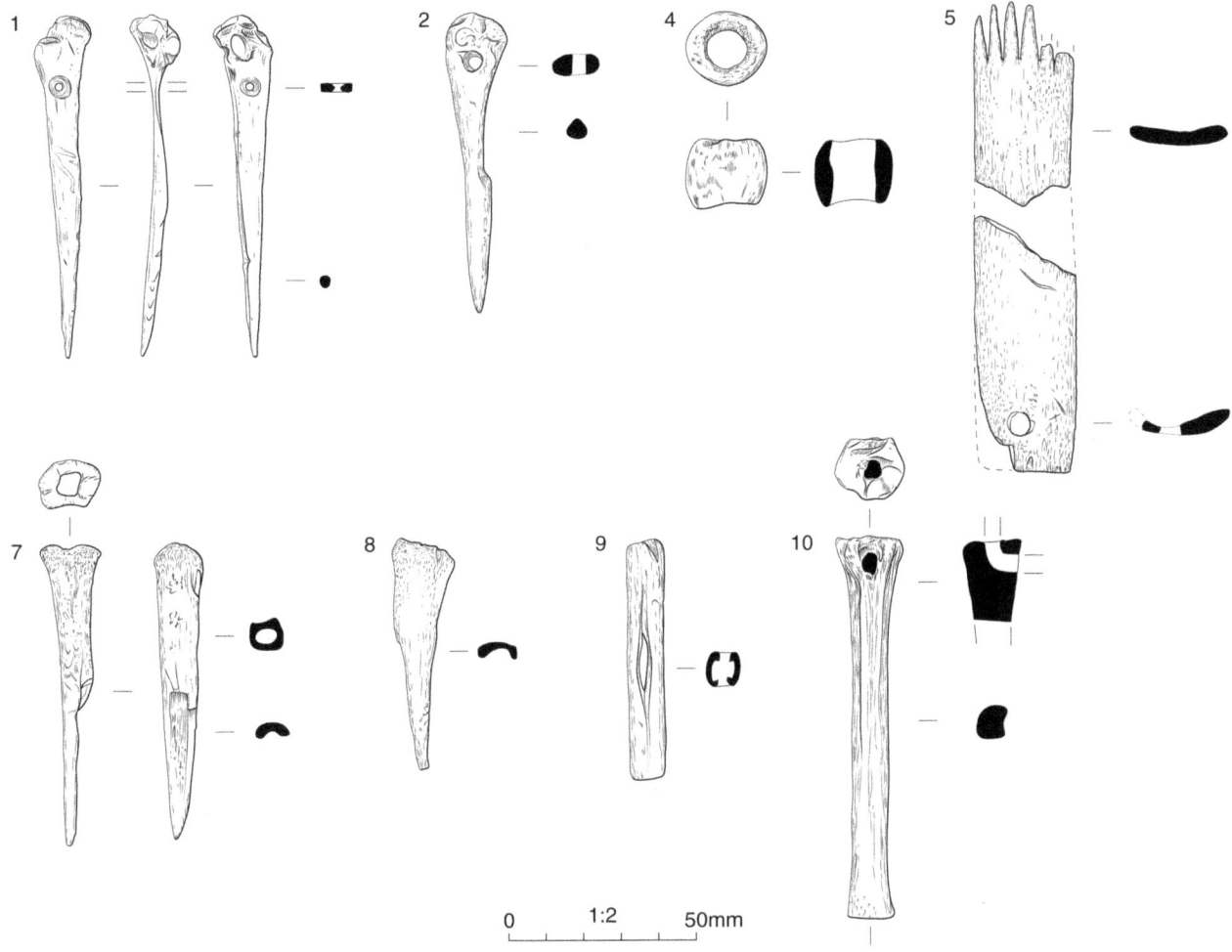

Figure 3.15 Worked bone objects: 1–10

close to the head which is formed form the bone joint. Surface shows polish from use. Length 80mm, width 16mm, depth 12mm. Period 4 pit 8068 (fill 8070) Ra. 1205. (Fig. 3.15, 2)

3   Bone point. Shaft is broken into two pieces and tapers to a point. Head is missing. Point is either broken or worn flat. Function unknown; possible pin, needle or textile awl. Surface shows polish. Length 100mm, width 11mm, depth 7mm. Period 4 pit 1426 (fill 1631) Ra. 1017. Not illustrated

4   Bead or toggle. Manufactured from a hollow section of bone. Circular in section, rounded ends. Surface is polished. Length 22mm, width 20mm, depth 16mm. Period 4 pit 2578 (fill 2580) Ra. 1106. (Fig. 3.15, 4)

Objects used in the manufacture or working of textiles

Iron Age weaving combs are relatively common finds from sites across Britain and a variety of plain and decorated styles have been recorded which as yet appear to show no strong regional or chronological patterning (Sellwood 1984a, 371–8). They are usually interpreted as weaving implements, although alternative uses such as combing sheep's wool when shearing, or as human hair combs, have also been suggested (Coles 1987, 105–17). Large groups include those from Danebury, Hampshire (Cunliffe and Poole 1991b, 354–7) and the Glastonbury and Meare 'lake villages', Somerset (Bulleid and Gray 1911; Coles 1987, 105–17). Local examples are known from Yarnton, Oxfordshire (Allen and Wallis 2011, 437–49), Bishops' Cleeve, Gloucestershire (Lovell *et al.* 2007, 99–102) and Potterne, Wiltshire (Seager Smith 2000, 228–9). Two fragments (a butt end and head) were recorded from two fills (1801 and 1802) of Period 4 pit 1802. These fragments do not join but are likely from the same comb. Also recorded were two bone points, likely utilised as awls and comparable to a similar group of objects recovered from Danebury, Hampshire (Sellwood 1984a, 387, nos. 3.139–3.176).

5   Weaving Comb. Head fragment, possibly from the same comb as object no. 6. Curved in section, widens towards the teeth. Four of the six teeth survive, those in the centre of the comb are longer in length. The teeth taper towards the apices and have rounded tips.

Undecorated. Manufactured from a horse long bone fragment. Width 27mm, depth 5mm. Period 4 pit 1802 (fill 1801). Ra. 1012 (Fig. 3.15, 5)

6   Weaving Comb. Butt fragment, possibly from the same comb as object no. 5. Plain, smoothed butt end, curved in section with a drilled perforation towards the end. Undecorated. Manufactured from a horse long bone fragment. Width 27mm, depth 5mm, perforation diameter 6mm. Period 4 pit 1802 (fill 1800)

7   Awl. Manufactured from a sheep/goat metatarsal. Head utilises the proximal end of the bone. Shaft removed at an acute angle and smoothed to a point. Surface shows polish from use. Length 79mm. Period 4 pit 2298 (fill 2301) (Fig. 3.15, 7)

8   Awl. Manufactured from a sheep/goat tibia. Bone splinter has been shaped to a long point. Tip is missing. Surviving length 63mm. Period 4 pit 3068 (fill 3062) (Fig. 3.15, 8)

Tools

Similar tools to object nos 9 and 10, manufactured from sheep long bones, were found at Danebury, Hampshire (Sellwood 1984a, 389, nos 3.177–3.198). Possible functions suggested for objects of this type include bobbins and spools. Another possible function for object no. 9 is a toggle.

9   Tool. Both ends of the bone removed and smoothed. Ends feature worn grooves. A central elongated perforation has been worked in the natural groove on either side of the bone. Shaft features multiple cut marks. Length 65mm. Period 4 pit 1585 (fill 1590) (Fig. 3.15, 9)

10   Tool. Manufactured from a sheep/goat metatarsal. Shaft surface is polished. Head utilises the proximal end and the distal end has been removed and cut flat. Two perforations drilled at right angles in the articular surface and proximal end of the shaft. Length 103mm. Period 4 pit 2592 (fill 2594) (Fig. 3.15, 10)

Other

11   Canid Canine Tooth. Polished surface suggesting that it has been well handled. Length 42mm. Period 4 pit 2258 (fill 2260). Not illustrated

Worked stone
Ruth Shaffrey

Introduction

The assemblage of worked stone comprises 36 fragments from a probable 31 objects: nine items broadly classified as querns, 21 weights, one whetstone and one other item. There are also 31 pieces of burnt stone weighing 4.1kg, recovered from nine contexts. The burnt stones are mostly heat cracked or shattered fragments of sandstone and quartzite, suggesting heating and rapid cooling, perhaps through cooking.

Weights

The largest category of finds is that of perforated stones (mainly chalk) used as weights, of which there are 18 large examples and three smaller ones. All were found in features assigned to Period 4 (Middle Iron Age) except for two unstratified weights. The 18 large examples were recovered from eight contexts and nine weights were from a single pit, 8118, which includes seven complete or almost complete weights and fragments from two others.

Overall, 11 weights are complete and a further three are substantively complete, so that the vast majority were fully functional at the time of deposition (Table 3.13).

The weights demonstrate a varied range of forms all of which correspond to Shaffrey's (2017a) classification, including oblong (Type 4), teardrop and/or oval (Type 1), shouldered (Type 2), triangular (Type 3) and irregular (Type 9) (Figs 3.16–3.17, 1–7). This range of forms need not affect function and may simply reflect who made the weights.

Table 3.13 Summary of larger weights

Context	Period	Ra.	Percent	Form	L (mm)	W (mm)	Th (mm)	Wt (g)	Lithology
Unstrat		0	100	Oblong	215	90	68	1274	Greensand
1631	4	1015	100	Teardrop	170	92	92	1243	Chalk
1874	4	1019	80	Teardrop	195	142	40	1030	Chalk
1874	4	1018		Fragment				57	Chalk
2054	4	1021	100	Oval	165	120	65	1410	Chalk
2910	4	1084		Fragment			47	293	Chalk
3066	4	1089	90	Oblong		130	52	1417	Chalk
3314		11107	100	Oval	165	113	35	723	Chalk
8070	4	1208	100	Irregular	250	120	58	1705	Limestone
8122	4	1221	50	Shouldered	145		85	920	Chalk
8122	4	1216	20	Teardrop?				270	Chalk
8122	4	1213	90	Teardrop	206	150	60	1629	Chalk
8122	4	1215	100	Teardrop	200	120	60	1844	Chalk
8122	4	1222	100	Shouldered	215	140	55	1728	Chalk
8122	4	1217	100	Teardrop	170	110	84	1034	Chalk
8122	4	1223	100	Oblong	192	95	75	1537	Chalk
8122	4	1211	100	Teardrop	200	115	70	1925	Chalk
8122	4		100	Triangular	165	147	85	1951	Chalk

What is more significant is the method of perforation and the weight of the objects because perforation changes the way the weights could have been suspended and the weight affects function. Ten of these weights are perforated through the thinnest dimension (the thickness) and six are perforated through the thickest part (the width): perforation through the width is typical of weights from Wiltshire (ibid., 237). The perforations are variable in diameter and neatness so that all could have been suspended with the use of cord (though none demonstrate any wear consistent with this) and at least two definitely could not have been suspended from a pole. The ten complete weights range in heaviness from 1034g to 1951g suggesting that matching weights was not of concern.

The group of nine weights from pit 8118 is of particular interest. They range in weight from 1034g to 1951g with projected weights for the fragments based on percentage surviving. Six weigh between 1728 and 1951g and might be considered a close group in terms of weight, although they include shouldered weights, teardrop shaped weights and a triangular weight. Groups of similar weights are a relatively common feature of Middle Iron Age pits in the region. The most well-known are four sets from pits at Danebury, the most comparable of which is a group of seven complete weights from one pit ranging from 1986.4g to 2210g (Brown 1984, 422).

Two much smaller disc-shaped weights were found in storage pit 9009 (Ras 1202 and 1203) and in the deliberate backfill of 8068, where it was probably associated with SK 8071 (Ras 1208 and 1225, Fig. 3.18, 8 and 9). The discs weigh 100g and 103g, which is at the very lowest range of weight suitable for use as loomweights and at the very upper end of what could be used for spinning. The diameter of the perforation of Ra. 1202 is very wide at 13mm which suggests that they were not spindlewhorls.

Catalogue of illustrated loomweights, weights and other worked stone objects
(Figs 3.16–3.18)

1　Large weight. Chalk. Irregular but roughly oblong-shaped weight with perforation of 7–15mm diameter through the thickness. Roughly straight with gouge marks visible on the lower face. Heavily burnt and blackened across the lower portion of two faces and grey on the other two. Measures 192 x 62–95mm x 50–75mm thick. Weighs 1537g. Ra. 1223. Period 4 (Iron Age) storage pit 8118 (first fill 8122)

2　Large weight. Chalk. Teardrop-shaped weight. Perforated through the thickness at the narrow end. Very heavily burnt and blackened across one face. Measures 170 x 80–92mm wide x 32–92mm thick. Weighs 1243g. Ra. 1015. Period 4 (Iron Age) pit 1426 (fill 1631)

3　Large weight. Chalk. Almost complete flat teardrop-shaped weight. Perforated at the narrow end through the width with narrow hole of 9mm diameter. Burnt and blackened on one face. Measures 206 x 150 x 50–60mm thick. Weighs 1629g. Ra. 1213. Period 4 (Iron Age) pit 8118 (first fill 8122)

4　Large weight. Chalk. Approximately oval weight perforated through width with irregular hole of 12–17mm diameter (definitely not hung on a pole). Some manufacturing marks visible across one face. Measures 165mm x 75–120mm x 35–65mm thick. Weighs 1410g. Ra. 1021. Period 4 (Iron Age) pit 2280 (fill 2054)

5　Large weight. Chalk. Crudely shouldered shaped flattish weight perforated at the narrow end through the width with wide hole of 12mm diameter. Burnt and blackened on one face. Measures 215mm long x 45mm wide on shoulders to 140mm wide across the body and 50–55mm thick. Weighs 1728g. Ra. 1222. Period 4 (Iron Age) pit 8118 (first fill 8122)

6　Large weight. Chalk. Triangular loomweight, heavily burnt and blackened across one face and the end. Perforated through the width with wide hole measuring 23mm at the edge and about 12mm internally. Some gouge marks visible from cutting of hole. Generally smooth all over. Measures 165 x 147 x 85mm thick. Weighs 1951g. Period 4 (Iron Age) pit 8118 (first fill 8122)

7　Large weight. Limestone. Large irregular weight perforated through the thickness towards one end. Gouge marks visible on both sides. Hole is 12mm diameter at narrowest point. Measures 250 x 120 x 58mm thick. Weighs 1705g. Ra. 1208. Period 4 (Iron Age) pit 8068 (fill 8070)

8　Spindlewhorl/loomweight. Chalk. Neat perforated flat disc, smoothed on one side with central perforation of 13mm diameter. Moderately burnt and blackened all over. Generally smooth finish. Measures 62mm diameter x 19mm thick. Weighs 100g. Ra. 1202. Period 4 (Iron Age) pit 9009 (fill 9010)

9　Spindlewhorl/loomweight. Chalk. Neat perforated flat disc, smoothed on one side and roughly flat but not neatly finished on the other with central perforation of 7mm at the central point to 11mm on the surfaces. Slightly burnt on one face. Measures 78mm diameter x 18mm thick. Weighs 103g. Ra. 1225. Period 4 (Iron Age) pit 8068 (fill 8070)

Not illustrated

Spindlewhorl/loomweight. Chalk. Three fragments of probable spindlewhorls or loomweights. The pieces do not adjoin and are not diagnostic, but possibly are from the same object. Burnt and blackened on the broken edges. Weighs 59g. Ra. 1203. Period 4 (Iron Age) pit 9009 (fill 9010)

Discussion of the weights

Weights of these forms and heaviness are very common finds on Middle Iron Age sites in the chalk downland areas of southern Britain but are entirely absent from other regions (Shaffrey 2017a, fig. 11.2). They have traditionally been

Figure 3.16 Worked stone weights: 1–4

0   1:5   250mm

Figure 3.17 Worked stone weights: 5–7

classified as loomweights, regardless of what they weigh, but most loomweights from known looms (that is from *in situ* deposits) weigh around 500g and almost all weigh under 1.5kg (ibid., 232). It is unlikely that heavy weights exceeding 1.5kg would have been used on a warp-weighted loom, which is the type of loom generally assumed to have been in use at this time (ibid.). One other possibility is that they were used on a 'Skolt-Lappish' loom where the warp threads were attached to a rod or pole that was weighed down with a weight at each end and possibly in the middle (Hoffman 1974, 87). Weights with wear suggesting suspension from a pole would increase the likelihood of this

being an accurate interpretation, but weights could have been hung indirectly from a pole via cords.

However, it is also worth noting that there is only limited other evidence for weaving from the site, or for general textile working. There is one fired clay triangular weight (McSloy, above), which some archaeologists interpret as loomweights, and there are the two smaller disc-shaped chalk weights described above as well as a single bone comb that may have been associated with weaving (Collier-Jones, above). A single fired clay spindlewhorl is suggestive of spinning, an associated task (Collier-Jones and McSloy, above, Fig. 3.9, 2) but other than the large weights, the

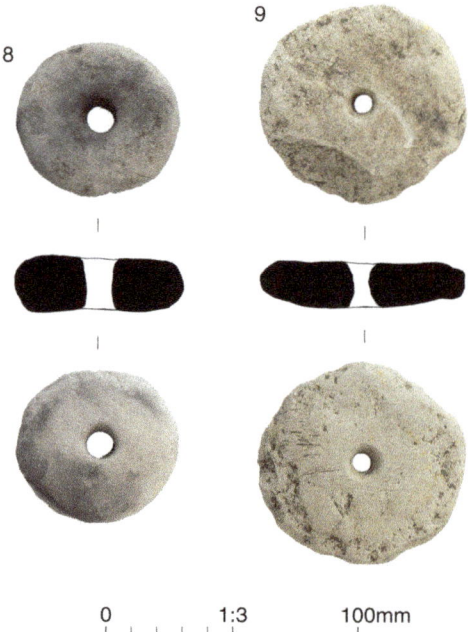

Figure 3.18 Worked stone spindlewhorls/loomweights: 8–9

evidence for weaving is limited. The weights could indicate the use of a 'Skolt-Lappish' type loom on the site (but without supporting evidence), however, an alternative use is as thatch weights for buildings.

Querns and other objects

The querns include three fragments of probable quern that are too small to be assigned to a type. Two adjoining fragments of micaceous sandstone have a pecked surface typical of querns, but also have a very smooth face suggesting use as a hone or grinding stone (fill 2940 in Iron Age pit 2938). A third fragment, this time of sarsen, has a pecked surface typical of querns (Iron Age pit 1057). Sarsen was not much used for rotary querns, and so it is more likely this was a saddle quern. A further fragment of saddle quern was also recovered from unphased layer 1047 (Ra. 1008). This fragment is of a coarse feldspathic gritstone containing frequent rock fragments. It is not typical of Millstone Grit or any stone known to have been used for saddle querns in the region and its provenance is uncertain.

In addition to the fragments, there are two complete items: one saddle quern (Ra. 1014 Fig. 3.19, 10) and one grain rubber (Ra. 1200, Fig. 3.19, 11), both from Period 4 Iron Age features. Saddle quern Ra. 1014 was part of a mixed deposit of domestic debris that had been placed in pit 1426 above a male skeleton (SK 1845). It is made of possible Old Red Sandstone, but from a boulder of it, rather than quarried. The sarsen grain rubber is also substantively complete and had been included in the final fill of pit 8068 (a capping over SK 8071). Skeleton SK 8071 has been radiocarbon dated to the Middle Iron Age. These are discussed further below.

Three rotary querns include a lower rotary quern of Lodsworth stone with a partially perforated socket that is typical in form for the Late Iron Age to Early Roman ditch in which it was found (Ra. 1088; Period 5.4 enclosure 1 ditch 22, fill 2957). Two rotary querns of Old Red Sandstone were found in backfill 2528 of Period 6 (Mid to Late Roman) oven 2827. One of these is an upper stone (Ra. 1085) and one is a lower stone (Ra. 1076). They could have formed a pair but, if so, the outermost 20mm of the upper stone would have overhung the lower stone. Both stones are charred because of direct exposure to fire.

The only other stone items of interest are a smoothed stone found in Period 5.3 ditch 8 (fill 3285) and an almost spherical lump of mineral, probably marcasite, which is unworked but was found in Period 4 pit 3068 (fill 3064). The smoothed stone has probably been used as a hone or other sort of processing tool, whilst the marcasite is probably best classed as a manuport (an unworked and unused stone that has been moved by people).

Catalogue of illustrated querns and other objects
(Fig. 3.19)

10 Saddle quern (Fig. 3.9, 10). Sandstone, probably Old Red Sandstone. Boulder with shaped grinding surface dished in both directions and worked with pecking. The grinding surface fills the whole upper surface of the quern. The base is curved/convex and the sides are roughly vertical but neither have been modified. Measures 275 x 160mm max width x 95mm max thickness. Weighs 5689g. Ra. 1014. Period 4 (Iron Age) pit 1426 (fill 1631)

11 Grain rubber (Fig. 3.9, 11). Sarsen. Rounded oblong rubber with rounded back roughly shaped but carefully chipped along the edges to give them a slightly rounded shape. The grinding surface is concave lengthwise but is slightly convex widthways. The grinding surface has been finished with neat pecking but has wear striations across the width of the stone. Measures 260mm long x 120–140mm wide x 65mm max thickness. Weighs 2956g. Ra. 1200. Period 4 (Iron Age) pit 8068 (fill 8069)

Querns and other objects not illustrated

Saddle quern. Gritstone. In hand specimen this is seen to be a feldspathic gritstone. A thin section reveals mostly polycrystalline quartz with many rock fragments. There is frequent feldspar, mostly perthite. The rock has been subject to compaction and pressure solution and as a result has little porosity or cement, although thin haematite rims are present around many of the grains. Fragment of probable saddle quern with one flat/very slightly concave pecked surface and one shaped/rounded back. Burnt and blackened on one face. Measures 60mm thick. Weighs 1108g. Ra. 1008. Unphased layer 1047

Figure 3.19 Worked stone: 10. saddle quern and 11. grain rubber

Possible quern. Fine-medium grained well-sorted grey-brown heavily micaceous sandstone. Two adjoining fragments of flat stone with one smoothed flat surface and one flat pecked surface with some wear. Pecked surface looks like that found on a quern but there are no original edges, and the very smooth face indicates reuse as a hone or other processing tool. Measures 100 x 68–82 x 25–28mm thick. Weighs 464g. Period 4 (Iron Age) pit 2938 (fill 2940)

Lower rotary quern. Old Red Sandstone. Of tapered form with thin straight vertical edges and sloped grinding surface that rises up to a gentle lip around the centre. The centre does not survive. Base is roughly worked into a flat shape. Edges are dressed. Grinding surface is neatly pecked but is worn completely smooth on the lip around the centre. Burnt and blackened on the base and edges. Measures 365mm diameter x 22–64mm thick. Weighs 4027g. Ra. 1076. Period 6 (Mid to Late Roman) oven 2827(fill 2527)

Lower rotary quern. Lodsworth Greensand. Central fragment with partially perforated spindle socket of 35mm deep. Grinding surface is pecked but has some worn areas and some rotational patterning. The circumference is missing. The lower face has been heavily re-used as a mortar so that there is a dished area, heavily smoothed inside, measuring 110 x >75 and 20mm deep at deepest point. Measures >340mm diameter x 60mm thick. Weighs 1283g. Ra. 1088. Period 5.4 (Late Iron Age to Early Roman) ditch 8 (fill 2957)

Upper rotary quern. Pebbly Old Red Sandstone/conglomerate of greyish red medium-coarse grained sandstone with frequent quartz pebbles including some pink quartz. Fragment of flat-topped type with straight vertical edges, slightly concave grinding surface and flat top. All surfaces have been neatly pecked although the grinding surface has some rotational wear and is smooth in patches on the outermost 10mm. The centre is missing. It is burnt and blackened in two patches, one on each face, suggesting two different burning episodes. Measures 410mm diameter x 34–39mm thick. Weighs 1749g. Ra. 1085. Period 6 (Mid to Late Roman) oven 2827 (fill 2528)

Quern. Sarsen. With one pecked flat face. No other faces are original, and it is burnt and blackened all over. Measures 100mm thick. Weighs 1042g. Ra. 1001. Period 4 pit 1057 (fill 1058)

Whetstone. Fine-grained grey, slightly micaceous sandstone. Central fragment of rectangular- sectioned, probably elongate whetstone. The faces are flat and smoothed and the arrises are slightly rounded. Measures >27mm long x 39mm wide x 10–12mm thick. Weighs 31g. Unstratified

Hone. Ferruginous sandstone. Thin flat stone smoothed on both faces with slight lip on one edge. Probably a hone or other processing tool. Measures >75 x 42–52mm wide x 18–24mm thick. Weighs 190g. Period 5.3 (Late Iron Age to Early Roman) ditch 8 (fill 3285)

Discussion of the querns and other objects

Two of the querns (saddle quern Ra. 1014 and rubber Ra. 1200) are complete. Saddle quern Ra. 1014 was part of a mixed deposit of domestic debris that had been placed in pit 1426 above a male skeleton (SK 1845). Rubber Ra. 1200 was included in the final fill of pit 8068, which contained a female skeleton (SK 8071). The use of stones as part of grave-capping processes has been under-appreciated because of a tendency to interpret them simply as backfill (Cooper *et al.* 2019, 241) but at a time when normal behaviour involved the fragmentation of querns prior to deposition, the inclusion of a complete saddle quern and a complete rubber in pits used for human burials is highly significant. They should be considered to have been deliberately placed and they are especially significant because querns are rarely found in mortuary contexts. Only 14 of 633 Iron Age querns included in a survey of quern deposition in south-western England were associated with human remains, and several of these only very loosely. Only one example from a pit at Sigwells, Somerset was in association with an articulated skeleton (Watts 2014, 114). The selection of a saddle quern for the male inhumation and a rubber for the female inhumation may have had symbolic importance. Ethnographic studies suggest that cereal processing was almost entirely a female task (Alonso 2019, 4320) and one would therefore anticipate that where querns were selected for use as grave cappings, that they would be for female skeletons. In other cultures, querns have been part of a female dowry, or given as a gift by a man to his new partner (ibid., 4320; Peacock 2013, 146) and it is not a stretch to imagine that at the end of such a relationship, as a result of his death, his partner may have marked that ending by giving up the quern.

The assemblage of querns is small but includes both saddle querns/rubbers and rotary querns and it covers the Iron Age and Roman periods. Saddle querns here are made of sarsen and other sandstones, including one of possible Old Red Sandstone. Rotary querns are made of Lodsworth stone and Old Red Sandstone. This is in keeping with what we know about quern use north of the Ridgeway in south Oxfordshire, where there were a series of changes in the provenance of querns during the Iron Age and Roman periods and as a result of the transition from saddle querns to rotary querns: sarsen and local gritstones were only used to make saddle querns, Lodsworth stone was only imported as rotary querns, and Old Red Sandstone was used for both types of querns (Shaffrey and Roe 2022).

Industrial debris
David Dungworth

Methodology

All of the material submitted was examined visually and recorded following standard guidance (HE 2015). The following categories of material were recognised:

Smithing hearth cake (SHC): Plano-convex (or concave convex) accumulations of slag that are approximately circular in plan. Smaller examples are usually associated with iron smithing (McDonnell 1991; Serneels and Perret 2003).

Non-diagnostic ironworking slag (NDFe): Most ironworking slag assemblages include a significant proportion of slag which lacks a diagnostic surface morphology that would allow the identification of the process(es) which produced them. In many cases, this is simply because the lumps of slag are small fragments of a larger whole; however, in some cases the lumps of slag are essentially complete but amorphous (HE 2015, fig. 18).

Vitrified ceramic lining (VCL): Fragments of highly fired (and often vitrified) ceramic are interpreted as fragments of a clay-built hearth (HE 2015, fig. 11).

Block tuyère: A large block of fired clay with a central hole which would allow air to be directed into a hearth or furnace. The outer surfaces are oxidised-fired while the inner portions are reduced-fired and vitrified.

Vitrified fuel ash (VFA): Vitrified fuel ash is a non-metallurgical waste material formed in a fire. Almost all organic fuels contain a small proportion of inorganic material. In many cases this will remain as ash; however, if the fire is hot enough this may vitrify (HE 2015, fig. 54).

Unidentifiable Slag (UID): Very small fragments of slag which lack any distinctive morphology that would identify process, and which even lack the colour and density of ironworking slags.

Iron concretion (Fe Conc): Naturally occurring lumps of soil that have been concreted by iron compounds (probably formed post-deposition).

Pyrites nodule: Naturally occurring nodules of iron pyrites (although most appears to have weathered to form iron oxides and hydrated iron oxides).

Results

Just over 4.5kg of metalworking slag and related materials were recovered (Table 3.14). In total, 3.3kg of the material was recovered from Iron Age contexts, and 0.9kg from Roman contexts (with the remaining material from late or unphased contexts, or not relevant to metalworking). The single most abundant category of material (48%) comprises seven smithing hearth cakes (in total 2.2kg). The size and shape of such smithing hearth cakes are quite distinctive and allow the positive identification of iron smithing. The absence of any diagnostic iron smelting slags suggests that smithing was the most significant metalworking activity. The non-diagnostic ironworking slag (0.7kg) could have been produced by smelting or smithing; however, the absence of smelting slags suggests that all the ironworking slags were produced by smithing. Five of the smithing hearth cakes (1.4kg) came from Iron Age contexts (all pits, 2056, 2167, 2265 and 2298), while two (0.7kg) came from

Table 3.14 Weights (in grams) of slag and related material

Context	Description	Period	Type	Comment	%	L	W	D	Wt
1190	Pit alignment	3	FC/Daub						16.7
1322	Ditch	5.1	Pyrites						10
1332	Ditch	5.1	NDFe						110
1333	Ditch	5.1	SHC		100	80	79	36	292
1382	Ditch	8.1	NDFe						22.7
1402	Ditch	5.1	Pyrites						15.5
1411	Pit	4	NDFe						112
1411	Pit	4	Pyrites						36.5
1424	Ditch	5.1	PBC						15.2
1500	Ditch	5.1	VCL						0.4
1564	Ditch	4	Pyrites						15.1
1589	Pit	4	NDFe						53.1
1631	Pit	4	Pyrites	Ra. 1016					16.1
1646	Pit	6	Pyrites						7.7
1725	Pit	4	NDFe						134
1731	Ditch	5.3	Pyrites						7.2
1733	Pit	5	Pyrites						37.2
1734	Pit	5	Pyrites						20.4
1734	Pit	5	SHC		?	86+	74+	52	468
1737	Pit	?	Pyrites						21
1777	Grave	4	VFA						120
1933	Pit	4	Pyrites						12.3
1942	Pit	4	VFA						74.6
1942	Pit	4	VFA						321
1955	Ditch	4	Pyrites						9.8
1962	Pit	4	NDFe	Ra. 1099					31.8
1972	Pit	4	NDFe						27.1
2014	Pit	4	NDFe						21
2014	Pit	4	VCL						9.3
2049	Pit	4	NDFe						16.2
2054	Pit	4	VCL						29.7
2056	Pit	4	SHC		?	81	63	25	116
2079	Pit	4	NDFe						2.5
2135	Pit	4	Pyrites						31.4
2166	Pit	4	SHC		100	101	90	44	399
2260	Pit	4	NDFe						107
2260	Pit	4	VCL						18.7
2260	Pit	4	Tuyère Block						756
2268	Pit	4	SHC		100	88	77	34	217
2268	Pit	4	SHC		>60	106	78+	43	402
2299	Pit	4	SHC		?	85	77	41	287
2308	Pit	4	Fe Conc						12.1
2451	External occupation	5	Coal						3.5
2475	Ditch	5	Coal						5.1
2681	Ditch	8.2	UID						0.7
2822	Oven?	6	Coal						11.8
3014	Ditch	5.2	PBC						2.7
3103	Pit	4	UID						11.7
3067	Pit	4	NDFe						34.3
8119	Pit	4	Crucible	uncertain form					22.9
8126	Natural?	?	UID						3.8
Total									**4528.8**

Late Iron Age to Early Roman contexts (ditch 9 and pit 1732). It is possible that smithing was carried out in both periods, but the later material could also be residual.

The vitrified ceramic lining (0.8kg) probably represents the remains of smithing hearth linings and/or superstructures but also includes several fragments of a block tuyère recovered from fill 2260 of Period 4 pit 2258 (Fig. 3.20). These fragments comprise around a quarter of the likely original extent of the block tuyère and have a bloated and partially vitrified face which probably faced into the hearth or furnace. The clay shows a variety of colours (from red-orange to black) that indicate that there was limited oxygen available inside the hearth or furnace. A perforation which extends through the tuyère would have allowed the delivery of air from bellows to the hearth/furnace and would have protected the organic bellows from heat damage.

Block tuyères are a relatively rare artefact in Britain (Tylecote 1986, 142–143); most hearths and furnaces were built with one or more perforations left in the walls at appropriate points during their construction (HE 2015, fig. 11). A few tubular tuyères are known (Tylecote 1986, 142–143) but block tuyères (rectangular or square) are very rare. There was an incomplete Iron Age block tuyère from Four Crosses in Powys (Havard *et al.* 2017, 26). This block tuyère had a flat, rectangular base 120mm wide. The top was missing but other fragments suggested a curved upper section. The association with copper ore and slag suggested that the Four Crosses block tuyère was used to help smelt copper. Parts of another prehistoric block tuyères were recently published from excavations at Poulton, Cheshire (Dungworth with Brooks 2021). The Poulton tuyère had not been subjected to high heat and it is not

0   1:2   100mm

Figure 3.20 Composite photograph of conserved and reconstructed fragments of a block tuyère

clear if it had been used. In addition, the air channel was at a steep angle unlike most where the air channel was close to horizontal.

Another block tuyère is known from the Roman fort at Carpow (Perthshire). The tuyère was 100mm square with a 24mm diameter perforation (Tylecote 1986, 142–143; Tylecote 1999, 569). It was found in a ditch fill with abundant iron slag and so was probably used in iron working although uncertainty exists over whether this was smelting or smithing. Block tuyères are also known from Roman sites in the Weald where they appear to have been used in iron smelting. Many of these are distinguished by

the presence of two (merging) perforations, suggesting that two bellows were used with each tuyère.

Block tuyères are much more common in France (Orengo *et al.* 2000) where dozens are known. Most of these appear to have been used in iron smithing and the author excavated one in a blacksmith's workshop at Mont Beuvray (Chadron-Picault and Pernot 1999, fig. 169). The available dating evidence suggests that block tuyères were employed in France from the Late Iron Age and through the Roman period.

Substantial quantities of vitrified fuel ash were recovered from fill 1942 of Period 4 pit 1917. This material is found in small quantities on most archaeological sites but is particularly abundant on later prehistoric sites (McDonnell 1986). It is not believed to be a waste product of metalworking and the chemical composition of those examples which have been analysed suggests a relatively simple combination of wood (or other plant) ash and some clay or soil. The present state of knowledge of this material does not allow the identification of the process which produced it (Dungworth 2016).

Pyrites was recovered from 13 contexts (combined weight 240.2g). Most of the nodules are quite small and weathered: the iron sulphide has largely been transformed in iron oxides and hydrated iron oxides. None of the nodules show obvious signs of having been used, for example as a part of a strike-a-light (Cave-Browne 1992). While the pyrites may have had some significance for past populations, nodules occur naturally in chalk and especially the lower chalk formations that outcrop at Wroughton.

Discussion

Iron smithing slag is routinely recovered during the excavation of Iron Age and Roman sites and the quantities recovered here provide no indication that the level of smithing was anything above the ordinary. The block tuyère is a rare find: it is only the fourth example from the UK known to the author. A block tuyère is portable and raises the possibility that the smith travelled with kit to enable smithing on more than site.

Chapter 4
Environmental evidence

Palaeoenvironmental remains were recovered from bulk samples taken from a wide variety of features across the site. These have provided charred plant macrofossils, wood charcoal, and land snails. In addition, a substantial animal bone assemblage was hand recovered. Further information has been provided with respect to diet by the analysis of lipids from pottery (see Chapter 3).

Plant macrofossils
Sarah F. Wyles

Introduction and methodology

A series of 72 bulk environmental samples and 14 small contiguous samples were processed and assessed for environmental remains from a range of feature types, mainly Iron Age pits. As a result of the assessment of these samples (Aitken and Wyles 2020), the charred plant remains from 35 samples were selected for further analysis. The breakdown of these by period is tabulated in Table 4.1. The assessment results for the unselected samples were either poorer or showed similar assemblages to those selected for further analysis. The results are recorded in Tables 4.2 to 4.5.

The bulk samples were processed following standard flotation methods, using a 250μm sieve for the recovery of the flot and a 0.5mm sieve for the collection of the residue. All identifiable charred plant remains from 32 of these samples were identified. Large quantities of charred plant remains were recovered in the remaining three samples, so these flots were subsampled, with only 10% of the 1mm, 0.5mm and 0.25mm flot fractions being fully sorted. In

Table 4.1 Breakdown of analysed samples by period

Period		Number of samples	Feature types
2	Beaker	1	Pit
4	Iron Age	28	Pits
5	Late Iron Age/Early Roman	1	Pit
6	Mid-Late Roman	4	Ovens
U	Undated	1	Pit
Total		**35**	

these cases, the subsampled remains have been multiplied up and marked with 'est.' (estimate) in Tables 4.3 and 4.5. In all of these cases, the remaining unsorted fractions were scanned to ensure that the full range of species was recovered from the assemblage. The plant remains were identified using a stereo-binocular microscope and with reference to modern seed reference material and the digital seed atlas (Cappers *et al.* 2006). Nomenclature follows that of Stace (1997) for wild plants, and traditional nomenclature, as provided by Zohary *et al.* (2012) for cereals.

Period 2: Beaker period

A very high number (nearly 1000) of hazelnut (*Corylus avellana*) shell fragments was recorded from pit 1245. There were also a few barley (*Hordeum vulgare*) grain fragments, a sloe (*Prunus spinosa*) stone fragment and a small number of weed seeds. This assemblage may be reflective of food preparation waste and domestic hearth remains and is likely to be indicative of the exploitation of hedgerows and woodland edge as a wild food resource.

Period 4: Iron Age

A total of 28 samples were analysed from 24 Iron Age pits across the site, and from the C-shaped enclosure ditch. The small quantities of charred plant remains recorded from the C-shaped enclosure ditch at the assessment included emmer (*Triticum dicoccum*) and spelt (*Triticum spelta*) glume base fragments and seeds of vetch/wild pea (*Vicia/Lathyrus* sp.) and bedstraw (*Galium* sp.). An exceptionally large charred plant assemblage was recovered from pit 2084, whilst there were high numbers of plant remains from 17 other pit samples, moderate numbers in a further eight and a smaller quantity in a further two pits. These assemblages can be divided into a number of different groups.

Pit 2084

The exceptionally large assemblage from pit 2084 was dominated by cereal remains, representing around 95%

Table 4.2 Charred and mineralised plant identifications from Period 2 and Period 4 pits

Columns are grouped by Period: **4 – Iron Age (Pits)** — cuts 1454, 1585, 1770, 1781, 2012, 1631, 1426, 1631, 1381, 1225, 1069, 1048; and **2 – Beaker (Pit)** — cut 1245. Columns below are presented in the left-to-right order of the original page.

Feature type / Taxonomy	Common name	2012	1781	1770	1585	1454	1631	1426	1631	1381	1225	1069	1048	1245
Context		2014	1782	1771	1587	1455	1631	1426	1631	1380	1227	1072	1051	1248
Sample		155	133	125	118	117	128	128	122	114	104	102	100	106
Vol (L)		18	20	20	20	20	20	20	19	20	19	20	20	16
Flot size		15	30	20	60	42	60	60	50	195	45	25	20	200
%Roots		50	5	5	20	30	2	2	10	2	75	50	10	50
Cereals														
Hordeum vulgare L. *sl* (grain)	barley	3	3	7	8	–	6	–	10	14	cf. 1	1	6	2
Hordeum vulgare L. *sl* (rachis frag)	barley	–	–	1	–	–	1	1	–	–	3	2	–	–
Triticum cf. *dicoccum* (Schübl) (grain)	emmer wheat	–	4	9	2	6	1	3	1	–	5	3	8	–
Triticum dicoccum (Schübl) (glume base)	emmer wheat	–	–	–	–	–	–	–	–	–	–	–	–	–
Triticum dicoccum (Schübl) (spikelet fork)	emmer wheat	–	–	–	2	–	–	–	–	–	–	–	–	–
Triticum spelta L. (grain)	spelt wheat	3	3	2	1	1	2	–	2	3	2	1	3	–
Triticum spelta L. (glume bases)	spelt wheat	3	30	20	7	27	1	–	7	–	11	5	22	–
Triticum spelta L. (spikelet fork)	spelt wheat	5	9	6	2	–	2	–	–	–	–	–	–	–
Triticum dicoccum/spelta (grain)	emmer/spelt wheat	–	1	6	2	7	2	2	2	5	11	6	13	–
Triticum dicoccum/spelta (germinated grain)	emmer/spelt wheat	1	–	–	–	1	–	–	–	–	–	–	–	–
Triticum dicoccum/spelta (spikelet fork)	emmer/spelt wheat	2	1	4	2	11	3	3	2	–	38	2	18	–
Triticum dicoccum/spelta (glume bases)	emmer/spelt wheat	–	25	24	8	43	11	4	4	–	62	1	49	–
Triticum sp. (grain)	wheat	3	1	2	–	–	2	2	4	2	1	–	–	1
Cereal indet. (grains)	cereal	14	13	9	12	9	11	11	3	5	18	9	10	1
Cereal frag. (est. whole grains)	cereal	5	4	7	4	5	5	5	3	5	7	6	8	1
Cereal frags (rachis frags)	cereal	–	–	2	–	–	–	–	–	–	–	–	2	–
Cereal frags (culm node)	cereal	–	1	2	–	–	–	–	1	–	–	1	3	–
Other species														
Ranunculus acris/repens/bulbosus L.	meadow/creeping/bulbous buttercup	–	–	–	–	–	2	2	–	–	–	–	–	–
Ranunculus sp.	buttercup	–	1	–	–	–	1	1	1	–	–	–	1	1
Papaver L.	poppy	–	–	–	–	–	2	2	1	–	–	–	–	–
Corylus avellana L. (fragments)	hazelnut	–	–	–	–	–	–	–	–	–	–	–	–	988
Corylus avellana L. (immature shell)	hazelnut	–	–	–	–	–	–	–	–	–	–	–	–	1
Chenopodium sp. L.	goosefoot	–	–	1	–	–	–	–	–	–	–	–	–	–
Chenopodium album L.	fat-hen	–	–	–	–	–	–	1	1	–	–	–	–	–
Persicaria lapathifolia/maculosa (L.) Gray/Gray	pale persicaria/redshank	–	1	–	–	1	–	–	1	–	–	–	–	–
Polygonum aviculare L.	knotgrass	–	–	1	–	1	3	–	–	–	–	–	1	1
Fallopia convolvulus (L.) Á. Löve	black-bindweed	–	–	1	–	–	–	3	–	–	–	–	1	–
Rumex sp. L.	docks	–	7	5	1	2	6	6	2	2	1	–	–	–
Rumex acetosella group Raf.	sheep's sorrel	–	2	1	1	–	3	3	–	2	–	–	–	–
Rumex crispus L. Type	curled dock	–	4	1	1	1	–	6	1	–	2	–	–	–
Viola sp. L.	violet	–	–	1	–	–	–	–	–	–	–	1	1	1
Brassica sp. L.	brassica	1	1	–	–	1	–	–	–	–	–	–	–	–
Brassica cf. *nigra* (L.) W.D.J. Koch	black mustard	–	1	4	1	–	1	1	–	–	–	–	–	–
Potentilla sp. L.	cinquefoils	–	–	1	1	–	1	1	–	–	–	–	–	–
Prunus spinosa L.	sloe stone	–	–	1	1	–	–	–	–	–	–	–	1	1
Prunus spinosa L.	sloe type fruit	–	1	1	–	1	–	–	–	–	–	–	–	–
Prunus spinosa L./*Crataegus monogyna* Jacq (thorns/twigs)	sloe/hawthorn type thorns	–	–	–	1	1	–	–	–	1	1	–	2	2
Aphanes arvensis L.	parsley-piert	–	1	1	1	1	–	–	–	–	–	–	1	1
Vicia L./*Lathyrus sp.* L.	vetch/wild pea	2	2	–	1	1	–	–	–	–	–	–	1	1
Vicia faba/Pisum sativum L.	celtic bean/pea	6	–	–	–	1	–	–	–	–	–	–	–	–

Species (Latin)	Common name														
Lathyrus cf. *nissolia* L.	grass vetchling	—	—	—	—	—	—	—	1	—	—	—	—	—	—
Pisum sativum L.	pea	—	1	3	—	2	—	1	cf. 1	—	—	2	1	—	—
Medicago/Trifolium sp. L.	medick/clover	3	—	—	2	—	—	3	3	1	2	1	2	2	—
Medicago sp. L.	medick	—	2	—	—	—	1	—	2	—	—	1	1	1	—
Trifolium sp. L.	clover	—	—	2	—	—	—	—	1	—	—	1	2	—	—
Linum usitatissimum L.	flax	—	1	—	1	—	—	—	—	—	—	—	—	—	—
Hyoscyamus niger L.	henbane	—	—	—	—	—	—	—	—	—	—	—	—	—	—
Galeopsis sp.	hemp-nettle	—	—	—	1	—	1	—	—	—	—	1	—	—	—
Prunella vulgaris L.	selfheal	—	—	—	—	—	—	—	—	—	—	—	—	—	—
Plantago lanceolata L.	ribwort plantain	—	—	—	1	—	2	—	2	—	—	1	1	—	—
Veronica hederifolia L. (charred)	ivy-leaved speedwell	—	—	—	—	—	—	2	—	—	—	—	—	—	—
Odontites vernus (Bellardi) Dumort.	red bartsia	2	2	2	—	—	2	2	2	—	—	3	3	1	—
Sherardia arvensis L.	field madder	3	3	—	—	—	3	1	1	—	—	3	—	—	—
Galium sp. L.	bedstraw	3	2	—	10	—	10	2	1	1	—	6	6	2	1
Galium aparine L.	cleavers	7	—	2	20	2	20	1	4	1	—	15	15	4	1
Valerianella dentata (L.) Pollich	narrow-fruited cornsalad	1	—	—	—	—	—	1	4	1	—	—	—	1	—
Carduus/Cirsium sp. L.	thistle	—	—	—	—	—	—	—	—	—	—	1	1	1	—
Anthemis cotula L. (seeds)	stinking mayweed	—	1	—	1	—	—	—	—	—	—	—	—	—	—
Tripleurospermum inodorum (L.) Sch. Bip.	scentless mayweed	—	—	—	—	—	1	1	—	—	—	1	1	3	—
Schoenoplectus lacustris Palla	club-rush	—	—	—	—	—	—	1	—	—	—	—	—	—	—
Isolepis setacea (L.) R. Br.	bristle club-rush	1	—	—	—	—	1	1	1	—	—	1	1	—	—
Carex sp. L. trigonous	sedge trigonous seed	4	4	1	1	—	—	1	6	1	1	1	5	—	—
Lolium/Festuca sp. L.	rye-grass/fescue	7	7	1	1	—	2	—	6	1	1	5	5	1	2
Poa/Phleum sp. L.	meadow grass/cat's-tails	5	5	—	—	2	2	2	1	—	—	5	2	1	1
Arrhenatherum elatius var. *bulbosum* (Willd) (*tuber*)	false oat-grass	5	4	—	1	—	—	1	1	—	1	1	1	1	1
Arrhenatherum elatius var. *bulbosum* (Willd) (*stem*)	false oat-grass	4	2	—	—	—	—	2	4	—	—	7	7	—	2
Avena sp. L. (grain)	oat grain	—	2	5	—	—	2	2	4	4	4	7	7	29	2
Avena L./*Bromus* L. sp.	oat/brome grass	8	6	3	5	1	5	1	5	3	6	8	8	33	5
Bromus sp. L.	brome grass	10	2	2	3	2	1	2	1	2	2	3	3	—	—
Monocot. Stem/rootlet frag		2	—	—	2	—	—	—	—	1	—	3	—	1	—
Bud		—	—	—	—	X	1	—	—	—	1	—	1	1	—
Rosaceae type thorns		—	—	—	—	1	—	—	—	—	—	—	—	—	—
Parenchyma/dung/vitrified charcoal		—	—	—	—	—	—	—	—	—	—	—	—	—	—
'Tuber'		—	—	2	2	1	1	1	—	—	—	1	1	—	—

Mineralised material

Species (Latin)	Common name														
Mineralised cf. immature grain		—	—	1	—	—	—	—	—	—	—	—	—	—	—
Mineralised *Chenopodium* type seed	goosefoot	—	—	—	—	—	—	—	1	—	—	1	—	—	—
Mineralised *Fallopia convolvulus* type seed	black-bindweed	—	—	—	—	—	—	—	—	—	1	—	—	—	—
Mineralised *Polygonum/Rumex* type seed	knotgrass/docks	—	—	—	—	—	1	2	1	—	1	1	—	2	—
Mineralised Brassicaceae type seed	brassicas	2	—	108	7	10	—	2	2	—	2	—	22	2	2
Mineralised *Linum* type seed	flax	—	1	1	—	1	1	1	—	—	cf.1	—	—	—	—
Mineralised Lamiaceae type seeds	dead nettles	—	—	—	—	—	—	—	—	—	4	—	—	1	—
Mineralised *Carduus/Cirsium* type seed	thistles	—	1	—	—	1	—	—	1	—	—	1	1	1	—
Mineralised large Poaceae type seed	grasses	—	—	—	—	—	—	1	—	—	1	—	—	—	—
Mineralised seeds		—	1	—	—	5	—	5	—	—	1	6	6	1	—
Mineralised stem		—	—	—	—	X	—	—	—	—	1	—	—	1	—
Mineralised matter		—	—	—	—	2	—	2	—	—	—	—	—	—	—
Mineralised nodule		2	2	12	—	2	—	3	—	—	2	3	3	2	2

Table 4.3 Charred and mineralised plant identifications from Period 4 pits

Taxonomy / **Cut**	Common name	2032	2043	2084	2235	2669	2835	2900	2928	2938	3080	3083
Period							4 – Iron Age					
Feature type							Pits					
Context		2034	2021	2085	2237	2671	2843	2904	2930	2940	3081	3085
Sample		158	165	169	173	237	234	239	241	242	252	253
Vol (L)		20	16	20	9	18	16	15	8	18	17	16
Flot size		40	10	330	15	20	15	20	10	15	7	25
%Roots		30	60	<1	75	10	10	5	<1	65	1	10
% 1.0mm fraction analysed				10								
% 0.5mm + 0.25 mm fraction analysed				10								
Cereals												
Hordeum vulgare L. *sl* (grain)	barley	3	1	est.1482	2	3	3	2	–	3	3	2
Hordeum vulgare L. *sl* (germinated grain)	barley	–	–	10	–	–	–	–	–	–	–	–
Hordeum vulgare L. *sl* (rachis frag)	barley	2	–	–	–	–	–	1	1	–	1	1
Triticum cf. *dicoccum* (Schübl) (grain)	emmer wheat	4	–	–	1	5	18	6	36	4	39	4
Triticum dicoccum (Schübl) (glume base)	emmer wheat	3	–	–	–	2	–	2	4	–	7	3
Triticum dicoccum (Schübl) (spikelet fork)	emmer wheat	4	cf. 1	355	2	–	1	5	2	1	2	2
Triticum spelta L. (grain)	spelt wheat	31	–	est. 52	11	30	50	25	117	26	113	19
Triticum spelta L. (glume bases)	spelt wheat	–	–	est. 23	1	1	–	2	–	–	–	–
Triticum spelta L. (spikelet fork)	spelt wheat	13	–	847	5	14	14	13	4	13	9	11
Triticum dicoccum/spelta (grain)	emmer/spelt wheat	–	–	26	1	–	1	–	–	–	–	–
Triticum dicoccum/spelta (germinated grain)	emmer/spelt wheat	22	–	est.70	3	24	23	33	32	6	27	27
Triticum dicoccum/spelta (spikelet fork)	emmer/spelt wheat	80	–	est. 30	12	89	193	173	263	51	227	102
Triticum dicoccum/spelta (glume bases)	emmer/spelt wheat	–	–	–	–	–	–	–	–	–	–	–
Triticum turgidum/aestivum (grain)	free-threshing wheat	1	–	–	–	–	–	–	–	–	–	–
Triticum sp. (grain)	wheat	3	–	32	–	2	1	8	3	1	–	2
Cereal indet. (grains)	cereal	15	–	92	15	18	10	24	5	14	15	11
Cereal frag. (est. whole grains)	cereal	9	1	125	5	8	6	10	4	8	5	7
Cereal frags (rachis frags)	cereal	3	–	–	–	–	–	1	–	–	–	–
Cereal frags (culm node)	cereal	2	–	–	–	–	1	1	–	1	–	–
Cereal frags (awns)	cereal	–	–	–	–	–	–	1	–	–	–	–
Cereal frags (coleoptile)	cereal	–	–	est. 1320	–	2	2	–	–	–	–	–
Other species												
Ranunculus sp.	buttercup	–	–	–	–	–	–	1	–	–	–	–
Corylus avellana L. (fragments)	hazelnut	–	–	–	–	–	–	–	–	–	1	–
Chenopodium sp. L.	goosefoot	–	–	–	–	1	1	1	–	–	–	–
Persicaria lapathifolia/maculosa (L.) Gray/Gray	pale persicaria/redshank	1	–	–	–	–	–	1	1	1	–	–
Polygonum aviculare L.	knotgrass	–	–	–	–	1	1	1	–	–	1	–
Rumex sp. L.	docks	1	–	est. 10	–	1	1	1	–	–	1	1
Rumex crispus L. Type	curled dock	–	–	–	–	–	–	2	6	–	–	2
Brassica sp. L.	brassica	–	–	est. 30	–	1	1	2	–	–	2	2

Taxon	Common name										
Prunus spinosa L./*Crataegus monogyna* Jacq (thorns/twigs)	sloe/hawthorn type thorns	1	–	–	–	1	1	–	3	1	2
Aphanes arvensis L.	parsley-piert	1	–	–	–	1	1	5	1	1	1
Vicia L./*Lathyrus* sp. L.	vetch/wild pea	1	–	–	1	1	5	5	1	2	1
Vicia faba/*Pisum sativum* L.	celtic bean/pea	–	–	–	–	–	–	–	1	–	cf. 1
Medicago/*Trifolium* sp. L.	medick/clover	–	–	–	1	1	5	5	5	–	2
Medicago sp. L.	medick	–	–	–	–	–	2	2	2	–	2
Trifolium sp. L.	clover	1	–	3	–	–	3	3	3	–	3
Lithospermum arvense L.	corn gromwell	1	–	–	–	1	–	–	–	–	–
Galeopsis cf. *tetrahit* L.	common hemp-nettle	–	1	–	–	–	–	–	–	–	–
Veronica hederifolia L. (charred)	ivy-leaved speedwell	1	–	–	1	–	2	2	–	–	–
Odontites vernus (Bellardi) Dumort.	red bartsia	1	–	6	–	–	–	–	–	–	–
Galium sp. L.	bedstraw	1	est. 10	1	4	1	1	4	1	1	1
Galium aparine L.	cleavers	–	–	1	1	1	–	1	1	1	–
Valerianella dentata (L.) Pollich	narrow-fruited cornsalad	–	–	–	1	–	1	1	–	–	–
Carex sp. L. trigonous	sedge trigonous seed	–	–	1	1	–	–	–	–	–	–
Lolium/*Festuca* sp. L.	rye-grass/fescue	2	est. 10	1	1	1	1	2	2	2	2
Poa/*Phleum* sp. L.	meadow grass/cat's-tails	2	est. 10	2	–	–	–	–	–	–	–
Arrhenatherum elatius Var. *bulbosum* (Willd) (tuber)	false oat-grass	2	–	–	2	–	–	5	5	–	–
Arrhenatherum elatius Var. *bulbosum* (Willd) (stem)	false oat-grass	1	–	–	–	–	1	1	–	1	1
Avena sp. L. (grain)	oat grain	1	3	1	1	2	2	2	1	1	2
Avena sp. L. (floret base)	oat floret	–	–	–	–	–	–	–	–	–	–
Avena L./*Bromus* L. sp.	oat/brome grass	14	est. 22	1	2	10	10	15	5	5	3
Bromus sp. L.	brome grass	10	est. 60	2	7	9	15	14	2	2	6
Monocot. Stem/rootlet frag		1	–	–	1	1	–	2	–	–	2
Rosaceae type thorns		–	–	–	–	–	–	–	–	–	–
Dung		cf. 1	–	–	–	–	–	–	–	2	–
Tuber		1	–	–	1	–	1	–	–	–	–

Mineralised material

Taxon	Common name										
Silicaceous stem/awns frags		–	++	–	–	–	–	–	–	–	–
Mineralised *Ranunculus* type seed	buttercup	–	–	–	1	–	–	–	–	–	–
Mineralised *Polygonum*/*Rumex* type seed	knotgrass/docks	2	–	–	1	1	–	–	–	–	–
Mineralised Brassicaceae type seed	brassica	2	–	–	5	5	2	–	1	–	1
Mineralised *Linum* type seed	flax	–	–	–	1	1	–	–	–	–	–
Mineralised *Plantago lanceolata* type seed	ribwort plantain	–	–	–	2	2	1	–	–	–	–
Mineralised large Poaceae type seed	grasses	–	–	–	1	1	–	–	–	–	–
Mineralised seeds		1	–	1	1	1	1	1	–	1	3
Mineralised nodule		17	–	–	15	15	–	–	–	3	1

Table 4.4 Charred and mineralised plant identifications from Period 4 and 5 pits

Period		4 – Iron Age						5 – LIA/ERB
Feature type		Pits						Pit
Cut		8068		8115		8118		2261
Context		8069	8098	8117	8121	8119	8122	2282
Sample		275	276	272	277	278	279	176
Vol (L)		10	17	14	9	18	20	19
Flot size		60	75	25	10	10	20	15
%Roots		10	35	25	50	60	25	25
Taxonomy	Common name							
Cereals								
Hordeum vulgare L. *sl* (grain)	barley	15	37	15	2	1	7	–
Hordeum vulgare L. *sl* (germinated grain)	barley	–	–	1	–	–	–	–
Triticum cf. *dicoccum* (Schübl) (grain)	emmer wheat	1	–	–	–	–	–	–
Triticum dicoccum (Schübl) (glume base)	emmer wheat	1	2	8	–	–	2	1
Triticum dicoccum (Schübl) (spikelet fork)	emmer wheat	–	–	–	1	–	–	2
Triticum spelta L. (grain)	spelt wheat	2	1	–	–	–	–	2
Triticum spelta L. (glume bases)	spelt wheat	1	2	25	–	–	2	13
Triticum dicoccum/spelta (grain)	emmer/spelt wheat	11	2	8	–	–	3	10
Triticum dicoccum/spelta (spikelet fork)	emmer/spelt wheat	1	–	12	–	–	–	6
Triticum dicoccum/spelta (glume bases)	emmer/spelt wheat	6	3	102	–	–	3	33
Triticum sp. (grain)	wheat	–	–	–	–	1	1	–
Cereal indet. (grains)	cereal	28	5	16	2	2	4	19
Cereal frag. (est. whole grains)	cereal	12	7	9	2	3	4	12
Cereal frags (rachis frags)	cereal	–	–	3	–	–	–	–
Cereal frags (culm node)	cereal	–	–	1	–	–	–	–
Cereal frags (awns)	cereal	–	–	1	–	–	–	–
Cereal frags (coleoptile)	cereal	–	–	4	–	–	–	–
Other species								
Juniperus communis L.	common juniper	–	–	–	cf. 1	–	–	–
Ranunculus sp.	buttercup	–	2	–	1	–	–	–
Chenopodium sp. L.	goosefoot	–	6	–	–	–	–	–
Chenopodium album L.	fat-hen	–	4	–	–	–	–	–
Atriplex sp. L.	oraches	–	–	–	–	–	1	–
Stellaria media L.	common chickweed	–	1	–	–	–	–	–
Persicaria lapathifolia/maculosa (L.) Gray/Gray	pale persicaria/redshank	–	2	–	–	–	–	–
Polygonum aviculare L.	knotgrass	–	9	1	2	–	–	–
Fallopia convolvulus (L.) À. Löve	black-bindweed	–	4	1	–	–	–	–
Rumex sp. L.	docks	–	29	1	–	–	1	1
Rumex acetosella group Raf.	sheep's sorrel	–	3	–	–	–	1	–
Rumex crispus L. Type	curled dock	–	25	–	–	–	1	1
Brassica sp. L.	brassica	–	11	3	–	–	6	1
Brassica cf. *nigra* (L.) W.D.J. Koch	black mustard	–	–	–	–	–	3	–
Prunus spinosa L./*Crataegus monogyna* Jacq (thorns/twigs)	sloe/hawthorn type	–	1	–	–	–	1	1
Aphanes arvensis L.	parsley-piert	3	–	–	–	–	–	–
Vicia L./*Lathyrus* sp. L.	vetch/wild pea	1	6	1	1	1	–	5
Medicago/Trifolium sp. L.	medick/clover	2	2	–	–	1	2	–
Medicago sp L.	medick	2	1	–	–	–	–	1
Trifolium sp. L	clover	3	1	–	–	1	1	1
Torilis sp. Adans	hedge-parsley	–	–	1	–	–	–	–
Veronica hederafolia L (charred)	ivy-leaved speedwell	2	–	–	–	–	–	–
Odontites vernus (Bellardi) Dumort.	red bartsia	3	2	–	1	–	–	–
Sherardia arvensis L.	field madder	–	1	–	–	–	–	–
Galium sp. L.	bedstraw	1	14	–	3	–	8	2
Galium aparine L.	cleavers	–	11	–	5	–	2	4
Valerianella dentata (L.) Pollich	narrow-fruited cornsalad	–	2	–	–	2	–	–
Anthemis cotula L. (seeds)	stinking mayweed	1	–	–	–	–	–	–
Tripleurospermum inodorum (L.) Sch. Bip.	scentless mayweed	–	–	1	–	–	–	–
Poaceae basal culm node	grass	1	–	–	–	–	–	–
Lolium/Festuca sp. L.	rye-grass/fescue	–	–	1	1	1	1	–
Poa/Phleum sp. L.	meadow grass/cat's-tails	2	2	–	–	1	1	–
Arrhenatherum elatius Var. *bulbosum* (Willd) (tuber)	false oat-grass	–	–	2	–	–	–	–
Avena sp. L. (grain)	oat grain	–	2	5	–	–	–	1
Avena L./*Bromus* L. sp.	oat/brome grass	6	3	4	–	–	2	8
Bromus sp. L.	brome grass	9	3	2	–	1	–	16
Rosaceae type thorns		–	–	3	–	–	–	–
Tuber		1	–	–	–	1	–	1
Mineralised material								
Silicaceous material		–	–	–	–	–	+	–
Mineralised *Polygonum/Rumex* type seed	knotgrass/docks	7	–	–	–	–	–	–
Mineralised Brassicaeae type seed	brassicas	3	6	–	2	–	1	–
Mineralised *Sherardia* type seed	field madder	–	1	–	–	–	–	–
Mineralised *Poa/Phleum* type seeds	meadow grass/cat's-tails	–	–	–	–	–	1	–
Mineralised seeds		2	–	–	–	–	–	–
Mineralised nodule		–	–	–	1	–	–	1

Table 4.5 Charred and mineralised plant identifications from Period 6 ovens and undated pit

Period		6 – Mid–Late Roman				Undated
Feature type		Ovens				Pit
Cut		2532		2827		2431
Context		2530	3181	3184	3185	2432
Sample		218	256	259	260	183
Vol (L)		20	8	9	9	9
Flot size		625	185	42	18	20
%Roots		<1	15	3	3	45
% 1.0mm fraction analysed		10	10			
% 0.5mm + 0.25 mm fraction analysed		10	10			
Taxonomy	Common name					
Cereals						
Hordeum vulgare L. *sl* (grain)	barley	239	85	26	48	1
Hordeum vulgare L. *sl* (grain still in husk)	barley	20	–	–	–	–
Hordeum vulgare L. *sl* (germinated grain)	barley	5	–	4	–	–
Hordeum vulgare L. *sl* (rachis frag)	barley	est. 11	1	2	–	–
Triticum cf. *dicoccum* (Schübl) (grain)	emmer wheat	–	–	–	–	1
Triticum dicoccum (Schübl) (glume base)	emmer wheat	est. 202	est. 150	20	4	1
Triticum dicoccum (Schübl) (spikelet fork)	emmer wheat	est. 44	12	7	–	–
Triticum spelta L. (grain)	spelt wheat	105	96	31	23	–
Triticum spelta L. (germinated grain)	spelt wheat	–	7	3	–	–
Triticum spelta L. (glume bases)	spelt wheat	est. 1358	est. 1200	422	30	1
Triticum spelta L. (spikelet fork)	spelt wheat	13	11	13	–	–
Triticum spelta L. (spikelet)	spelt wheat	2	–	–	–	–
Triticum dicoccum/spelta (grain)	emmer/spelt wheat	309	447	75	90	18
Triticum dicoccum/spelta (germinated grain)	emmer/spelt wheat	24	3	2	9	–
Triticum dicoccum/spelta (spikelet fork)	emmer/spelt wheat	est. 390	est. 465	127	8	4
Triticum dicoccum/spelta (glume bases)	emmer/spelt wheat	est. 1374	est. 2980	630	57	2
Triticum turgidum/aestivum (grain)	free-threshing wheat	4	4	–	2	–
Triticum sp. (grain)	wheat	55	72	8	20	3
Cereal indet. (grains)	cereal	93	173	108	35	23
Cereal frag. (est. whole grains)	cereal	55	140	43	15	14
Cereal frags (rachis frags)	cereal	est. 75	est. 12	–	1	–
Cereal frags (culm node)	cereal	2	2	1	–	–
Cereal frags (awns)	cereal	–	est. 68	5	–	–
Cereal frags (coleoptile)	cereal	est. 34	2	20	12	–
Other species						
Ranunculus acris/repens/bulbosus L.	meadow/creeping/bulbous buttercup	–	–	1	–	–
Ranunculus sp.	buttercup	–	–	1	1	–
Papaver L.	poppy	est. 20	–	–	–	–
Corylus avellana L. (fragments)	hazelnut	1	–	1	–	–
Chenopodium sp. L.	goosefoot	–	–	1	–	–
Chenopodium album L.	fat-hen	–	–	–	–	1
Atriplex sp. L.	oraches	–	–	1	–	–
Persicaria lapathifolia/maculosa (L.) Gray/Gray	pale persicaria/redshank	3	–	–	–	2
Polygonum aviculare L.	knotgrass	–	1	–	–	–
Fallopia convolvulus (L.) À. Löve	black-bindweed	–	1	–	–	–
Rumex sp. L.	docks	est. 51	86	14	3	7
Rumex acetosella group Raf.	Sheep's sorrel	5	5	2	–	2
Rumex crispus L. Type	curled dock	est. 103	110	22	3	3
Malva sp. L.	mallow	–	–	1	–	1
Brassica sp. L.	brassica	est. 11	1	–	1	2
Potentilla sp. L.	cinquefoils	–	–	–	–	7
Vicia L./*Lathyrus sp.* L.	vetch/wild pea	6	2	2	3	3
Medicago/Trifolium sp. L.	medick/clover	est. 22	est. 11	2	1	3
Medicago sp. L.	medick	–	–	–	1	–
Linum usitatissimum L.	flax	–	–	cf. 1	–	–
Bupleurum sp. L.	Hare's-ears	est. 10	–	–	–	–
Prunella vulgaris L.	selfheal	–	–	–	–	5
Plantago lanceolata L.	ribwort plantain	2	–	1	1	–
Odontites vernus (Bellardi) Dumort.	red bartsia	–	–	–	–	23
Galium sp. L.	bedstraw	–	–	1	1	–
Valerianella dentata (L.) Pollich	narrow-fruited cornsalad	1	–	–	–	–
Cardus/Cirsium sp. L.	thistle	–	1	–	–	–
Centaurea cyanus L..	cornflower	–	–	–	2	–
Anthemis cotula L. (seeds)	stinking mayweed	–	est. 22	1	2	2
Tripleurospermum inodorum (L.) Sch. Bip.	scentless mayweed	est. 10	1	–	–	2
Festuca sp. L	Fescue	7	10	–	1	–
Lolium/Festuca sp. L.	rye-grass/fescue	est. 166	est. 314	20	4	14
Poa/Phleum sp. L.	meadow grass/cat's-tails	est. 20	est. 22	1	1	9
Avena sp. L. (grain)	oat grain	20	est. 30	4	8	7
Avena sp. L. (floret base)	oat floret	est. 12	–	2	–	–
Avena L./*Bromus* L. sp.	oat/brome grass	est. 34	est. 117	12	6	9
Bromus sp. L.	brome grass	22	est. 35	3	3	4
Parenchyma/dung/vitrified charcoal		+	+	–	–	–
Dung		+	+	–	–	–
Mineralised material						
Silicaeous material		+++	–	–	–	–
Silicaeous stem/awns frags		+++	+++	+++	+++	–

of the assemblage, with grains outnumbering the chaff elements. Barley grains were more numerous than those of spelt wheat in this assemblage. There is also some evidence for germination on a number of the grains, as well as a large quantity of coleoptile fragments. Germination can be a result of poorly stored grain but also can be a deliberate stage within the malting process, as part of beer making. Lodwick (2017) has defined this and noted that 'accidental charring may happen at three stages: malted grains within their spikelets, which have become accidentally burnt (type B); germinated grains (malt) once they have been removed from their spikelets (type C); and waste or 'comings' (glume bases and coleoptiles), once they have been removed from the cereal grains after de-husking and used as fuel (type A)'. It is possible that this assemblage may include some type A and type C remains. The level of germination seems to be too high to be a result of poorly stored grain. This is the only assemblage where such a high level of evidence for germination was noted, while low levels of evidence for germination were recorded in five of the other 27 assemblages.

The weed seeds in this assemblage were mainly those of the larger or intermediate seed size species such as oats (*Avena* sp.), brome-grass (*Bromus* sp.) and rye-grass/fescue (*Lolium/Festuca* sp.), of species with seeds with appendages such as docks (*Rumex* sp.), and of twining/binding species such as bedstraw. These are all species typical of grassland, field margins and arable environments and are likely to have been brought in with the crops.

Glume-rich samples

The large plant assemblages recovered from pits 1048, 1225, 1454, 2032, 2669, 2835, 2900, 2928, 2938, 3080, 3083 and 8115 were dominated by chaff remains, which represented between 54 and 88% of the assemblages. The cereal remains were predominantly those of spelt, with small quantities of emmer and barley.

Again, the weed seeds in these assemblages are generally species of grassland, field margins and arable environments and are likely to have been brought in with the crops. They were mainly those of the larger or intermediate seed-size species such as oats, brome-grass and rye-grass/fescue (*Lolium/Festuca* sp.), as well as species with seeds with appendages such as curled docks (*Rumex crispus*), species with seed heads such as scentless mayweed (*Tripleurospermum inodorum*), and twining/binding species such as cleavers (*Galium aparine*) and black bindweed (*Fallopia convolvulus*).

These pit assemblages are generally indicative of waste derived from a late stage of crop processing involving the dehusking of hulled grain stored as semi-cleaned grain or in spikelet form (Hillman 1981;1984). The weed seeds would have been incorporated with the crop-processing waste. The larger and intermediate weed seeds, those from seed heads and those from twining/binding species, may remain with the spikelets in storage and become released when the spikelets are pounded to dehusk the hulled grain for use.

Less well processed assemblages

The samples from pits 1770 and 1781 produced high numbers of charred plant remains. Although the cereal remains outnumbered the weed seeds in these assemblages, the weed seeds were more numerous than the grains and chaff elements taken separately. The cereal remains were dominated by those of spelt, with smaller numbers of barley and emmer wheat. They also contained a few culm nodes. The weed seeds included those of cleavers and brome grass and were mainly those of species which would be left in with the grain during the earlier stages of crop processing (Hillman 1981; 1984). It may be that these samples represent waste material from the processing of crops which had been less well processed prior to storage (as semi cleaned grain or in spikelet form) than the waste material in the glume-rich samples discussed above. This could be due to pressure of time at harvest.

Domestic hearth /food production/settlement waste material

Nine of the pits produced assemblages which appear to be indicative of domestic hearth/food production/settlement waste. High numbers of charred remains were recorded from pits 1426 and 8068, moderate numbers from pits 1069, 1381, 1585, 2012, 2235 and 8118, and a small amount from pit 2043. The cereal remains included those of spelt, emmer and barley. Remains of other potential crops and food sources included those of flax (*Linum usitatissimum*), peas (*Pisum sativum*), and black mustard (*Brassica nigra*).

There were also a few charred flax seeds from pit 1381 and mineralised flax seeds from pits 1225, 1426, 1585 and 2669.

Mineralised and silicaeous remains

Significant numbers of mineralised seeds and other remains were recovered from pits 1225, 1426, 1585, 1770 and 8068. These included mineralised seeds, grains, stems and nodules. This material may have come from the dumping of settlement waste material or be the result of manuring. There was no clear evidence that any of the analysed pits had primary functions as cess pits. A number of the charred weed seeds, such as fat-hen (*Chenopodium album*) and henbane (*Hyoscyamus niger*), thrive in nitrogen-rich soils and may be indicative of animal grazing and manuring in the area.

Silicaeous awn and stem fragments were noted in assemblages from pits 2043 and 8118 and these may be related to the burning of chaff elements as fuel.

Period 5: Late Iron Age–Early Roman

A large charred plant assemblage was recorded from pit 2261. The assemblage was dominated by cereal remains, with the chaff elements outnumbering those of grain. The cereal remains included those of spelt and emmer and the weed seeds included those of brome grass, vetch/wild pea and cleavers. This assemblage may be representative of late-stage crop processing waste.

Period 6: Mid–Late Roman

Four samples were analysed from oven 2827. Exceptionally large assemblages were recovered from the oven end (*c.* 250 identifiable items per litre of soil) and from flue 3181 (*c.* 840 identifiable items per litre of soil), and high numbers from oven fills 3184 and 3185.

The assemblages were dominated by chaff, which represented 71–76% of these assemblages, with the exception of fill 3185 which was more grain-rich. The cereal remains were predominantly those of spelt, with smaller amounts of emmer and barley. Again, the weed seeds were generally those likely to have been brought in with the crops, including those of larger or intermediate seed-size species, species with seeds with appendages, species with seed heads, and twining/binding species. The chaff-rich assemblages are likely to represent late stage crop processing waste being used as tinder/fuel in the oven.

It is thought that crop-processing ovens were used for a variety of functions during the Romano-British period, including the drying of whole ears or even sheaves especially after a wet summer; the parching of fully ripe spikelets of glume wheats to render the glumes brittle and facilitate their removal by pounding and subsequent winnowing; the drying of fully processed grain or spikelets prior to storage; the drying of fully processed grain to harden it prior to milling; and the roasting of germinated grain to stop the germination process as part of the malting process (van der Veen 1989). The assemblages recovered suggest that oven 2827 had been used for the parching of crops which had already been processed by winnowing, threshing and sieving, and possibly for the drying of cleaned grain to harden it prior to milling. However, it should be noted that these assemblages only reflect the final uses of the oven and it is possible that it was used for a variety of the functions detailed above.

Unphased

The sample from unphased pit 2431 produced a high number of plant remains. The assemblage was dominated by the weed seed component and this included seeds of red bartsia (*Odontites vernus*), rye-grass/fescue, meadow grass/cat's-tails (*Poa/Phleum* sp.), oats, brome-grass, sheep's sorrel (*Rumex acetosella*), curled docks, cinquefoils (*Potentilla* sp.) and selfheal (*Prunella vulgaris*). These are all species typical of grassland, field margins and arable environments. The cereals include remains of spelt, emmer and barley. This assemblage may be indicative of waste material from the processing of crops which had been less well processed prior

to storage, or waste material from a slightly earlier stage of crop processing. The assemblage would be compatible with assemblages from Period 4 Iron Age pits on this site but would equally be compatible with the sort of assemblages expected from Periods 3, 5 or 6.

Discussion

Period 2: Beaker period
The predominance of hazelnut shell fragments has been recorded from other Beaker deposits in southern Britain, such as at south-east Amesbury (Wyles and Stevens forthcoming) and this dominance of hazelnut fragments and other wild food remains may be indicative of the exploitation and general reliance on these wild food resources as a significant part of the diet during this period (Moffett *et al.* 1989; Stevens 2007; Robinson 2000).

Period 4: Iron Age
The range of crops recorded in these assemblages, mainly barley, spelt and emmer (with spelt being more dominant than emmer), together with small amounts of peas/beans, flax and black mustard, is compatible with this date, as spelt appears to have been the predominant wheat during the Iron Age period in this part of southern Britain (Greig 1991). Spelt was the predominant wheat in other Iron Age assemblages from the area, such as at Ridgeway Farm, Purton, Wiltshire (Wyles 2017a), and Groundwell West, Wiltshire (Stevens and Wilkinson 2001), although in some assemblages at Latton Lands, Wiltshire (Griffiths 2009) there was more barley and emmer wheat.

The assemblages at the Collection Management Facility from this period suggest some local crop processing. There is an indication of waste derived from a late stage of crop processing involving the dehusking of hulled grain stored as semi-cleaned grain or in spikelet form after it had been processed by winnowing, threshing and sieving (Hillman 1981; 1984). A few of the assemblages appeared to represent cereals that had been less well processed prior to storage or possibly material from an earlier stage of processing. This supports the evidence for local crop processing activities provided by the crop/food processing finds from the site such as a saddle quern from pit 1426, a grain rubber from pit 8068 and a possible quern fragment from pit 2938. The storage of hulled grain as semi-cleaned grain or in spikelet form allowed the time-consuming final stage crop processing to be carried out as the grain was required over the year, rather than being done at busy harvest time.

The waste chaff elements from crop processing may have been used as tinder/fuel and the silicaeous awn and stem fragments noted in assemblages from pits 2043 and 8118 may also be related to the burning of chaff elements as fuel. Quantities of silicified awns have been noted in other Iron Age assemblages such as at Steart Point, Somerset (Wyles 2017b) and at Kenn Moor and Banwell Moor on the north Somerset levels (Jones 2000). There is also a suggestion of some malting, as part of the brewing process being caried out on site.

The weed seeds were generally those of grassland, field margins and arable environments and were dominated by seeds of the larger or intermediate seed-size species, species with seeds with appendages, species with seed heads, and twining/binding species. Such seeds are all likely to remain with the grains until the final late stage crop processing took place prior to use and this pattern has been seen on other sites such as Ridgeway Farm, Purton (Wyles 2017a), Yarnton, Oxfordshire (Stevens 2011), Gravelly Guy, Oxfordshire (Moffett 2004) and Ashville Trading Estate, Abingdon, Oxfordshire (Jones 1978). In contrast, the assemblages at Groundwell West (Stevens and Wilkinson 2001) were dominated by small-seeded weed species, suggesting a lower degree of processing prior to storage. The presence amongst the Collection Management Facility assemblages of low growing weed species indicates a low harvesting height, probably using a sickle which would be a typical harvesting method for the period (Hillman 1981).

There is an indication of the use of a number of different environments, such as lighter drier calcareous soils favoured by species such as field madder (*Sherardia arvensis*), narrow-fruited cornsalad (*Valerianella dentata*) and corn gromwell (*Lithospermum arvense*), heavier damper soils where species such as sedge (*Carex* sp.), bristle club-rush (*Isolepis setacea*) and club-rush (*Schoenoplectus lacustris*) thrive, and hedgerow/woodland edge environments typical of species such as hazel. The damper species may possibly have been brought on to site with material for use as floor covering from places such as by the stream in nearby Markham Bottom, while the crops are likely to have been grown on the nearby calcareous slopes.

There is an indication of possible local manuring provided by the significant numbers of mineralised seeds, grains, stems and nodules recovered from five of these pits. In addition, a number of the charred weed seeds, such as fat-hen and henbane, thrive in nitrogen-rich soils and may also be indicative of animal grazing and manuring in the area.

Period 5: Late Iron Age–Early Roman
The assemblage recorded from pit 2261 suggests a continuation of the crop production and the crop processing regime indicated by the Iron Age samples.

Period 6: Mid–Late Roman
The crop remains recovered in the assemblages from this period were those of spelt, with smaller amounts of emmer and barley. This continuation of the range of crops in the Roman period was also seen in assemblages from the nearby site at Ridgeway Farm, Purton (Wyles 2017a). The range of weed seeds would also suggest a continuation of growing crops on the lighter calcareous soils in the vicinity.

It is thought that crop-processing ovens were used for a variety of functions during the Romano-British period and these assemblages suggest that oven 2827 had been used, at least for the final use, for the parching of crops which

had already been processed by winnowing, threshing and sieving, and possibly for the drying of cleaned grain to harden it prior to milling.

Summary

The range of crops and food sources recorded in these assemblages are compatible for the periods. There is evidence for local crop production and processing during the Iron Age, with a small indication for other settlement activities such malting as part of the brewing process and flax processing possibly for weaving. The crops appear to have been grown on the local light calcareous soils and there is a suggestion of some local manuring/animal grazing from these assemblages. The local crop production and processing regime appears to have continued into the Roman period on this site. The results from this site fit into the wider pattern for these periods and add to the information for this area.

Molluscan analysis
Sarah F. Wyles

Introduction and methodology

A series of 14 small contiguous samples (28 litres of soil) for molluscs were taken from Period 4 (Iron Age) C-shaped enclosure ditch. It was hoped that the mollusc assemblages would provide some information on the nature of the local landscape.

The mollusc samples were processed following standard methods, with a flot and residue mesh of 0.5mm. The molluscs were identified according to Anderson (2005) with habitat preferences according to Kerney (1999) and Davies (2008) (Table 4.6).

Results

The number of mollusc shells from the C-shaped ditch was generally low, in particular from the lower fills.

A moderate mollusc assemblage was recorded from a later (Period 5, Late Iron Age to Early Roman) fill of the ditch (fill 2367, sample 195) which included Late Iron Age to Early Roman pottery, and this was dominated by remains of the intermediate species *Trochulus hispidus* and *Deroceras/Limax*. This is suggestive of a possible period of stabilisation and grassy vegetation within the ditch. A moderately high number of mollusc shells was recovered from another late fill, 2355 (sample 191), probably Late Iron Age or Early Roman but lacking pottery, and the assemblage from that deposit was dominated by those of *Vallonia costata* and *Vallonia excentrica*. This may be indicative of some arable activity in the immediate vicinity at this stage. It is likely that the monument was dug in an open landscape. The assemblages were too small to warrant full detailed analysis.

Table 4.6 Assessment of the mollusc samples from C-shaped ditch

Feature							C-shaped ditch section 2357							
Context			2369					2368	2367	2366		2356		2355	
Depth (m)	1.2–1.28	1.1–1.2	1.0–1.1	0.9–1.0	0.8–0.9	0.7–0.8	0.6–0.68	0.5–0.6	0.4–0.5	0.33–0.4	0.28–0.33	0.18–0.28	0.1–0.15	0–0.1
Sample	225	224	223	200	199	198	197	196	195	194	193	192	191	190
Weight (g)	1500	1500	1500	1500	1500	1500	1500	1500	1500	1500	1500	1500	1500	1500
Open country species														
Vertigo pygmaea	–	–	–	–	–	–	–	–	–	–	–	–	C	C
Vallonia costata	–	–	–	–	–	–	C	–	–	–	–	–	A	C
Vallonia excentrica	–	–	–	–	–	–	–	–	C	–	–	–	A	C
Helicella itala	–	–	–	–	–	–	–	C	–	–	–	–	C	C
Intermediate species														
Trochulus hispidus	–	–	–	C	–	–	–	A	A	C	–	C	B	C
Cepaea sp.	–	–	–	–	–	–	–	–	C	+	+	–	–	–
Cochlicopa sp.	–	–	–	–	–	–	–	–	C	C	–	–	C	C
Punctum pygmaeum	–	–	–	–	–	–	–	–	–	C	–	–	C	–
Deroceras/Limax	–	–	–	–	–	–	C	C	A	–	C	C	B	–
Shade-loving species														
Carychium tridentatum	–	–	–	–	–	–	–	–	C	–	–	–	–	–
Aegopinella nitidula	–	–	–	–	–	–	–	–	C	–	–	–	–	–
Burrowing species														
Cecilioides acicula	–	–	–	–	–	–	–	C	–	C	–	C	–	C
Total	**0**	**0**	**0**	**1**	**0**	**0**	**4**	**14**	**55**	**6**	**2**	**2**	**65**	**10**

Key: C = 1-4, B = 5-9, A = 10+

Wood charcoal
Dana Challinor

Introduction

Sixteen samples were submitted for the analysis of the charcoal, but only 12 merited examination. These comprised samples from the following: a Beaker (Period 1) pit; nine Iron Age (Period 4) pits; and two from a Mid to Late Roman (Period 6) oven. Samples from additional features and periods were unproductive of charcoal. The analysis sought to examine domestic fuel use, offering an insight into selection processes and the exploitation of local woody resources.

Methodology

Charcoal >2mm in transverse section was considered for identification, though preference was given to larger >4mm fragments which could be assessed for maturity. Where available, 30–50 fragments per feature were randomly selected for identification. The charcoal was fractured and sorted into groups based on the anatomical features observed in transverse section at X7 to X45 magnifications. Representative fragments from each group were then selected for further examination using a Meiji incident-light microscope at up to X400 magnification. Identifications were made by comparison with identification keys (Gale and Cutler 2000, Hather 2000, Schweingruber 1990) and modern reference material. Heartwood was identified by the presence of multiple tyloses across more than one growth ring and sapwood was identified by the absence of

tyloses. In the absence of pith and/or bark, roundwood was attributed to fragments which exhibited strong or moderate ring curvature. Additional observations on features relating to pre- and post-burning conditions (vitrification, vivianite or iron staining, presence of insect tunnels and fungal hyphae) were also recorded. Classification and nomenclature follow Stace (2019).

Results

The results are presented by period in Tables 4.7–4.9. Generally, charcoal was well preserved, with moderate or abundant assemblages of mid-sized (4–6mm) fragments. Condition was good to fair and there were low levels of indeterminate fragments (4%); with the exception of the assemblage from pit 1048, in which the charcoal was small, scrappy and vitrified, with indeterminate fragments representing 40% of the assemblage. The reason for the poorer preservation in this pit is unclear, but there were also multiple small twig fragments that were not identifiable due to insufficient visible anatomical structure.

Table 4.7 Charcoal results from Beaker pit (showing fragment counts)

	Feature no.	1245
	Context no.	1248
	Sample no.	106
Corylus avellana L.	hazel	31 (ri)
Bark		19

r = roundwood; i = insect tunnels; brackets ( ) = present in some fragments only

Table 4.8 Charcoal results from Middle Iron Age pits (showing fragment counts)

	Cut no.	1048	1381	1426		1454	1585	1781	2265	8115
	Context no.	1051	1380	1631	1846	1455	1587	1782	2268	8117
	Sample no.	100	114	128	138	117	118	133	174	272
Prunus spinosa L.	blackthorn	13 (r)				8r	9r	14r		
Prunus sp.	blackthorn/cherry					12r	5r	5r	4r	8r
Maloideae	hawthorn grp			3r		1r	8r		6 (r)	8r
Rhamnus cathartica L.	buckthorn									6r
Quercus sp.	oak	2	30 (sh)	16 (rs)	19 (rs)	3	6	10 (h)	3	
Corylus avellana L.	hazel			1r	1r	5r				
Alnus/Corylus	alder/hazel	(1r)								3r
Acer campestre L.	field maple			9 (r)				1r	2 (r)	1r
Cornus sanguinea L.	dogwood	(2r)								
Fraxinus excelsior L.	ash								1	
Bark							2			
Indeterminate		12 (t)		1t		1t			4	4 (t)

r = roundwood; h = heartwood; s = sapwood; t = twig; brackets = cf. identification or present in some frags only

The presence of at least nine taxa was positively identified:

Rosaceae: *Prunus* spp., blackthorn/cherry, including confirmed *P. spinosa* (blackthorn)
Maloideae, hawthorn group: comprising *Pyrus* (pear), *Malus* (apple), *Sorbus* (rowan/service/whitebeams), *Crataegus*, (hawthorn)
Rhamnaceae: *Rhamnus cathartica*, purging buckthorn
Fagaceae: *Quercus* sp., oak
Betulaceae: *Corylus avellana*, hazel
Salicaceae: *Populus/Salix*, poplar or willow
Sapindaceae: *Acer campestre*, field maple
Cornaceae: cf. *Cornus sanguinea*, dogwood
Oleaceae: *Fraxinus excelsior*, ash

Roundwood fragments were frequent, some with preserved pith and/or bark and including some small twig remains. Ages of small diameter roundwood (≤10mm) ranged between 1 and 7 years. Some larger roundwood was recorded in the assemblage from oven 2532, with diameters up to 35mm and age ranges of 9 to 16 years. Oak heartwood was infrequent, with tyloses only visible in occasional fragments. Insect tunnels were observed in *Corylus* fragments from pit 1245 and in *Prunus*, *Quercus* and *Populus/Salix* fragments in oven 2532. The shape of the tunnels was generally small and asymmetric but those in the oak were large and oval, some with frass (insect excreta).

Table 4.9 Charcoal results from Mid to Late Roman oven 2532 (showing fragment counts)

	Feature no.	2532	2827
	Context no.	2530	3181
	Sample no.	218	256
Prunus sp.	cherry type	4ri	1r
Quercus sp.	oak	12rsi	26 (rhs)
Corylus avellana L.	hazel	1r	3r
Populus/Salix	poplar/willow	33ri	

r = roundwood; h = heartwood; s = sapwood; i = insect tunnels; brackets ( ) = present in some frags only

This is consistent with galleries left by the Cerambycidae (long-horned beetles) that tend to inhabit dead wood on the ground and suggests that the wood had been pre-seasoned prior to use as fuel.

Discussion

Period 2: Beaker pit (1245)

The charcoal assemblage from pit 1245 comprised hazel, including many fragments of roundwood (exhibiting moderate or strong ring curvature). There was also a notable quantity of charred bark. While this is likely to have detached from the hazel roundwood, it is also unusual for such a significant quantity and size of bark fragments to be preserved in charcoal assemblages and it is possible that the bark represents deliberate fuel used on the fire. Certainly, some of the larger bark fragments were inconsistent with the thin bark that might be expected as detached from small diameter roundwood. The charred plant remains assemblage included a high number of hazelnut shells, sloe stones and cereal grains (Wyles, above), which indicates domestic food waste. The absence of any other taxon in the charcoal, notably *Prunus spinosa*, suggests that the sloe stones were not accidentally included with wood fuel. Although small kindling-type pieces do not always survive the burning process, the excellent preservation of the bark suggests that the fire (or at least the part of the fire represented) did not reach sufficiently high temperatures to burn to extinction and/or was deliberately extinguished.

Period 4: Middle Iron Age pits (1048, 1381, 1426, 1454, 1585, 1781, 2265, 8115)

With the exception of pit 2265, all of the pits examined produced quantities of charred cereal grain and other mixed domestic waste. This included pit 1426, which additionally contained the skeleton of an adult male (see Clough, Chapter 5). The charcoal assemblage from pit 1426 was dominated by oak, with some field maple,

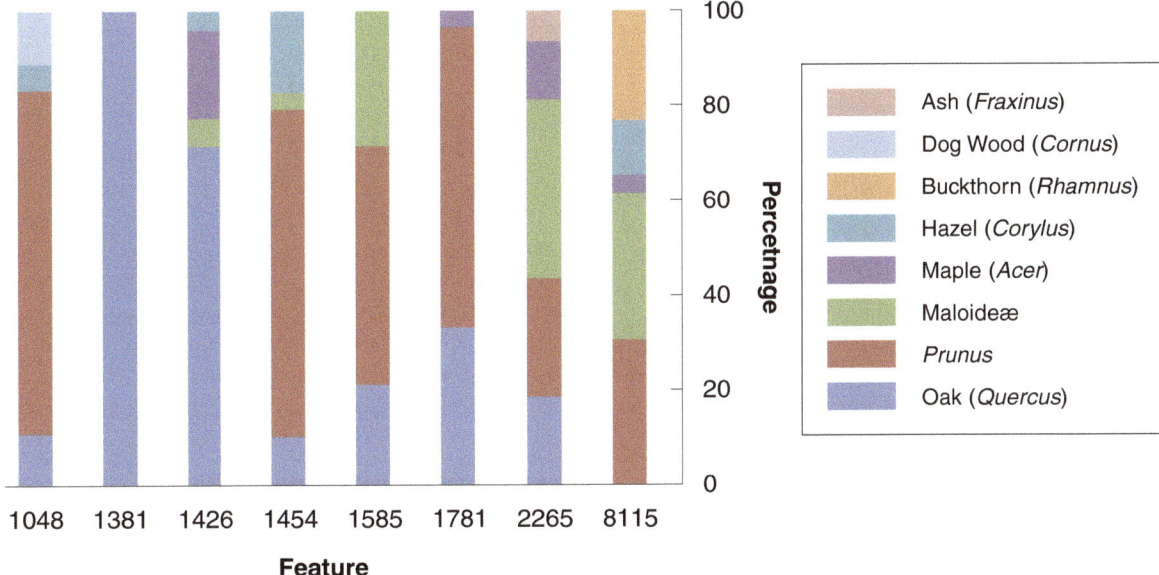

Figure 4.1 Taxonomic composition of charcoal from Middle Iron Age pits

Maloideae type and hazel. Although this pit, along with pit 1381, contained more oak than others, the assemblages are broadly consistent, exhibiting a range of taxa. These included a range of shrub/small trees, such as blackthorn, Maloideae, buckthorn and dogwood, all of which were present as roundwood, indicating the use of branchwood or small stems. Although the individual pit assemblages varied in taxonomic composition and abundance, it is clear that oak, *Prunus* and Maloideae were the most abundant and frequent taxa across the Iron Age assemblage (Fig. 4.1). This indicates some consistency in fuelwood supplies, utilising branchwood from scrub/hedgerows supplemented with larger trunkwood (oak, hazel, field maple) to provide longer, more sustained heat. A comparable picture was observed in the charcoal assemblages from Middle Iron Age pits and ditches at Cotswold Community, where almost the same range of taxa (*Prunus*, Maloideae, buckthorn, field maple, hazel, oak and ash) were exploited for fuel (Challinor 2010). In addition, the majority of the charcoal was from small diameter roundwood.

Period 6: Mid to Late Roman oven 2532

The samples analysed from oven 2532 comprised the fill of the fire pit (2530) and one fill from the main oven chamber (3181). Unsurprisingly, there was a vast quantity of well-preserved and large charcoal in the fire pit, while the material from 3181 was significantly sparser and smaller. The assemblages were similar, but there was a greater quantity of oak in the main chamber fill and a signficant amount of poplar/willow in the fire pit. This is probably because of the way that oak produces a large amount of ash, which would readily blow through the flue and into the chamber. Added to which, oak charcoal fractures easily along its large rays meaning that it can be over-represented in small material. All of the charcoal from oven 2532 came from roundwood, which was generally wide

(moderate ring curvature) and up to 25mm in diameter (incomplete). Heartwood was rarely observed with only a couple of fragments in context 3181, suggesting that the majority of the fuel was supplied from younger wood. The material is consistent with coppiced stems, but could have been sourced from unmanaged young trees or branches. The presence of insect tunnels in most taxa suggests that the wood had been seasoned prior to burning. Poplar and willow, certainly, benefit from being well-seasoned as they are traditionally considered poor fuels (Edlin 1949, 156), but all of the hardwood taxa represented burn better and with greater heat output if seasoned (Warren 2006).

If the oven was used for crop processing (or for malting), it is interesting to make some comparisons with the fuel used in similar structures elsewhere in the area. A Mid Roman crop-processing oven from Cotswold Community was fuelled almost exclusively by oak, but a slightly later (Mid to Late Roman) oven at the same site contained only a small quantity of *Prunus* charcoal (Challinor 2010). At Bath Road, Melksham, four crop-processing ovens also produced a range of taxa, including *Prunus*, Maloideae, hazel, oak, poplar/willow and ash, with notable variations between individual assemblages (Challinor 2018a). Particularly noteworthy, however, is that the majority of the charcoal derived from wide or narrow diameter roundwood, with no evidence for mature wood. Moreover, this picture was replicated at Beanacre, Wiltshire where ten Roman ovens (some associated with crop processing, some associated with doemstic waste) produced a range of taxa, showing inconsistency between individual oven assemblages and a significant use of young roundwood for fuel (Challinor 2018b). In conclusion, there was variation in the choice of fuel types used in Romano-British crop-processing ovens, but they were generally fuelled by young stems from a range of species, potentially supplied from coppice, and sometimes supplemented with more mature trunkwood.

Animal remains

Matilda Holmes

Introduction

A total of 5342 fragments of animal bones and teeth were recovered by hand from 500 contexts; 1741 could be identified to taxon. The assemblage is from features ranging in date from the Beaker period to the Mid to Late Roman period, although the majority are from Iron Age and Late Iron Age to Early Roman deposits, and these will be analysed in detail. Other periods are less well represented and will only be summarised in terms of species represented.

Methodology

Bones were identified using the author's reference collection. Due to anatomical similarities between sheep and goat, bones of this type were assigned to the category 'sheep/goat,' unless a definite identification (Zeder and Lapham 2010; Zeder and Pilaar 2010) was made. Horses, donkeys and mules were separated based on long bone measurements and teeth (Davis *et al.* 2008; Eisenmann 1986; Johnstone 2006) and dogs and foxes using metapodial measurements (Ratjen and Heinrich 1978). Frogs and toads were separated following criteria in Ratnikov (2001). Bones that could not be identified to species were, where possible, categorised according to the relative size of the animal represented (micro – rat/vole size; small – cat/rabbit size; medium – sheep/pig/dog size; or large – cattle horse size). Ribs were identified to size category where the head is present, vertebrae where the vertebral body is present, and maxilla, zygomatic arch and occipital areas of the skull were identified from skull fragments. Due to problems with the identification of post-cranial bones of micro-mammals, only their mandibles and maxillae were identified to taxa.

Tooth wear and eruption were recorded using guidelines from Grant (1982) and Payne (1973), as were bone fusion, metrical data (von den Driesch 1976), anatomy, side, zone (Serjeantson 1996) and any evidence of pathological changes, butchery (Lauwerier 1988) and working. The condition of bones was noted on a scale of 0–5, where 0 is fresh bone and 5, the bone is falling apart (Behrensmeyer, in Lyman 1994, 355). Other taphonomic factors were also recorded, including the incidence of burning, gnawing, recent breakage and refitted fragments. All fragments were recorded, although articulated or associated fragments were entered as a count of 1, so they did not bias the relative frequency of species present. Details of Associated Bone Groups (ABGs) were recorded in a separate table. Where bones from both sides of the body of a single individual could be identified from an ABG, only one set of bones were measured. A number of sieved samples were collected but because of the highly fragmentary nature of such samples, a selective process was undertaken whereby fragments were recorded only if they could be identified to species and/or element or showed signs of taphonomic processes.

Bones were included in analysis if they came from features that could be securely phased. Quantification of taxa used a count of all fragments (NISP – number of identified specimens), and that of anatomical elements was done using a restricted count of epiphyses only, based on Grant (1975). Mortality profiles were constructed based on tooth eruption and wear of mandibles (Grant 1982; Jones 2006; Jones and Sadler 2012) and bone fusion (O'Connor 2003). Redistribution of different carcass parts was investigated, whereby the more robust, dense elements are most likely to survive in terms of preservation if whole carcasses are disposed of (after Brain 1981). Cattle and sheep/goats were sexed on the basis of the morphology of pelves (Davis 2000; Greenfield 2006) and pigs by their canines (Schmid 1972).

Taphonomy and condition

Bones were in good to fair condition, but variable, with a high proportion of refitted fragments and recently broken bones suggesting they were friable upon excavation (Table 4.10). Many refitted fragments did not exhibit recent breakage, indicating they were broken some time ago in situ, or at least without much subsequent disturbance. This is exemplified by the high proportion of mandibles containing teeth that could also be refitted. Root etching (Fig. 4.2, 1) was also commonly recorded, most notably on the Late Iron Age to Early Roman assemblage. This is typically caused by acid produced by the roots of vegetation or fungi (Lyman 1994; Tjelldén *et al.* 2015) and implies that much of the assemblage was in an environment that allowed growth of vegetation to come into contact with bones over a period of time. The mechanics of this are poorly understood, and whilst it is possible that the bones were affected recently (West and Hasiotis 2007), the depth of deposition of much of the material suggests that it happened historically.

Prior to burial, some bones must have been available for dogs to chew, as approximately a tenth to a fifth of the assemblage showed signs of canid gnawing (Table 4.10). One large mammal bone from pit 2203 (fill 2205) had been heavily gnawed by rodents. The high proportion of teeth remaining in their respective mandibles further indicates fairly rapid accumulation and minimal post-depositional movement.

Few butchery marks were recorded, but this may reflect the effects of root etching that can easily obliterate knife cuts. Butchery marks represent carcass reduction in a systematic way, and evidence of techniques relating to skinning, disarticulation, jointing and splitting the carcass into sides was observed, as well as evidence for marrow and meat removal. Burnt bones were rarely recorded, and although small quantities of burnt bone were recovered from many of the Iron Age pits, there were no large groups to indicate that bones were routinely exposed to fire during cooking or as fuel or as a means of disposal.

Several primary contexts were evident from the presence of loose epiphyses recovered alongside their corresponding

Table 4.10 Condition and taphonomic factors affecting the hand-collected assemblage identified to taxa and/or element

Condition	Beaker	LBA – Early Iron Age	MIA settlement	C-shaped enclosure	Late Iron Age – Early Roman	Mid–Late Roman
Fresh			1			
Very good			32	11	1	
Good		1	410	53	85	4
Fair		1	269	34	166	1
Poor	1	5	66	4	87	1
Very poor		3	10	2	3	
Total	1	10	788	104	342	6
Refitted long bones	1=6	33=5	888=124	217=33	384=72	4=2
Refitted mandibles			32%	50%	50%	
Recent break		5	20%	29%	21%	2
Gnawed		2	12%	23%	20%	2
Loose mandibular teeth*		2	38	8	48	1
Teeth in mandibles*			148	23	60	
Etching	1	9	20%	18%	57%	
Butchery			3%	6%	4%	
Burning	1		2%		1%	

*deciduous and permanent 4th premolar and molars. Teeth included where stated; percentages given for the larger assemblages

Table 4.11 Associated bone groups by period

Phase	Feature	Context	Taxon	Details
MIA	Pit 8118	8122	Canid	Disarticulated remains of at least four perinates. Mandibles were all at the same stage of eruption (dp4 erupted but unworn and M1 unerupted) = 1–4 months. Ra. 1220
MIA	Pit 8118	8122	Cattle	Skeleton, largely complete mandible wear stage C. 1224/1210
MIA	Pit 8118	8122	Mixed	Group of micro-mammal (including field vole) and frog/toad (including frog) bones. Ra. 1220
MIA	Pit 6030	6035	Dog	Skeleton, largely complete (no bacculum), 15–24 months. 3x lumber vertebrae with bent dorsal processes
MIA	Pit 1068	1067	Dog	Skeleton, largely complete (no bacculum), adult
MIA	Pit 2844	2845	Cattle	Foot from hind leg (distal tibia, tarsals, metatarsal, 1st and 2nd phalanges). Adult, gnawed, tibia disarticulation marks
MIA	Pit 1381	1353	Sheep/goat	Partial skeleton (left humerus, radius, metacarpal, tibia) perinatal.
MIA	Pit 1669	1671	Dog	Disarticulated femur and pelvis, probably same adult animal
MIA	Pit 1669	1671	Sheep/goat	Perinatal humerus and metacarpal, probably same animal
MIA	Pit 1454	1455	Sheep/goat	Disarticulated remains of at least three perinates
MIA	Pit 2567	2569	Cattle	Pair of hind leg (distal tibia, astragalus, calcaneus), calf
MIA	Pit 1984	1962	Dog	Mostly complete skeleton of an adult male. Missing skull and 3rd phalanges, possibly skinned. Pitting evident on lumber vertebrae and bones of the upper fore and hind legs
MIA	Pit 3150	3151	Horse	Hind leg (tibia, tarsals, metatarsal, lateral metatarsal). Massive exostosis of metatarsal, tarsals and lateral metatarsal, see Fig. 4.2, 2
LIA–ER	E1 ditch 4	2821	Cattle	Vertebrae (thoracic and lumber vertebrae and sacrum). Not old adult
LIA–ER	E1 ditch 8	2727	Cattle	Vertebrae (thoracic and lumber vertebrae). Older adult
LIA–ER	E1 ditch 8	2870	Cattle	Vertebrae (thoracic vertebrae). Older adult
LIA–ER	E1 ditch 9	2819	Cattle	Two third phalanges, probably from the same animal
M–L R	Pit 1645	1697	Cattle	Ribs, thoracic vertebrae, lumber vertebrae and sacrum. Nearing old adult age as some of the vertebrae were just starting to fuse
M–L R	Pit 2363	2362	Sheep/goat	Partial skeleton (vertebrae, skull, fore and hind limbs), perinatal
M–L R	Pit 2363	2362	Domestic fowl	Partial skeleton (vertebrae and sternum, wings and tibia), juvenile

metaphyses, implying minimal post-depositional disturbance. These included Period 4 (Iron Age) pits 6030 (fill 6028), 1784 (fill 1785), 2567 (fill 2568) and 2258 (fill 2260). Numerous ABGs were recorded, and these are summarised in Table 4.11. Several possible origins are represented by these ABGs, including possible butchery waste in the form of cattle vertebrae, as observed Period 6 (Mid to Late Roman) pit 1645 and Period 5 (Late Iron Age to Early Roman) ditches associated with enclosure 1. Several complete and partial skeletons were also recovered

from pits. Most came from Period 4 (Iron Age) storage pits, some containing single animals, others multiple. Pit 8118 contained the remains of four puppies, a cattle skeleton and several disarticulated skeletons of micro-mammals and frogs/toads. Other pits included the remains of four adult dogs, two cattle (one adult, one calf), five perinatal sheep/goats and an adult horse. It is notable that the cattle and horse were represented by lower hind leg bones. Mid to Late Roman pit 2363 contained the partial skeletons of a lamb and juvenile domestic fowl. A large number of skulls

Figure 4.2 Animal bone 1) Examples of root etching observed on fragmented bone; 2) Equid metatarsus showing deformations of the proximal articulation (oblique view)

were also recovered, many of which also came from Iron Age pits (Table 4.12), more than one being recorded from pits 1851 and 2203.

There were no isolated deposits of primary butchery, skin-processing or craft-working waste, although some ABGs described above may have been resulted from the early stages of butchery.

Results by period

Period 2: Beaker pit
A fragmentary piece of roe deer antler was recovered from pit 1245 (fill 1247). It was burnt but showed no signs of working or wear.

Period 3: Late Bronze Age to Early Iron Age
A few animal remains were recovered from Pit alignments 1 and 2. Cattle and horse were best represented (Table 4.13) with a few finds of sheep/goat and pig represented by scraps of disarticulated bones and teeth.

Table 4.12 Animal skulls by period

Phase	Feature	Context	Skull	Taxon
MIA	Pit 1851	1944/1860	Skull	Horse x2, cattle x2 (1944); horse (1860)
MIA	Pit 2203	2205&6	Skull	Cattle x2
MIA	Pit 3068	3067	Skull	Cattle
MIA	Pit 3113	3116	Skull	Canid
MIA	Pit 1430	1435	Skull	Cattle
MIA	Pit 1770	1771	Skull	Sheep
MIA	Pit 2223	2224	Skull	Sheep/goat
MIA	Pit 1724	1726	Horn cores	Cattle
MIA	Pit 2258	2260	Skull	Horse
MIA	Pit 2280	2277	Horn cores	At least 4x sheep/goats
MIA–RB	C-ditch	2356	Skull	Horse
MIA–RB	C-ditch	2398	Skull	Canid
LIA–ER	Ditch 13	2152	Skull	Cattle
LIA–ER	Ditch 11	2804	Skull	Cattle
LIA–ER	Ditch 8	2244	Skull	Cattle

Table 4.13 Species representation (NISP). H = Hand collected; S = samples

Taxa	Beaker	LBA – Early Iron Age	Middle Iron Age		MIA C-shaped enclosure	Late Iron Age – Early Roman		Mid–Late Roman	
	H	H	H	S	H	H	S	H	S
Cattle		9*	320*	3	66	199*		3	
Sheep/goat		2	512*	27	55	213	1	4*	
Sheep			53		7	13			
Goat			1						
Pig		2	44	7	10	23		1	
Equid		4	52*		6	46			
Canid			21*	1	4	3			
Red deer			1		1	1			
Roe deer	1		2			1			
Deer					1				
Hare			1						
Micro-mammal			26	143			16		1
Field vole			6	51			1		1
Water vole			3	3					
Mouse				3					
Wood mouse			13				1		1
Shrew				2					
Mole				4					
Domestic fowl			1			3		1*	
Small passerine				1					
Buzzard			1						
Toad				1					
Frog				2					
Frog/toad			12	9	1		3		
Total identified	**1**	**17**	**1058**	**268**	**151**	**502**	**22**	**9**	**3**
Unidentified mammal	1	24	218		22	130			
Large mammal	2	30	1002		118	591		6	
Medium mammal	2	6	1068		54	318		4	
Bird			3			1			
Total	**6**	**77**	**3349**		**345**	**1542**		**19**	

* Associated bone groups included as a count of 1

Table 4.14 Species represented by phase and feature (NISP)

Taxa	Middle Iron Age						
	BSP	LP	SP	P	RH12	RH9	G1364
Cattle	57	138*	90*	32*	3		
Sheep/goat	91*	223	196*	52	2	1	1
Pig	7	17	16	3			
Equid	3	24	25*				
Canid	3*	9*	4	4*			
Wild mammal	1	1	1	1			
Domestic fowl			1				
Total	**162**	**412**	**333**	**92**	**5**	**1**	**1**

Taxa	Late Iron Age–Early Roman															
	E1	RH1	RH5	E1.1	Str A	D1	D13	D18	D19	E2	E3	DW A	D20	E4	O2827	Other
Cattle	99*	2	2	14	7	2	29	6			12	4			4	18
Sheep/goat	115	1		11	4	3	39	1		1	15	2		1	7	26
Pig	13			1			1	1			3			1	1	2
Equid	24		1	2	1		6		1	1	1	2	1		1	5
Canid	1							2								
Wild mammal							1					1				
Domestic fowl	2										1					
Total	**254**	**3**	**3**	**28**	**12**	**5**	**76**	**10**	**1**	**2**	**32**	**9**	**1**	**2**	**13**	**51**

Taxa	Mid–Late Roman				
	G 2295	G 2309	G 2315	G 2352	Pit
Cattle		1	2		
Sheep/goat	1	1	1		1*
Pig				1	
Equid					
Canid					
Wild mammal					
Domestic fowl					1*
Total	**1**	**2**	**3**	**1**	**2**

* Associated bone groups included as a count of 1. PA= pit alignment; BSP= bell-shaped pit; LP= large storage pit; SP= small pit; P= other pit type; RH= roundhouse; D= ditch; DW = droveway; E = enclosure; O = oven; Str = structure; G = grave

Period 4: Iron Age

The Iron Age settlement

A considerable assemblage was recovered from the Iron Age settlement. A few animal remains came from roundhouses 12 and 9 (Table 4.14), amongst which cattle and sheep/goat were identified. It is unusual to have so few bones and teeth associated with roundhouses, and they may have been affected by truncation, or else the ditches were regularly cleaned out and the waste disposed of elsewhere. A small piece of sheep/goat tibia was identified from grave 1364 (fill 1365) that contained a neonate skeleton (SK 1366), along with a further ten fragments of unidentified bone. It is most likely that these were residual, incorporated during backfilling of the grave, rather than being deliberate inclusions.

Nearly all the assemblage came from pits. There was little difference in species proportions between the fills of large, small and uncategorised pits (as identified during analysis of the pits; details in the site archive) (Table 4.14). Sheep/goats were most common, followed by cattle (Table 4.13). Horse, pig and canid remains were next most common, along with occasional finds of red and roe deer, hare, domestic fowl,

buzzard and smaller, background species including field vole, water vole and frog/toad. Further micro-mammals were recorded in the environmental samples, including field vole, water vole, wood mouse, common shrew, mole and toad.

The micro-mammals and frogs/toads are most likely to have been pit falls, rather than the result of predator meals. They can give some indication of the environment: shrews, mice and voles require cover; shrews prefer areas of shrubby grassland and woodland, while field voles like grassland, heathland and moorland and wood mice are found in woodland and grassland. The water vole and frogs/toads require an open water source.

A domestic fowl bone came from pit 2012. Finds of domestic fowl in Iron Age settlements are unusual as this is the period when chickens were introduced to Britain and, as rarities, may have been high status animals (Sykes 2012). However, only a single coracoid was recovered, which does not allow further appraisal. Wild mammal remains are also unusual on Iron Age sites, particularly roe deer and hare (Hambleton 2008). Roe deer were represented by a radius and humerus, the former from a subadult. The hare femur was unfused at the proximal end and broken midshaft, with

Table 4.15 Species representation by anatomical element in order of expected preservation, most robust fragments at the top (epiphysis count). Hand collected bones

Element	MIA C-shaped enclosure		Middle Iron Age settlement				Late Iron Age–Early Roman			
	C	S/G	C	S/G	P	E	C	S/G	P	E
Mandible**	2	6	12	53	2		6	14	3	
Metacarpal p	3	1	15	20		1	6	2		1
Metatarsal p	1	1	8	22	1		4	5		
Humerus d	1	2	9	15	2		8	4		1
Tibia d	1		14	11		3	3	7	1	2
Radius p	4	2	12	15	2	3	12	4		2
Pelvis	2	2	10	12		3	4	4	1	2
Scapula	2		14	14	1	1	6	1	1	3
Metacarpal d	1		2	9		1	3	3		1
Metatarsal d			2	9			1	3		2
Femur p			2	12	1	3	2	2	1	
Radius d	1	2	3	6	1	1	4	2		1
Tibia p			6	8		2	1	1		1
Femur d		1	10	6	2	2	1	2		
Humerus p			4	5	2			1		
1st phalanx*	1	1	2	2	1	1		1		1
2nd phalanx*	1		1		1	1	1			1
3rd phalanx*			1				1			
Total	22	12	129	176	14	22	60	47	4	20

*numbers adjusted for frequency bias; **mandibles with 4th deciduous premolar and permanent molars only.
C = cattle; S/G = sheep/goat; P = pig; E = equid/ horse; p = proximal; d= distal

singe marks close to the break. It is likely that both the roe deer and hare were hunted. A fragmentary piece of red deer antler was also recovered, but this could have been gathered as a shed antler or have come from a hunted animal; there were no signs of working.

Cattle and sheep/goat bones were recovered from all parts of the carcass (Table 4.15), and generally in order of expected preservation, suggesting that animals were culled, processed and disposed of on site. However, an over-abundance of cattle distal femurs, and sheep mandibles and proximal femurs was apparent suggesting that some carcass parts were brought in from elsewhere. Conversely, there were fewer finds of cattle distal metapodials than expected, and it is possible that these bones were removed for working. Sample sizes were too small for pig and horse remains to produce meaningful data, although again bones came from all parts of the carcass.

Some cattle were culled as young adults for meat, evident in those at wear stages C, E and F (Table 4.16), and in the peak in unfused bones at the intermediate fusion stage (Table 4.17). Others were older, culled as adults at stages G and G/J, and would have been kept for secondary products such as milk and/or for traction. Several porous bones and mandibles at wear stage A imply the presence of perinatal calves and that breeding took place in or around the site. Two female animals were identified from pelvis morphology. One loose third mandibular molar had a reduced posterior column due to malocclusion from the upper tooth row. Some large cattle bones were noted, but the wither heights calculated were fairly small, between 1090mm and 1160mm (mean 1120mm).

Table 4.16 Tooth wear data by phase

Cattle			Sheep/goat			Pig		
Stage	4	5	Stage	4	5	Stage	4	5
A	2		A	1		A		
B	1		B	8		B		
C	3		C	17	2	C	2	1
D		1	D	6	6	D	2	1
DE		1	E	8	1	DE		1
E	2	3	F	1	1	E		
F	1	1	G	4		F		
G	5		GH	7	2	G		
GJ	2	1	H	2		H		
H		1	J			J		
J		1						
Total	16	9	Total	56	12	Total	4	3

Sheep/goats were culled at all ages, from wear stages A to H (Table 4.16), with a peak in immature animals at wear stage C. This is consistent with the high proportion of unfused bones from the intermediate stage (Table 4.17). A high quantity of porous bones (45) coupled with perinates at wear stages A and B suggest that lambs were commonly to be found in and around the site and included animals culled for meat. One pelvis was from a male animal. Two mandibles had signs of alveolar recession in the area of the 4th premolar and first molar, one at stage one, and one at stage 2–3 (Levitan 1985). Wither heights ranged from 510mm to 590mm (mean 540mm).

Although there were few pig bones, mandibles at wear stage D and the high proportion of unfused long bones (Tables 4.16 and 4.17) imply that they were commonly

Table 4.17 Fusion data by phase

Cattle	4			C-shaped enclosure		5		6	
	U	F	%F	U	F	U	F	U	F
Neonatal		20	100		4		10		
Early	5	56	92		15		33		1
Intermediate	10	14	58	1	1		7		
Late	5	18	78		1	2	6		
Final	6	12	67	1	1	5	9	1	
Total	**26**	**120**		**2**	**22**	**7**	**65**	**1**	**1**

Sheep/goat	4			C-shaped enclosure		5		6	
	U	F	%F	U	F	U	F	U	F
Neonatal	8	27	77		1		6		
Early	19	43	69		7	3	15		
Intermediate	24	16	40			3	12		
Late	27	12	31		3	4	4		
Final	16	17	52	2		9	5		
Total	**94**	**115**		**2**	**11**	**19**	**42**		

Pig	4			C-shaped enclosure		5		6	
	U	F	%F	U	F	U	F	U	F
Neonatal		1							
Early	4	3				1	1		
Intermediate						1			
Late						2			
Final	2								
Total	**12**	**4**				**4**	**1**		

culled young for meat. Some perinates were also evident from porous bones, suggesting that there was a breeding population at the site, though no adults are represented. Of three mandibular and three maxillary canines, only one was from a female.

Although the canid remains may have included fox, all those that could be definitely identified were dogs. The dog remains were morphologically similar, coming from animals between 450mm and 570mm tall at the shoulder. Most canid and all horse remains were fused, suggesting that they were largely adult, with an emphasis on their use for herding, hunting, riding and transport. Several puppies were evident as ABGs, and it is likely that dogs were bred in and around the settlement. As well as the horse hind limb from pit 3150 with exostosis around the hock area, another fragment of tibia from pit 2258 (fill 2260) had lesions along the shaft, and thickened bone, suggesting it had an infection. Two bones were complete enough to produce wither heights, coming from small ponies 1070mm and 1200mm tall (10.2 and 11.3 hands high, respectively).

C-shaped enclosure

The C-shaped ditch contained cattle and sheep/goat in similar proportions (Table 4.13), with a few finds of pig, horse and canid (dog or fox). Because this was a long-lived feature, the recovered bone assemblage spans the late prehistoric through to the Late Roman periods. A butchered red deer tibia implies hunting, and a small, poorly preserved antler fragment was also recovered. A frog/toad bone was also present, indicating a source of water close by.

Bones were recovered from all parts of the carcass (Table 4.15), suggesting that animals were culled, processed and consumed at the site. They were generally in order of

expected preservation, but there were fewer than expected sheep/goat metapodials which may suggest that these were retained for bone working or that joints of meat, including the bones of the upper limbs (humerus, radius and pelvis) and heads, were brought into the area. However, the sample is too small to be certain. One cattle horn core had been chopped through, most likely in an effort to remove the horn sheath for working.

Mortality data took the form of tooth wear and eruption (Table 4.16) and long bone fusion (Table 4.17). A calf was present at wear stage B, as well as an older adult at stage G; this is consistent with the fusion data that includes young and mature animals. Two pelves were morphologically consistent with the presence of males.

Sheep/goats were largely adults when culled (wear stages E to GH), combining meat production with a few years of wool and/or dairy use (Table 4.16). The porous bone of a lamb was also recovered, suggesting they were bred close by. Two pelves were complete enough to identify a female and a male.

Two immature pigs were recorded at wear stage C (Table 4.16) indicating that these were slaughtered for meat. One canine came from a male. An unfused canid proximal radius indicates the presence of a young dog. A horse metatarsal had lipping at the proximal end and had been butchered at the distal end consistent with disarticulation of the lower leg.

Period 5: Late Iron Age to Early Roman

A substantial assemblage was recovered from the Late Iron Age to Early Roman deposits; it is treated as one period as all subdivisions produced similar species proportions (Fig. 4.3). Sheep/goats were slightly more common than

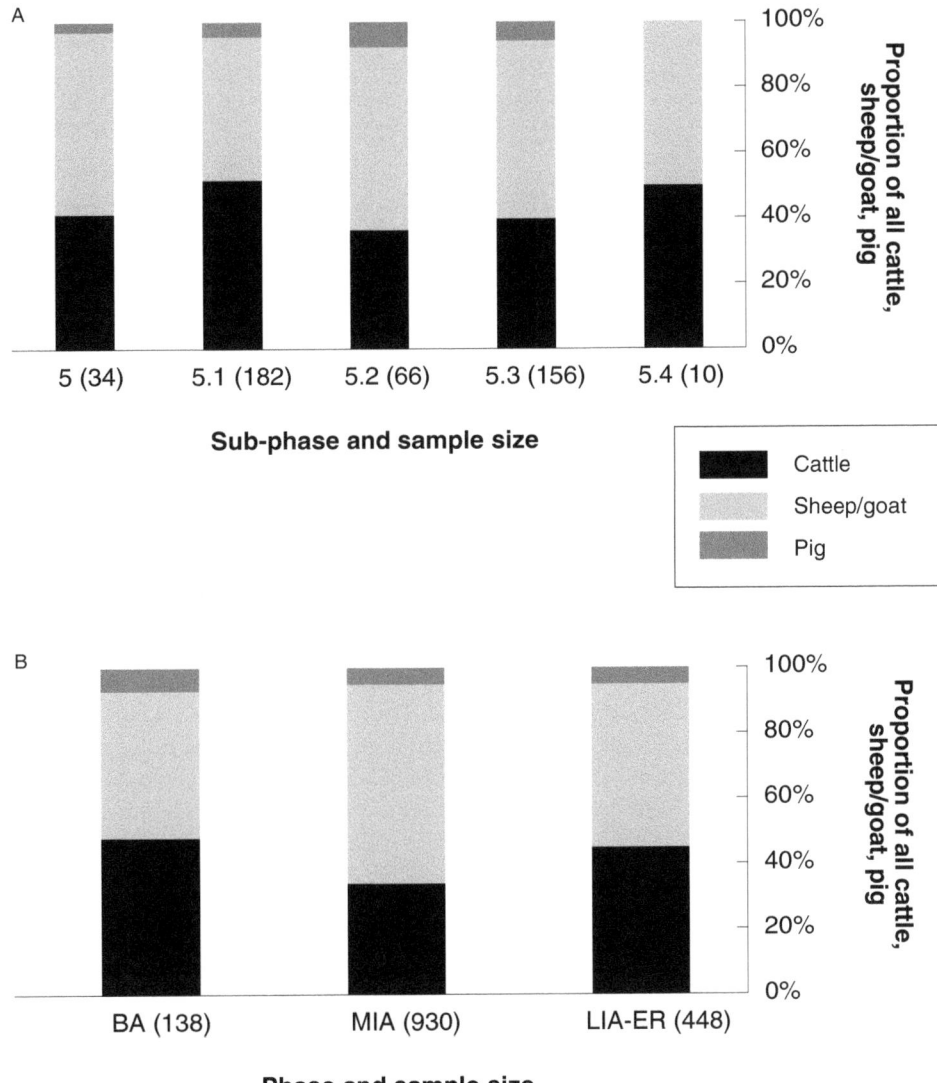

Figure 4.3 A) Proportion of all cattle, sheep/goat and pig Period 5, by sub-phase; B) proportion of all cattle, sheep/goat and pig by period

cattle, with smaller quantities of equid (horse or donkey, of which only horse was positively identified) and pig remains. Canids, red and roe deer and domestic fowl were also recovered, with the addition of micro-mammals (field vole and wood mouse) and frog/toads from the bulk soil samples. The field vole and wood mouse imply areas of cover close by, and the frogs/toads indicate open water. The red deer was represented by a first phalanx, and the roe deer by a metatarsal. These post-cranial bones provide evidence for hunting.

Unsurprisingly, given its longevity, the majority of animal remains come from ditch fills associated with enclosure 1 (Table 4.14), although substantial assemblages were also recovered from a boundary ditch re-cut, ditch 13. As for Period 4, very little zooarchaeological material came from the two roundhouses, and it is likely the ditches of these were periodically cleaned. Repeated findings of cattle vertebrae in ditches 4 and 8 of enclosure 1 suggests that they may have resulted from primary butchery events that took

place close by. All carcass parts of the main domesticates were represented, largely in order of expected preservation (Table 4.15), although with an over-representation of cattle radii, which may indicate that some joints of meat were brought in from elsewhere.

Cattle were culled at all ages. Subadult animals bred and culled for meat were evident from mandible wear stages of D to F (Table 4.16), while older, working animals used for power and/or milk were represented by wear stages G to J. A second phalanx had lipping and exostosis consistent with the use of an animal for traction. Two pelves that could be sexed came from a female and male. Several very large cattle bones were noted, but the wither heights reflected relatively small animals 1040mm to 1150mm tall (mean 1110mm). A third mandibular molar had a vestigial posterior column, which is a congenital trait.

Sheep/goats were culled at all ages, but with a peak in subadults at wear stage D (Tables 4.16 and 4.17), suggesting that most were used for meat, with a few older animals kept for wool, dairying and breeding. A few porous bones represent lambs, suggesting that sheep were bred close by. Two male animals were identified from pelvis fragments, and a polled animal was also present. Metrical data were scarce and produced two wither heights of 590mm and 600mm.

Pigs were culled young, with a focus on meat production, as indicated by both the tooth wear and fusion data (Tables 4.16 and 4.17). Two mandibular canines were from females, while two maxillary canines were from males. Equid bones were all fused, indicating adults used for riding or draught. This is reflected in a second phalanx with slight lipping to the proximal articulation and enthesophytes on the anterior aspect. These deformations may result from traction or old age. A single unfused epiphysis represents a subadult animal. One bone was complete enough to calculate a wither height of 1330mm, a pony 13 hands high.

Domestic fowl were represented by a coracoid and two femurs, both from adults, one of which was in lay and the other not. The presence of a female in lay suggests that chickens were bred or used for eggs on the settlement.

Period 6: Mid to Late Roman (AD 250 – 410)

Very few bones were recovered from Mid to Late Roman deposits. A group of cattle ribs and vertebrae radiocarbon dated to cal. AD 131–335 (SUERC-100019, see Table 5.10) were recovered from pit 1645. The partial skeletons of a sheep/goat and domestic fowl came from pit 2363 (Table 4.11), the rest from grave fills (Table 4.14). All graves containing animal remains (2295, 2309, 2315 and 2352) were part a group of surrounding posthole 2887. However, the bones were fragmentary and are unlikely to have formed grave goods or offerings of food. Two, from graves 2309 and 2313, had been gnawed, again suggesting that they were not deliberate depositions. It seems more likely that the animal remains associated with this group of graves were residual and incorporated with the backfills.

Discussion

The size of the assemblage, particularly in Periods 2, 4 and 5, has allowed detailed consideration of the diet, nature of the site, animal economy and special deposits to be undertaken.

Diet

With the exception of the symbolic deposits discussed below, the disarticulated nature of the assemblages coupled with butchery marks suggests that most of the animal bones and teeth result from food waste. Cattle and sheep/goat remains dominate all assemblages, but with a predominance of sheep/goats in the Iron Age (Fig. 4.3). However, even when sheep/goats are more common than cattle, it is likely that beef would have made up a greater proportion of the meat diet due to the relative sizes of individual animals. Lamb would have been widely available and pork less so. It is also likely that horsemeat may have

been consumed as horse bones were treated in much the same way as cattle, and a butchered metatarsal came from the Period 2 assemblage. Small-scale hunting in all periods is implied by finds of red and roe deer bones, and venison would have been an occasional treat. The consumption of hare and domestic fowl is not a given in prehistoric society; on his arrival in Britain, Caesar observed that Britons did not eat hare, cockerel or goose, instead using them for sport (McDevitte and Bohn 1869, book 5, chapter 12). However, the presence of a broken and singed hare bone implies some form of processing. Dogs are less likely to have been eaten, as they are more often recovered as partial or complete skeletons, suggesting they were treated differently to other livestock in death.

Nature of the site

A diverse group of micro-mammals, frogs and toads have provided some information regarding the site environment. Most are non-specific, simply requiring cover where they can hide from people and predators, but the water voles, frogs and toads would have required an open water source close by. While most of these small creatures would be almost invisible to those living in the area, water voles are more noticeable as they create relatively large burrows in the banks of rivers and ponds that are easily spotted, and they are often active during the day.

In all phases whole animals were culled, processed and consumed on site. However, there is some indication in the Iron Age and Late Iron Age to Early Roman periods that some meaty joints were also brought in. This may indicate households of different status receiving the better cuts of meat, or occasional meetings of groups of people from further afield, bringing joints of meat with them.

The homogeneous nature of the animal remains produced from the Iron Age pits and many of the Late Iron Age to Early Roman features suggests that they came from a similar source, with dumps of material either originating from a central midden, or from domestic households who consumed similar meat diets. This is consistent with the dearth of material associated directly with the roundhouses that implies they were regularly cleared of rubbish. The taphonomy of the animal remains implies that while bones may have been left unburied long enough for dogs to access, the presence of teeth in mandibles suggests that the delay in burial was not protracted.

Animal economy

Variable species proportions can be observed at other Late Iron Age to Early Roman sites in the region (Table 4.18), implying that mixed husbandry regimes were established on a site-by-site basis, dependent on local conditions and preferences. The predominance of sheep/goats in the Iron Age is more consistent, present between 47% and 76% of the major domesticates in all the nearby sites. The overall mean at local sites was 60%, and the proportion of sheep/goats at the Collection Management Facility (61%) sits firmly in the middle. Hambleton (1999) recognised that

Table 4.18 Comparative sites from neighbouring counties. Data from Hambleton (2009) and Allen et al. (2015). Total = total number fragments cattle, sheep/goat and pigs; numbers of cattle, sheep/ goats and pigs given as a proportion of the total

Period	Site type	Site	County	Total	Cattle	Sheep/goat	Pig
MBA	settlement	Bishops Cannings Down	Wiltshire	2069	61	36	2
MBA	settlement	Brean Down	Somerset	599	42	57	2
MBA–LBA	settlement	Dean Bottom	Wiltshire	3223	37	59	4
MBA–LBA	settlement	Middle Farm	Dorset	403	45	54	1
MBA–LBA	settlement	Poundbury	Dorset	538	83	14	3
MBA–LBA	settlement	Rockley Down	Wiltshire	180	48	49	3
LBA	settlement	Brean Down	Somerset	1728	48	49	2
LBA	settlement	Burderop Down	Wiltshire	4167	30	62	8
LBA	**droveway**	**Collection Management Facility**	**Wiltshire**	**138**	**48**	**45**	**7**
LBA	settlement	Runnymede Bridge	Berkshire	1534	28	42	30
LBA	settlement	Runnymede Bridge	Berkshire	2724	58	28	14
LBA	settlement	Runnymede Bridge	Berkshire	2103	33	29	38
LBA	occupation	Sandy Lane	Gloucestershire	209	58	25	17
MIA	settlement	Battlesbury Bowl	Wiltshire	433	31	58	10
MIA	settlement	Battlesbury Bowl	Wiltshire	2726	31	58	11
MIA	hillfort	Bury Hill	Hampshire	509	30	66	4
MIA	hillfort	Cadbury Castle	Somerset	2904	19	64	17
MIA	settlement	Cannards Grave	Somerset	525	33	60	7
MIA	occupation	Chalton Site 15	Hampshire	186	15	76	9
MIA	settlement	Claydon Pike	Gloucestershire	554	49	47	5
MIA		**Collection Management Facility**	**Wiltshire**	**930**	**34**	**61**	**5**
MIA	hillfort	Danebury	Hampshire	32581	22	65	13
MIA	hillfort	Danebury	Hampshire	7004	18	66	16
MIA	occupation	Halfpenny Lane	Oxfordshire	210	41	51	8
MIA	banjo enclosure	Micheldever Wood	Hampshire	2309	36	50	14
MIA	settlement	Mingies Ditch	Oxfordshire	1538	34	59	7
MIA	settlement	Old Down Farm	Hampshire	1534	26	68	6
MIA	banjo enclosure	Owslebury	Hampshire	4081	34	51	15
MIA	settlement	Rope Lake Hole	Dorset	385	35	58	8
MIA	settlement	Slade Farm	Oxfordshire	178	39	55	6
MIA	enclosure	Suddern Farm	Hampshire	4112	27	70	3
MIA	settlement	Tuckwells Pit	Oxfordshire	535	27	71	2
MIA	settlement	Watkins Farm	Oxfordshire	921	44	47	9
MIA	settlement	Winnall Down	Hampshire	2404	35	54	11
LIA–ERB	settlement	Abbotstone Down	Hampshire	647	50	40	10
LIA–ERB	settlement	Balksbury Camp	Hampshire	463	21	46	33
LIA–ERB	enclosure	Brighton Hill South	Hampshire	1811	52	40	8
LIA–ERB		**Collection Management Facility**	**Wiltshire**	**448**	**45**	**50**	**5**
LIA–ERB	settlement	Compact Farm	Dorset	2131	21	74	5
LIA–ERB	hillfort	Ditches	Gloucestershire	4340	47	38	15
LIA–ERB	enclosure	Easton Lane	Hampshire	202	59	34	7
LIA–ERB	settlement	Figheldean	Wiltshire	484	35	58	7
LIA–ERB	settlement	Old Down Farm	Hampshire	414	37	54	9
LIA–ERB	settlement	Owslebury	Hampshire	13609	39	42	18

sheep farming was integral and widespread in the economy of Wessex during this period, potentially reflecting a specialisation of trade and wool production, or arable production and the need for manure.

Cattle husbandry did not change much between the Iron Age and Late Iron Age to Early Roman periods, the mortality data in both periods being consistent with animals kept for meat and secondary products (Fig. 4.4). Similar mortality profiles exist for the sheep/goat assemblage for the same periods, although there was a greater emphasis on meat production, with over 80% of animals culled as sub- and young adults before reaching wear stage G (Fig. 4.4). Slightly more sheep/goats were kept into old age in the Iron Age for wool, dairy or breeding. The sheep/goats from the C-shaped ditch were the oldest, with more of an emphasis on secondary products; just under half survived to old adulthood bit the mixed date of these deposits is noted above.

The presence of perinatal lambs, calves, piglets and puppies in all the major phases implies that breeding populations were kept in and around the site. This serves to emphasise how the agricultural focus would have been implicit and woven into the daily lives of people and animals. The Iron Age assemblage produced a relatively high proportion of very young lambs (18% of mandibles at wear stages A and B) and calves (14%), which suggests a considerable quantity of breeding mortalities.

Special deposits

This assemblage has been notable for the potentially symbolic depositions present in all the major phases. The horse and canid skulls recovered from the C-shaped ditch suggests that these species were treated differently to other livestock, possibly because of the close bonds formed with people during their long working lives. Hunting was not commonly undertaken in prehistoric societies that were

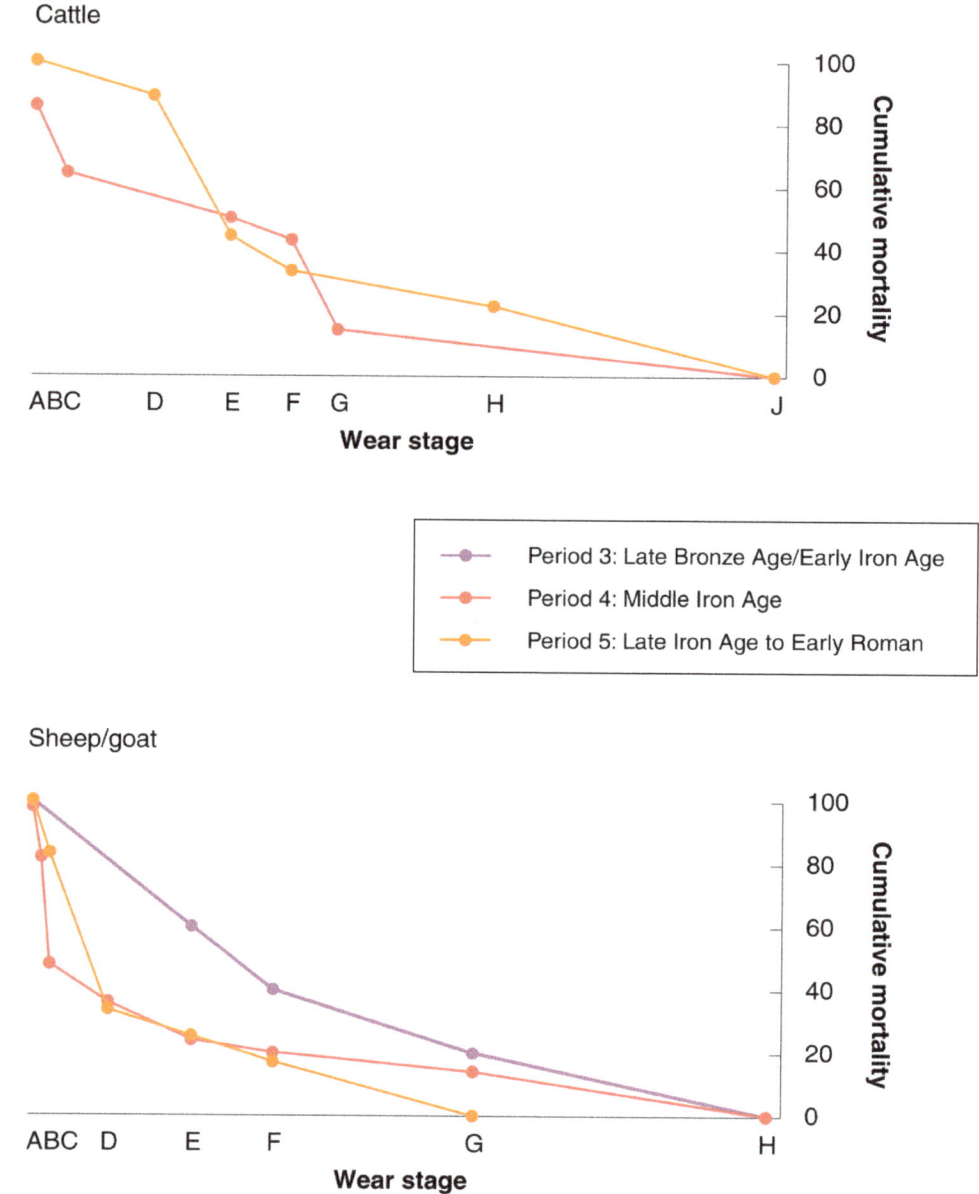

Figure 4.4 Cattle, cumulative mortality (top); sheep/goat, cumulative mortality (bottom)

focused on animals within the domestic sphere (Sykes 2014) but may have been carried out to mark special occasions (Serjeantson 2011). The presence of an Iron Age domestic fowl early in the history of the introduction of this species may reflect its use for symbolic purposes in death, particularly as it is unlikely to have been used for meat, rather being of more cosmological significance (Sykes 2012).

The deposition of ABGs and skulls in Iron Age pits is well established, particularly in southern England, where excavations at sites such as Danebury (Grant 1984, 1991), Battlesbury Bowl (Hambleton and Maltby 2008, 91), Winnall Down (Maltby 1985), Old Down Farm (Maltby 1981) and Suddern Farm (Hamilton 2000) have produced comparable types of ABGs to those recovered from the Collection Management Facility, albeit in greater

proportions (Morris 2011, table 4.3). As at the Collection Management Facility, the deposition of cattle, horse and sheep/goat partial skeletons is commonly recorded in contemporary assemblages, while dogs and perinatal mortalities are more often complete burials (ibid., 57), implying a widespread, repeated activity.

Caution is sounded against treating special deposits as separate to the rest of the zooarchaeological assemblage (Hill 1995; Morris 2008), and the presence of ABGs and skulls alongside animal bones and teeth more obviously derived from food waste at this site emphasises the potential mixing of intentions. The deposition of cattle and horse skulls and partial skeletons (sets of vertebrae and limb bones) suggest that they represent an offering following primary butchery of the carcass – although they could easily be interpreted as butchery waste. Similarly, given the relatively high proportion of perinatal sheep/goat remains recovered in the Iron Age assemblage, it is possible that the lambs disposed of in the pits were birthing fatalities. Yet the importance of sheep farming in the animal economy of this region in this period make it likely that these lambs became more than incidental losses, and were deliberately placed in pits, maybe to ensure fertility in the flock, or as an offering.

Discussion of the environmental remains

Clare Randall

Period 2: Beaker period

The plant and wood charcoal remains which date to the Beaker period appear to indicate the remnants of domestic fuel. The large number of hazelnut shell fragments recovered is fairly typical of this period (see Wyles, above) and clearly indicates the importance of the exploitation on wild foods (Moffett *et al.* 1989; Stevens 2007; Robinson 2000), perhaps also supported by the single sloe stone fragment. However, cultivation, or at least a degree of consumption of cultivated crops in the area is indicated by a few barley grain fragments. The wood charcoal largely comprised hazel, including many fragments of roundwood and charred bark, which was possibly used deliberately as a fuel. The single fragment of animal bone was a fragmentary piece of roe deer antler. The picture which is provided is of a landscape in which woodland was important and regularly exploited; the evidence for clearance and cultivation is limited.

Period 3: Late Bronze Age to Early Iron Age

The only evidence which was recovered which relates to the Late Bronze Age to Early Iron Age pit alignments was a very small amount of animal bone. This included the remains of cattle, sheep/goat and pig, which is entirely consistent with the regional pastoral economy (Hambleton 2008), as well as a few horse bones. These proportionally appear over-represented, which may be an artefact of the small assemblage. However, it may also relate to the location of deposition, perhaps deliberately marking the alignment.

Period 4: Iron Age

The Iron Age has provided us with the most extensive evidence for the plant and animal economy and the local environment. This is probably related to the number of well-preserved assemblages recovered from many of the numerous pits which characterise this period of the use of the site. The material was not evenly distributed, with an exceptionally large charred plant assemblage recovered from pit 2084.

In the main, the plant remains appear typical of settlement waste derived from different stages of crop processing with many deposits dominated by chaff remains. This was probably destined for consumption within the settlement and finds of quern fragments and rubbers within the settlement attest to the location of the processing, whilst the presence of low growing weeds suggests cutting of the cereal stems low to the ground (and possibly suggesting utilisation of the straw). The cereals were predominantly spelt wheat, with some emmer and barley, which is entirely in keeping with contemporary regional assemblages. Other minority specimens suggest other potential crops: flax, peas, and black mustard.

Weed seeds were all typical of grassland, field margins and arable environments, probably brought in with the crops, but suggesting a patchwork of land use in the surroundings. Some were typical of the well-drained calcareous soils of the ridge, whilst others suggest lower lying and wetter areas, indicating that there was access to and use of the different elements of the surrounding landscape. Some material was mineralised, and whilst the evidence for pits being used for the disposal of cess is not clear, this may represent the result of manuring, given the presence of nitrogen loving weeds.

The wood charcoal recovered presents a broadly consistent picture with a range of shrubs and small trees, such as blackthorn, Maloideae, buckthorn and dogwood. These all included branchwood or small stems. Oak, *Prunus* and Maloideae were the most abundant and frequent taxa and suggests consistency in obtaining fuelwood probably from areas of scrub (perhaps on the valley side) or hedges. Some larger trunkwood of oak, hazel, or field maple suggests areas of more established woodland which were available for exploitation.

In considering the animal economy and wild species the assemblage was dominated by sheep/goat but with cattle a significant component. This would align it with the sheep/goat dominated pastoral economies of the chalk uplands to the south, rather than the more balanced or cattle-oriented approaches of the Upper Thames Valley (Hambleton 2008, 43). The mixed structure of the sheep/goat population is typical of a balanced approach to the production of meat and secondary products as well as maintaining a breeding herd. The culling profile of the cattle is slightly different with older animals probably relating to both the production of dairy products and use for traction, suggesting some integration with the arable economy. The importance of sheep/goats and cattle in producing dairy products is underlined by the lipids identified from Iron Age pottery which suggest that whilst some vessels were used for processing animal fats (e.g., cooking meat, and both porcine and ruminant fats have been identified), the majority of the tested vessels (particularly bowls) were used for specialised processing of dairy products (see Dunne *et al.*, Chapter 3). In several of these cases, vegetable waxes were also present, suggesting the use of plants in processing or flavouring cheese, and demonstrating the integration of the products of the local area.

Horse, pig and canids were also represented, completing a fairly typical Iron Age assemblage with the horses and dogs likely used to provide transport and livestock management roles. The presence of a few domestic fowl, is slightly more unusual, as chickens were not common in Britain until the Roman period (Best *et al.* 2022) and were likely to have only been kept in small numbers around the settlement. The occasional finds of red and roe deer, and hare, are also a typical picture of limited exploitation of wild mammals, although the presence of post-cranial elements suggest active hunting. Other wild species were probably incidental inclusions reflecting the local environment with buzzard, field and water vole, wood mouse, common shrew, mole and frog/toad. All these species occur in open grassland environments as well as more wooded areas; amphibians roam some distance from ponds as do water voles.

Period 5: Late Iron Age–Early Roman

The Period 5 assemblages were more limited in both scale and scope. A large charred plant assemblage was, however, recorded from pit 2261 and was dominated by cereal chaff of spelt and emmer with weed seeds including those of brome grass, vetch/wild pea and cleavers. This assemblage may be representative of late-stage crop processing waste, and the weeds are reflective of arable land. There is nothing to indicate a change in approach from the preceding period. The range of species reflected in the animal bone assemblage is also similar to that of the Iron Age, and in similar relative proportions, and also incorporating a minor element of exploitation of wild mammals. However, there was less indication of the use of cattle for secondary products, and lipids in the pottery suggest that there was a reduction in the processing of dairy products during this period, with more vessels being used for the preparation of meat. There is also limited evidence for the use of pottery in cooking pork (see Dunne *et al.*, Chapter 3).

A moderate land mollusc assemblage from the C-shaped enclosure was dominated by remains of the intermediate species and suggests a period of stabilisation of the feature and grassy vegetation within the ditch. The species within another possibly contemporary fill may indicate some arable activity nearby, and an open landscape is probable at this time. The small vertebrate assemblage contained similar species to the Iron Age, also suggesting an open landscape and it is likely that the patchwork of habitats was retained into the Roman period, despite the establishment of clearer land boundaries.

Period 6: Mid–Late Roman

Due to the nature of the later Roman archaeology, there was a narrower scope of material to inform on the economy or environment. The charred plant remains largely came from the oven and its flue within the C-shaped enclosure. The assemblage of cereal remains in this oven was predominantly spelt, with smaller amounts of emmer and barley typical of the assemblages in the region in this period and it was dominated by chaff, although one fill was more grain rich. The chaff-rich assemblages represent late-stage crop processing waste which was used as tinder/fuel to fire the oven which seems to have been used for the parching of crops which had already been processed by winnowing, threshing and sieving. The weed seeds present were probably brought in with the crops and reflect continued production on the light calcareous soils in the area. The animal economy of the period is difficult to comment on as there were very few animal remains, although this included the partial skeletons of a sheep/goat and domestic fowl, suggesting that there was a similar range of species being exploited to that seen in the earlier Roman period.

The wood charcoal from the oven was of oak and willow/poplar. Much of this was roundwood, and it was possibly the result of coppicing. Insect tunnels were observed, and this may relate to the storage and seasoning of the wood, given that willow/poplar does not burn well when fresh. This might suggest that there was further infrastructure associated with the activity represented by the oven, but which was outside the area of the excavation.

Chapter 5
Human remains, radiocarbon and isotopic analyses

Introduction

This chapter presents the osteological analysis of all the human bone and a grave catalogue, the radiocarbon dating of the human bone and other remains, and the isotopic analysis of the human bone.

Osteological analysis
Sharon Clough

From the excavations at Collection Management Facility, Science and Innovation Park there were 11 Iron Age burials which had been made within graves or cut into pits, one ditch burial dating to the Late Iron Age or Early Roman period, one burial from the within the Iron Age C-shaped enclosure dating to the Roman period, an isolated grave of similar date and a Late Roman period cemetery of 17 individuals. A further four Roman period features contained partial human remains, which may or may not be truncated graves.

Methodology

Skeletal remains were recorded and analysed in accordance with the following guidelines; Mitchell and Brickley (2017), and Mays *et al.* (2018). Skeletal remains were recorded as presence/absence into Excel, long bones divided into five sections. Surface preservation, which is the condition of the bone cortex, was assessed using the grading system defined by McKinley (2004), ranging from 0 (excellent) to 5+ (extremely poor). Where surface preservation was variable, the overall condition was noted for the majority of the bones, and this was taken as the preservation grade.

The degree of fragmentation was recorded as either low, medium or high. Assessing fragmentation is quite subjective but can indicate where it was not possible to record metrical data, or easily observe pathological lesions. The completeness of the skeleton was assessed and expressed as a percentage, where 100% is all possible bones are present.

Age was estimated using standard ageing techniques (O'Connell 2018). For non-adults age was estimated using the stage of dental development (Moorrees *et al.* 1963), dental eruption (AlQhantani *et al.* 2010), measurements of long bones and other appropriate elements, and the development and fusion of bones (Scheuer and Black 2000; for neonates, Gowland and Chamberlain 2002). In adults age was estimated using the pelvis (Brooks and Suchey 1990; Lovejoy *et al.* 1985) and ribs (İşcan *et al.* 1984; 1985), dental attrition (Miles 1962) was noted, but as it is not always reliable, in particular for Roman period populations, it was only included where no other methods were available.

Age categories used in the text:

Neonate	38–40 weeks–1 month
Infant	1 month–1 year
Young child	1–2 years
Middle child	3–5 years
Older child	6–12 years
Adolescent	13–17 years
Young adult	18–25 years
Prime adult	25-35 years
Mature adult	35–45 years
Older adult	45+ years
Adult	18+ years
Non-adult	Less than 18 years

Sex was estimated using standard osteological techniques, such as those described in Cox and Mays (2000) and Ferembach *et al.* (1980). The pelvis was preferentially used over other areas, as the shape of the skull can be influenced by factors such as age (Walker 1995). Measurements of bones were used to supplement the morphological assessment or where no other indicators were available. Where provided results from aDNA analysis or peptide analysis confirmed the osteological assessment of sex and this is included in the catalogue.

Stature depends on two main factors, heredity and environment and can only be established in skeletons if at least one complete (or where fragmented it can be united without affecting the total length) and fully fused long bone

Table 5.1 Summary of the Iron Age burials

Cut number	Skeleton number	Fill number	Radiocarbon date	Biographic information (age/sex etc.)
Main excavation area				
1222	1206	1205	SUERC-94037	Older adult female
1207	1209	1208	SUERC-100009	Young adult female
1364	1366	1365		Neonate
1384	1489	1386		12–13 years
1658	1659	1660	SUERC-100014	Mature adult female
1781	1778	1779	SUERC-100012	Older adult female – spine joint disease
1426	1845	1632	SUERC-94041	Mature adult male – infection lower legs. Crush fracture vertebrae. Right elbow OA
1925	1926	1926		Neonate
1947	3235	1951?	SUERC-100015	Mature adult female
8068	8071	8070	SUERC-100011	Young adult female – systemic infection
330m north of the main excavation area (see Fig. 1.5)				
10003	10005 and 10005b	10004	SUERC-94043	SK 10005 prime adult/young adult female. SK 10005b 10–12 years child

is present, and the sex has been estimated. Where possible, bones from the legs were used in preference to those of the upper limb as these carry the lowest error margin (Trotter 1970) and for ease of comparison with other assemblages the left femur is preferred. Stature is then calculated using the regression formula developed by Trotter (1970) which has been proven to be sufficient for British archaeological populations (Mays 2016).

Further leg measurements were obtained from the femora and tibiae and used to calculate the shape and robusticity of the femoral shaft (platymeric index) and the tibial shaft (platycnemic index; Bass 1987).

Non-metric traits are discontinuous changes on the skeleton which do not affect an individual in life and occur in a minority of skeletons. They have been suggested to have hereditary affiliation between skeletons (Saunders 1989). It is now thought that although there may be a genetic tendency, some can be produced by mechanical stress or environment (Kennedy 1989). The non-metric traits described by Finnegan (1978) and Berry and Berry (1967) were observed and recorded. Only the results for the adult skeletons are presented and only those traits where there was at least one instance recorded is detailed.

Skeletal pathology and/or bony abnormality were described and differential diagnoses explored with reference to standard texts (e.g. Ortner and Putschar 1981; Resnick 1995; Aufderheide and Rodriguez-Martin 1998; Waldron 2009). Where it was considered appropriate the extent and range of pathology was explored by calculating crude prevalence rates (CPR – the number of individuals with a condition out of the total number of individuals observed) and true prevalence rates (TPR – the number of elements or teeth with a particular condition out of the number of elements or teeth observed).

The dentition was recorded using the Zsigmondy/Palmer system (Hillson 1996) and coded 1–5 (1 present in occlusion, 2 present but loose, no alveolar, 3 missing ante-mortem, 4 missing post-mortem (alveolar present), 5 probably congenitally absent, blank – bone and tooth missing) pathologies were recorded with reference to Dias and Tayles (1997) (caries, granulomas, abscess), Brothwell (1981) (calculus) and Ogden (2008) (periodontal).

Results

Period 4: Iron Age

There were ten burials dating to the Iron Age within the main area of excavation and another located some distance away (around 300m to the north) and these are summarised in Table 5.1.

All except one burial were articulated inhumations and positioned in various degrees of flexion on the left or right side, or face down. The interred body position and the resulting skeletal arrangement were not necessarily the same, as movement can occur if the body is left uncovered for a period of time, there are voids within the backfill (from the inclusion of rocks for example), clothing or bindings deterioration rate etc. It is for example, entirely possible that a tightly bound body, placed propped up at the side of a pit, may end up facedown unintentionally. So, any inferences from the final body position must be considered against post-depositional movement.

Completeness/condition

Completeness of the skeleton was influenced by the extent of vertical truncation on the feature. The shallower features, or where the skeleton lay near the top of the feature, tended to have less completeness, usually the highest element, the head, had been removed, along with extremities, such as feet (Table 5.2). SK 1659 is an example of this where only the torso and parts of an arm and leg survived. The older child (SK 10005b) from grave 10003 had the least amount of skeleton surviving (10%). This individual was not recognised during excavation and had been mixed in with SK 10005 in the same bag as the bones of the shoulder area and teeth of that individual. Surviving elements were proximal femur, thoracic vertebral bodies and arches and teeth. This would suggest that they had been directly underneath the adult skeleton, perhaps in a crouched position.

The bone surface condition varied from 2–5 with most 2 or 3. Both of the sets of skeletal remains from burial 10003 (located away from the main area) had a very poor bone surface condition which affected observation of many features and may have contributed to the lack of elements from the non-adult. SK 1209, despite having 75% of the skeleton present (mostly the cranium was absent) had poor bone surface condition, grade 4, which may have affected observation of some more subtle changes. Despite the suggestion that infants and neonates are often absent due to their poorer chances of bone survival (Lewis 2007) the neonates SK 1366 and SK 1926 were in no better or worse condition than the adults.

Age and sex

There were eight adults and four children in total from the Iron Age burials. The burial was located away from the others (10003) contained two individuals, an adult female and a child *c.* 10–12 years, all the other burials had only one individual.

The adult burials in pits and graves within the settlement area were nearly all female with only one male burial (aged 35–45 years). The female ages were young (18–25 years), mature (35–45 years) or older (45+ years) with the 25–35 years age group not represented. There was one older child or adolescent aged 12–13 years, there were no children, but there were two neonates.

The combination of pit burials and scattered graves do not represent a cemetery as such, but individual interments over a period of time and are a funerary rite allocated to certain individuals, while the location of the majority of disposals of the dead is unknown. Therefore, examining the demography of the group is unlikely to be representative of the living.

Some trends though have been observed from 514 inhumations across 100 sites (Roth 2016). Male inhumations are more frequent than female (ibid., 65), which is in contrast to the results from the Collection Management Facility. The study (Roth 2016) also identified that age distribution of those interred during the Iron Age in general reflects an expected distribution for a normal attrition, with a high number of neonates, few children and adolescents and the majority were adult when they died. There are individual sites where this is not the case, which may reflect local conditions. Given the small number of burials from the Collection Management Facility, the absence of children may be reflective of the low quantity of examples rather than a deliberate exclusion.

Metrics

Only two of the adults had a left femur complete enough for stature estimation, SK 1209 had a right femur and SK 8071 a left humerus (Table 5.3).

Average stature for the period is quoted as: males 164–174cm (mean 168cm) and for females 154–164cm (mean

Table 5.2 Completeness and bone surface condition of the Iron Age skeletal remains

Skeleton number	Completeness (%)	Bone surface (Grade 1–5+)
1206	80	3
1209	75	4
1366	60	3
1489	80	2
1659	20	3
1778	60	3
1845	90	2
1926	20	3
3235	80	2
8071	90	2
10005	40	5
10005b	10	5

Table 5.3 Stature estimation for the Iron Age adult individuals

Skeleton number	Long bone (cm)	Calculated stature (cm) (after Trotter 1970)
1209 (female)	Right femur, 41.5	156.6 (±3.72)
1845 (male)	Left femur, 44.0	166.1 (±3.72)
3235 (female)	Left femur, 39.2	150.9 (±3.72)
8071 (female)	Left humerus, 28.0	152 (±4.45)

Table 5.4 Platymeric index of the femur

Sex	Hyperplatymeric (<74.9)	Platymeric (75.0–84.9)	Eurymeric (85.0–99.9)	Stenomeric (>99.9)
Male	–	1	–	–
Female	3	2	–	–

Table 5.5 Platycnemic index of the tibia

Sex	Hyperplatycnemic (<55.0)	Platycnemic (55.0–62.9)	Mesocnemic (63.0–69.9)	Eurycnemic (>69.9)
Male	–	–	1	–
Female	–	–	3	2

162cm) (Roberts and Cox 2003). This information is based, however, on about 100 individuals for males and 70 for females as inhumation burials in the period are scarce. It would suggest though that the male (5 ft 5 inches) is about average for the period, but that the females are all shorter than the mean and two are below the range; SK 3235 is particularly petite at 4ft 11 inches (150.9cm).

Platymeric indices

Measurements were taken from the femur and tibia to calculate platymeric and platycnemic indices (Table 5.4 and 5.5) which indicates the extent of flattening of the shafts from back to front. The flattening of the neck of the femur is likely to be due to mechanical adaptation and appears to vary dependent on time period and population (Brothwell 1981, 89). Similar to platymeria, platycnemia is likely to be caused by mechanical activity. Earlier populations are more likely to be platycnemic, so it is interesting that the Iron Age individuals at the Collection Management Facility were all mesocnemic or eurycnemic.

Table 5.6 Nonmetric traits amongst the Iron Age individuals

Non-metric trait	Number of individuals
Tibia squatting facet	3
Humeral septal aperture	1
Patella notch	1
Calcaneal double facet	3
Lambdoid ossicle	1 (7 left 1 right)

Non-metric traits

Non-metric traits are used in the study of human variation; some are affected by environmental factors whereas others are genetic in origin. Clusters of traits thought to be genetic may suggest familial relationships. Cranial traits are often considered to be more hereditary than post-cranial, unfortunately in the present assemblage the cranial traits were not as observable since the cranium was the most often area affected by truncation.

The lower limb non-metric traits were the most commonly observed and are likely activity related (Table 5.6). In particular, the distal tibia squatting facet develops from long periods spent in the squatting position and is commonly observed in archaeological populations (Brothwell 1981, 90). The low quantity of traits observed is partly due to preservation and number of individuals, but may also indicate a homogenous population, conducting similar activities and from a similar genetic background.

Dental and oral health

There was a total of 187 adult teeth, of which 131 were in sockets available for observation. A further 23 were absent ante-mortem, and probably lost after suffering caries.

There were two individuals who appeared to have very little dental attrition for their age (SK 1206 and SK 1209). Dental variation was present in the dentition of SK 1489 (non-adult) where the upper left second incisor was out of line (crowding). SK 8071 had an absent upper second incisor, there was no space in the dental arcade and none either for the third molars except the lower right. The second deciduous molar was retained, and it is likely that the upper right deciduous canine was also retained as there was an alveola for it.

Periodontal disease was only observed in the alveolar margins of SK 1845, affecting 23 sockets at grade 2 or 1. A single example of caries was observed in the dentition of three skeletons. For the period 3.2% of total burials or 4.8% of sexed adults had carious lesions (Roberts and Cox 2003, 100). With three of the eight adults in the present group affected, this is over a third and therefore much higher than frequency rates observed elsewhere. However, the low number of individuals with observable teeth probably over-inflates the observed rate.

Calculus affected four dentitions, and in two dentitions all the teeth were affected. In the other two, three or more teeth were affected. Levels of calculus for this period were as low as 5.4% of all individuals (Roberts and Cox 2003, 100), whereas in the present assemblage half of the adults

were affected, although again, this is based on a small number of examples. A single abscess was observed on SK 1845, in the maxillary left first molar.

Skeletal pathology

Skeletal pathological lesions are described here by individual as the quantity of individuals is low and therefore prevalence rates will be highly over inflated (as demonstrated in the dental section).

SK 1206, older adult female, fourth lumbar vertebra had large osteophytes on the anterior body extending in a superior direction. The other lumbar vertebrae were absent, so not available for observation. *Cribra orbitalia* was present in the left orbit.

SK 1209, young adult female, had a distinctive tendon insertion on both humerii. The insertion for the deltoid was raised and slightly pointed.

SK 1489, 12–13-year older child/adolescent, the long bones measured short compared to the dental age. This is based on data from modern populations (Maresh 1970) and it may be that they are not applicable to an Iron Age individual. Or it may indicate that growth had been affected by poor diet or ill health (Lewis 2007, 66). *Cribra femora* was present bilaterally, this porosity on the femoral neck has an uncertain aetiology and may indicate metabolic or physiological distress (Erkelens 2017).

SK 1778, older adult female, had spinal degenerative joint disease, however, poor preservation prevented full observation.

SK 1845, mature adult male, had a crush fracture to second to fourth lumbar vertebrae. The fourth lumbar vertebra was shaped as a wedge, third lumbar had an indentation to the superior body, second lumbar had a slight wedge-shape. Some minor osteophytes had developed on the body perimeter in response. Further there was a healed rib fracture on a right side rib near to the costal end. One rib had an indentation in an oval shape instead of a complete fracture. The stage of healing for both fractures was similar, but it is not possible to determine if they had occurred at the same event.

In addition to the trauma the bilateral distal tibiae had on all sides periostitis in the form of active grey woven bone, the fibulae were also affected (Fig. 5.1). The medial surface had the greatest quantity and on the right side some extended up to mid shaft. On the lateral side it was present just inferior to proximal joint surface. The bilateral nature of the infection suggests either something systemic, or a skin ulceration at the ankles/lower legs. Without any other areas of the skeleton affected it is not possible to determine the aetiology.

SK 1845 had further skeletal changes with bilateral erosive lesions on the medial aspect of the first metatarsal heads, these were small cortical defects with smooth sides. They may be caused by impingement of the blood supply. Similar lesions were observed on the third metatarsal proximal joint surface with the cuneiform (affecting both bones) on the

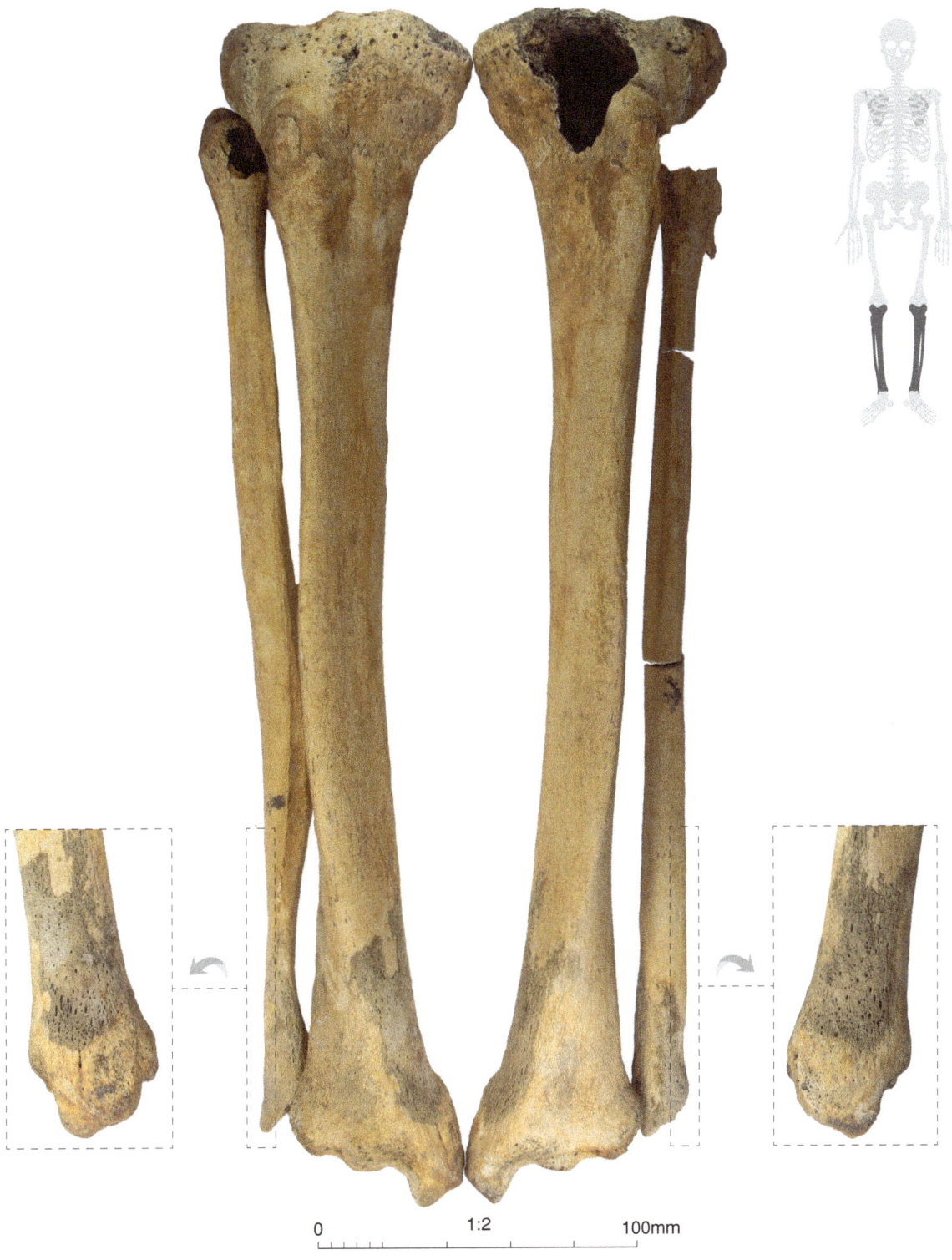

Figure 5.1 Left and right tibia and fibula of SK 1845, mature adult male, with periostitis on the lower shaft medial and lateral surfaces of both bones

inferior aspect and they are probably related. The posterior parietal bones and occipital had 'orange peel' porosity on the ectocranial surface. The aetiology of this is unknown, but may relate to scalp infection, or be a part of older age changes as it is commonly observed in older adults. The right elbow had osteoarthritis in the form of eburnation on

the ulna head lateral surface and the corresponding distal humerus posterior joint surface.

SK 3235, mature adult female, had exotosis on the left humerus lateral upper shaft (which had a post-mortem break just below, so could not observe fully). This is the deltoid muscle attachment site in which which it was noted

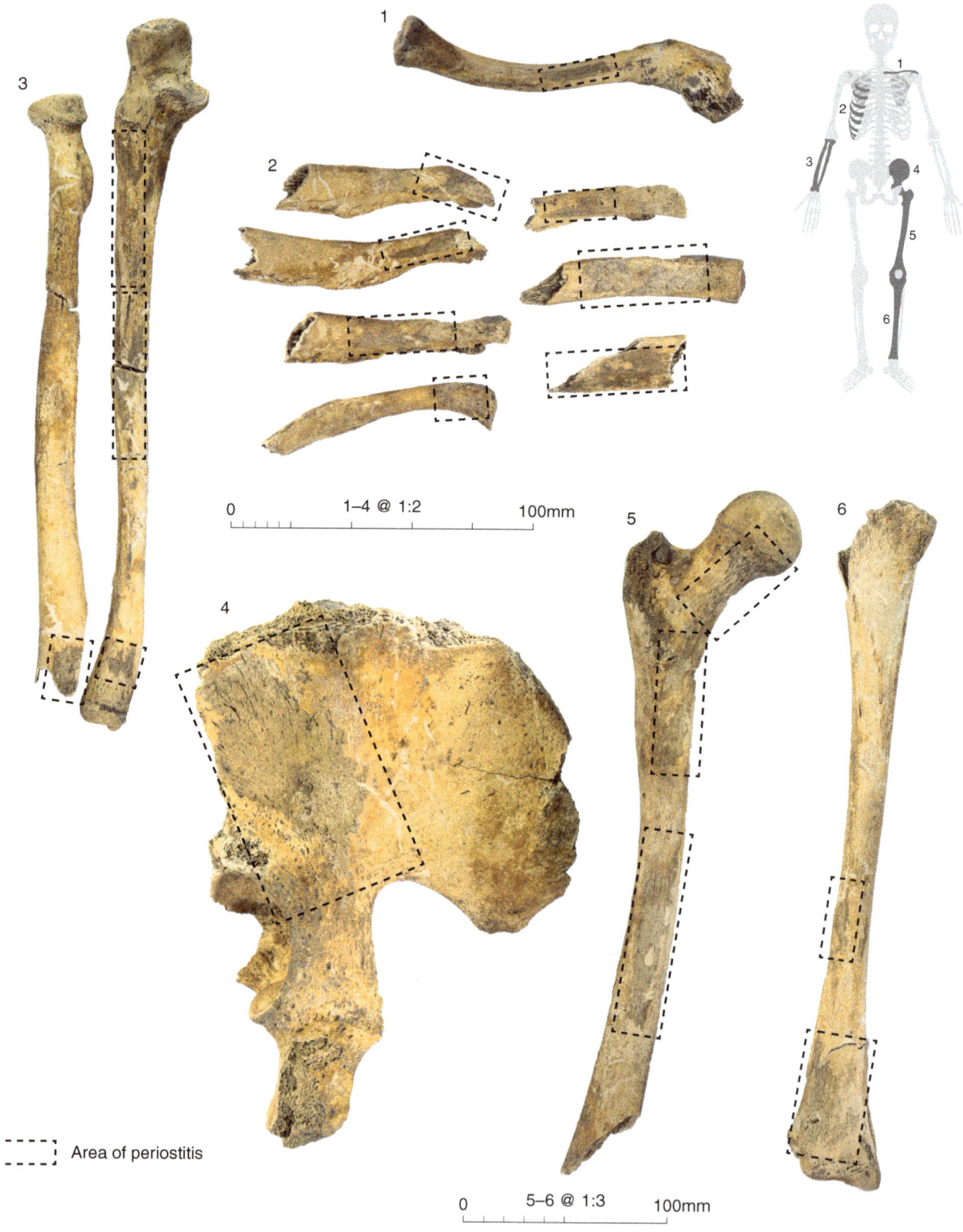

Figure 5.2 SK 8071, young adult female: multiple areas of periostitis 1) inferior side of the left clavicle, 2) rib shafts, 3) right radius and ulna, 4) left hip bone or os coxa posterior side, 5) posterior left femur, 6) posterior left tibia

SK 1209 had a prominent insertion point. It is possible that a specific activity is affecting the muscle which is used in the movement of the shoulder sideways, front and back.

SK 8071, young adult female, had a systemic infection which caused periostitis to occur all over the skeleton (a proliferative periosteal reaction). A grey layer (active) of periostitis was present often running along the deep muscle attachment sites all over both sides of the skeleton (Fig. 5.2). Due to the generalised nature of the periosteal reaction, it is not possible to determine the aetiology of the ailment. It was though active at the time of death and affected the whole body, so likely to have caused the individual to be quite unwell for a period of time. There were also endocranial lesions of the capillary type and *cribra orbitalia* (grade 3, after Stuart-Macadam 1991) and *cribra femora*, both which indicate metabolic and physiological ill health.

The female had a developmental anomaly of a bifid sacrum (Fig. 5.3). The age at death mean that the sacrum had not quite fused, but the spinous processes should have been more complete and were not fused below the first sacral vertebra. The first sacral spinous processes almost joined, but not quite. Further anomalies were dental with the retention of deciduous second molar in the mandible. There was an alveola for a deciduous canine and also possibly the upper second incisors. None of these anomalies would have particularly noticeable or affected daily life in anyway.

Period 5: Late Iron Age–Early Roman

SK 1076 was recovered from a ditch. It was estimated to be a mature adult female, 65% completeness and grade 3 bone surface. Ancient DNA analysis confirmed the estimate of female. In addition to the 65% completeness of the skeleton 12 loose teeth were recovered, and four had been lost ante-mortem, which affected the dental attrition. Nine of the teeth had calculus on the roots and there was alveolar height loss.

Stature was estimated to be 150.7cm (± 3.72) for the right femur. The femur was left 74 and right 76 on the platymeric index. These indices are the same as those observed for the Iron Age individuals. There was no observable pathology, though for example, the vertebral bodies were not preserved, an area where lesions are commonly observed.

Period 6: Mid–Late Roman

SK 2446 C-shaped enclosure

An older adult female with 80% completeness and bone surface grade 3 was recovered from within the C-shaped enclosure. Though fairly complete the fragmentation meant that no metrics were possible. It was possible to observe squatting facets and double calcaneal facets on both sides. The dentition comprised nine teeth, three were absent ante-mortem and 11 were absent post-mortem but the alveolar were present. There was an apical granuloma on the left maxillary canine and a cyst on the left mandible at the apex of both premolars with a smooth thin edge.

The neck vertebrae (cervical) had evidence of degeneration of the joints, which is commonly observed in older adults. The mid spine (thoracic vertebrae) had Schmorl's nodes, but no evidence of further joint degeneration. The left ischial tuberosity (pelvis) had what may have been a healed fracture, or a result of extensive muscle trauma. There was smooth extra bone growth creating a wave-like crest, then the remainder was a rough irregular surface, elements of which were porous. There was no normal morphology remaining, but this was isolated since the rest of the ischium was normal and the acetabulum unaffected. Avulsion

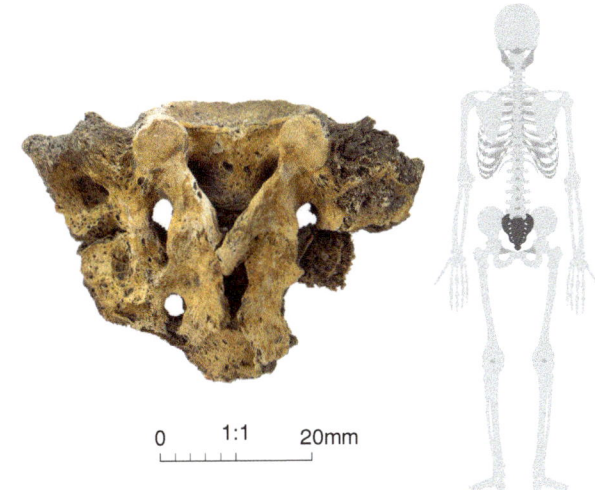

Figure 5.3 SK 8071, young adult female: posterior view of sacrum, bifid sacral arch at the first sacral level

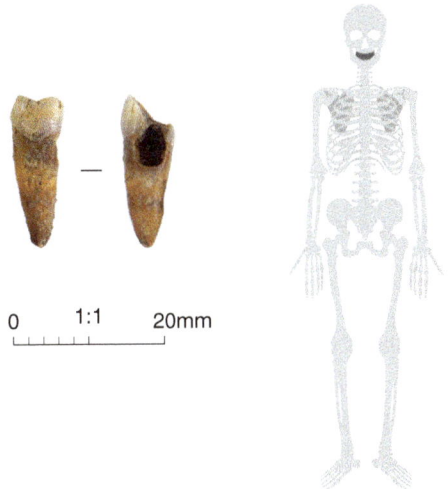

Figure 5.4 SK 12053, older adult male: angled wear on the first maxilla incisor tooth

fractures can occur at this location, however, the bony changes were not consistent with a healed fracture as such.

Isolated grave SK 12053

This grave located away from the others contained the remains of an older adult male, it was 50% complete and the bone surface was grade 1.

No pathological lesions were observed, and the remaining dentition suggested that either he had an odd bite or there was extra masticatory wear, since only the incisors had very angled wear, and not adjacent premolars (Fig. 5.4). However, the ante-mortem loss of the molars may have meant that they had been used to chew with. There was a caries on the right maxilla first and second incisor.

Cemetery

There were 17 graves which lay close to one another and are considered as a contemporary group. They all contained a single interment.

Table 5.7 Roman cemetery summary

Cut number of grave	Skeleton Number	Completeness	Age	Sex	Comments
2295	2297	80%	Older adult	Female	on left side coffin nails and hobnails
2309	2311	70%	Older adult	Female	supine extended
2315	2314	80%	Mature adult	Female?	Prone?
2316	2318	80%	Older adult	Female	supine extended; hobnails
2320	2321	75%	Older adult	Male	supine flexed; hobnails
2323	2324	90%	Older adult	Male	supine extended
2326	2327	80%	Older adult	Male	supine extended slightly flexed; hobnails
2329	2330	80%	Older adult	Female	supine extended right side angle; hobnails
2332	2333	80%	Older adult	Male	supine extended; hobnails and cleats
2335	2336	80%	Older adult	Female	supine extended left side lean; hobnails
2338	2339	90%	Older adult	Female	supine extended; hobnails and cleats
2341	2342	85%	Mature adult	Male	supine extended flexed legs to left
2344	2345	80%	Older adult	Female?	supine extended; hobnails and cleats
2349	2350	90%	Older adult	Male	supine extended
2352	2353	90%	Older adult	Male	supine extended
2863	2865	70%	Young adult	Female	prone
2878	2879	90%	6–8 years	N/A	prone

f?– possibly female ,   m? – possibly male,   N/A – not applicable since it is a non-adult

Completeness

All the 17 individuals were over 70% complete. With no intercutting of graves and limited vertical truncation the majority of the skeleton was available for observation in most cases.

Bone surface condition

Five were grade 4, 11 were grade 3 and two were grade 2, this meant that the majority had erosion to the bone surface which obscured observation of the more subtle changes. Fragmentation was generally high, which reduced the availability of long bones for measurements.

Demography

As with many other Roman period cemeteries there is a notable lack of those under 18 years of age (Table 5.7). One individual out of 17 was a child of 6–8 years and there were no neonates. The bias towards adult burial in cemeteries of this period is often observed and the dearth of neonates is often explained by the preference for burying this age group closer to the home (Moore 2009). However, the lack or low numbers of all the other children and adolescents is not so easily explained, other than perhaps we are incorrect in our assumption that there would be a high mortality rate in the age group in this period.

There were nine adult females to seven adult males buried in the cemetery. The slightly more females is interesting when it is commonly observed that for Roman period cemeteries there are always more males, particularly in the urban cemeteries (Pearce 2011). Another small rural Roman cemetery at Childrey Warren, Oxfordshire (Clough 2023, 60) had a similar imbalance in favour of the females and it has been suggested that perhaps this is where the 'missing' females from urban cemeteries are (ibid., 60), they are in the rural cemeteries.

The age groups for the adults indicate that most of them were over 45 years when they died, and some were likely to be much older, but the limitations of the aging methods and extent of the skeletal preservation means it cannot be more accurate.

Stature estimation

Only eight of the adults had long bones complete enough for stature estimation. None were the left femur, which is the most commonly used for comparison with other sites. There were three right femora (all male) and the remainder were humerii; estimates from lower limbs bones are more precise. The range and mean (Table 5.9) were comparable with other Roman contemporary sites.

Non-metric traits

As with the earlier periods, non-metric variation was low and in most cases was observed on a single individual. As this was the case the true prevalence rates have not been given here (Table 5.8). Only the double calcaneal facet was present on more than two individuals (total seven) which out of the 16 adults is nearly half the population. This would suggest that it is 'normal' variation for this group.

Dental and oral health

The total (adult) dentition was 201 with 18 of those as loose teeth and 132 lost ante-mortem (and 48 post-mortem). Of the teeth present in the entire assemblage there were 14 examples of caries, all but two were one per individual, and SK 2324 had four.

Calculus affected nine individuals, totalling 61 teeth with some level of calculus. SK 2318 and SK 2865 had the most teeth with calculus. The presence of calculus can cause periodontal disease and this was present for 89 alveolar, across six individuals. Two of these had all their teeth affected and it caused complete root exposure in some instances. Six individuals each had two or three abscesses and SK 2336 had a cyst on the right maxilla canine.

Enamel hypoplasia was almost not present at all with only one line observed on SK 2350, though with calculus affecting the teeth it may have obscured some observations.

The calculus was generally medium, slight or flecks on one side, so unlikely to affect observation to a great extent. With only one skeleton having a growth arrest period resulting in an enamel defect does indicate that food and health during childhood was generally consistently sufficient so as to not result in a permanent indicator. Non-metric variation of the teeth was not present. One skeleton SK 2327 all of the mandibular teeth had been lost ante-mortem (edentulous). Chipping or cracking of the upper incisors was present on SK 2321 and SK 2353.

With only 16 adult dentitions to observe the true prevalence rates (TPR) have not been calculated as this is likely to over inflate incidence. Access to wider variety of foods and consuming more sucrose in their diet it has been observed that compared to the Iron Age the Roman period has an increase in dental disease (Roberts and Cox 2003).

Pathology

Joint disease was the most common affliction observed on the skeleton. This is a reflection of the age of the population as joint disease increases with age (Rogers and Waldron 1995). Joint disease affected 15 of the individuals either on the spine or ex-spine (or both).

Non-spinal – joint degeneration

There were two individuals (SK 2321 and SK 2327) with evidence for joint degeneration in the form of osteophytes both were older adults males. For SK 2321 it affected the hip joint, the bilateral acetabulum on the superior edge of the articular surface and SK 2327 it also affected the hips and included the shoulder joints, mid-clavicle to manubrium and first distal pedal phalanx (big toe).

Non-spinal osteoarthritis

The wrist bone, and in particular the base of the thumb, were the most commonly affected joint with osteoarthritis (OA). OA affects only synovial joints and the prevalence increases with age. The thumb and DIP joints are more commonly found to be affected in women (Rogers and Waldron 1995, 32), so it is interesting that in this assemblage there are more men with the condition.

SK 2336 older adult male and SK 2345 older adult female? both had the right thumb base affected with OA. For the male (SK 2336) the left had joint affected, but not by eburnation (indicative of OA), and distal phalanges had osteophytic growth. SK 2327 older adult male, had left and right wrists affected in addition to the right thumb base. This individual also had extensive cervical spine OA (below).

SK 2350 older adult male, the left wrist had OA affecting the distal left ulna and lunate joints surfaces. The left hip had extensive changes, which were possibly secondary to trauma or a developmental condition. It had resulted in extensive osteophytic growth approximately 30mm and had re-shaped the joint surface. Eburnation and porosity/subchondral pitting were present in both the acetabulum and femoral head.

Table 5.8 Non-metric variation amongst the Roman skeletons

Non-metric trait	Skeleton number
Retained metopic suture	SK 2318 and SK 2350
Lambdoid ossicles	SK 2324 (and ossicle at lambda) and SK 2350
Inca bone	SK 2353
Atlas double facet	Right side SK 2339
Squatting facet	SK 2330 and SK 2350
Third trochanter	Left and right SK 2314
Double calcaneal facet	SK 2318, 2321, 2327, 2336, 2339, 2350 and 2353
Humeral septal aperture	SK 2865

Table 5.9 Collection Management Facility estimated stature compared with other Roman sites

Site	Male cm	Female cm
Collection Management Facility (8 individuals, 4 male, 4 female)	Range 165.9–167.8 (mean 167)	Range 159.8–164.8 (mean 161.3)
Bridges Garage, Cirencester (Holbrook *et al.* 2017)	170.11 mean	158.29 mean
Combined sites (Roberts and Cox 2003)	Range 159–178 (mean 169)	Range 150–168 (mean 159)
Childrey Warren (Clough 2023)	Range 1.67–1.79 (mean 1.71)	Range 1.54–1.67 (mean 1.6)

Spinal – joint degeneration

The spines of seven individuals (SK 2311, SK 2330, SK 2333, SK 2339, SK 2342, SK 2345, SK 2350) were affected by either osteophyte growth, porosity, Schmorl's nodes or a combination of all three. These changes are considered a normal part of aging (Rogers and Waldron 1995, 25) and are observed very commonly in archaeological populations.

With such low numbers of individuals, it was not possible to examine this by location in the spine, age or sex, but to note that it affected both the mature and older adults and all parts of the spine.

SK2350, male older adult, entire spine was affected by joint degeneration and in addition the thoracic and lumbar facets of the vertebral bodies had eburnation indicative of osteoarthritis.

Spinal osteoarthritis

SK 2327 male older adult, had extensive OA in the cervical spine (neck). This affected all the cervical vertebrae bodies and articular facets, with eburnation present in CV1, 2 and 4. The first three lumbar vertebrae were broken, making observation difficult, but LV4 and 5 were affected by body porosity and osteophytosis. SK 2336 and SK 2353 both older adult males had similar locations for OA on the right sacrum articular facet for fifth lumbar vertebra.

Diffuse idiopathic skeletal hyperostosis (DISH)

SK 2324 older adult male, the fourth to tenth thoracic vertebrae had the classic 'candle-wax' appearance of additional bone growth of diffuse idiopathic skeletal hyperostosis (DISH) running down the right-hand side (Fig. 5.5). Thoracic vertebrae 7–8 were completely fused

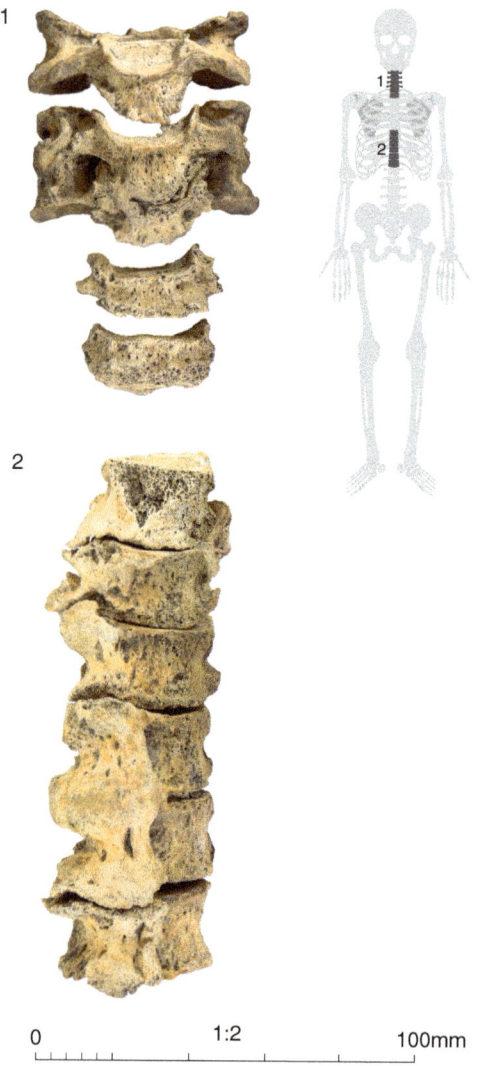

Figure 5.5 SK 2324, older adult male: 1) cervical vertebrae fusion between CV4 and CV5, 2) Diffuse Idiopathic Skeletal Hyperostosis (DISH) bone growth on the right side of the thoracic vertebrae

by the bone growth. The lumbar vertebra 3–4 had excessive growth on middle and left side of the bodies. Lumbar vertebra 1–2 and TV12 also had large outgrowths of osteophytes on the middle left side. Cervical vertebra 4–5 were also fused at body and facets (Fig. 5.5), with OA on the left CV2–3 facets and the bodies had porosity.

DISH is more prevalent in males than females and increases with age, it is associated with diabetes and obesity (Rogers and Waldron 1995, 54). The inference here is that SK 2324 may have had access to better and/or more foods than his counterparts which resulted in him becoming obese and developing DISH.

Fractures

Healed fractures were observed on four male individuals (all older adult). These were most commonly rib fractures (SK 2327, SK 2350 and SK 2324). SK 2324 also had the right tibia and fibula fused together at the proximal joint which

most likely has been caused by direct trauma. SK 2333 had compression fracture to the third lumbar vertebra, causing vertical height reduction of the body. In addition, the right first metacarpal proximal joint surface had a possible fracture as the surface was uneven and sloped.

Other trauma

In SK 2350, male older adult, the left and right big toe (first metatarsal) had a cortical defect, as a small circular indent on the concave surface. The articulating proximal phalanx joint surface was wider as a result with an irregular patch of bone. This is probably caused by pressure on the joint resulting in impingement of blood supply.

SK 2353, male older adult, had a possible peri-mortem cranial sharp force trauma (Fig. 5.6). The right parietal bone had an elongated opening with depressed bent bone, with radiating fracture lines. The lower edge is irregular and top edge internal and sharp. Something elongated and sharp and at a steep angle had penetrated the endocranium, there were no other signs of weapon trauma. Taphonomic processes, however, may also have caused the opening, so the origin is uncertain.

Infection

The only non-adult in the cemetery SK 2879, 6–8 years had infection in the form of fine grey periostitis as a layer on the surface of three ribs at the sternal end (Fig. 5.7). In addition, there were endocranial lesions on the parietal and occipital bones (Fig. 5.8). These may be related and indicate a systemic infection. They were also short for the dental age (long bone length indicated 5.5 years, Maresh (1970), whereas the teeth indicated 7–11 years. This could be genetic (since height is 80% inherited Lettre (2011)), though coupled with the evidence for an infection, this may have reduced/stopped growth. There was also bilateral *cribra femora* and bilateral *cribra orbitalia* type 2 (after Stuart-Macadam 1991), which indicate metabolic or physiological distress (Erkelens 2017).

SK 2327, a male older adult, had on the right-side maxillary sinus indication of chronic sinusitis. The whole floor of the sinus was covered in remodelled bone as a thickened layer. There was microporosity but thickened and striated and not web-like. Left side was affected to a much lesser extent. It is to be noted that there was much dental loss (ante-mortem) and thinning and remodelling of the alveolar bone. Chronic sinusitis is often associated with living in conditions of high air pollution, such as open fires and is seen more commonly in urban assemblages (Waldron 2009,115). The right mandible body at the level of the molars of SK 2314, mature adult ?female, had infection in the form of grey fine periostitis. It is was probably caused by the dental disease present in the molars.

Cribra femora

Other than the child (SK 2879) there was only one other individual with *cribra femora* (CF) – SK 2865 the only young adult female. The orbits were not observable for

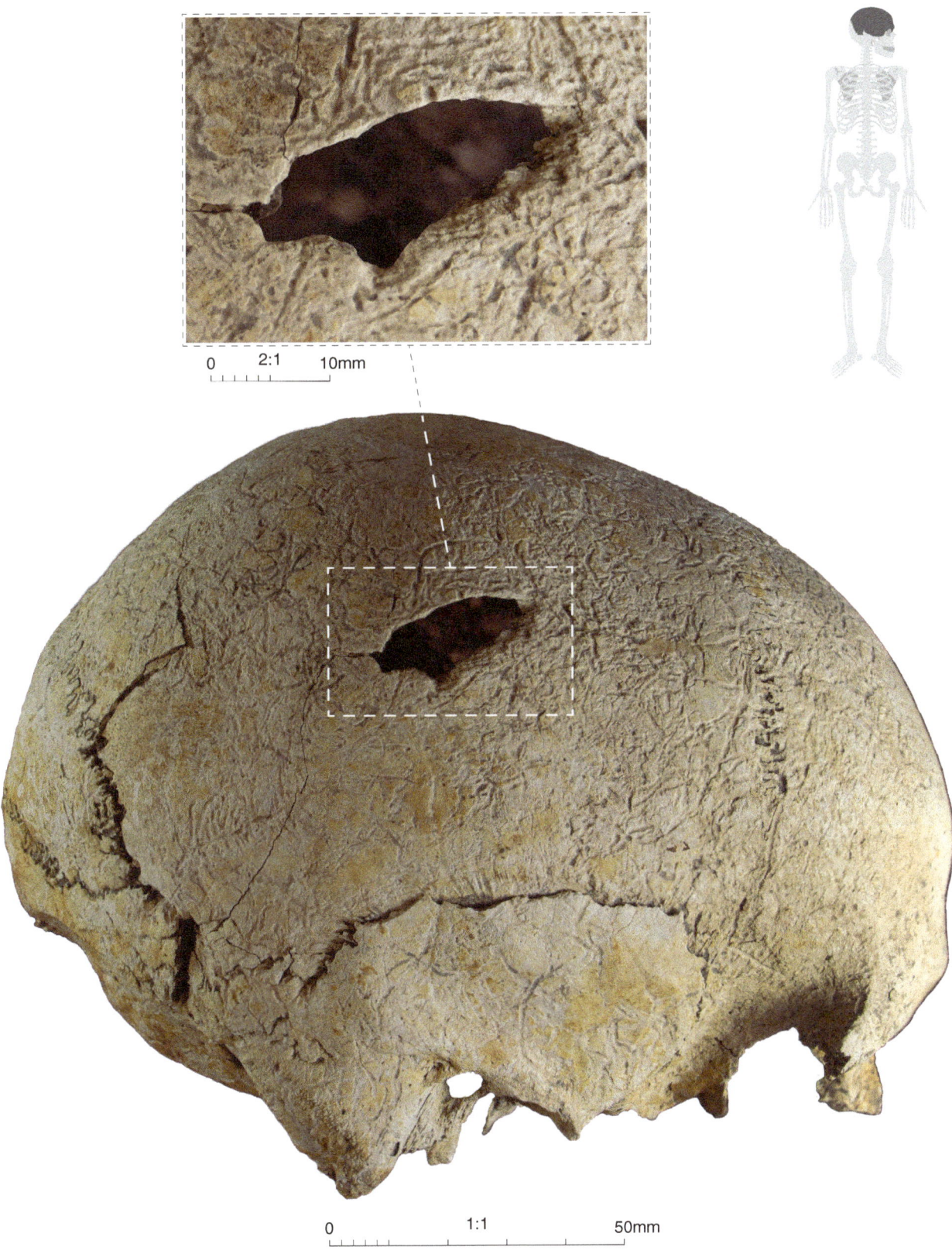

Figure 5.6 SK 2353, male older adult: possible perimortem cranial sharp force trauma on the right parietal bone

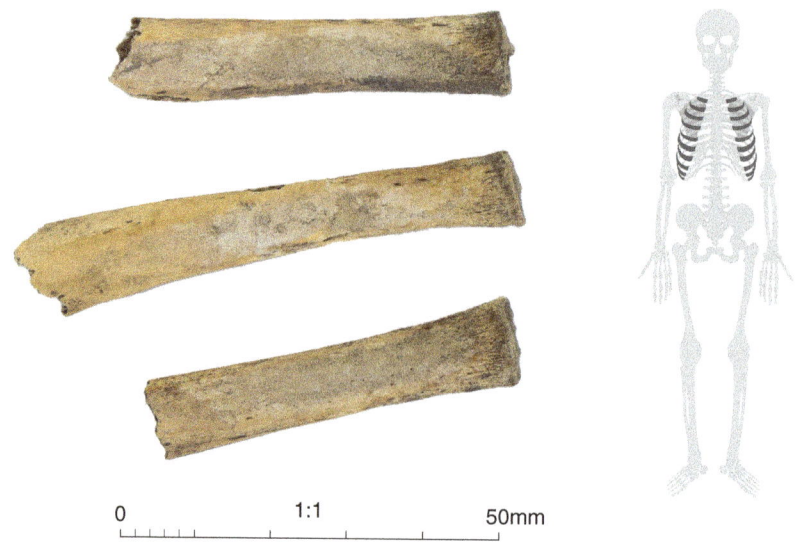

Figure 5.7 SK 2879, 6–8 year old child: periostitis on the sternal rib ends

Figure 5.8 SK 2879, 6–8 year old child: endocranial lesions on the occipital bone

cribra orbitalia. CF is of unknown aetiology and could be part of the development process (Erkelens 2017) which may explain the only two cases are on the youngest individuals. However, it has been suggested to co-occur with *cribra orbitalia* and indicate metabolic distress (ibid.).

Age-related conditions

Arachnoid granulations were present in the endocranium of older adult male SK 2327 and SK 2318 (older adult female) who also had HFI (hyperostosis frontalis interna) on the frontal bone. SK 2336 though male also had HFI and the cranium was thickened (which commonly accompanies HFI), but the rest of the skeleton was thin, almost osteoporotic. HFI is associated with post-menopausal females, but not exclusively so (Hershkovitz *et al.* 1999) and occurs when hormone imbalance leads to the growth of bone masses in the inner skull.

SK 2314 mature adult probable female had additional bone growth to the left mandible on the anterior and inferior to the coronoid process. The bony nodule may have formed due to the right side mandibular tooth loss.

The second metatarsal and articulating cuneiform on the right foot of SK 2353 (male older adult) had a form of joint destruction of which an aetiology could not be ascertained, but is likely caused by an injury to the forefoot. The left calcaneus had a lip of bone on the lateral side which has been associated with hyperextension of the toes (Stirland 1996). The right foot second metatarsal on the medial joint surface became concave due to destruction of the joint surface the second cuneiform (lateral) had additional bone growth on the superior side which was flat and smooth. Where it articulated with the metatarsal it was also concave and irregular on the surface. The cuboid and third and fourth metatarsals were also affected but to a lesser extent with mostly minor osteophytosis and slightly irregular joint surfaces. The lesions were not caused by osteoarthritis or gout due to their destructive nature, lack of new bone growth or porosity/periostitis.

SK 2324 male, older adult, the left humerus on the distal medial condyle adjacent to the joint surface had a small rounded nodule of bone 6mm in diameter and 4mm deep. This is not the usual location for entheseal changes, so may be trauma related.

Other Roman period skeletal remains

There were partial human remains recovered from non-grave features which have all been dated to the Roman period. From the top of droveway ditch A, ditch 3 (cut 1030, fill 1031) were recovered: adult sized cranial fragments and single lower second incisor, left clavicle shaft fragment, distal humerus and proximal ulna fragments, a metatarsal and fibula shaft fragment. As the elements are from different areas of the body and consistent in size and taphonomy, it suggests that this may be a very heavily truncated burial.

From rectangular pit 6052 (fill 6051) was recovered a single fragment of an adult sized ulna shaft. It is not clear how this fragment has come to be located in the pit.

From ditch terminal 2245 part of structure A (fill 2246) were recovered a neonate sized right humerus, distal half of radius and mid shaft femur fragment. The length of the humerus was 63mm indicating an age of approximately 40–44 weeks. As the elements recovered are from the upper and lower limbs, this is probably a neonate burial.

A single fragment of a neonate distal third of femur was recovered from pit 2754 (fill 2755). It is possible that this was also a neonate burial, but it may also have become incorporated into the pit fill through other means.

Discussion

Burials from two different time periods were excavated from the site at the Collection Management Facility. During the Iron Age, 11 of the pits were used as the location for deposition of the dead, either within the pit or in graves cut into the fills. These individuals were chosen for this particular practice of inhumation, when the majority of the dead were disposed of in a non-archaeologically recognisable manner. Placing the dead in pits in the Iron Age in the south of England is fairly common and not unexpected.

The Iron Age burials comprised adults, two neonates, and one adolescent. The adults were female dominant, with only one male. This male had multiple pathologies which had affected the skeleton. A female skeleton had a systemic pathology, which could not be specifically identified, though it would have been obvious in life and likely contributed to the early death. As pit burials occur in small numbers, comparison to other examples is limited.

Close to Segsbury hillfort, to the east and along the ridgeway, three Iron Age pit burials, two with non-adults and one with an adult female were recovered (Clough 2023). Other pit burials occur in the Upper Thames Valley where they are frequent finds in most Iron Age settlements, whilst earth cut graves also appear (Lambrick with Robinson 2009). The burials from the present site conform to the regional pattern. The double burial (SKs 10005 and 10005b) located quite some distance from all the group of pits within the settlement it is hard to interpret due to the limited excavation area around the burial, it may not be completely isolated as it appears. Double burials are not common, but there are other examples from pit burials. A fine example was not too far away at Watchfield, Oxfordshire (Birbeck 2001) where the double burial (intertwined adult female and non-adult) lay central to the entrance way to an enclosure.

Some of the Iron Age and Roman period burials took place as apparently independent of any others. These were ditch burial SK 1076, burial in the C-shaped enclosure SK 2446, and SK 12053 to the east of the C-shaped enclosure and located a long way from any others. As they were not included in the cemetery it seems that these individuals warranted particular individual attention, a chronological gap, or there was an ignorance of contemporary burials. Isolated burials frequently occur in and near ditches during the Roman period, particularly at the edges of cultivated land (Pearce 1999). The individual within the boundary of the C-shaped ditch does not appear osteologically to be different to any of the others. It is then perhaps status in life that caused the location for their burial.

The location of the Late Roman period cemetery of 17 individuals, may reference the Iron Age pit burials, despite the hundreds of years between their occurrences. Small cemeteries such as these are fairly common and reflect the national trend for organised inhumation cemeteries which date to the 3rd and 4th centuries AD. The lack of intercutting of the graves suggests duration of up standing markers. Those buried in the graves were all adult (except one), and as such are unlikely to reflect the living population. The greater number of females was also identified at another small cemetery not too far along the ridgeway at Childrey Warren, Oxfordshire (Clough 2023). With small numbers of individuals, it is easy to overinflate any bias, further investigation of the potential for small rural Roman cemeteries to contain the 'missing' females notably absent from urban cemeteries is much needed.

The skeletal pathologies were all those expected in a rural population and reflected the better access to food than urban counterparts. With the exception of possible trauma to SK 2353, no weapon or interpersonal violence, trauma or lesions were present, mostly older age-related degeneration and accidents of everyday life. This is observed for the rural population (Smith *et al.* 2018) where the evidence for the adult population indicates a hard physical, strenuous lifestyle.

In the immediate area of the site on the higher ground there are a few Late Roman inhumation burials scattered around. Blackland, Calne (Philips 2005), Maltshovel Lane, Lambourn (Richards 1976), Alfred's Castle (Gosden and Lock 2013). These all contain 3–9 individuals and those from Alfred's Castle were neonates from around a villa. The larger cemeteries are around the towns (e.g., *Durocornovium* – Wanbrough), or closer to the river Thames, areas of higher population. The group of 17 Late Roman burials at the present site is larger than these other rural sites. It is though a very similar size to the cemetery further along the Ridgeway near Wantage and close to the hillfort at Segsbury (Clough 2023).

Grave catalogue

Period 4: Iron Age

Skeleton 1206 (grave 1204, fill 1205)
(Fig. 2.14)
Grave: north/south aligned grave
Human remains: Older adult female; prone, tightly folded, head to north. 80% skeletal recovery, bone surface grade 3

Pathology and trauma: *Cribra orbitalia* present in left orbit. Fourth lumbar vertebra had large osteophytes on the anterior body extending in a superior direction, other lumbar vertebrae were absent
Dental: Very little dental attrition for their age. One small distal carious lesion on the second premolar, and a small quantity of calculus observed across majority of teeth. One tooth had been lost ante-mortem
Non-pathological traits: Bilateral squatting facets and bilateral calcaneal double facets present
Grave goods: none
Grave fill finds: none
Date: Radiocarbon date (human rib) *759–462 cal. BC (93.0%) and 438–421 cal. BC (2.4%) (95.4% probability)* (SUERC-94037)
Scientific samples: Isotopes – C and N see Hamilton (below)

Skeleton 1209 (grave 1207, fill 1208)
(Fig. 2.15)
Grave: north/south aligned
Human remains: Young adult female; tightly folded, head to north. 75% skeletal recovery, bone surface grade 4. Calculated stature 156.6cm (±3.72)
Pathology and trauma: Distinctive tendon insertion on both humerii; the deltoid tuberosity was raised and slightly pointed
Dental: Very little dental attrition for their age. Calculus observed on maxillary premolars and first molars
Non-pathological traits: Bilateral squatting facets and bilateral humeral septal apertures present
Grave goods: none
Grave fill finds: none
Date: Radiocarbon date (human rib) *514–366 cal. BC (95.4% probability)* (SUERC-100009)
Scientific samples: Isotopes – C and N see Hamilton (below)

Skeleton 1366 (grave 1364, fill 1365)
(Fig. 2.12)
Grave: square grave
Human remains: Neonate; tightly crouched. 60% skeletal recovery, bone surface grade 3
Pathology and trauma: none observed
Dental: none
Non-pathological traits: None observed
Grave goods: none
Grave fill finds: none
Date: Iron Age
Scientific samples: none

Skeleton 1489 (pit 1384, sealed by pit fills)
(Fig. 2.17)
Grave: placed in partially filled storage pit
Human remains: child aged 12–13 years; crouched position on left side, head to north. 80% skeletal recovery, bone surface grade 2
Pathology and trauma: Long bones measured short for dental age. *Cribra femora* present bilaterally

Dental: none observed

Non-pathological traits: None observed

Grave goods: n/a

Grave fill finds: n/a

Date: Iron Age

Scientific samples: none

Skeleton 1659 (grave 1658, fill 1660)

(Fig. 2.18)

Grave: north/south aligned

Human remains: Mature adult female; crouched on left side, skull absent due to truncation but would have been to the north. 20% skeletal recovery, bone surface grade 3

Pathology and trauma: none observed

Dental: Calculus present on buccal and lingual surface on left central mandibular incisor

Non-pathological traits: None observed

Grave goods: none

Grave fill finds: none

Date: Radiocarbon date (human rib) *362–242 cal. BC (61.5%) and 236–150 cal. BC (33.9%) (95.4% probability)* (SUERC-100014)

Scientific samples: Isotopes – C and N see Hamilton (below)

Skeleton 1778 (within pit 1781; grave 1777, fill 1779)

(Fig. 2.19)

Grave: north-east/south-west aligned

Human remains: Older adult female; crouched, head to south-west. 60% skeletal recovery, bone surface grade 3

Pathology and trauma: Spinal degenerative joint disease present

Dental: Much reduced alveolar height where teeth remains, with calculus present on roots. 13 teeth lost ante-mortem

Non-pathological traits: Bilateral calcaneal double facets present

Grave goods: none

Grave fill finds: Middle Iron Age pottery

Date: Radiocarbon date (human rib) *358–279 cal. BC (51.6%) and 231–112 cal. BC (43.8%) (95.4% probability)* (SUERC-100012)

Scientific samples: Isotopes – C and N see Hamilton (below)

Skeleton 1845 (pit 1426, sealed by pit fills)

(Fig. 2.21)

Grave: on base of storage pit 1845

Human remains: Mature adult male; prone, very tightly flexed. 90% skeletal recovery, bone surface grade 2. Calculated stature 166.1cm (±3.72)

Pathology and trauma: Posterior parietals and occipital displayed 'orange peel' porosity. Active periostitis present bilaterally on all surfaces of the distal tibiae, and present across both fibulae with a concentration on the medial surfaces. Periodontal disease observed on alveolar bone of 23 sockets at grade 2 or 1. An abscess was present on the first left maxillary molar. Bilateral erosive lesions on

the medial aspect of the first metatarsal heads consisting of small cortical defects with smooth sides. Similar, likely related, lesions present on the third metatarsal proximal joint surface with the cuneiform on the inferior aspect, which affected both bones. OA present in right elbow, with eburnation on the lateral surface of the ulna head and the corresponding posterior joint surface of the distal humerus.

A crush fracture to second to fourth lumbar vertebrae was observed. The second lumbar had a slight wedge shape, the third lumbar had an indentation to the superior body, the fourth lumbar was wedge shaped. Some minor osteophytes had developed on the body perimeter of the first and second lumbar in response. In addition a healed fracture was present near the costal end of a right side rib, alongside an oval shape indentation on another rib

Dental: Periodontal disease at grade 2 on the maxilla and grade 1 on the mandible, with calculus present across the majority of recovered teeth. An apical granuloma was observed on the left maxillary first molar, which exposed the roots distally. 5 teeth lost ante-mortem

Non-pathological traits: Bilateral calcaneal double facets present

Grave goods: n/a

Grave fill finds: n/a

Date: Radiocarbon date *391–346 cal. BC (35.7%) and 316–206 cal. BC (59.7%) (95.4% probability)* (SUERC-94041)

Scientific samples: Isotopes: tooth enamel C, O and Sr – see Hamilton (below)

Skeleton 3235 (pit 1947, sealed by pit fills)

(Fig. 2.23)

Grave: placed on floor of storage pit

Human remains: Mature adult female; crouched. 80% skeletal recovery, bone surface grade 2. Calculated stature 150.9cm (±3.72)

Pathology and trauma: Exostosis on the left deltoid tuberosity of the humerus

Dental: A single small distal carious lesion on the left maxillary lateral incisor. 4 teeth had been lost ante-mortem

Non-pathological traits: None observed

Grave goods: n/a

Grave fill finds: n/a

Date: Radiocarbon date (human rib) *359–277 cal. BC (54.4%), 258–248 cal. BC (1.1%) and 233–120 cal. BC (40.0%) (95.4% probability)* (SUERC-100015)

Scientific samples: Isotopes – C and N see Hamilton (below)

Skeleton 8071 (pit 8068, sealed by pit fills)

(Fig. 2.25)

Grave: placed on pit floor, up against pit side

Human remains: Young adult female; tightly folded, head to north. 90% skeletal recovery, bone surface grade 2. Calculated stature 152cm (±4.45)

Pathology and trauma: *Cribra femora* observed alongside *cribra orbitalia* grade 3. Active periostitis present bilaterally throughout skeleton, often associated with deep muscle attachment sites. Endocranial lesions of the capillary type were also observed

Dental: none observed

Non-pathological traits: A maxillary lateral incisor was absent from the dentition, and no corresponding space in the dental arcade. There was also no space for the third molars, with the exception of the right mandibular third molar, which had erupted. The second deciduous molar was retained, and it is likely that the maxillary right deciduous canine was also retained as there was an alveola for it. The sacrum is bifid, with the spinous processes appearing incomplete and do not join below S1. S1 almost joins, but not quite.

Bilateral patella notch and bilateral lambdoid ossicles present

Grave goods: n/a

Grave fill finds: n/a

Date: Radiocarbon date (human rib) *362–242 cal. BC (62.8%) and 236–154 cal. BC (32.6%) (95.4% probability)* (SUERC-100011)

Scientific samples: isotopes tooth enamel C, O, and Sr see Hamilton (below)

Skeleton 10005 (grave 10003, fill 10004)

(Fig. 2.16)

Grave: circular grave, interred with SK 100005b

Human remains: Prime/young adult ?female; crouched position on her left side (?originally crouched, seated). 40% skeletal recovery, bone surface grade 5

Pathology and trauma: None observed

Dental: A single large carious lesion on the mesial surface of the right mandibular third molar

Non-pathological traits: None observed

Grave goods: none

Grave fill finds: none

Date: Radiocarbon date (human femur) *466–386 cal. BC (95.4% probability)* (SUERC-94043)

Scientific samples: isotopes tooth enamel C, O, and Sr see Hamilton (below)

Skeleton 10005b (grave 10003, fill 10004)

(Fig. 2.16)

Grave: circular grave, interred with SK 100005

Human remains: Child 10–12 years; likely under the chest area of SK 10005, identified in post-excavation. 10% skeletal recovery, bone surface grade 5

Pathology and trauma: None observed

Dental: None observed

Non-pathological traits: None observed

Grave goods: none

Grave fill finds: none

Date: Iron Age see above (SUERC-94043)

Scientific samples: none

Period 5.2: Late Iron Age to Early Roman

Skeleton 1076 (grave 1083, sealed by ditch fills)

(Fig. 5.9)

Grave: shallow cut into base of Period 5 Ditch 3, flowing the NE/SW ditch alignment

Human remains: Mature adult female; extended supine. 65% skeletal recovery, bone surface grade 3

Pathology and trauma: none observed

Dental: Probable periodontal disease on mandible; alveolar height loss and calculus on roots observed. Four teeth lost ante-mortem

Non-pathological traits: Right tibial squatting facet present

Grave goods: none

Grave fill finds: chalk pebbles

Date: Radiocarbon date (human tibia) cal. AD 30–40 cal. AD (1.8%) and 60–212 cal. AD (93.7%) (95.4% probability) (SUERC-94036)

Scientific samples: sex confirmed through aDNA analysis

Isotopes – C and N see Hamilton (below)

Period 6: Mid to Late Roman

Skeleton 2297 (grave 2295, fill 2296)

(Fig. 5.10)

Grave: north-east/south-west aligned

Human remains: Older adult female; extended, slightly flexed position on left side, head to north-east. 80% skeletal recovery, bone surface grade 4

Pathology and trauma: none observed

Dental: Periodontal disease grade 3 observed across mandible and maxilla. Calculus present buccally on majority of left mandibular teeth, and lingually on second right mandibular molar. A small carious lesion present on the CEJ on second left mandibular molar. 8 teeth lost ante-mortem

Non-pathological traits: None observed

Grave goods: none

Grave fill finds: hobnails, carpentry nails, 2nd–4th-century pottery

Date: Mid to Late Roman

Scientific samples: none

Skeleton 2311 (grave 2309, fill 2310)

(Fig. 5.11)

Grave: North-east/south-west aligned

Human remains: Older adult female; slightly flexed supine extended position, head to north-east. 70% skeletal recovery, bone surface grade 4

Pathology and trauma: Osteophyte growth observed in the lower spine. Porosity and osteophyte growth present on the cervical spine

Dental: 20 teeth lost ante-mortem

Non-pathological traits: None observed

Grave goods: none

Grave fill finds: none

Figure 5.9 SK 1076, grave 1083

Figure 5.10 SK 2297, grave 2295, looking north-east

Figure 5.11 SK 2311, grave 2309, looking south-east

Figure 5.12 SK 2318, grave 2316, looking south-east

Figure 5.13 SK 2321, grave 2320, looking north-east

Date: Mid to Late Roman
Scientific samples: none

Skeleton 2314 (grave 2315, fill 2313)
(see Fig. 2.41)
Grave: north/south aligned
Human remains: Mature adult female; extended prone, head to north, hands flexed at elbows in a 'falling' position. 80% skeletal recovery, bone surface grade 4
Pathology and trauma: Additional bone growth on the left mandible on the anterior and inferior coronoid process, which may have formed due to tooth loss and significant tooth wear on the right mandible. Fine grey new growth periostitis present on the right mandible body, probably caused by dental disease present in molars
Dental: An apical abscess was observed on the buccal surface of the right maxilla above the first and second premolars. Grade 3 periodontal disease present on the alveolar bone around central mandibular incisors and the left mandibular lateral incisor. Grade 4 periodontal disease present on the second right mandibular molar, which had led to complete root exposure on the buccal surface. 7 teeth lost ante-mortem
Non-pathological traits: Bilateral third trochanter on femora
Grave goods: none
Grave fill finds: none

Date: Radiocarbon date (human rib) cal. AD 247–405 (95.4% probability) (SUERC-100013)
Scientific samples: isotopes tooth enamel C, O and Sr see Hamilton (below)

Skeleton 2318 (grave 2316, fill 2317)
(Fig. 5.12)
Grave: north-east/south-west aligned
Human remains: Older adult female; extended, supine, head to south-west. 80% skeletal recovery, bone surface grade 4
Pathology and trauma: Hyperostosis frontalis interna (HFI) is present on the frontal bone, alongside pacchoniam granulations on the occipital bone
Dental: Majority of recovered teeth possessed calculus. Carious lesion observed on the right mandibular first molar buccal surface at the CEJ
Non-pathological traits: Retained metopic suture and bilateral calcaneal facet
Grave goods: none
Grave fill finds: hobnails (Ra. 1041), Roman pottery
Date: Mid to Late Roman
Scientific samples: none

Skeleton 2321 (grave 2320, fill 2322)
(Fig. 5.13)
Grave: north-east/south-west grave

Human remains: Older adult male; slightly flexed, head to north-east. 75% skeletal recovery, bone surface grade 3

Pathology and trauma: Osteophytes present bilaterally on the superior edge of the acetabulum, signalling joint degeneration

Dental: A small carious lesion was present on the mesial surface of the right maxillary second molar. An apical abscess was observed on the buccal surface of the left maxilla above the central incisor, while two further apical abscesses were recorded on the buccal surfaces above the right maxillary first and second molars. Grade 2 periodontal disease was present on the left mandible, alongside chipping and cracking of the maxillary incisors. 7 teeth lost ante-mortem

Non-pathological traits: Bilateral double calcaneal facet

Grave goods: flint flake (Ra. 1038)

Grave fill finds: hobnails, carpentry nail, Roman pottery

Date: Mid to Late Roman

Scientific samples: none

Skeleton 2324 (grave 2323, fill 2325)

(Fig. 5.14)

Grave: north-east/south-west grave

Human remains: Older adult male; extended supine, head to north-east. 90% skeletal recovery, bone surface grade 3

Pathology and trauma: Fourth to the tenth thoracic vertebrae displayed the 'candle-wax' appearance of additional bone growth running down right-hand side that characterises DISH, with TV7-8 completely fused by the bone growth. The lumbar vertebra 3-4 had excessive growth on middle and left side of the bodies. Lumbar vertebra 1-2 and TV12 also had large outgrowths of osteophytes on the middle left side. Cervical vertebra 4-5 were also fused at body and facets, with OA on the left CV2-3 facets. The CV bodies had porosity indicative of IVD. The left humerus on the distal medial condyle adjacent to the joint surface had a small rounded nodule of bone 6mm diameter and 4mm deep, potentially relating to trauma as this is not the usual location for entheses. A possible healed fracture on small fragment of rib shaft was recorded. The right tibia and fibula appear irregular with additional bone and microporosity and were fused at the proximal joint, likely as a result of direct trauma or dislocation

Dental: A small carious lesion was present on the distal surface of the left maxillary lateral incisor. Large caries were recorded on the proximal surface of the left and right mandibular second molar, and at the CEJ of the right mandibular third molar. Apical abscesses were present above the left maxillary canine, right maxillary first premolar, and left mandibular first molar. Calculus was present several of the teeth, predominantly on the mandibular incisors and canines. 6 teeth lost ante-mortem

Non-pathological traits: Bilateral lambdoid ossicles present

Grave goods: none

Grave fill finds: none

Figure 5.14 SK 2324, grave 2323, looking north-east

Date: Mid to Late Roman

Scientific samples: none

Skeleton 2327 (grave 2326, fill 2328)

(Fig. 5.15)

Grave: north-east/south-west grave

Human remains: Older adult male; slightly flexed, head to south-west. 80% skeletal recovery, bone surface grade 3

Pathology and trauma: Right-side maxillary sinus is covered in remodelled bone as a thickened layer, indicative of chronic sinusitis. There was microporosity but thickened and striated and not web-like. Left side was affected to a much lesser extent. Extensive OA was recorded in the cervical vertebral bodies and articular facets, with eburnation present in CV1, 2 and 4. Lumbar vertebrae 4 and 5 were affected by body porosity and osteophytosis, with further analysis of LV1-3 hindered by preservation. There was also OA present bilaterally in the wrists and the base of the right thumb. Osteophytes associated with degenerative joint disease were present in the hips, shoulders, and mid-clavicle to manubrium. The first distal pedal phalanx displayed complete degeneration of the joint. Arachnoid granulations were present in the endocranium. There were a minimum of four healed rib fractures, but fragmentation prevents further analysis

Dental: 7 teeth were lost ante-mortem, alongside thinning and remodelling of the alveolar of the maxilla, potentially associated with the chronic sinusitis. The entire mandible was edentulous (ante-mortem)

Figure 5.15 SK 2327, grave 2326, looking north-west

Figure 5.16 SK 2330, grave 2329, looking north-west

Non-pathological traits: Bilateral double calcaneal facet present

Grave goods: none

Grave fill finds: hobnails, Roman pottery

Date: Mid to Late Roman

Scientific samples: none

Skeleton 2330 (grave 2329, fill 2331)

(Fig. 5.16)

Grave: north-east/south-west aligned grave

Human remains: Older adult female; extended supine, head to south-west. 80% skeletal recovery, bone surface grade 2

Pathology and trauma: Schmorl's nodes, IVD porosity, and minor osteophyte growth present on the spine

Dental: Small caries on the left mandibular first premolar and the right mandibular canine, both located on the buccal surface of the root. 14 teeth had been lost ante-mortem

Non-pathological traits: Squatting facet present

Grave goods: broken leaf-shaped Early Neolithic flint arrowhead (Ra. 1039) found close to waist

Grave fill finds: hobnails, Roman pottery

Date: Mid to Late Roman

Scientific samples: none

Skeleton 2333 (grave 2332, fill 2334)

(see Fig. 2.39)

Grave: north-east/south-west grave

Human remains: Older adult male; supine extended, head to south-west. 80% skeletal recovery, bone surface grade 3

Pathology and trauma: There is some evidence of DJD in the spine, but full analysis is prevented by poor preservation. A compression fracture to the body of the third lumbar vertebra was observed, with the vertical

Figure 5.17 SK 2336, grave 2335, looking north-east

height of the body reduced unevenly and a concave surface in centre. The right first metacarpal proximal joint surface articulating with the trapezium had a possible fracture as the surface was uneven and sloped; the left side of the MC1 was unobservable, but the trapezium has eburnation

Dental: A single large carious lesion on the right maxillary third molar, located on the buccal surface of the root. Severe periodontal disease leading to the full exposure of the roots was observed, particularly on the molars of the right maxilla. Calculus was present on the roots. Teeth exhibit heavy wear, with only the roots remaining on many of the teeth. 16 teeth had been lost ante-mortem

Non-pathological traits: None observed

Grave goods: none

Grave fill finds: Hobnails and cleats, late 3rd to 4th-century pottery

Date: Mid to Late Roman

Scientific samples: none

Skeleton 2336 (grave 2335, fill 2337)

(Fig. 5.17)

Grave: north-east/south-west grave

Human remains: Older adult female; slightly flexed, a little on left side, head to north-east. 80% skeletal recovery, bone surface grade 3

Pathology and trauma: The cranium is thickened, similar to that seen in Paget's disease, but is likely to be hyperostosis frontalis interna (HFI) which is common in post-menopausal females. The rest of the skeleton is thin, bordering on osteoporotic. The right articular facet of the sacrum has eburnation, indicative of OA. There are minor osteophytes on the lower lumbar and thoracic vertebrae. There is evidence of OA at the joint surface of the first metacarpals bilaterally. The right MC1

joint surface has eburnation on the proximal lateral surface, with porosity and minor osteophytes (1mm). The left MC1 joint surface has porosity and minor osteophytes (1mm) on the proximal superior surface, but no eburnation was observed. Both the trapeziums are missing. The proximal joint surface of both distal phalanges have pointed irregular osteophyte growth. The right scaphoid has a slight ridge of osteophyte growth on the joint surface for the radius

Dental: A single large smooth walled carious lesion on the right mandibular second premolar measuring 9mm was observed. The right maxillary canine had a cyst on the root CEJ, located on the buccal side with the crown still intact. 11 teeth had been lost ante-mortem

Non-pathological traits: Right calcaneal double facet present

Grave goods: none

Grave fill finds: hobnails, Roman pottery

Date: Mid to Late Roman

Scientific samples: none

Skeleton 2339 (grave 2338, fill 2340)

(Fig. 5.18)

Grave: north-east/south-west grave

Human remains: Older adult female; extended supine, head to north-east. 90% skeletal recovery, bone surface grade 3

Pathology and trauma: Schmorl's nodes were observed on the spine

Dental: A single carious lesion was observed on the left mandibular second molar on the CEJ, located on the buccal surface. A moderate amount of calculus was present on the buccal and lingual surfaces on the right mandibular second premolar and first molar. 8 teeth had been lost ante-mortem

Figure 5.18 SK 2339, grave 2338, looking north

Figure 5.19 SK 2342, grave 2341, looking north-east

Non-pathological traits: Right atlas double facet and right calcaneal double facet present

Grave goods: none

Grave fill finds: hobnails and cleats, late 3rd to 4th-century pottery

Date: Mid to Late Roman

Scientific samples: none

Skeleton 2342 (grave 2341, fill 2343)

(Fig. 5.19)

Grave: north-east/south-west

Human remains: Mature adult male, slightly flexed, a little on left side, head to the north-east. 85% skeletal recovery, bone surface grade 3

Pathology and trauma: The cervical vertebrae had degenerative joint disease on the facets and body. The lumbar and thoracic vertebrae had osteophyte growth

Dental: none

Non-pathological traits: None observed

Grave goods: none

Grave fill finds: late 3rd to 4th-century pottery

Date: Mid to Late Roman

Scientific samples: none

Skeleton 2345 (grave 2344, fill 2346)

(Fig. 5.20)

Grave: north-east/south-west

Human remains: Older adult ?female; extended supine, head to south-west. 80% skeletal recovery, bone surface grade 4

Pathology and trauma: Cervical vertebrae display porosity on the bodies. OA, eburnation, and osteophytes were recorded on the distal joint surface of the MC1. Eburnation was observed on the trapezium. The left hand was not affected

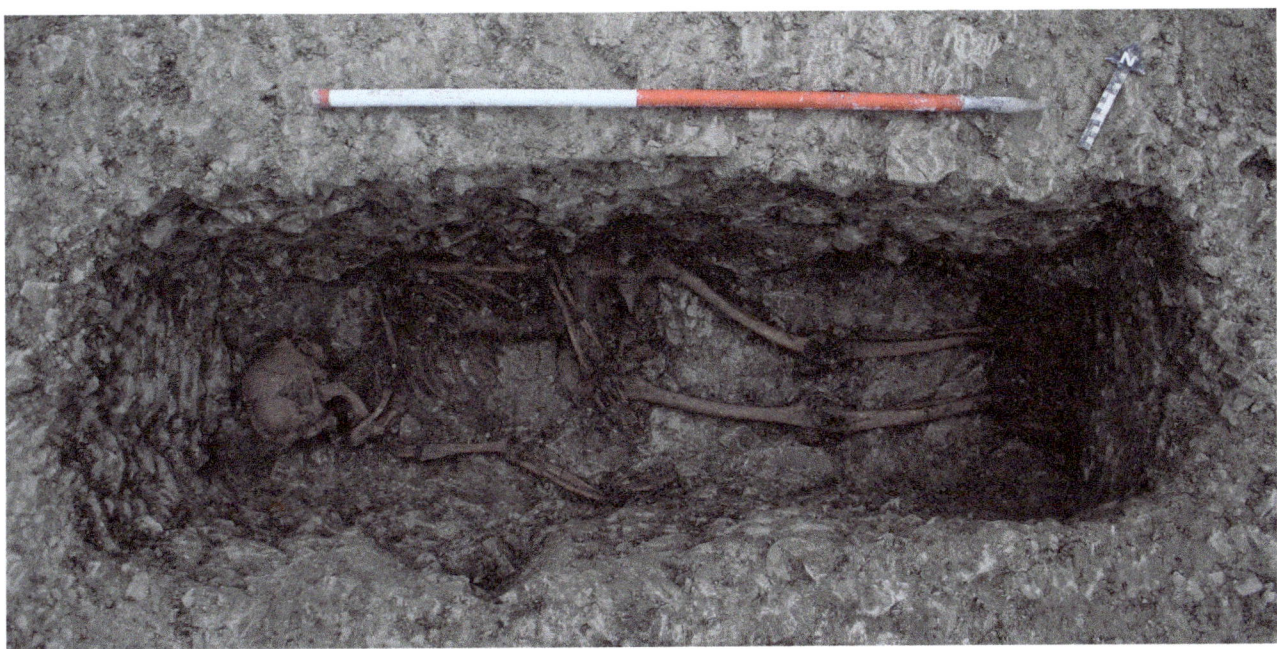

Figure 5.20 SK 2345, grave 2344, looking north-east

Dental: Calculus was observed on the buccal and lingual surfaces on the mandibular teeth, extending to the roots. The alveolar bone was porous with alveolar height reduction on all teeth, indicating periodontal disease. A periapical granuloma was recorded on the right mandibular central incisor. 6 teeth had been lost ante-mortem

Non-pathological traits: None observed

Grave goods: none

Grave fill finds: hobnails and cleats

Date: Mid to Late Roman

Scientific samples: none

Skeleton 2350 (grave 2349, fill 2351)

(Fig. 5.21)

Grave: north-east/south-west aligned

Human remains: Older adult male; supine extended, head to south-west. 90% skeletal recovery, bone surface grade 3

Pathology and trauma: A single occurrence of linear enamel hypoplasia was recorded on the right mandibular canine. OA was recorded on the left wrist, with eburnation on the distal ulna and corresponding lunate joint surfaces. OA in the left hip had led to extensive changes; extensive osteophytic growth of approximately 30mm had re-shaped the joint surface, alongside eburnation, porosity and subchondral pitting on the acetabulum and femoral head. The right acetabulum only displayed slight lipping. The knees and ankles were not affected. The cervical vertebrae bodies displayed degenerative joint disease. The thoracic and lumbar vertebrae bodies had osteophytes and Schmorl's nodes, while the TV and LV facets had eburnation indicative of osteoarthritis. Cortical defects were recorded on the MT1 bilaterally,

Figure 5.21 SK 2350, grave 2349, looking east

Figure 5.22 SK 2353, grave 2352, looking north-east

presenting as a small circular indent on the concave joint surface. The articulating proximal phalanx joint surface was wider as a result with an irregular patch of bone. 5 healed rib fractures were observed, originating from a lower posterior location

Dental: A single large carious lesion was recorded on the left mandibular first molar, located on the CEJ. Left mandibular and maxillary teeth have calculus on the buccal and lingual surfaces. 11 teeth had been lost ante-mortem

Non-pathological traits: Retained metopic suture and left lambdoid ossicles observed. Right squatting facet and bilateral double calcaneal facet present

Grave goods: none

Grave fill finds: none

Date: Mid to Late Roman

Scientific samples: none

Skeleton 2353 (grave 2352, fill 2354)

(Fig. 5.22)

Grave: north-east/south-west

Human remains: Older adult male; supine extended, head to north-east. 90% skeletal recovery, bone surface grade 3

Pathology and trauma: OA was recorded on the right sacrum articular facet for fifth lumbar vertebra, alongside degenerative joint disease in the spine. The second metatarsal and articulating cuneiform on the right foot had some form of joint destruction with an unknown aetiology. The left calcaneus had a lip of bone on the lateral side. The right second metatarsal on the medial joint surface became concave due to destruction of the joint surface. The second cuneiform (lateral) had additional bone growth on the superior side which was flat and smooth. Where it articulated with the metatarsal it was also concave and irregular on the surface. The cuboid and third and fourth metatarsals were also affected but to a lesser extent with mostly minor osteophytosis and slightly irregular joint surfaces. The

lesions were not caused by osteoarthritis or gout due to their destructive nature, lack of new bone growth or porosity/periostitis. The right parietal had an elongated opening with radiating fracture lines and depressed bent bone at the corners. The lower edge is irregular and the top edge is internal and sharp. The shape of the opening suggests a possible peri-mortem cranial sharp force trauma, as the colouration is consistent with the rest of the bone indicating it is not a recent break

Dental: A single small carious lesion on the right maxillary central incisor. Periodontal disease graded between 3 and 4 was located across all alveolar bone. Two periapical granulomas were recorded, one above the left maxillary second premolar and one above the left mandibular lateral incisor. Calculus was observed on the right maxillary canine, the left mandibular canine, and the left mandibular first molar. Chipping and cracking of the maxillary incisors was noted. 9 teeth had been lost ante-mortem

Non-pathological traits: Bilateral squatting facet and bilateral double calcaneal facet present. Inca bone also observed

Grave goods: none

Grave fill finds: iron hobnails and cleats

Date: Mid to Late Roman

Scientific samples: none

Skeleton 2446 (grave 2389, fill 2445)

(see Fig. 2.38)

Grave: north/south grave within prehistoric C-shaped enclosure

Human remains: Older adult female; extended supine, head to north. 80% skeletal recovery, bone surface grade 3

Pathology and trauma: The cervical vertebrae had evidence of degeneration of the joints, while the thoracic vertebrae had Schmorl's nodes but no evidence of further joint degeneration. The left ischial tuberosity had smooth

Figure 5.23 SK 2865, grave 2863, looking north-east

Figure 5.24 SK 2879, grave 2878, looking east

extra bone growth creating a wave-like crest, with the remainder of the surface being rough and irregular, elements of which were porous. There was no normal morphology remaining, but this was isolated since the rest of the ischium was normal and the acetabulum unaffected. Avulsion fractures can occur at this location, however, the bony changes were not consistent with a healed fracture as such

Dental: A single apical granuloma was located above the left maxillary canine. A cyst was recorded at the apex of the left mandibular premolars, which had thin smooth edges and porous alveolar bone. Three teeth had been lost ante-mortem

Non-pathological traits: Bilateral squatting facets and bilateral double calcaneal facets were observed

Grave goods: none

Grave fill finds: carpentry nails

Date: Radiocarbon date cal. AD 122–338 (95.4% probability) (SUERC-94042)

Scientific samples: Isotopes – C and N see Hamilton (below)

Skeleton 2865 (grave 2863, fill 2864)

(Fig. 5.23)

Grave: north-east/south-west

Human remains: Young adult female; extended prone, head to south-west. 70% skeletal recovery, bone surface grade 2

Pathology and trauma: Bilateral *cribra femora* were present

Dental: Calculus was recorded on the buccal surfaces of the majority of the maxillary teeth, and on the lingual surfaces of the majority of the mandibular teeth

Non-pathological traits: Bilateral humeral septal apertures present

Grave goods: none

Grave fill finds: none

Date: Mid to Late Roman

Scientific samples: none

Skeleton 2879 (grave 2878, fill 2880)

(Fig. 5.24)

Grave: north/south

Figure 5.25 SK 12053, grave 12052, looking north

Human remains: Child 6–8 years; extended, prone, head to north. 90% skeletal recovery, bone surface grade 3

Pathology and trauma: Bilateral *cribra femora* and bilateral *cribra orbitalia* type 2 were present. Fine grey periostitis was present on three rib surfaces at the sternal end. The parietal and occipital bones had endocranial lesions

Dental: none observed

Non-pathological traits: none observed

Grave goods: none

Grave fill finds: none

Date: Mid to Late Roman

Scientific samples: none

Skeleton 12053 (grave 12052, fill 12054)

(Fig. 5.25)

Grave: east/west

Human remains: Older adult male; extended supine, head to west. 50% skeletal recovery, bone surface grade 1

Pathology and trauma: None observed

Dental: Two small caries were recorded on the right maxillary central and lateral incisors. The remaining dentition suggested that either he had an odd bite or there was extra masticatory wear, since only the incisors had very angled wear, and not adjacent premolars. However, the ante-mortem loss of the molars may have meant that they had been used to chew with. 5 teeth had been lost ante-mortem

Non-pathological traits: None observed

Grave goods: none

Grave fill finds: none

Date: Radiocarbon date (human rib) cal. AD 246–402 (95.4% probability) (SUERC-100010)

Scientific samples: Isotopes – C and N see Hamilton (below)

Radiocarbon dating
Emma Aitken and Alistair J. Barclay

The following report discusses the results and the chronology of the site. In addition, Hamilton (below) discusses the results on human bone along with their carbon, nitrogen, oxygen and strontium isotopes.

Radiocarbon dating was undertaken in order to confirm the dates of graves 1083, 1204, 1426, 2389, and 10003, oven 2827, pits 1245, 1288, and 1658, graves 12052 and 2315, small storage pit (cuts 2938 and 1777), large storage pit (cuts 8068, 1947, and 1984), and Pit alignment 2 (cut 1645), and ditch 2433 from C-shaped ditch 1. The samples were analysed during August 2020, September 2021, November 2021 and at Scottish Universities Environmental Research Centre (SUERC), Rankine Avenue, Scottish Enterprise Technology Park, East Kilbride, Glasgow, G75 0QF, Scotland. The methodology employed by SUERC Radiocarbon Laboratory is outlined in Dunbar *et al.* (2016).

The uncalibrated dates are conventional radiocarbon ages. The radiocarbon ages were calibrated using the University of Oxford Radiocarbon Accelerator Unit calibration

Table 5.10 Details of the radiocarbon dates for the prehistoric features. Calibrated using the IntCal 20 curve. Where stated the dates derive from the model presented in Figure 5.27

Lab No.	Feature	Material	δ ¹³C	δ ¹⁵N	C/N ratio	Radiocarbon age	Calibrated radiocarbon age 95.4% probability	Probability density estimate cal. BC at 95.4% unless otherwise stated
Beaker								
SUERC-100004	Context 1248 Pit 1245	Charred plant remains: Hazelnut shell frag (*Corylus avellana*)	-23.6‰			3787 ± 29 BP	2338–2325 cal. BC (1.1%) 2300–2134 cal. BC (92.8%) 2080–2062 cal. BC (1.5%)	
Iron Age								
SUERC-94037	SK 1206 Grave 1204	Human bone: Left rib from an older adult female, tightly folded	-20.8‰	9.7‰	3.4	2465 ± 26 BP	758–678 cal. BC (32.7%) 672–462 cal. BC (60.2%) 437–420 cal. BC (2.5%)	*759–462 cal. BC (93.0%) 438–421 cal. BC (2.4%)*
SUERC-94041	SK 1845 Grave 1426	Human bone: Left rib from a mature adult male, prone and very tightly flexed	-20.4‰	9.5‰	3.3	2247 ± 26 BP	389–348 cal. BC (29.3%) 312–206 cal. BC (66.2%)	*391–346 cal. BC (35.7%) 316–206 cal. BC (59.7%)*
SUERC-94043	SK 10005 Grave 10003	Human bone: Left femur from a young adult female, crouched/seated	-20.4‰	8.6‰	3.3	2369 ± 26 BP	538–530 cal. BC (1.6%) 518–391 cal. BC (93.8%)	*466–386 cal. BC*
SUERC-100005	Context 2940 Small Storage Pit (cut 2938)	Charred plant remains: Spelt wheat grain (*Triticum spelta*)	-22.7‰			2135 ± 29 BP	348–311 cal. BC (14.0%) 206–51 cal. BC (81.5%)	*354–286 cal. BC (39.8%) 210–96 cal. BC (55.7%)*
SUERC-100009	SK 1209 Pit 1288	Human bone: Rib from a young adult female, tightly folded	-21.1‰	10.6‰	3.5	2340 ± 29 BP	515–366 cal. BC (95.4%)	*514–366 cal. BC*
SUERC-100011	SK 8071 Large Storage Pit (cut 8068)	Human bone: Rib from a young adult female, tightly folded	-20.6‰	8.7‰	3.3	2175 ± 29 BP	360–241 cal. BC (52.0%) 236–147 cal. BC (40.4%) 137–110 cal. BC (3.1%)	*362–242 cal. BC (62.8%) 236–154 cal. BC (32.6%)*
SUERC-100012	SK 1778 Grave 1777	Human bone: Rib from an older adult female, crouched	-20.6‰	9.3‰	3.4	2157 ± 29 BP	355–281 cal. BC (34.2%) 231–96 cal. BC (58.8%) 73–56 cal. BC (2.5%)	*358–279 cal. BC (51.6%) 231–112 cal. BC (43.8%)*
SUERC-100014	SK 1659 Grave1658	Human bone: Rib from a mature adult female, couched	-21.7‰	9.4‰	3.5	2172 ± 29 BP	360–272 cal. BC (45.5%) 265–242 cal. BC (3.5%) 236–106 cal. BC (46.5%)	*362–242 cal. BC (61.5%) 236–150 cal. BC (33.9%)*
SUERC-100015	SK 3235 Large Storage Pit (cut 1947)	Human bone: Rib from a mature adult female, crouched	-20.5‰	8.5‰	3.2	2163 ± 29 BP	356–279 cal. BC (39.3%) 257–247 cal. BC (1.2%) 233–100 cal. BC (53.9%) 68–59 cal. BC (1.1%)	*359–277 cal. BC (54.4%) 258–248 cal. BC (1.1%) 233–120 cal. BC (40.0%)*
SUERC-100020	Context 1962 Large Storage Pit (cut 1984)	Animal bone: Dog rib	-20.4‰	8.0‰	3.3	2181 ± 29 BP	364–151 cal. BC (95.0%) 128–124 cal. BC (0.4%)	*364–164 cal. BC*
SUERC-100021	Context 6035 Bell-Shaped Storage Pit (cut 6030)	Animal bone: Dog rib	-20.6‰	8.6‰	3.3	2209 ± 29 BP	376–194 cal. BC (93.4%) 187–177 cal. BC (2.1%)	*379–196 cal. BC*
SUERC-100660	Context 2436 C-shaped ditch 1 Ditch 2433	Animal bone: Canid	-20.4‰	8.2‰	3.2	2140 ± 24 BP	348–311 cal. BC (16.7%) 206–91 cal. BC (72.5%) 79–53 cal. BC (6.3%)	*351–296 cal. BC (39.5%) 208–102 cal. BC (55.9%)*

programme OxCal v4.4.4 (Bronk Ramsey 2020; Bronk Ramsey 2009) using the IntCal20 curve.

Selected radiocarbon dates (Iron Age) have been statistically modelled using the online OxCal program (v4.4.4) (https://c14.arch.ox.ac.uk/oxcal/OxCal.html) (Bronk Ramsey 2009; 2020). The main focus is on the prehistoric burials and, to a lesser extent, the Iron Age settlement. The results from this model are discussed below and are presented in the radiocarbon figures and the tables below. The model has good individual and overall agreements.

Discussion

The single result SUERC-100004 with a calibrated range of 2300–2134 cal. BC (92.8%) (at 95.4% probability) from

Beaker pit 1245 indicates an early Beaker or Chalcolithic date (before 2150 BC) (Table 5.10 and Fig. 5.26), which is in accordance with the style of pottery (see Banks, Chapter 3).

The 12 radiocarbon dates from the Iron Age phase of activity on the site were placed in a simple phased model (Fig. 5.27). Eight of these results were on human bone, three were on animal bone and one was on charred cereal. All of the samples were from discrete features and, therefore, the model contains no sequences, although the samples are listed by phase (grave, isolated graves, burials in pits, pits and C-shaped enclosure). Three of the human burials may have been stored for an unknown period of time and, therefore, their results are treated as *terminus pro quems* and are modelled using the OxCal '*After*' function.

OxCal v4.4.4 Bronk Ramsey (2021); r:5 Atmospheric data from Reimer et al. (2020)
R_Date SUERC-100004
2600
2500
2400
2300
2200
2100
2000
1900
Calibrated date (cal. BC)

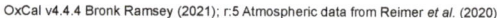

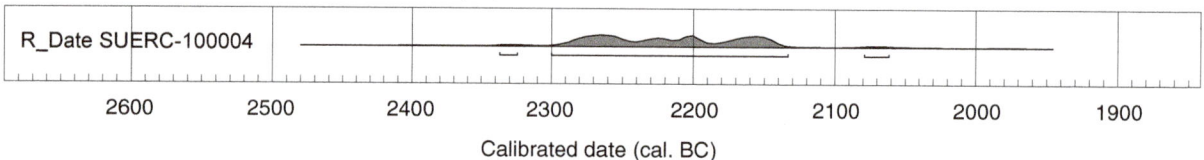

Figure 5.26 Calibrated radiocarbon date for the Beaker pit

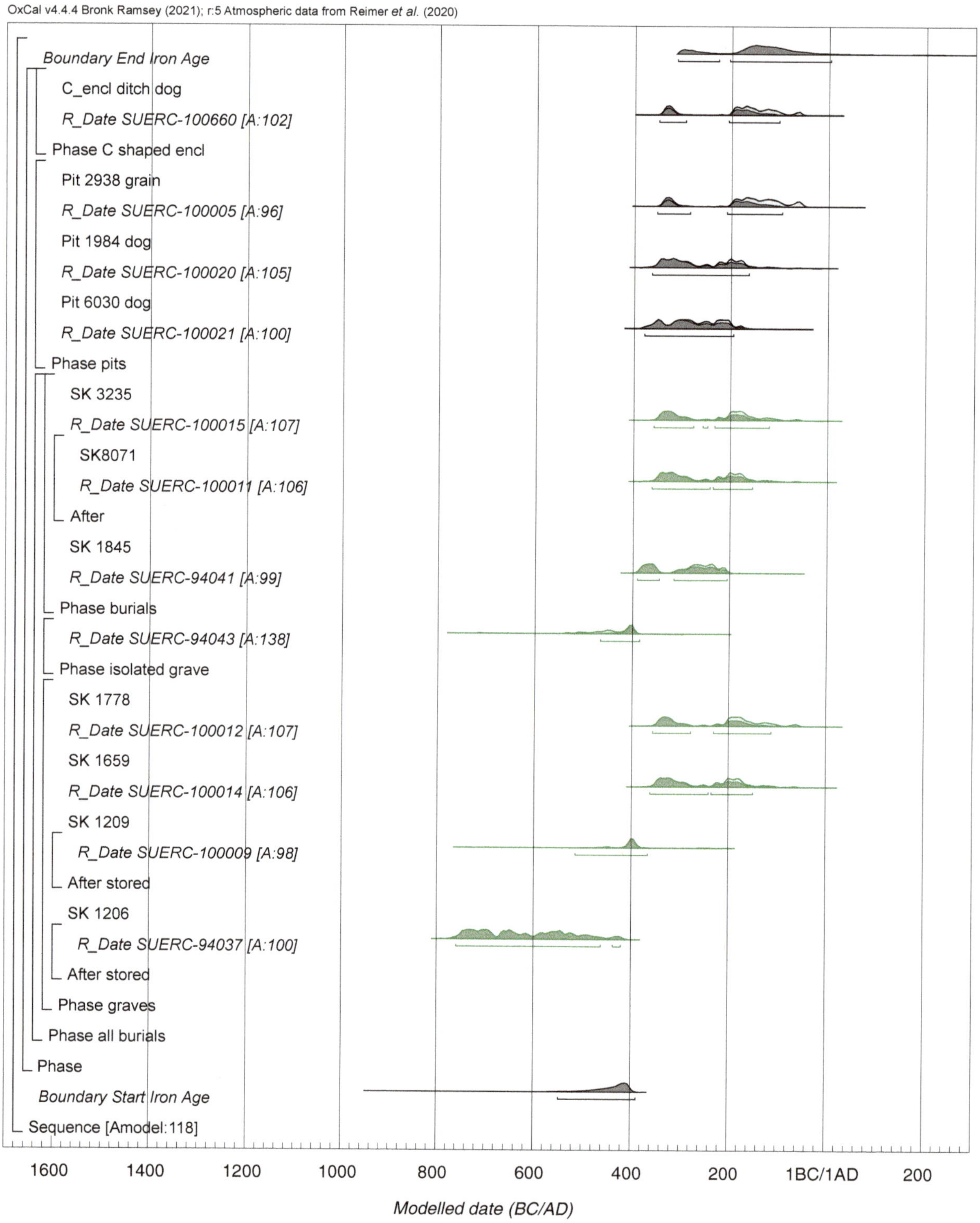

OxCal v4.4.4 Bronk Ramsey (2021); r:5 Atmospheric data from Reimer et al. (2020)
Boundary End Iron Age
C_encl ditch dog
R_Date SUERC-100660 [A:102]
Phase C shaped encl
Pit 2938 grain
R_Date SUERC-100005 [A:96]
Pit 1984 dog
R_Date SUERC-100020 [A:105]
Pit 6030 dog
R_Date SUERC-100021 [A:100]
Phase pits
SK 3235
R_Date SUERC-100015 [A:107]
SK8071
R_Date SUERC-100011 [A:106]
After
SK 1845
R_Date SUERC-94041 [A:99]
Phase burials
R_Date SUERC-94043 [A:138]
Phase isolated grave
SK 1778
R_Date SUERC-100012 [A:107]
SK 1659
R_Date SUERC-100014 [A:106]
SK 1209
R_Date SUERC-100009 [A:98]
After stored
SK 1206
R_Date SUERC-94037 [A:100]
After stored
Phase graves
Phase all burials
Phase
Boundary Start Iron Age
Sequence [Amodel:118]
1600
1400
1200
1000
800
600
400
200
1BC/1AD
200
Modelled date (BC/AD)

Figure 5.27 A simple phased model (OxCal) of all radiocarbon results obtained for the settlement and its burials (green)

Whilst the individual date on each of these burials would be an accurate measurement of their age at death, this may not be the same as the date of burial (see Chapter 6).

The burials all fall within a period from the 5th century BC to sometime in either the late 4th, 3rd or 2nd century BC (see Fig. 5.26 and Tables 5.10–5.11). The duration of burial at the site appears to have lasted from between *62 to up to 335 years* (modelled as '*Span Iron Age burials*' at 95.4% probability; Fig. 5.28). The Iron Age burials coincide with the beginnings of the settlement, although domestic activity appears to have extended beyond the use of the site for burial (see Table 5.11). However, this could just reflect that burial was taking place elsewhere or away from the area of settlement contained within the limits of the excavation described here. Table 5.12 presents the radiocarbon dated burials in probability order. This indicates that SK 1206 was

Table 5.11 Selected parameters deriving form the model presented in Figure 5.27

Parameter name	68.3%	95.4%
First grave	*416–392 cal. BC*	*466–386 cal. BC*
Last grave	*326–289 cal. BC (14.2%)*	*334–243 cal. BC (24.7%)*
	210–147 cal. BC (54.1%)	*235–108 cal. BC (70.7%)*
Span Iron Age burials	*79–108 years (9.8%)*	*66–312 years*
	192–286 years (58.4%)	
Start Iron Age	*458–398 cal. BC*	*548–389 cal. BC*
End Iron Age	*306–284 cal. BC 6.7.8%*	*314–228 cal. BC (17.5%)*
	182–78 cal. BC (61.6%)	*206 cal. BC–4 cal. AD (77.9%)*

the earliest then SK 10005, followed by SK 1209 and SK 8071. All four burials are earlier than SK 1659, SK 3235 and SK 1778 (Fig. 5.29 and Table 5.12). Burial SK 1778 is

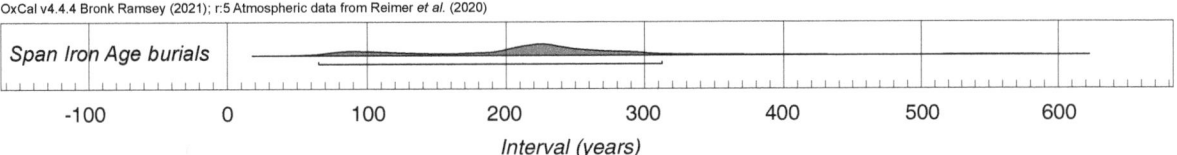

OxCal v4.4.4 Bronk Ramsey (2021); r:5 Atmospheric data from Reimer *et al.* (2020)

Figure 5.28 Iron Age burials – estimate for the duration ('Span') derived from the model shown in Figure 5.27

Table 5.12 Probability order of all the radiocarbon dates on Iron Age burials. Generated using the 'Order' function and from the OxCal model shown in Figure 5.27 and summarised in Figure 5.29. The table should be read from the left hand column across each row. The stated value is the probability (%) that the radiocarbon date listed in the lefthand column is older than each radiocarbon date in the row (e.g., SK 1206 has a 99% probability of being older than SK 10005)

	Order	SK 1206 SUERC-94037	SK 10005 SUERC-94043	SK 1209 SUERC-100009	SK 1845 SUERC-94041	SK 8071 SUERC-100011	SK 1659 SUERC-100014	SK 3235 SUERC-100015	SK 1778 SUERC-100012
SK 1206	SUERC-94037	0	99	98	100	100	100	100	100
SK 10005	SUERC-94043	1	0	62	99	100	100	100	100
SK 1209	SUERC-100009	2	38	0	98	99	99	99	99
SK 1845	SUERC-94041	0	0	2	0	64	65	68	70
SK 8071	SUERC-100011	0	0	1	36	0	51	54	56
SK 1659	SUERC-100014	0	0	1	35	49	0	53	56
SK 3235	SUERC-100015	0	0	1	32	46	47	0	52
SK 1778	SUERC-100012	0	0	1	30	44	44	48	0

Table 5.13 Radiocarbon results for Roman features. Calibrated ranges are all unmodelled

Lab no.	Feature	Material	δ¹³C	δ¹⁵N	C/N ratio	Radiocarbon age	Calibrated radiocarbon age 95.4% probability
SUERC-94036	SK 1076 Grave 1083	Human bone: Right tibia from an older adult female, extended	-20.2‰	9.3‰	3.4	1913 ± 26 BP	30–40 cal. AD (1.8%) 60–212 cal. AD (93.7%)
SUERC-94042	SK 2446 Grave 2389	Human bone: Right femur from an older adult female, extended supine	-19.8‰	10.4‰	3.4	1862 ± 26 BP	122–338 cal. AD
SUERC-100003	Context 3184 Oven 2827 (cut 2827)	Charred plant remains: Spelt wheat grain (*Triticum spelta*)	-23.1‰			1689 ± 29 BP	256–284 cal. AD (16.0%) 326–422 cal. AD (79.4%)
SUERC-100010	SK 12053 Grave 12052	Human bone: Rib from an older adult male, extended supine	-21.5‰	7.5‰	3.5	1738 ± 29 BP	246–402 cal. AD
SUERC-100013	SK 2314 Grave 2315 (cut 2315)	Human bone: Rib from an mature adult female, extended prone	-20.2‰	9.0‰	3.3	1732 ± 29 BP	247–405 cal. AD
SUERC-100019	Context 1697 Isolated pit (cut 1645)	Animal bone: Cattle rib	-22.4‰	4.2‰	3.4	1811 ± 29 BP	130–144 cal. AD (1.9%) 154–260 cal. AD (60.2%) 278–335 cal. AD (33.4%)

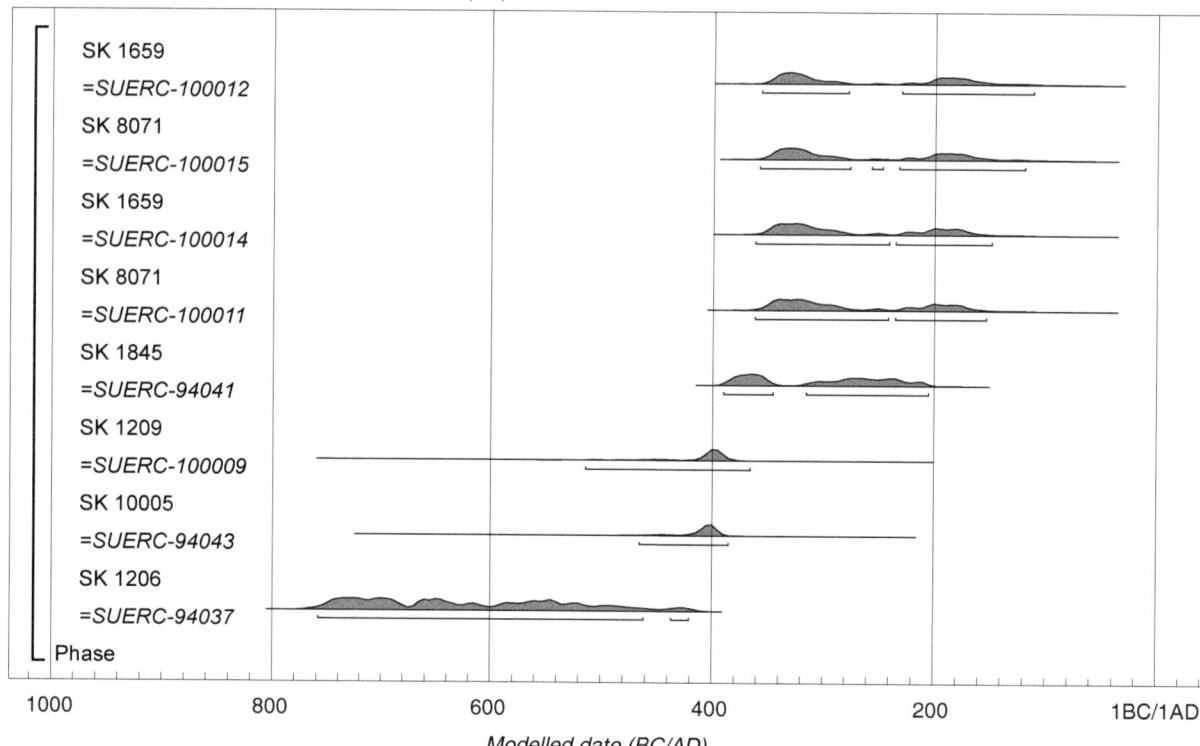

Figure 5.29 Iron Age burials – results derived from the model shown in Figure 5.27 placed in probability order

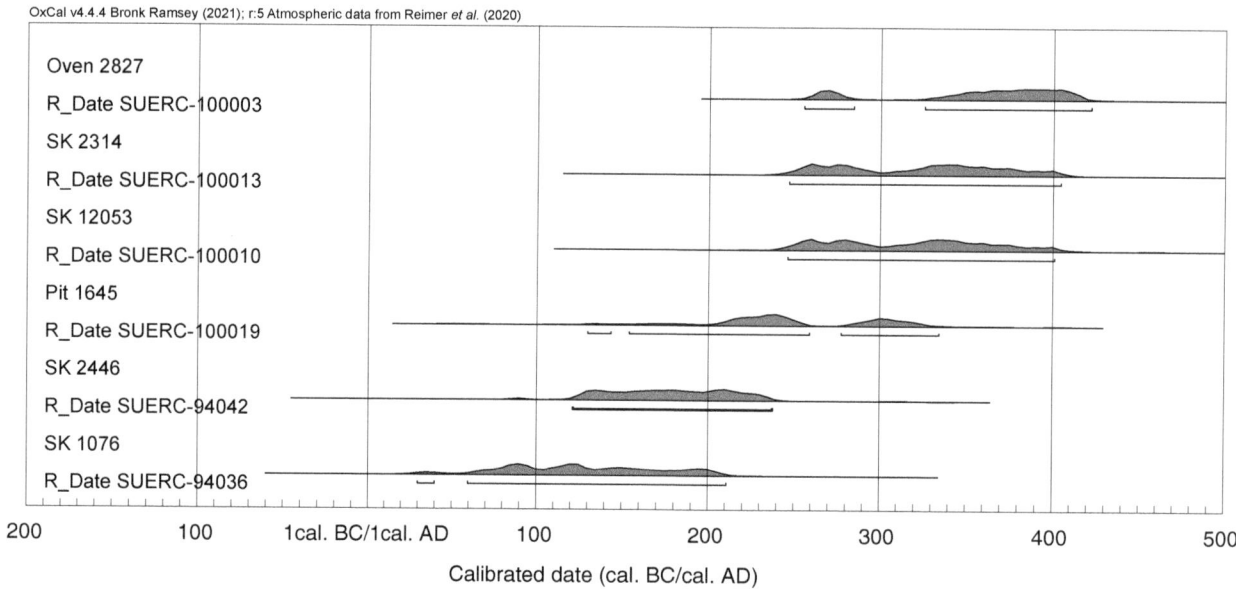

Figure 5.30 Calibrated radiocarbon dates for the Roman period

later than everything else but the difference is slight and the later burials in particular are effected by the bimodal nature of the calibration curve that corresponds with the Middle Iron Age period.

Other Iron Age activity that was radiocarbon dated includes three samples (2 x dog bones and a single grain: SUERC-100005, 100006 and 100020) from three Iron Age pits. A fourth sample (SUERC-100660) was on dog remains recovered from the upper ditch fills of the C-shaped enclosure and provides a *terminus ante quem* for the digging

of its ditch possibly in the earlier centuries of the Middle Iron Age.

Six dates were obtained for Roman features including four human burials, grain from an oven (crop dryer) and animal bone from a pit near one of the pit alignments (Table 5.13 and Fig. 5.30). When calibrated the dates span much of the Roman period. The earliest date (SUERC-94036) is on burial SK 1076 (grave 1083) and dates to the Early Roman period. Burial SK 2446 (grave 2389) is slightly later and its calibrated range falls mostly within the 2nd

Table 5.14 Radiocarbon dates and isotope results from the bone samples of skeletons

Lab Code	Sample	Material	$\delta^{13}C_{\text{V-PDB}}$ (‰)	$\delta^{15}N_{\text{AIR}}$ (‰)	C:N	Radiocarbon age (BP)	Calibrated date (95% probability)
SUERC-94041	SK 1845	left rib	-20.4	9.5 ±0.2	3.3	2247 ±26	390–200 cal. BC
SUERC-100013	SK 2314	rib	-20.2	9.0 ±0.2	3.3	1732 ±29	cal. AD 240–410
SUERC-100011	SK 8071	rib	-20.6	8.7 ±0.2	3.3	2175 ±29	360–110 cal. BC
SUERC-94043	SK 10005	left femur	-20.4	8.6 ±0.2	3.3	2369 ±26	540–390 cal. BC
Dated skeletons with no associated Sr or O isotope measurements							
SUERC-94036	SK 1076	right tibia	-20.2	9.3	3.4	1913 ±26	cal. AD 30–220
SUERC-94037	SK 1206	left rib	-20.8	9.7	3.4	2465 ±26	760–420 cal. BC
SUERC-94042	SK 2446	right femur	-19.8	10.4	3.4	1862 ±26	cal. AD 120–240
SUERC-100009	SK 1209	rib	-21.1	10.6	3.5	2340 ±29	520–360 cal. BC
SUERC-100010	SK 12053	rib	-21.5	7.5	3.5	1738 ±29	cal. AD 250–380
SUERC-100012	SK 1778	rib	-20.6	9.3	3.4	2157 ±29	360–50 cal. BC
SUERC-100014	SK 1656	rib	-21.7	9.4	3.5	2172 ±29	360–100 cal. BC
SUERC-100015	SK 3235	rib	-20.5	8.5	3.2	2163 ±29	360–50 cal. BC

century cal. AD. Of Middle Roman date is cattle bone (SUERC-100019), whilst burials SK 12053 and 2314 are of Late Roman date. A sample of charred grain from the oven that was built within the Iron Age C-shaped enclosure is potentially of Late Roman, 4th-century date, and as such represents some of the latest Roman activity on the site. A sample of cattle bone from pit 1645 is of Mid-Late Roman date (SUERC-100019) and appears to be associated with a probable boundary ditch rather than the pit alignment.

Radiocarbon dating and isotopic analyses of human remains

Derek Hamilton

Ten ribs and two femurs from Iron Age and Roman period burials were subjected to radiocarbon dating and a suite of isotopic analyses at the Scottish Universities Environmental Research Centre (SUERC), East Kilbride, UK. Additionally, molars or premolars from four of the individuals were submitted for strontium and oxygen isotope analyses. The light stable isotopes on the radiocarbon-dated bone samples suggest there was either no or minimal marine protein in the diets of these individuals, and so no correction has been made for the Marine Reservoir Effect (MRE).

Methods

Radiocarbon dating

The bones were pretreated following Dunbar *et al.* (2016). Briefly, samples were sanded, weighed, and placed in a beaker with 100 mL of 1M HCl at room temperature for 24–48 hrs or until fully demineralised. If more than 48 hrs are required, the sample is rinsed and the acid replenished. After demineralisation the sample is rinsed to near neutral pH and 100 mL of ultrapure MillQ® water is added. The sample is placed on a hotplate at ~80ºC until fully solubilised. The solution is then passed through GF/A filter paper and reduced to 5–10 mL prior to freeze-drying.

For graphitisation, 10–20mg of the collagen is weighed into a clean quartz insert and placed into a precleaned quartz combustion tube containing copper oxide to provide the oxygen for the reaction and silver foil to remove gaseous impurities (Vandeputte *et al.* 1996). The resulting carbon dioxide is then cryogenically purified and a 3 mL subsample reduced to elemental carbon (graphite) using the two-step iron and zinc process proposed by Slota *et al.* (1987). The graphite is then pressed into aluminium target holders and measured on either the SUERC 5MV tandem or 250kV single-stage AMS.

The radiocarbon results (Table 5.14) are conventional radiocarbon ages (Stuiver and Polach 1977). They have been calibrated using the internationally agreed terrestrial (IntCal20) calibration curve of Reimer *et al.* (2020) and the OxCal v.4.4 computer program (Bronk Ramsey 2009). The $\delta^{13}C$ and $\delta^{15}N$ values on the bones collagen suggest there was either no or minimal marine protein in the diets of these individuals, and so no correction has been made for the Marine Reservoir Effect (MRE).

$\delta^{13}C$ and $\delta^{15}N$ stable isotope methods

Sayle *et al.* (2019) fully describe how the simultaneous $\delta^{13}C$ and $\delta^{15}N$ values were obtained by combusting approximately 1–1.5mg of collagen, which was weighed into a tin capsule and subsequently introduced to a single combustion reactor containing tungstic oxide and reduced copper wires held at 1020ºC. Samples were introduced via the Thermo Scientific MAS Plus Autosampler alongside a pulse of oxygen to aid combustion. The resulting N_2 and CO_2 gases produced in the reactor were separated using a temperature variable GC column (70–240ºC), and then transferred to a Thermo Scientific DELTA V Advantage IRMS via a Thermo Scientific ConFlo IV Universal Interface (Thermo Fisher Scientific, Bremen, Germany). Optimising the gas chromatography separation and helium carrier gas flow during sample analysis in the EA IsoLink IRMS System enabled simultaneous $\delta^{13}C$ and $\delta^{15}N$ values of archaeological bone collagen to be obtained in approximately 10 minutes, providing sharp peak shapes. There is 20% duplication of all samples in each run. Results are reported (Table 5.14) as per mil (‰) relative to the internationally accepted standards V-PDB and AIR with 1σ precisions of ±0.1‰ and ±0.2‰ for $\delta^{13}C$ and $\delta^{15}N$, respectively.

Table 5.15 Isotope results from the tooth enamel of skeletons

Lab Code	Sample	Period	Material	$\delta^{13}C_{V\text{-}PDB}$ (‰)	$\delta^{18}O_{V\text{-}PDB}$ (‰)	$\delta^{18}O_{VSMOW}$ (‰)	$^{87}Sr/^{86}Sr$	Sr_{conc} (ppm) [$\pm 2\sigma$ %]
GU63663	SK 1845	Iron Age	Lower left 2nd molar	-13.2 ±0.02	-4.21 ±0.06	26.58	0.70821 ±0.0015	111.1 [0.3]
GU63664	SK 2314	Late Roman	Lower left 1st premolar	-14.4 ±0.09	-4.57 ±0.12	26.21	0.70864 ±0.0014	86.0 [0.3]
GU63665	SK 8071	Iron Age	Upper right 2nd premolar	-14.1 ±0.02	-4.35 ±0.01	26.44	0.70837 ±0.0010	55.3 [0.2]
GU63666	SK 10005	Iron Age	Lower left 2nd molar	-14.0 ±0.05	-4.83 ±0.07	25.94	0.70843 ±0.0011	82.0 [0.2]

$^{87}Sr/^{86}Sr$ analysis

Strontium isotope analysis was made on the tooth enamel from the four burials (Table 5.15). A small fragment of tooth was removed from the junction of the occlusal surface and one of the side faces of the tooth, with preference given to the best-preserved location. The fragment was placed in a 10 M NaOH solution and heated to approximately 80°C for 8 hrs and then allowed to cool. The dentine was scraped from the enamel using a dissecting needle and the procedure repeated until all the dentine had been removed. The sample was then repeatedly rinsed with 0.5 M HCl to remove all traces of the NaOH and finally rinsed with ultra-pure water. The isolated enamel sample was then oven dried overnight and transferred to a labelled glass vial to await analysis.

Strontium was separated from the enamel sample using conventional extraction chromatography using the Sr.Spec (Eichrom) crown ether, and loaded onto a single Re filament using a Ta_2O_5 activator for mass spectrometry. The total procedural blank was <200 pg. The sample was analysed on a VG Sector 54–30 mass spectrometer operated in dynamic (3 cycle) multi-collection mode. Instrumental mass fractionation was corrected to $^{86}Sr/^{88}Sr$ = 0.1196 using an exponential fractionation law. Data were collected as 12 blocks of 10 ratios. NIST SRM-987 was used as a quality control monitor. A small volume of a high-purity Sr-84 spike was weighed carefully and added to the sample prior to dissolution and analysis, and the amount of Sr-84 relative to sample Sr was measured during the TIMS analysis for $^{87}Sr/^{86}Sr$.

$\delta^{18}O$ and $\delta^{13}C$ analysis on carbonate

To analyse the biogenic carbonate ($\delta^{18}O_{carb}$) in the tooth sample, the excess material that was removed for strontium analysis was crushed using the Retsch® Micro-mill sample preparation kit, until it passed freely through a 400 μm stainless steel sieve (Retsch®). The sample was then sent in glass vials to Iso-Analytical (Cheshire, UK) where it was processed for both $\delta^{18}O$ and $\delta^{13}C$ analysis.

The sample (~7 mg) was weighed in duplicate into Exetainer™ tubes and then flushed with 99.995% helium. After flushing, phosphoric acid was added to the samples and they were allowed to react in the acid overnight to allow complete conversion of carbonate to CO_2. Reference and control materials were prepared the same way.

The CO_2 gas liberated from samples was then analysed by Continuous Flow-Isotope Ratio Mass Spectrometry (CF-IRMS). Carbon dioxide was sampled from the Exetainer™ tubes into a continuously flowing He stream using a double-holed needle. The CO_2 was resolved on a packed column gas chromatograph and the resultant chromatographic peak carried forward into the ion source of a Europa Scientific 20-20 IRMS where it is ionised and accelerated. Gas species of different mass are separated in a magnetic field then simultaneously measured using a Faraday cup collector array to measure the isotopomers of CO_2 at m/z 44, 45, and 46.

The phosphoric acid used for digestion had been prepared for isotopic analysis in accordance with Coplen *et al.* (1983) was injected through the septum into the vials. The reference materials used during analysis was: IA-R022 (Iso-Analytical working standard calcium carbonate, $\delta^{13}C_{V\text{-}PDB}$ = –28.63‰ and $\delta^{18}O_{V\text{-}PDB}$ = –22.69‰), NBS-18 (carbonatite, $\delta^{13}C_{V\text{-}PDB}$ = –5.01‰ and $\delta^{18}O_{V\text{-}PDB}$ = –23.20‰), IA-R066 (chalk, $\delta^{13}C_{V\text{-}PDB}$ = +2.33‰ and $\delta^{18}O_{V\text{-}PDB}$ = –1.52‰) and ILC1 limestone.

Acid preparations of samples and controls were measured directly against acid preparations of the working Iso-Analytical calcium carbonate standard. This procedure removes the need to apply separate corrections for temperature dependent isotope fractionation. The results obtained for the NBS18 and IA-R066 controls are used to check and correct the data as required.

Results

The results of the analyses on the samples are given in Figures 5.31 and 5.32. As mentioned above, the $\delta^{13}C$ and $\delta^{15}N$ values from the bones suggest little or no marine component to the diets. Interestingly, the nitrogen value for SK 12053 is considerably lower than the other individuals, suggesting their dietary protein likely was derived primarily from grains and terrestrial herbivores, while the two individuals with elevated $\delta^{15}N$ values (SK 1209 and SK 2446) might have incorporated more higher trophic level foods in their diets, such as pig or freshwater fish.

Turning to the strontium and oxygen values on the tooth enamel (Fig. 5.33), the White Chalk that underlies the Collection Management Facility, Science and Innovation Park has an expected strontium isotope range of 0.7079

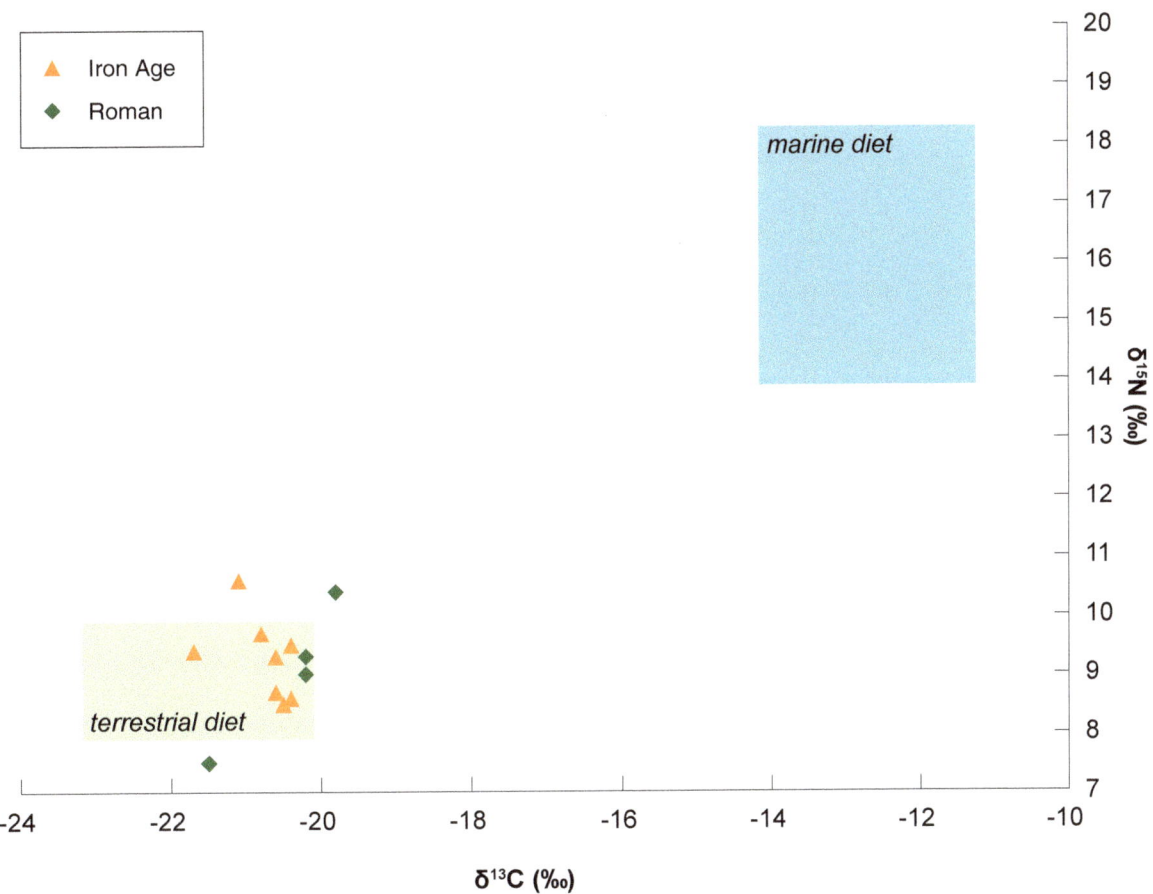

Figure 5.31 Biplot of δ¹⁵N versus δ¹³C for the human remains from the Collection Management Facility. The boxes for the expected values of fully terrestrial versus fully marine values are based on the data of Mays (1998, fig. 9.2)

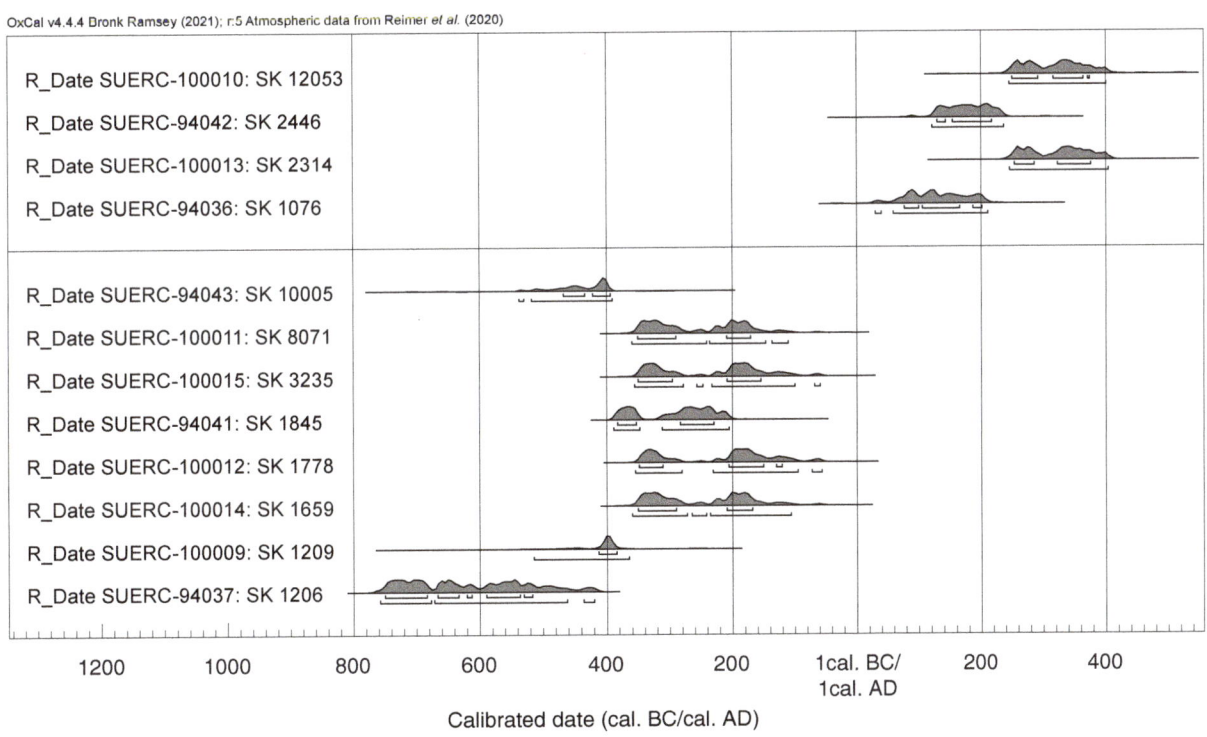

Figure 5.32 Probability distributions for the calibrated radiocarbon dates on human remains from the Collection Management Facility

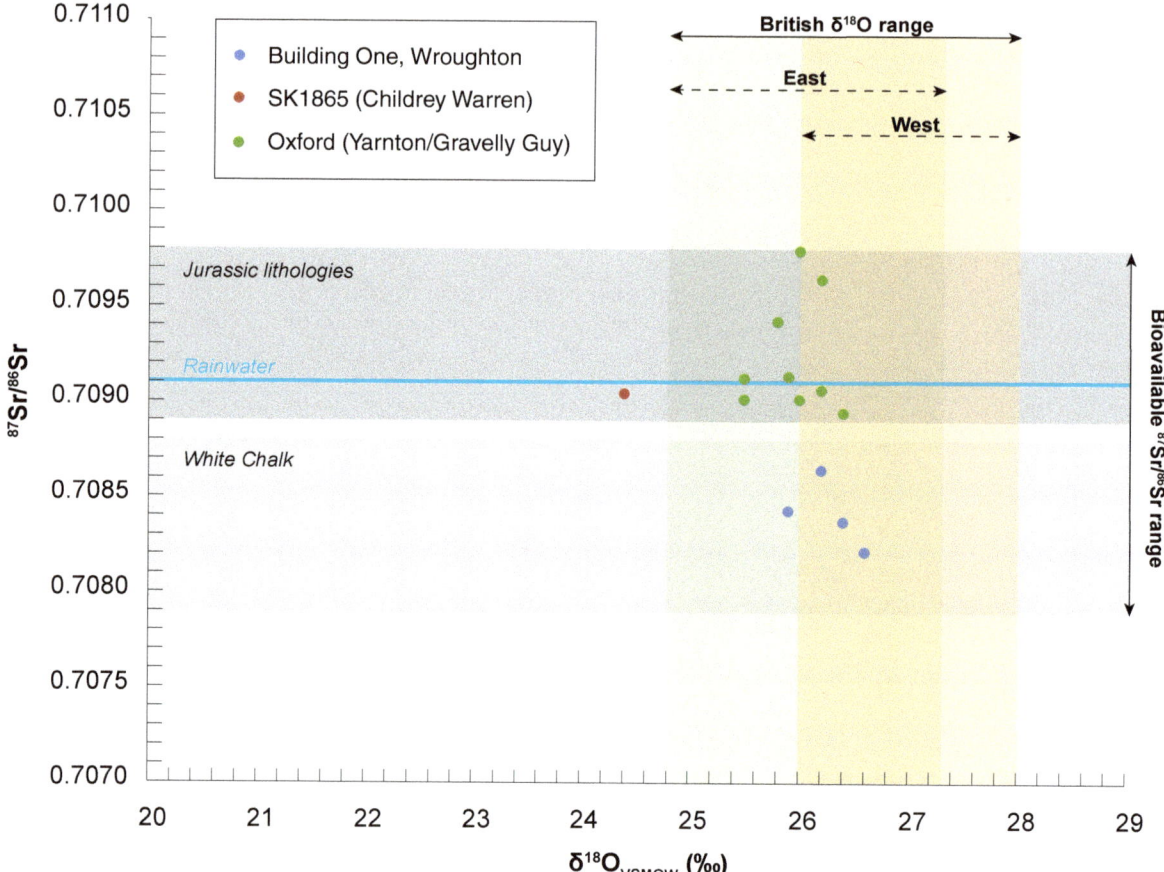

Figure 5.33 Plot of $^{87}Sr/^{86}Sr$ *and* $\delta^{18}O_{carb}$ *‰ (VSMOW) for the human tooth enamel samples from the Collection Management Facility. These data are compared to recently measured samples from near Childrey Warren (Gault/Upper Greensand formations) and the sites of Yarnton and Gravelly Guy, near Oxford (Kellaways and Oxford Clays)*

and 0.7088 (Moore and Montgomery 2023). However, the site lies less than 2km south of the Jurassic period lithologies that are more radiogenic and have an expected range of 0.7089–0.7098 for those geologic units that stretch approximately 15km to the north (e.g. West Walton, Corallian, Kellaways and Oxford Clays) (Moore and Montgomery 2023). This range is consistent with

unpublished strontium isotope data from Iron Age burials from Yarnton and Gravelly Guy, as well as a recently excavated Iron Age burial near Childrey Warren. The strontium isotope ratios from these four individuals are consistent with individuals that were raised on food from the White Chalk, suggesting the majority of their dietary protein came from local sources.

Chapter 6
Discussion

Clare Randall

At the edge of an escarpment overlooking the clay vale of the River Ray, the Collection Management Facility, Science and Innovation Park site lacks any shelter and is open to the elements, seemly unpromising for settlement. There is no water source within the site, and the nearest clean water was probably springs located off the edge of the scarp. However, people were attracted to the area from the Mesolithic period onwards, and the free-draining substrate and wide visibility of the surrounding landscape may have played a part.

The earliest evidence

No Mesolithic or Neolithic features were identified, although there were a handful of flints of Mesolithic and Mesolithic or Early Neolithic date, residual in later features. It is possible that a couple of these, such as the Early Neolithic leaf-shaped arrowhead found within a Roman grave and a flake from a Neolithic polished flint axe within one of the pits of a Late Bronze Age to Early Iron Age pit alignment may have been collected and curated. Whilst scant, this evidence is of use, as to date no other Mesolithic or Neolithic remains have been recorded nearby. The immediate area is mostly devoid of known sites and monuments of pre-Bronze Age date, although a possible but untested stone circle has been suggested at Coate just to the north of the site (Barclay *et al.* 1995, 73 and fig. 37) and the Avebury monument complex, along with the suggested activity under the present town of Marlborough, lies just to the south. Certainly, the various valleys that cut through the downs would have been natural and obvious routeways through the chalk hills, which would have linked the various river catchments of the Thames Valley (see Hey *et al.* 2011a and figs 14.9 and 14.10).

Pit deposits associated with the use of Impressed (Peterborough) Ware and Grooved Ware that can define the later Neolithic are also under-represented in the immediate area, although this could simply be a factor of a lack of development and research excavation (see Barclay 2024; Guarino and Barclay 2023). The same probable pattern of low-level activity appears to continue into the Beaker and Early Bronze Age period during the late 3rd and early 2nd millennium BC, although a number of barrows are known, particularly on the chalk downs including a small number of cemeteries.

The Beaker pit

The earliest dated feature was a small, bowl-shaped pit which contained nearly 80 sherds of Beaker pottery. It also contained the majority of flints from the site, part of a burnt antler, a concentration of charred hazelnut shells, barley grains and a charred sloe stone. The radiocarbon determination of 2338–2062 cal. BC was obtained from one of the hazelnut shells. Whilst this was the only feature of this date, it was located close to the north-western limit of the excavation so it is possible that additional features lay to the north. However, pits of this date are often found in small groups or in isolation (Hey *et al.* 2016).

The finds within pit 1245 are consistent with domestic activity but may also have been part of a continuum of the selection of material for specific deposition. Typologically the pottery appears to be early and fits the character of early domestic assemblages and is similar to the material found at Dean Bottom on the Marlborough Downs some 7km north-west of Marlborough (Gingell 1992). One unusual feature is the occurrence of bone temper, although this has been noted on a number of sites in Wiltshire and also in Oxfordshire (e.g. Yarnton, Oxon: Barclay *et al.* 2016, 98).

Such pits are a feature of the Neolithic to Early Bronze Age periods and are well attested within the Thames Valley (Hey with Robinson 2011), for example at Gravelly Guy, Oxfordshire (Bradley and Lambrick 2004, 35); they are perhaps less common in the Wiltshire and Gloucestershire part of the Upper Thames catchment, although sporadic evidence for Beaker pits and activity was found along the line of the A419/417 road scheme (Mudd *et al.* 1999) and from Horcott, Fairford (Pine and Preston 2004); and Cotswold Community (Powell *et al.* 2010), and on the Marlborough

Downs. The pit at the Collection Management Facility seems to echo these examples, including Marlborough Downs, including Burderop Down (Gingell 1992).

Apart from the solitary Beaker pit there was no evidence for activity of Bronze Age date from the immediate site despite the occurrence of barrows and later Bronze Age settlement evidence within the vicinity.

The pit alignments

Pit alignments dating to the Late Bronze Age to Early Iron Age are well known in the Thames Valley (Lambrick with Robinson 2009), north into the Midlands (Buteux and Chapman 2009), spreading over to the east of England (Pollard 1996), and into the north of England (Waddington 1997) and Scotland (Barber 1985), although the distribution is patchy (Rylatt and Bevan 2007, 220). They are not well represented in the Wessex region with some notable exceptions near to the Iron Age hillfort at Old Sarum (Old Sarum and Greentrees School, Wessex Archaeology 2013; 2016), where a pair of parallel lines of pits terminated at a settlement of later Bronze Age date. Its course possibly extended to a small group of barrows and beyond over a distance of a kilometre, where its alignment also coincided with a Wessex linear ditch, perhaps suggesting a boundary function or land division. Near the barrows other perpendicular rows of posts ran from the main alignment towards one of the barrows. Waddington (1997, 22) identified two forms of pit alignment, single and double rows, of which the single rows were more common; the Collection Management Facility pit alignments comprising two sets of largely parallel rows, one double, the other multiple, appears to be one of the more complex examples. The triple arrangements are rarely maintained along the length of the monument (Lambrick with Robinson 2009, 60), and this holds true for Pit alignment 2 at the Collection Management Facility.

At the Collection Management Facility, the western Pit alignment 1 is a neater group of features, with two rows of apparently paired pits, whereas Pit alignment 2 is more complex with perhaps three main rows of pits, altered, and added to in places, although interpreting this is complicated by the impingement onto it of later settlement features, which gave it a false segmented appearance. In the case of alignment 2, however, there is a sense that it may have been renewed over a period of time. How much this had to do with its proximity to the area in which settlement arose is not possible to say.

The two Collection Management Facility pit alignments are poorly dated, containing few datable finds, a common factor in Upper Thames Valley alignments (Lambrick with Robinson 2009, 60). At Willow Brook Centre, Bradley Stoke, South Gloucestershire (now subsumed into the northern side of Bristol) two broadly parallel single alignments of pits were positioned about 25m apart. No datable material was recovered from the pits, but they were dated to the later Bronze Age or Early Iron Age on stratigraphic grounds (Simmonds 2011, 17). At Roughground Farm, Lechlade (Glos) the two short lengths of pits in single lines, only contained scraps of Iron Age pottery (Allen *et al.* 1993 47). At the Collection Management Facility, the flake removed from a Neolithic polished flint axe found in one pit is clearly residual, but other finds are limited to a small sherd of Early Iron Age pottery. Although there was no stratigraphic relationship between the two alignments the more easterly, Pit alignment 2 was in several locations stratigraphically earlier than elements of the Iron Age settlement. It is assumed that both alignments were broadly contemporary although, the date of their establishment and use is unknown. Whilst they have been categorised here as Late Bronze Age/Early Iron Age, they may only just precede the establishment of the settlement (although pinpointing that commencement is not without problems, see below). The Iron Age buildings and pits largely respected the alignments, with most features (but not all) located to the east of them, suggesting a degree of contemporaneity, that the earlier features remained at least partially visible, or there was a strong recollection of the presence of some form of boundary.

Alignments may have functioned as symbolic landscape or territorial divisions, rather than necessarily physical barriers to either people or livestock (Thomas 2003; Cunliffe 2005, 432; Buteux and Chapman 2009, 104–5). Where these alignments did not create a physical barrier, they may still have created a 'cognitive' barrier (Waddington 1997, 22), but the functional and social explanations need not be mutually exclusive (cf Rylatt and Bevan 2007, 219). The separation between pits, which would have affected their permeability as a boundary, may have been affected by truncation (cf Buteux and Chapman 2009, 104). Most of the pits were around 1m in diameter and spaced at a similar distance apart. This is typical for this type of monument (cf Rylatt and Bevan 2007, 221), and similar to those seen in the Upper Thames Valley (Lambrick with Robinson 2009, 60) and further afield. The pair of alignments at St Ives, Cambridgeshire had significant gaps between the pits (Pollard 1996, 98–102).

The evidence for post-pipes in these alignments is variable, with many not containing indications of timbers (Barber 1985, 151; Waddington 1997, 24; Simmonds 2011, 32), and the evidence generally pointing to pits being left open to silt (Rylatt and Bevan 2007, 220). None of the Upper Thames Valley examples in the Lechlade area has shown evidence for posts (Lambrick with Robinson 2009, 60). A few of the pits at the Collection Management Facility provide some indication that they may have contained upright posts, although this is only arguable for small numbers of features in each alignment, and all have a degree of ambiguity. If the holes did contain timbers, this could have supported a post and rail arrangement of fence. However, some pits were shallow and there was variability in diameter and spacing, particularly in Pit alignment 1, although this is probably due to the degree of later plough damage. Barber has suggested that pits in alignments may have been used to create an upcast bank (1985, 162), although the profile of most examples appears to argue against this (Waddington 1997, 24). The Collection Management Facility pits, with steep or vertical sides do not seem to fit the quarry-scoop model, and there is certainly no trace of a bank or filling from one side.

Whilst there is therefore no evidence that pit alignments provided an impervious barrier, the permeability of the alignments should not perhaps be over emphasised with respect to the movement of livestock. Cattle in particular can be influenced in movement by their perception of barriers and people within their wide field of vision, utilising their flight response and animals can become 'hefted', not only to a space but to habitual movement (Randall 2010a, 65–66). Therefore, it is possible that there is an element of practicality, enabling movement through a landscape with livestock which reduces the numbers of people needed to move animals, but did not require a solid boundary – something that may not have been desirable for social reasons.

Whilst over 300 pits were exposed along the two alignments, both clearly extended to the north-west and south of the excavated area, making them substantial features which represent a significant investment in time and effort. The size of these monuments is akin to that seen at Shorncote/Cotswold Community, near Cirencester, Gloucestershire which was 500m in length (Davies 2018), and an example known from crop marks over 900m at Long Wittenham (Lambrick with Robinson 2009, 65), or the Greentrees School/Old Sarum example (Wessex Archaeology 2013; 2016) given above. Given the number of pits in some alignments, they may have constituted a major communal work, with the pits suggesting gang construction where the achievement of any one individual or group was more evident (Buteux and Chapman 2009, 104). This might explain the variability in spacing and number of rows in the Collection Management Facility Pit alignment 2. However, these monuments generally appear to have often been short lived, suggesting that the act of their creation which was more important than their functional existence and that the pit digging had some mnemonic connotation (Pollard 1996, 110–111). There is little to suggest this in the Collection Management Facility example, although the deliberate placement of later Iron Age pits which contained highly specific deposits might indicate that this area had been appropriate for this type of activity.

It has been suggested that pit alignments are associated with landscape demarcation (Barber 1985, 162; Pollard 1996, 112). Around 20 pit alignments around the confluence of the Trent and Tame rivers in Staffordshire seem to have demarcated areas of land, and each 'parcel' appears to have encompassed different resources afforded by the landscape (Buteux and Chapman 2009, 106). In the Upper Thames, the alignments appear to divide sections of land within the river bends (Lambrick with Robinson 2009, 65), a pattern which has also been seen in the upper Severn (Wigley 2007). The Collection Management Facility

site topography is clearly different from the latter, and it is not possible to identify a block of land which it divides or demarcates but it does seem to have occurred at a point in the landscape where differing resources met or were accessible from – water in the valley, wetland and upland grazing and perhaps woodland, especially on the slopes.

The orientation of both the alignments at the Collection Management Facility means that rather than dividing the upland area from the lowland by running along the edge of the scarp, which lies at the north end of the excavated area, both run south from the break in slope. They both appear to originate at the scarp edge, and converge as they exit the excavation area, 300m to the south. If contemporary, they perhaps defined a routeway which opened out at the northern end onto the slopes down into the valley and heading south led up onto the higher ground of the Marlborough Downs. The alignments diverge towards the plateau edge, and if they had a practical function, would work efficiently if they defined the sides of a droveway for bringing livestock up from valley grazing, the splayed 'entrance' from the lower ground acting as a funnel entrance for efficient stock handling (cf Randall 2021, 57–58), and a common feature for tracks entering a more controlled landscape from an open one (Randall 2010b, 211). The orientation aligns with the head of a south-west/north-east oriented valley, Markham Bottom, within which a spring rises. This would therefore give direct access to a clean source of water. Further to the east, to the south of modern Wantage, and about 1.5km to the north-east of Segsbury Camp hillfort, a double pit alignment identified on the line of the Childrey Warren water pipeline ran north-south, perpendicular to the slope leading from the high ground of the Berkshire Downs into the Vale of the White Horse, close to and parallel with a stream which now rises just to the north. In this case a pit rich in Early Iron Age pottery located nearby was felt to underline the symbolic nature of the boundary (Guarino and Barclay 2023, 169). This is a similar situation to that seen at the Collection Management Facility with pit 1048, and possibly by pit 8068.

There is no information on the livestock population from the site during this period, so it is difficult to postulate the nature of the husbandry regime or consider seasonal or more regular movement, of either animals or people. Extensive later Bronze Age field systems on the Marlborough Downs, including around Barbury hillfort have been suggested to have been part of a grazing regime for cattle which would have utilised the valley during the summer, and over wintered on the higher ground, that would also have been used for arable and sheep (Gingell 1992, 156, fig. 96). If this were the case, then delineation or demarcation of routeways or the location of water courses in during the Late Bronze Age–Iron Age transition, into the Early Iron Age may have marked places which had been long understood.

Cattle and sheep/goat are well attested in the Iron Age phase of activity at the Collection Management Facility, and given the lack of water on the plateau, regular access to the River Ray, particularly for cattle, which have a considerable need for water on a daily basis (Smith Thomas 2005, 16; Reynolds 1987, 41), and especially when used for dairy products, would have been a practical necessity that the landscape division could have organised. The seasonally variable availability of land and grazing in the Upper Thames Valley has been noted, as has an increase in livestock keeping during the Middle Iron Age (Hey 2007), and whilst there may be greater variability in the approach to production in the valley than suggested by a model of movement between gravel terraces on a seasonal basis (cf Hingley 1984), the facilitation of movement onto the plateau adds an additional series of possibilities for husbandry approaches and the relationships between local groups. In this context, the lack of evidence of the individuals buried on the site during the Iron Age (albeit in a small sample) having lived anywhere other than on the chalk (see below) is intriguing.

The general association of pit alignments with water and watercourses is emphasised (Buteux and Chapman 2009; Pollard 1996, 113) and Rylatt and Bevan (2007, 221–2) supply numerous examples. Their suggestion, however, that pit alignments were constructed to contain water at some points in the year (Rylatt and Bevan 2007, 231), on the chalk literally does not hold water. Pit alignments of the Late Bronze Age and Early Iron Age in the Welsh Marches have a strong relationship with topography and drainage with about a third running perpendicularly or at an angle away from watersheds and half running towards or perpendicularly towards the head of a valley (Wigley 2007, 124–5). Iron Age settlement and land boundaries appears to have been more extensive in the area between the rivers Coln and Leach and their confluence with the Thames, and in several cases around modern Lechlade, linear boundaries appear to have originated as pit alignments, although they are not common in the Upper Thames Valley as a whole (Hey 2007, 167). A double alignment of similar scale to the Collection Management Facility examples, and with similar sized pits, dated to the Late Bronze Age or Early Iron Age has been excavated at Shorncote. There are Late Bronze Age and Early Iron Age sites in the area, and the suggestion from palaeobotanical material in a watering hole that at the beginning of the 1st millennium BC there was still relatively dense woodland in this area (Hey 2007, 168).

If the alignment marked a territorial boundary, it seems that access to the watercourse on the edge of the downs was a significant factor in its placement, a practicality probably related to livestock husbandry which may have accumulated more symbolic associations. The significance of the alignments appears to have lingered into the period of the establishment of the settlement (suggested by the general avoidance of the area of the pits), and the co-location of pit alignments with settlement has been noted elsewhere (Waddington 1997, 24–5). If the pits also signify division of space and perhaps tenure, the location of settlement against the pit alignments would imply settlement at the edge of a territorial unit. The longevity of the meaning of some of these features has, however,

been noted elsewhere (Pollard 1996; Powell *et al.* 2010), although this is not universal (Simmonds 2011). As will be mentioned below, the general location and orientation of the Collection Management Facility examples seems to be echoed in a ditched track which was established during the Late Iron Age/Early Roman transitional period, perhaps echoing both functional practicality and long-standing understanding of territory.

The settlement

There is relatively little evidence for Iron Age settlement in the immediate area, and there appears to have been limited study, including of the hillforts which are closest to the site. More settlement is of course known to the north, with the well-known settlements of the Upper Thames Valley, although even here, there is a propensity for sites to occupy the gravel terraces adjacent to the Thames or its tributaries (Hey 2007, 158). Across the Severn-Cotswolds during this period both enclosed and unenclosed settlements occur, and there is variability within the latter, with a tendency to shift across an area of landscape (Moore 2006, 92). Whilst the complete form of the settlement at the Collection Management Facility cannot be discerned due to truncation and removal of more ephemeral features by later ploughing, and its total extent was not revealed, extending as it did beyond the limits of excavation, a significant portion was available for investigation. It is possible that the poor understanding of the general settlement pattern in the area is partly due to the ploughing of the uplands (as suggested for the Berkshire Downs, Barclay *et al.* 2003, 256), and reduced visibility of unenclosed as opposed to enclosed sites.

Chronology

In common with the pit alignments, the date of inception of the Iron Age settlement is not entirely clear. A few Early Iron Age pottery sherds came largely from contexts which contained other either very broadly datable or more evidently Middle Iron Age pottery. There seemed to be a slight concentration of sherds with earlier affinities in the north-eastern part of the settlement, although it was not possible to clearly identify any given feature as being likely to be of specifically Early Iron Age date. In addition, there are several radiocarbon dates which fall within the Early to earlier Middle Iron Age (8th–4th century BC). These were all on human burials which were made within the north-western part of the settlement area, and together suggest that the earliest activity may have been in the northern part of the excavated area, adjacent to, but respecting Pit alignment 2. However, the tightly flexed nature of these burials suggests that they may have been curated (see below); the deposition of the remains may have been more contemporaneous with the main floruit of settlement activity, and therefore misleading in suggesting the date of inception of the activity. An Early Iron Age phase of settlement could exist beyond the present limits of archaeological investigation.

Nevertheless, the bulk of the evidence for the settlement suggests a broadly Middle Iron Age date, extending into the Late Iron Age. Clearly Late Iron Age material is scarce but does include some pottery with La Tène style decoration that may date into the 2nd and 1st centuries BC, which are scattered across the settlement area.

Nature and layout of the settlement

Most of the Iron Age occupation occurred in a broadly north/south band across the western half of the excavated area. As mentioned above, this largely respected the course of Pit alignment 2, although at some points this was impinged on. There were some outlying pits to the west, including one, 8118, which was on the line of Pit alignment 1, and perhaps was deliberately referencing it – it contained a more complex than usual group of finds and articulated animal burials. To the south-east, was a group of three roundhouses (8, 9 and 13), which seem deliberately separated from the main group. No physical boundaries to these areas of occupation were found, and the settlement was probably unenclosed and multi-focal. That it extended beyond the excavated area is also suggested by further Iron Age pits found immediately east of the site during the 2006 evaluation (OA 2006; Fig. 1.5), so dispersed groups of buildings which may have shifted over time are perhaps to be imagined. To the north, the edge of the scarp would have constrained the extent of the settlement, supported by a lack of remains noted in this area (OA 2005; Fig. 1.5). To the west and south the masking properties of dumped material associated with the airfield precluded the geophysical survey from identifying features (WYAS 2013). However, there have been finds of Iron Age material in the surrounding landscape, including an Iron Age brooch at Clouts Wood immediately to the north of the site (HER entry MWI15213; Fig. 6.1). As Moore has pointed out, an 'unenclosed' settlement may well have been perceived as 'bounded' in other ways than a physical barrier (2006, 98)

In a couple of areas roundhouses are in close proximity to each other. It is possible that in some cases an arrangement of house and ancillary structure pairings could be suggested (e.g., roundhouses 4 and 12), but it would require considerable refinement of the dating evidence to propose this. However, if this were the case then the pairing of dwellings may have been employed to house a growing extended family group. However, in this example, it is equally likely that one structure may have been the replacement for another; the extrapolated ground plans touch, suggesting that they may not have been standing at the same time. However, there is also no direct stratigraphic evidence to demonstrate that any single building succeeded another.

This is likely to be a function of the dispersed and shifting nature of the settlement and this is in keeping with other open sites in the Thames Valley (Lambrick with Robinson 2009, 94), such as Shorncote/Cotswold Community (Barclay and Glass 1995; Hearne and Adam 1999; Hearne and Heaton 1994). The broad pattern of Iron Age settlements in the Upper Thames Valley, is of small, enclosed settlements on the valley sides and floodplain and open settlements on the higher gravel terraces (Hingley 1984; Hey 2007, 159), and this holds true on the south side of the river systems to the east (e.g. open settlements of contemporary date on the Childrey Warren water pipeline route (Guarino and Barclay 2023, 170)). Given that the local settlement pattern is unclear, it is difficult to apply comparisons, but at first glance it appears that an open settlement on the chalk upland escarpment may represent a different approach to landscape organisation and exploitation on the Marlborough Downs. The more dispersed settlement pattern of the Thames upper reaches compared to that lower down the river has been suggested to be possibly related to late clearance of woodland (Hey 2007, 167), but it is not known if this may also account for areas closer to the Collection Management Facility site.

The buildings

Almost nothing survived of the roundhouses themselves and so details of their architecture are lacking but this is not unusual for the Upper Thames Valley (Lambrick with Robinson 2009, 133). There are few extant postholes, probably due to the degree of later plough truncation. The identified structures were surrounded by shallow ditches interpreted as eavesdrip gullies. These were 10m–12m in diameter and if it is assumed that the building wall lines were roughly 1m inside the gullies, the buildings may have ranged from 8m to 10m in diameter, which would be on the larger side of those seen in the Thames Valley (cf Lambrick with Robinson 2009, 141), although there are no known examples near to the Collection Management Facility site. Further structures at Wroughton Airfield may have lacked these shallow gullies or had them ploughed away, and so remain undetected. There certainly may be more which remain as yet unseen within the broader confines of the airfield site.

Whilst at first glance the numerous pits which also made up the settlement appear to have been scattered across the site, it is worth noting here that a fair number of them fall within the footprint of, or seem closely associated with particular roundhouses (e.g., roundhouses 3, 10, and 8 and 13 in the south-eastern area). In many cases these may have preceded or succeeded the use of the building, which suggests that there was indeed longevity to the settlement and that its internal arrangement changed over time. Clearly an open pit within a building may have constituted a hazard. However, it is possible that some, suitably covered, may have been contemporary with the building. A number of pits, located within the footprints of roundhouses have also been identified as part of a settlement, probably of similar date, at Site 4 of the Childrey Warren water pipeline, near Segsbury Camp (Guarino and Barclay 2023,

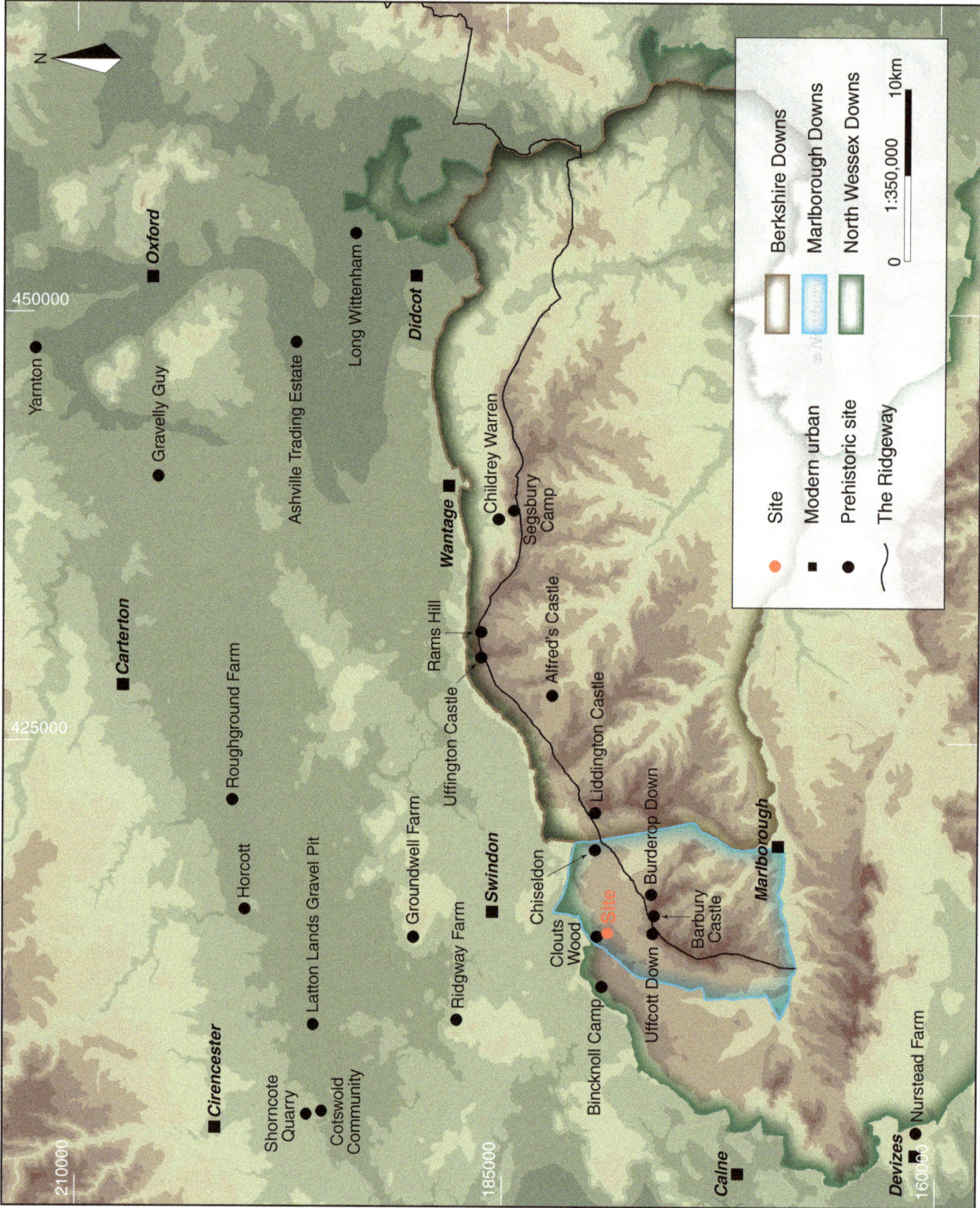

Figure 6.1 Selected Iron Age sites in the surrounding landscape

30). It is possible that some pits may have had a structural role, but others possibly provided storage. The possibility of contemporaneity is increased when considering some of the less usual contents of pits (further explored below); of six pits which contained notable dumps of sarsen stone (excepting those associated with human remains), four of them lay in the central area of a roundhouse structure defined by a gully (roundhouses 8, 10, 12 and 13). The use of stone in structured deposits has also been noted elsewhere, albeit with characteristics specific to the site; at Gravelly Guy animal associated bone groups were often laid in pits on a layer of burnt limestone (Lambrick and Allen 2004, 241).

When considering the use of the buildings, few finds or ecofacts came from the roundhouses, with the majority having been retrieved from pit fills. This is at least in part likely to relate to the degree of plough truncation, which has removed all of the probable floor levels of these buildings. This precludes identifying any specific functions of particular structures. However, this situation is not unusual, with most contemporary houses in the region producing limited material (Moore 2006, 101; Lambrick with Robinson 2009, 148).

The pits

As mentioned above, the settlement was at least in part defined by a broad and dispersed scatter of over 150 pits. These were variable in size, shape and depth. Some were no more than shallow scoops, whereas others were substantial and deep features, although these were in the minority. Most pits over 0.5m in diameter were broadly circular with straight sides and a flat base, although this may have at least partially related to the geology; some had undercut sides. There is little evidence of specific categories of pits as have been employed for Danebury (Cunliffe and Poole 1991a, 160) amongst other sites. Most of the larger examples appear to have been dug with straight sides to a flat base created by the natural substrate. Where there is variation in the sides, this appears to result from undercutting or collapse and may indicate cleaning out and reuse or pits that were left open for a period of time before eventual filling.

The original purpose of the pits is difficult to elucidate. Experimental work associated with storage has been carried out on large features (Reynolds 1974; Hill *et al.* 1983) and interpretations of their contents which relate to this also made in relation to large pits (Cunliffe 1992). It therefore remains unclear as to the effectiveness for the same purposes of shallower features with a greater surface area to volume contained. It seems unlikely that with an average depth of around 0.75m these pits would have provided the necessary volume to achieve an effective storage environment or escape the worse of water percolation. Consequently, it does not appear that the Collection Management Facility pits were largely intended to provide large scale or systematic storage for cereals; the dispersed and somewhat random

pattern of the pits, as well as not being in an enclosed area, suggests that control of the contents by the group or specific households was not a concern. If some of the larger pits which would be over a volume threshold more practical for seed corn storage (cf Hill *et al.* 1983) were used for this purpose, then these may have been associated with individual households.

In many cases pits appear to have undergone a variety of processes of infilling including episodes of gradual silting and more rapid and deliberate deposition of high volumes of often largely sterile material derived from the local subsoil and underlying chalk natural. Most pit contexts contained few, if any, finds, but some were rich in material of various types or contained more notable items and objects. These will be discussed further below, but it is worth noting that much of the information on the economy and wider connections of the settlement is derived from the material deposited in these features. The mixture of materials and homogeneous nature of the pottery assemblages suggests that food waste and other domestic debris was probably stored for a period above ground before final disposal. Canid gnawing on some animal bones indicates that they were available to the dogs on the settlement before deposition.

The economy

Food and farming

A mixed economy is suggested, with arable and pastoral farming both having been undertaken. Charred plant remains from the site were dominated by cereals: emmer and spelt wheats and barley. In several deposits there were large amounts of cereal chaff, indicating the disposal of the cleanings of the crop, and the use of the by-products as a domestic fuel. Further processing of grain is attested by the numerous fragments of querns distributed around the settlement. The plants are indicative of household consumption of arable crops. One mature woman (SK 3235) bore indications of engagement in long-term repetitive activity that affected her left shoulder, and depending on which was her dominant hand, it may have been occupational in origin, possibly related to crop processing or use of a quern, although this might be expected to be more bilateral in its expression. Another younger woman (SK 1209) did display bony development of the tendons of both shoulders, which could have a been a response to this sort of work.

Whilst there is no indication of fields within the excavation area, an iron tip from a ploughshare, a rare discovery of what was probably a common object, would seem to indicate that arable agriculture was carried out by people from this settlement. Crops were mainly barley, and spelt and emmer wheat, which are typical of this period and location. The weed seeds were those of grassland, field margins and arable environments, but were often large seeded plants, which often are retained into late stage processing, but also that the crop was harvested close to the ground, as these are taller and climbing plants. We might surmise that the straw was used for a variety of purposes around the settlement. Some of the weeds indicate cultivation of the light drier calcareous soils, but some are indicative of heavy damp soils and hedgerow/woodland edge environments. Some of these may have been brought to the site in material for use as floor covering and would have been available by the stream in Markham Bottom. The crops are likely to have been grown on the nearby calcareous slopes. Crops also included some peas/beans (often under-represented), black mustard and flax which may have been grown for linen or for linseed oil, or both. Mineralisation of some seeds suggests incorporation into midden heaps and may indicate that manuring was practiced.

There are similarities to other Iron Age assemblages from the area in which spelt is the predominant wheat, such as at Ridgeway Farm, Purton, Wiltshire (Wyles 2017a), and Groundwell West, Wiltshire (Stevens and Wilkinson 2001), although it differs from Latton Lands, Wiltshire (Griffiths 2009) where there was more barley and emmer wheat. The weed seeds at the Collection Management Facility reflect grassland, field margins and arable environments, probably remaining until the final late stage crop processing, and similar to Ridgeway Farm, Yarnton, Oxfordshire (Stevens 2011), Gravelly Guy, Oxfordshire (Moffett 2004) and Ashville Trading Estate, Oxfordshire (Jones 1978).

Consumption of cereals was probably mainly as flour, but a small number of spelt and barley grains had partially germinated and may indicate that brewing was undertaken. Considering the use of the pottery associated with the settlement, most sherds are from were jars or bowls, with jars being the most common form. Lipid analysis indicated that the jars were used for a variety of foods, including the processing and/or cooking of dairy products but also cooking animal products and plants, which perhaps suggests stews and broths. In contrast, bowls seem to have had a more specialist use for serving or cooking dairy products. This is in keeping with evidence from other sites (see Dunne *et al.*, Chapter 3).

The animal bone assemblage is typical in that it is dominated by livestock species. Most abundant were sheep/goats, with cattle the next numerous, although the relative meat yield of the carcasses would have levelled this in terms of diet. Cattle were killed at their prime meat-bearing age, and as older animals suggesting that they were also kept for breeding, dairying, and/or traction. Sheep/goats were killed at all ages which indicates the probable exploitation of a full range of products, meat, wool and dairy products. The latter was clearly, from the results of the lipid analysis, a significant part of the diet. Pigs were lesser in terms of abundance as is generally the case, and were, in common with most sites of this period, killed at their prime meat-bearing age. However, the remains of calves, lambs and piglets attest to their being reared around the settlement. Wild animals (red and roe deer, and hare) contributed little to the assemblage.

Dogs were present, and bred on or near the settlement, as a number of puppies were identified and they were probably used for herding, guarding, hunting or as companion animals, whilst horses were present in small numbers and probably used for riding and traction; there is no evidence that either dogs or horses were consumed in this location.

There appears to have been some patterning by element in the disposal of sheep/goat and cattle bone. Some butchery may have been undertaken beyond the excavated area, with the non-meat bearing extremities discarded elsewhere and suggested by an over-representation of cattle and sheep/goat femurs. However, sheep/goat mandibles were well represented suggesting the disposal of the entire carcass; their robust nature may, however, indicate that there are preservational issues in play. Given that the full extent of the settlement was not uncovered, it is not possible to say whether there was any exchange of joints of meat rather than culling and consumption of animals arriving on the hoof, or what relationships there may have been with other settlements in the area. There is also little evidence for disposal of waste from specific consumption events. A single chicken bone came from pit 2012, and whilst this is unusual for this date, it is in accordance with recent dates for chicken in southern Britain spanning this period, although individual chicken bones can be intrusive (Best *et al.* 2022, 874, 877). This bone came from the upper fill of the pit and as chicken was present during the Roman use of the site it is possible that it was intrusive, or that the pit only finally filled in later.

The landscape in which crops and animals were raised was one of grassland, arable and woodland. Wood fuel used by the inhabitants came from a range of species with oak, hazel and field maple supplemented by various species gathered from hedgerows or scrub. The animal remains include cover-loving species such as shrews which favour shrubby grassland and woodland; field voles prefer grazed grassland; wood mice are found in woodland and grassland. There were frogs/toads which would have inhabited ditches and open, damp pits as well as natural damp/wet areas such as streams and hollows. Weeds seeds suggest the exploitation of materials from the damp stream sides.

Manufacturing and trade

The pottery was probably made locally or within a few kilometres of the site. Craft activities probably included horn working, possibly suggested by horn cores from at least four sheep/goat found in pit 2280. Bone working took place, indicated by a small number of items but this was most likely for domestic consumption. There is considerably more evidence for the working of textiles, presumably related to the wool produced by flocks and perhaps linen from the flax which may have been cultivated. Chalk weights may have been loomweights (although see Shaffrey, Chapter 3) occurred in several features as well as a fired clay weight in pit 2043 spindlewhorl (pit 3083), a second spindlewhorl made from a pottery sherd (pit 9009), and two pieces probably from the same bone weaving comb in pit 1802.

Metalworking was also apparently undertaken, although a location for this has not been identified. Smithing hearth cakes and other industrial residues occurred in various places across the settlement and are indicative of small-scale smithing which probably only served the immediate needs of this small community. Importantly, the remains included a fired clay block tuyère was recovered from pit 2258, a rare artefact in Britain (see Chapter 3; Tylecote 1986, 142–143). This could have been used for working both ferrous and non-ferrous metals, but as it is a portable item, it may be that the user was not a resident of the site, but peripatetic. Evidence for ironworking, at least in the Upper Thames Valley is limited. Sites where activity areas associated with metalworking can be identified, such as Brooklands sewage works are further down the Thames to the east (cf Lambrick with Robinson 2009,182). In keeping with most of the evidence from the region (Lambrick with Robinson 2009, 218) the evidence from the Collection Management Facility is for smithing, not smelting and is dependent on redeposited material.

People, burials and structured deposition

There is little to suggest that the inhabitants of the settlement were of high status, or that there was much differentiation between individuals. The pottery from the settlement includes only a few decorated sherds and other finds were sparse and primarily functional. Personal dress and adornment items were restricted to a shale bracelet fragment, a bone bead or toggle, and two bone pins. This picture is very similar to most local sites in the wider region of the Upper Thames Valley.

Human bodies were disposed of within the area covered by the settlement, but also to the north of the main excavation site. According to several radiocarbon dates this ostensibly occurred over a long period of time. The remains of 11 individuals were found within pits and or placed in purpose-dug graves; this seems to represent two separate traditions or practices. The people included a range of ages and both sexes, although with an apparent bias towards females. One was a neonatal baby, two were children (one buried with an adult), seven were adult woman and one was an adult male. Crouched inhumation is increasingly recognised across the region, and into the Thames Valley and the southern chalk uplands, within settlements, in some cases in definable cemeteries (e.g., Yarnton, Oxon (Stansbie *et al.* 2011, 62), Thame, Oxon (Ellis and Davies 2024), Rowbarrow, Salisbury (Powell 2015), and Suddern Farm, Hants (Cunliffe and Poole 2000), and as off-site burials (Moore 2006, 111).

Three burials produced dates largely within the Early Iron Age. One of these individuals (SK 10005 which also contained a child 10005b) was in a grave seen in an evaluation trench to the north of the main excavation, just off the edge of the plateau on the upper slopes above the stream in Markam Bottom. This suggests that settlement

and burial occurred across an extensive part of this landscape, possibly spreading over the area to the north to the point where the terrain became very steep. This was, however, the only burial seen which contained multiple individuals interred at the same time. The young woman, SK 10005 had strontium and oxygen isotope values suggesting that she originated on the chalk, rather than on Jurassic geology which occurs only about 2km to the north of the site, in common with individuals buried within the settlement area (see Hamilton, Chapter 5). It remains unclear how extensive the area deemed suitable for burial was.

Two other bodies which yielded early dates (SKs 1206 and 1209) were located within the settlement area. These burials were in purpose-made shallow oval cuts. SKs 1206 and 1209 were only a few metres apart and both oriented north-south. It may relevant that they were only about six metres to the east of Pit alignment 2, which at this point had a north-south orientation. Several other burials (SKs 1659, 1489 and 1778) two of which produced dates within the Middle Iron Age, were also made in purpose-cut oval graves that were also generally north-south aligned. These were more widely scattered across the north of the settlement area, although SK 1489 was close to the early pair of burials. SK 1659 was the only one to sit within the footprint of one of the roundhouses, 12 but may or may not have been deposited when it was standing. All the individuals were in a crouched position with the head generally to the north, and there were no obvious grave goods. The isotopic values from the young woman SK 1209 showed higher trophic levels in the foods in her diet, such as would be provided by pig or freshwater fish (see Hamilton, Chapter 5). It is notable that she also had little dental wear for her age (see Clough, Chapter 5), so she seems to have consumed a different diet from other individuals from the site, perhaps relating to the earlier date of her death or some different status which she enjoyed, although development of the insertions of the deltoid muscles in her upper arms suggests she may have engaged in some manual labour.

Whilst many burials in the Severn-Cotswolds region and across the central southern chalk uplands during this period were made within pits, earth-cut graves, often oval and shallow, are known elsewhere (e.g., in a cemetery context at Yarnton (Bell *et al.* 2011, 185)). In some cases, they were cut into the fills of other features such as Roughground Farm, Gloucestershire (Allen *et al.* 1993). At Gravelly Guy the majority of Early and Middle Iron Age human remains (a total of 20) were found in features within the settlement (Lambrick and Allen 2004, 228; Wait 1985). Whilst most were placed within pits and assigned to the pit-burial tradition (cf Whimster 1981), it was noted that several were not in 'storage' pits but in shallower or bowl-like features (Lambrick and Allen 2004, 230), suggesting some variation in the burial rite. What is different about the burials at Gravelly Guy is that the majority of them were of children and infants. Some of these burials had objects included in the deposits including a bone toggle, spindlewhorl, and iron spearhead amongst other objects; one infant was buried with foetal sheep and goats and an adult goat (Lambrick and Allen 2004, 232–3).

Further burials, some of which had Middle Iron Age radiocarbon dates appear to have been made into disused pits. SK 1845 was face down in very tightly flexed position on the base of pit 1426, and directly covered by large chalk and sarsen fragments and structural daub that retained wattle impressions. This was covered by a fill containing charcoal, pottery and animal bone, apparently settlement debris, but also a complete saddle quern, a chalk loomweight, a piece of slag and a possible pin (see Chapter 3). These items seem to reference most aspects of life in the settlement, from food production and consumption to textile and metal working, encapsulated in one feature and which in other periods would be referenced as 'domestic' burials – a body buried with material gathered from a household (see Barclay and Bradley 2017, 155; Gilchrist 2008). The sarsen blocks are clearly not incidental, as noted by Shaffrey (Chapter 3) and there may be a relationship between the worked and unworked stone in this context. The only burial made to the west of Pit alignment 2, SK 8071 was also a very tightly flexed burial, placed onto an initial thin silt in pit 8068, leaning against the pit wall. The body was covered with a dump of chalk and sizeable sarsen stones, interleaved with lenses of charcoal and that also contained pottery, a limestone loomweight, a spindlewhorl, two bone pins, and a stone rubber (which would have been used with a quern). This was capped by two large sarsens. There are clearly similarities in the treatment of these two individuals, which have echoes in a third pit burial. SK 3235 was placed, lying in a crouched position, generally north-south on the base of pit 1947. In this case there was a smear of charcoal on the base of the pit, the body had been covered in clay silt, but this was capped over with a dump of pure chalk.

When considering these burials there are two possible scenarios with respect to their date and the development of practice. On the face of things, we have a group of Early Iron Age burials which were made into earth-cut graves. This was a practice that continued into the Middle Iron Age. At some point, broadly contemporary with that continued earth-cut grave use, a practice of pit burial, which included some practices echoing other acts of deposition, was adopted for certain individuals. However, in an adjustment to this scenario, we need to consider the possibility of curation of remains, particularly, but not exclusively, for the burials associated with the earlier dates. Given the tightly crouched and possibly wrapped nature of the remains, it is possible that we are dealing with preserved bodies.

The curation of human remains is increasingly recognised in later British prehistory (e.g., Brück and Booth 2022a). Preservation and curation of Chalcolithic and Early Bronze Age articulated remains on Cranborne Chase, Dorset has been demonstrated via a number of histological and taphonomic methods (Smith *et al.* 2016) and a number of examples occurring with disarticulated material, with

some indication that this increased from the Middle to Late Bronze Age (Brück and Booth 2022b). Burials at Cladh Hallan in the Outer Hebrides, dating to the Late Bronze Age–Early Iron Age were not only preserved and retained over some period of time but had been manipulated, including the creation of at least one composite body from parts of three individuals (Parker Pearson *et al.* 2005). Therefore, the identification of additional examples of curated remains should not be surprising. At Suddern Farm, where crouched burials were made in a cemetery of earth-cut graves (Cunliffe and Poole 2000, 168), Cunliffe has suggested that these may be the result of burial after a period of excarnation (2000, 132). However, the Collection Management Facility burials are far more tightly flexed, in a way which suggests that a great deal of soft tissue could not have been present, and probably represent better potential examples of the retention and manipulation of human remains prior to deposition. However, as none of the skeletons were recovered in their entirety, it is difficult to say whether the loss of some peripheral elements occurred prior to burial as one might expect, if the remains had been kept for a period of time.

If the burials that returned the earliest dates were curated, this would suggest that the deposition of all the burials in earth-cut graves may have taken place at broadly the same time, but that some of the individuals interred had been retained for some considerable duration before burial. They may represent ancestors who were brought to the area when the settlement came into being, and at some point, their burial was deemed appropriate, perhaps to cement a relationship to this new place – a collective foundation deposit. This should perhaps be considered in relation to the marking of space by the immediately adjacent pit alignments discussed above. If this scenario were the case then we may be seeing remnants of three different ways of dealing with the dead throughout the Early and Middle Iron Age, moving from the preservation and retention of ancestors, through the development of individual earth-cut burial, and incorporation at some point during the Middle Iron Age the inclusion of the human body in complex depositional practices which carried meaning beyond that of body disposal.

Disentangling this is not easy, partly because of the broad dating of much of the pottery and paucity of material in some key contexts. There is, however, some stratigraphic information which suggests complexity in the chronology of the adoption of practices. The earliest dated human remains were of an older adult female (SK 1206) who had been placed within a grave cut into the edge of storage pit 1222. The body was in a very tightly folded position, indicating some form of binding, and she appears to have been placed face down, which may have been the result of the orientation of the body not being clear if it was a wrapped bundle. One of her ribs produced a date of *759–421 cal. BC* (SUERC-94037). However, whilst apparently having died during the Early Iron Age, the grave was cut into an earlier pit. As outlined above, there is a limited independent indication of the date of inception of the settlement, and unfortunately this pit did not contain any datable material. It should also be said that several of the other early cut graves which returned later radiocarbon dates also cut earlier, backfilled, features. The grave of a child SK 1489 was dug into the three-quarter filled pit 1488; SK 1778 was in a grave cut into the upper fill of pit 1777. Neither of these pits contained anything out of the ordinary. A programme of additional histological study would be desirable to determine whether curation was indeed carried out.

Whilst the radiocarbon result for SK 1206 (SUERC-94037) provides an accurate date range for this individual at the point of death, it only provides a *terminus post quem* for the date of burial at Collection Management Facility. In the OxCal model presented in Chapter 5 (Fig. 5.27), It is possible that the individual died at some point during the 8th to 5th centuries (*759–421 cal. BC at 95.4% probability*), although the Early Iron Age plateau makes this difficult to ascertain with any precision. However, this burial appears to predate all other radiocarbon dated activity at the site, for which the latter has a modelled start date of within the later 7th to the start of the 4th century or even within the 5th century BC (modelled as *Start Iron Age 548–369 cal. BC at 95.4% probability*) with most of the human burials and other deposits falling no earlier than the end of the 5th century BC and mostly within the 4th to 2nd.

In addition to the early burial discussed above, the seven remaining radiocarbon dated burials have been placed into probability order and as the plot of the dates appears to show several burial events over a period of a century or more. The earliest of the remaining seven burials is SK 10005, which is of a similar date to SK 1209 both having been made around 400 BC. It is probable that SK 1845 was made next, whilst SK1659, 1778, 8071 and 3235 could all have been made during a similar phase of activity (see Radiocarbon, below). Unfortunately, the bimodal nature of the section of the calibration curve corresponding with the Middle Iron Age (400–50 BC) indicates that the burials could all of happened within either a short or long period of time (modelled *Span 'all graves' 79–108 years (9.8%) and 192–286 (58.4%) at 68.3% probability* and see Fig. 5.28).

It seems clear that there are two treatments of the human body that were used regularly, and possibly contemporaneously. On the one hand there is an apparently simple crouched burial in a shallow earth-cut oval grave which does not appear to have included objects, other than some pottery, but may have been incidental. Some of these were cut into the fills of earlier backfilled features; it is unclear if this was an inevitable result of reuse of the settlement area or whether it was deliberate. On the other hand, the human body was incorporated into pits in a way which is in many ways more reminiscent of a sub-set of the pits on the site that contained more complex deposits and are discussed further below. There are some very clear links between them in the use of particular materials

such as sarsen blocks, and some objects such as querns and loomweights.

In two out of the three burials made deliberately into pits the complexities of the deposition of the body described above have echoes in other depositional behaviours. However, these also need to be related to the biography and health status of the individuals concerned. In the case of SK 1845, the individual displayed poorer oral health than others (extensive periodontal disease), changes to the surface of the vault of the skull (possibly duc to scalp infection or aging), osteoarthritis in the right elbow, healed fractures to the vertebral bodies in the lower back (three adjacent collapsed lumbar vertebrae), healed fractures to two ribs, and bilateral erosive lesions in the feet which may have been caused by impingement of the blood supply (see Clough, Chapter 5). This individual also had indications of an extensive infection around both ankles which appears to have been active at the time of death, although it is not clear exactly how extensive it was. The pattern of multiple healed injuries classes as recidivist injury, but as Redfern notes, this is difficult to tell apart from the victims of abuse (2016). Coupled with indications of hard work, and general poor health, it is possible that this individual falls within the range of treatments which might suggest subordination, captivity or enslavement, as suggested for Late Iron Age individuals from Fishbourne, Isle of Wight or Gussage All Saints, Dorset (Redfern 2020). However, it is to be noted that rather than having an origin at variance with the rest of the population as sometimes occurs in these cases, SK 1845 had strontium and oxygen isotope values indicating an origin on the chalk, similarly to other individuals (see Hamilton, Chapter 5).

This was also the case for the young woman SK 8071. She had a lack of unification of the process of the sacrum, but this is unlikely to have affected her in life, However, her skeleton also had indications of metabolic ill health of some long standing; she had suffered a widespread systemic infection at the time of her death. Periostitis often affected many of the deep muscle attachment sites all over both sides of the skeleton, but the generalised nature of the periosteal reaction, means that it is not possible to identify the origin of the infection. However, the nature of the illness, which seems likely to have been involved in this individual's death may well have also been related to the manner of her burial. The third individual SK 3235, a mature adult female, was petite at only 4' 11", and her left upper arm showed a bony development which may have related to repeated use of her arm. It may be that she also may have had a different status which made a pit burial suitable for her; like SK 1845, from the isotopic evidence it does not appear that having an origin different from that of the other inhabitants was the cause, although she may have come from further to the south of the settlement.

There were few finds from the roundhouse gullies. In contrast, excavation of the pits has yielded a substantial artefactual and ecofactual assemblage. However, consideration of the contents of pits (Appendix 1) shows

Table 6.1 Combinations of items in more complex pit deposits

Pit	Weights	Querns	Bone objects	Metal objects	Other objects	Sarsen blocks	Chalk dumps	Charcoal	Articulated animals	Skull	Human remains
1426		X	X	X	Daub and slag	X		X			X
1430						X				X	
1851							X			X	
1947							X				X
1984					Slag		X	X	X		
2258				X	Polished dog tooth and tuyère	X		X		X	
2265				X	Smithing heath cakes		X				
2280	X				Group of horn cores			X			
2938				X	Hone or grinding stone		X	X			
3068	X		X		Marcasite lump		X		X		
8068	X				Spindlewhorl and grain rubber	X	X	X			X
8118	X								X		
9009	X				Spindlewhorl			X			

that, in common with many contemporary sites, most features contained few finds, palaeoenvironmental or indeed other materials. Where pottery and bone were present, this was often in low concentrations and effectively the result of re-deposition of refuse which would have been generally present within the settlement. However, against this background, there are features whose contents stand out. A number of these have been described in detail in Chapter 2.

The occurrence of 'special' or structured deposits in Iron Age contexts, and pits in particular, has been well rehearsed by many authors over the last three decades and a range of explanations offered from the functional to the ritual (Bersu 1940, 53; Wait 1985; Cunliffe 1992; Poole 1995), some of which are predicated on assumptions about the function of the pits themselves (Hill 1995; Fitzpatrick 1997, 83) and pit digging itself suggested to be a ritual activity (Cunliffe and Poole 1991, 162; Gwilt 1997, 161–2). One issue in dealing with this subject is in deciding what is 'special'. In this case, anything which stands out from the general background of pottery and animal bone has been considered. This means that aside from apparently 'obvious' inclusions such as human remains or articulated animals, it is possible to include consideration of the juxtaposition of a wider range of materials, including concentrations of apparently more prosaic material, lenses of charcoal and dumps of stone that stand out from the norm for the site.

At one end of the spectrum, in this case, are the inclusions of human bodies in pits that have been outlined above, in particular SK 1845 and SK 8071. Given the frequency of the inclusion of disarticulated human remains in Iron Age pits as part of the suite of depositional behaviours (e.g., Hill 1995), the Collection Management Facility site is unusual in that this does not occur. The combination of other characteristics and objects in those cases is instructive as several of them recur in other pits with complex deposits. First amongst these is the utilisation of dumps of sarsen stones and blocks. These occurred in combination with a variety of materials including charcoal deposits, metal

objects, querns but also both animal skulls and human burials (Table 6.1). There may also be a connection between the use of dumps of sarsen, and its use for the manufacture of some of the querns (see Shaffrey, Chapter 3). The stone is likely to have been available for collection on the upland chalk and was generally common on the Marlborough Downs (Whittaker 2019). Sarsen was also combined in some places with dumps of chalk or chalk blocks; chalk dumps were in turn a frequent inclusion where there were other notable materials and appears to have served as a frequent sealing deposit. It is also interesting to consider the spatial distribution of pits which contain sarsen or deposits of chalk blocks. There appears to be an association between pits containing sarsen with houses, where they occur within the footprint of buildings in four instances (Fig. 2.12). Piles of stones themselves have been counted as 'special deposits', occurring on the bases of pits at Danebury, with associated bone groups placed under, within and over them (Poole 1995, 262, 274).

The majority of more 'unusual' finds occurred as single instances in pits, and this included single examples of weights (possibly for the loom), fired clay and worked bone objects, as well as substantially complete pots and occasional smithing hearth cakes. These are in many cases probably reflective of the general range of discard practices. The find of an iron ploughshare tip in one pit, that contained little else which would make it stand out, was nevertheless perhaps suggestive of more deliberate action, as the object was not worn out, and could have been recycled if it were beyond use; other examples have come from hillforts (see McSloy, Chapter 3). In addition, there are cases where multiple items occur in combination, and which may indicate complex and deliberate depositional behaviour. One group of objects that recur in combination with others are weights which occurred in combination with spindlewhorls on at least two occasions and appear in the same deposits and features as a variety of other objects, although this did not include metal. Worked bone objects and metal objects are rarer and it is difficult to discern any particular associations between them and the other materials they appear with, although they both seem to be more likely to occur with the range of objects and materials classed as 'other' in Table 6.1.

Human remains occurred in three pits and in all cases additional materials were recovered, although in one case this was only a charcoal deposit. However, it is noticeable that human bodies did not occur in the same features which contained animal remains, although other materials, such as sarsen, metal objects, charcoal or stone weights were associated with both. This might imply that whilst that both humans and animals were afforded some similarities in treatment, they were segregated.

Associated bone groups, and most particularly articulated animal bodies or parts of bodies have also become synonymous with 'special' or 'structured' deposition, and in particular with deposition in Iron Age pits. They have had in the past a range of explanations (Morris 2008, 2) but have become an oft defining element of 'structured' deposition (e.g., Wait 1985; Wilson 1992). The issues around inclusion of isolated animal skulls as automatically 'special' has been highlighted by Morris (2008) and there is a tendency to over interpret isolated skulls due to their recognisability. Individual skulls have been commented on in Chapters 2 and 4, but without evidence of articulation with adjacent elements, it is possible that they are merely incidental. As with all deposits, their immediate context needs to be taken into account, and some seem immediately to be significant particularly where there are multiple skulls of more than one species in one feature (e.g., pit 1851).

Aside from skulls, entire animals and partial remains such as articulated limbs occurred; the deposition of differing proportions of different species is an echo of that seen in similar deposits at Gravelly Guy where larger species were better represented as skulls, dogs as whole bodies and livestock as partial limbs (Lambrick and Allen 2004, 238). The species included were cattle, sheep/goat, dog and horse, and as is common (Morris 2008, 83) the incidence of dog and horse appears more elevated than their general representation in the co-mingled settlement assemblage as whole might suggest. However, different explanations can be advanced for different types of material.

Single animal skulls occurred in a number of pits, and some may be significant as they were combined with other materials. A cattle skull on the base of pit 3068 was covered by dumps of chalk, that included not only general pottery and animal bone but a chalk weight and a lump of marcasite, which had probably been collected as an eye-catching unusual stone. The top fill contained a worked bone point. Pit 1430 also contained a cattle skull on the base, in this case having sarsen blocks placed against it in the pit centre. A group of very large sarsen blocks in the centre of the base of pit 2258 was overlain by a deposit in which was a horse skull, and a polished dog's tooth. This also included a dribble of copper alloy and a fired clay tuyère. Other cases are probably more incidental. The only dog skull present occurred in the upper fill of a shallow pit

and may have been incidental or re-deposited. Sheep/goat skulls in pits 1770 and 2223 also appear to be of general animal bone waste rather than placed. An articulated cattle foot in the initial fill of large pit 2844 was not associated with any other obvious material. It had been gnawed by a dog prior to deposition, showed evidence of cut marks and probably represents discarded butchery waste. This is probably the explanation for the cattle hind hock amongst a dump of burnt flint and charcoal in pit 2527, and a partial horse hind leg in pit 3150.

Multiple animals also occurred in pit 1454, where there were the remains of at least three neonatal sheep/goat. Sheep/goat are the most common components of ABGs of animal carcasses during the Iron Age in southern Britain (Morris 2008, 85). The rest of this pit contained material which is most reminiscent of general settlement waste, and it raises the possibility that in cases like this the most obvious explanation would be the serendipitous disposal of lambing fatalities. The partial remains of a single neonatal sheep/goat in the uppermost fill of pit 1381 can probably be explained in such a way.

The deposition of a largely complete dog carcass in the middle fills of pit 1454 was also largely devoid of other materials other than a piece of industrial waste. The placement of the body, in the centre of the pit, however, suggests that the remains were deliberately positioned; the toes and head were missing, leading to the suggestion of skinning (albeit with no cut marks noted), and this suggests a more complex process of deposition, although there may have been a functional element. Pit 6030 provides a further example of an entire dog, placed in the centre on the base of the pit. Again, in this case, there were no other unusual deposits, unless a fragment of iron knife from the top fill is included; this may have been incidental. A further dog skeleton in pit 1068 and partial remains in pit 1669 were also not accompanied by other materials, but did also occur on the base or in the lower part of pits, suggesting that whilst it may not have been appropriate to include dog remains in more complex depositional behaviours, dogs attracted a specific mode of disposal which may have been related to their position, use or role in the community.

However, in other cases, the claim to less prosaic activity is clearer. Pit 8118 is interesting as it combines one of the more complex groups of associated animal remains with a suite of other objects. The initial fill of the pit contained pottery, co-mingled bone from sheep/goat and cattle, but also the remains of four neonatal dogs and an entire cattle skeleton. With this was included nine chalk weights, possibly for the loom with six close enough in weight to suggest a set, and the best part of a slack-shouldered jar. In this context, it seems that it is most likely that a Beaker/Early Bronze Age thumbnail scraper was not residual but collected and placed as an old object, and deliberately included. Deposits of this type often include lithic objects, particularly arrowheads and axes and/or metalwork, such as the burial of a Bronze Age spearhead as a possible foundation deposit in a Middle Iron Age context at Yarnton (see Hey *et al.* 2011a, 73; Bradley 2002, 53–54; Chaffey and Barclay 2013, 221–222). The pit 8118 deposit also contained the remains of microvertebrates, including frogs and at least one field vole. At more than a metre deep, this is beyond the capacity of these animals to escape (Whyte 1988), and they represent classic pit fall victims. The utility of microvertebrates in understanding the duration of pit filling and pauses in the process has been recognised elsewhere (Randall 2010b, 98). In this particular case, the likelihood of the pit standing open over an extended period is supported by the formation of a chalk deposit from the collapse of the pit sides, succeeded by a gradual filling of the rest of the feature. The location of this pit away from the main settlement area, not only appears to have referenced the earlier Pit alignment 1, but if left open would not have created a practical hazard. It underlines that performance and display were integral to the practice, and it appears that it was intended not to immediately to place things beyond access, but to display them.

Whilst taking into account the caveats with respect to animal skulls being automatically regarded as special, where these occur in multiples or in combination with other materials, they are due further consideration. The contents of pit 1851 included a total of five skulls; the deposit sequence was one of the more complex. Into a half-filled pit a sub-adult horse skull had been placed and covered over. Later, a hole appears to have been dug in the fill into which was placed two cattle and two adult horse skulls and was covered by a chalk-rich deposit. The only other material in the pit was pottery, but the actual process of deposition itself was a clearly complicated act, as it involved the deliberate excavation of a hole within a half-filled feature. Pit 2203 contained two cattle skulls, placed on the base of a pit which may have been open for some time before they were placed on opposite sides, and had dumps of chalk-rich material dumped over them from the respective sides of the pit. The rest of the pit appears to have then been left to fill gradually. This is an unusual deposit, however, in that the feature which contained it was elongated rather than of a typical shape.

There is also evidence that pit filling was also not a continuous or single event. Pit 8118 described above is one example, but there are others (e.g., pit 2210). This is something that has been noted elsewhere with the numbers of pits at Danebury, Hampshire enabling categorisation into fast and slow fill cycles and deposits interpreted as successions of events, separated in time by anything from a day to a year (Poole 1995, 250, 275). Hill suggests timescales of years, with possibly gaps of decades between deposition in individual pits, with a possible seasonal element. Frequent natural silting episodes of pits at Winklebury, Hampshire indicated openness, possibly taking years to be filled (1995, 75, 92–3). This complex phenomenon has also been demonstrated for later Iron Age pits at Sigwells, Charlton Horethorne, Somerset (Randall 2010b, 98).

Whilst the exact meaning of each class of material or the individual combinations of materials and objects is not possible to identify, it is clear that there was an appropriate suite of materials and actions. Some of these were clearly specific to the place, such as the inclusion of sarsens, available from the immediate landscape and perhaps a deliberate reference to the topographical location. There was also a tendency for pauses in pit filling which suggests further that there were elements of performance in their placing and an intention to display the act over a period of time. This might suggest that in some cases, and not just in those involving human remains, that acts of commemoration were part of this practice. The visibility of some of these deposits also may have related to marking space, something which has been alluded to above in relation to burials and the earlier pit alignments.

The C-shaped enclosure

The date of construction of the C-shaped enclosure in the south-eastern part of the site remains uncertain. The lowest fill was almost pure chalk and probably accumulated rapidly possibly derived from an accompanying bank, although the location of this is unclear. There was a lack of finds and environmental evidence from the lowest fills. However, it was certainly open during the Mid to Late Iron Age with the partial remains of a dog which was in a middle fill radiocarbon dated to *351–296 cal. BC (39.5%) and 208–102 cal. BC (55.9%)* (SUERC-100660). The enclosure remained visible into the Mid to Late Roman period, with the upper ditch continuing to accumulate material.

The function of the enclosure is difficult to discern. It was a substantial feature, with a steep-sided cut some 2.5m wide and 1.3m deep, which would have provided a substantial barrier. The enclosed area was roughly 33m by 15m. The profile in at least one location suggests that it had been cleaned out or recut at least once, suggesting longevity during its initial phase of use. The adjoining ditch attached at the southern end of the C-shape may have provided drainage or elaboration. Given the degree of truncation seen elsewhere on the plateau it is possible that the feature partially enclosed a building or other structure, the ephemeral evidence for which may have been lost due to truncation. What is clear is that whilst probably contemporary with at least part of the life of the Iron Age settlement, it was spatially separate from it with the enclosed area facing away from the plateau edge and towards the higher ground of the Marlborough Downs. It was also the only ditched enclosure of this date. It seems that it was most likely used for some specific function, different from that of the main settlement area. However, it did attract similar depositional practices to those seen within the settlement. Aside from the dog remains which were radiocarbon dated, two further skulls, one of dog and the other of horse were recovered from the ditch, and it may be that it was, like the pits in the settlement regarded as a suitable place for deposition of specific items.

Whilst clearly dissimilar from the incomplete circuit at the Collection Management Facility, curvilinear enclosures dating to the Iron Age which appear to have attracted ceremonial practices occur in the greater south-west. At Grimstone Down, Dorset, a small sub-circular enclosure with opposing gaps in the ditches and an internal diameter of about 8m, with a concentric arc of ditch with a putative diameter of 40m associated with earlier and contemporary features including unusual deposits was located on a prominent location in a similar upland chalk setting close to the edge of an escarpment (Randall *et al.* 2016). In Cornwall, a 60m diameter feature akin to a hengiform enclosure has been excavated at Hay Close, St Newlyn East but dated to the Iron Age (Jones 2014), whilst at Camelford, a penannular enclosure about 20m across produced a Late Iron Age date and evidence for structured deposition (Jones and Taylor 2008). At Tremough, Penryn a Late Iron Age to Romano-British enclosure was about 50m in diameter contained a single large pit, which may have contained a substantial post akin to a totem pole (Jones *et al.* 2015).

The Iron Age setting

The Collection Management Facility Iron Age settlement sat within a landscape that contained hillforts but the settlement structure of which is otherwise poorly understood. Barbury Castle, 2.7km to the south is clearly visible from the site on the southern skyline. It is at the western extent of a string of hillfort enclosures located along the Ridgeway with Liddington Castle, Uffington Castle and Ram's Hill to the east. Several of the Berkshire group have their origins in the 8th century BC, associated with All Cannings Cross style ceramics (Barclay *et al.* 2003, 257), although there is no excavated evidence of similar origins for Barbury. Others such as Alfred's Castle, further down the dip slope, were later (Lock and Gosden 2003). Although no modern excavation has been undertaken within Barbury Castle, a geophysical survey as part of the *Wessex Hillforts Project* demonstrated that its interior was packed with roundhouses and pits (McQueen 2009), although probably not all in use simultaneously. The degree of contemporaneity with the activity at the Collection Management Facility is unknown. A small excavation undertaken in 1875 within the hillfort interior recovered a so-called blacksmith's hoard. These comprise possibly elite objects; parts of a chariot and chariot harness fittings, sickles, spearheads and other metalwork (SM ref. 1014557 list entry), although these lack their original context, and have much in common with potentially ritually deposited metal objects on other hillfort sites. Also in the wider landscape, and better dated to the Middle Iron Age, the Chiseldon Cauldron hoard, consisting of 12 cauldrons and two cattle skulls buried in a pit (Baldwin and Joy 2017), was recovered a about 5km east of the Collection Management Facility.

About 2.5km to the west of the Collection Management Facility site is Bicknoll Castle or Camp (HE List 1005685; Fig. 6.1). This is the site of a Norman motte and bailey castle, but it may have its origins as an Iron Age promontory fort, occupying a spur of land on the edge of the chalk escarpment overlooking the valley to the north, and flanked to the east by a north-south valley with a spring, a very similar landscape location to the settlement and pit alignments at the Collection Management Facility. There are also undated enclosures on the lower ground to the north which could relate to a broader picture of settlement. Further cropmarks have been recorded on the downs south of the site closer to Barbury Castle, whilst Iron Age pottery has been found on Uffcott Down (MWI15209).

The pattern of settlement in the immediate environs of hillforts and in their wider hinterlands remains patchily understood. The *Danebury Environs Programme* (Hampshire) found that settlement in the hinterland was reasonably dispersed and there was little evidence of settlement close to the hillfort itself (Cunliffe 2000, 170–1), whilst there is also an apparent lack of contemporary settlement adjacent to Maiden Castle, Dorset with these examples suggesting models of centralisation (Sharples 2010). However, the uniformity of this is debatable. In southern Somerset, the immediate surroundings of Cadbury Castle included settlement and field systems both immediately adjacent to the hillfort and more widely in the surrounding landscape, with the biggest determinant in the Middle Iron Age being topography and soil type (Tabor 2008). At Battlesbury, a hillfort in south-west Wiltshire, a probably open settlement of roundhouses accompanied by pits and four-post structures was present outside the defences at Battlesbury Bowl (Ellis and Powell 2008), and there appeared to have been contemporary settlement outside the ramparts at Castle Hill, Oxfordshire (Allen *et al.* 2010). On the Berkshire Downs the unenclosed settlement at Towe Hill demonstrates that they existed in a broader landscape where they were contemporary with the earliest hillforts (Barclay *et al.* 2003, 257).

It is possible that the Collection Management Facility settlement was broadly contemporary with the hillfort at Barbury Castle. There seem to be findspots of later prehistoric material fairly close to the hillfort in this case (see Fig. 6.1). The Collection Management Facility site and hillfort are intervisible and separated by only 2.7km, but the date and use of Barbury Castle is poorly understood, as it has not been investigated under modern conditions. Along with other hillforts along the Ridgeway, including Liddington Castle and Uffington, Barbury Castle may have been sited both with reference to control movement along the Ridgeway. The suggestions that routeways between the valley and the high ground during the Early Iron Age at the Collection Management Facility may have related to regular or seasonal movements of livestock raises other issues of mobility and seasonality of occupation within this landscape, but which are at present difficult to approach due to poor knowledge of the patterns of settlement or land division.

The Collection Management Facility settlement lies on the edge of two distinct regions, the Wessex Downs and the Upper Thames Valley, and shows links across both regions.

For example, whilst much of the ceramic assemblage sits easily with contemporary sites from the Upper Thames Valley, the saucepan pots are more typical of the Wessex region. Comparable vessels dating to between the 4th–1st centuries BC were recorded at Brickley Lane, Devizes, Wiltshire (Timby 2002, 221) and Danebury Hillfort, Hampshire (Cunliffe 1984, 234). The scarcity of decorated sherds (<1%) together with the relative predominance of burnishing, is also indicative of Middle and Late Iron Age handmade traditions in the area which are commonly represented by highly burnished finewares and coarsewares with limited decoration. Just under 2% of the Middle Iron Age assemblage at Watkins Farm were decorated (Allen and Robinson 1993, 42) whilst the Middle Iron Age group from Latton Lands was entirely undecorated (Edwards 2009, 63). Most of the worked stone objects have been created from materials which could be sourced in the immediate vicinity (e.g., sarsen) but a coarse feldspathic gritstone quern fragment is of unknown provenance.

The Late Iron Age–Early Roman settlement and fields

As the date for the ending of the Iron Age settlement is ambiguous, it is difficult to say whether there was a complete hiatus in the use of the landscape at the end of the first millennium BC or how long that lasted. The place name of the nearby small town at Wanborough (*Durocornovium*) has been suggestive of a tribal grouping called the *Cornovii* in this area (Fig. 6.2), whilst *Dobunnic* coinage dominates across this area (Rivet and Smith 1979, 350; Corney 2001, 6). At what point affiliations emerged or how this might be reflected in the local settlement pattern is unclear. However, as far as the site at the Collection Management Facility is concerned it is apparent that a new approach to settlement commenced during the Late Iron Age–Early Roman transitional period, and involved for the first time, substantial land division. Ditch 18 (recut as ditches 13 and 19) provided a long-lasting element throughout this period, and positioned near the edge of the scarp, apparently defined the northern limits of the inhabited or enclosed area.

The initial activity then involved the creation of other land boundaries, appended to which was a series of ditches forming enclosure 1. This was effectively D-shaped and, 65m by 70m; it clearly related to adjoining boundaries that appear to have formed a system which extended more broadly across the landscape but does not appear to have aimed at apportioning all of it. Truncated by later ploughing it is difficult to discern an obvious entrance to enclosure 1, but this may have been in the area of the rounded south-east corner. It is also difficult to identify evidence for associated banks, and if the ditches were originally relatively slight, it is possible that low banks may have been hedged, but there is no direct evidence for this.

Within the southern half of this enclosed space were two roundhouses, 1 and 5. They were represented by gullies and

a few postholes, but other structural evidence appears to have been removed by later ploughing. The dating evidence from these two buildings was broad. Given the lack of chronological resolution it is difficult to say whether they were contemporaneous with one building subsidiary to the other, providing both a dwelling or storage (although the similar size of both at around 12m in diameter probably argues against this), or whether one building replaced the other over time. It is difficult to say how long this phase of use as settlement lasted within the wider period of time over which the enclosures in their various configurations were in use.

The houses were slightly larger than those of the main Iron Age settlement, and although it is noted that Late Iron Age houses seem to have been variable in size (Moore 2006, 102), these seem to be large for this period. This is not assisted by the broad dating of the structures and the tendency of circular construction to continue into the Roman period (Hingley 1989). It seems likely that, notwithstanding some interruptions to the circuits of both gullies due to later truncation that both buildings had entrances to the east-south-east, which appears to have been the dominant direction throughout the Iron Age (Lambrick with Robinson 2009, 132). In neither case are there any clearly associated internal features which appear to be structural, not even at the doorways. It is hard to tell, however, whether this is due to truncation by ploughing or construction methods; there was a general move away from post-built construction over time in the Thames Valley and Cotswolds (Lambrick with Robinson 2009, 137; Moore 2006, 101), but given the unclear ground plans of the houses in the Iron Age settlement, it is difficult to make an argument for this at the Collection Management Facility. Settlements of this period in the Cotswold region vary in form, and there is considerable evidence of continuity in the region from the every end of the Iron Age into the earliest Roman period (Moore 2006, 164, 167), and this seems to be the case here, with a number of re-workings and development of the layout over multiple sub-phases of activity, and the potential for a more gradual change in use.

Within enclosure 1, in its northern part, was almost square enclosure 4, 15m by 13m, with a well-defined 3.5m-wide entrance in the centre of its south side. Its northern side was parallel to ditch 14, the northern side of enclosure 1, which was only separated from it by a gap of a metre. There is a bend in ditch 14 at the point it almost meets the north-west corner of enclosure 4, suggesting that enclosure 4 was one of the earlier elements of the layout that was being referenced and respected in the design of enclosure 1. The fills of the ditch of enclosure 4 produced dating evidence broadly covering the Late Iron Age–Early Roman transitional period. There was only one feature that can possibly be attributed to it, pit 1820 which remains undated.

The lack of structures within enclosure 4 does not assist in discerning its function. If early in the sequence of development of land boundaries it possibly stood alone.

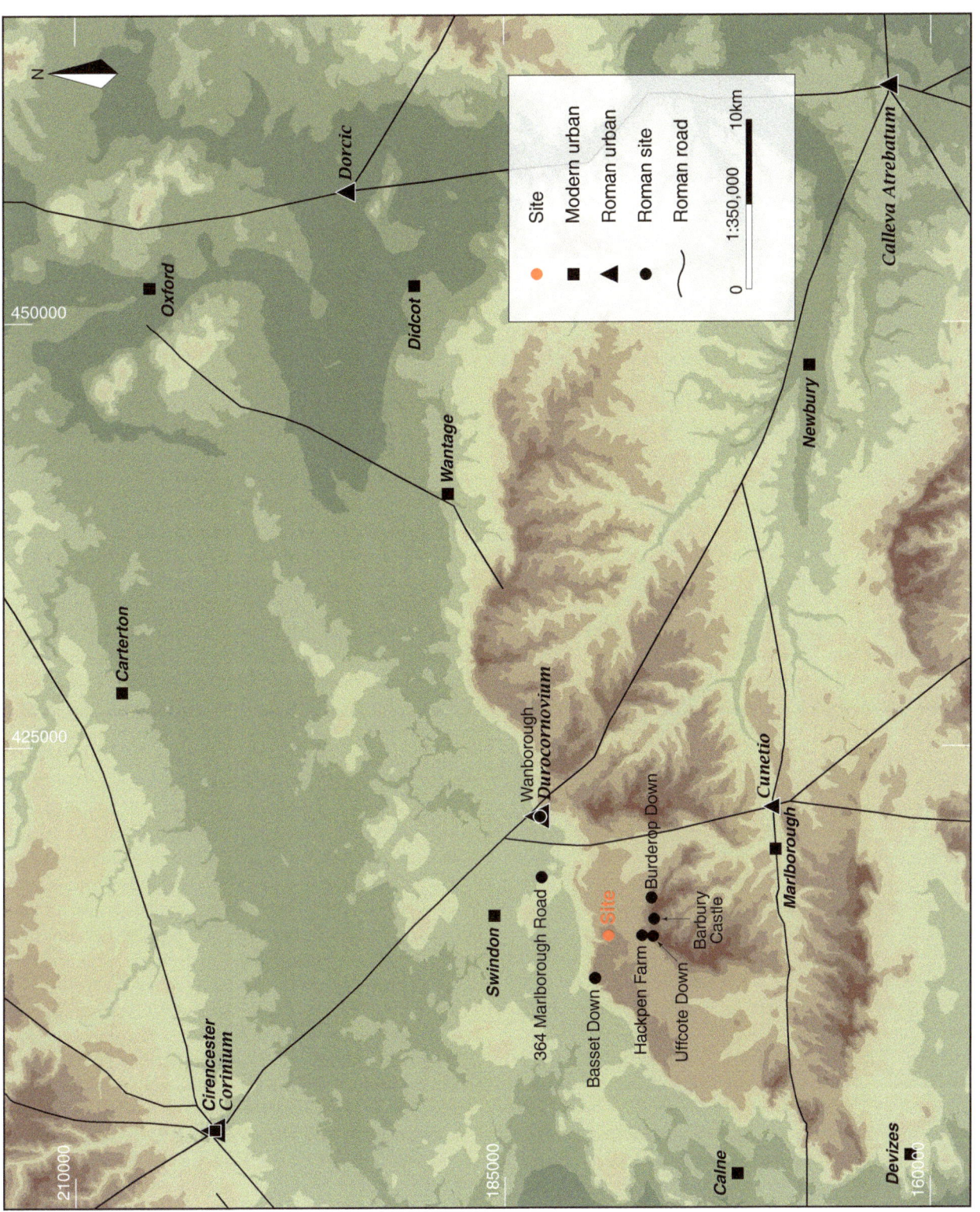

Figure 6.2 Selected Roman sites in the surrounding landscape

Truncation may have removed shallow structural features which might have signified domestic use, or it may have provided a small corral. The southerly facing entrance may be of significance in its relationship to the houses positioned to the south, depending on their degree of contemporaneity. The form of the enclosure is a familiar and common type which occur in the wider region, and often date throughout the Iron Age and into the Late Iron Age or the transitional period and as mentioned above settlement at the end of the Iron Age could take multiple forms (Moore 2006, 45–50, fig. 4.6, 163). There is in this case some evidence of metalworking being carried out in the immediate area with vitrified hearth lining with traces of copper alloy coming from the ditch fills of enclosure 5.

Also positioned within enclosure 1, to the north of roundhouse 5 was structure A. The two flat-based trenches appeared to represent the south-western corner of a rectangular building, with the trenches probably being beam slots. Early Roman pottery came from these, so structure A may be a relatively late development within Period 5, perhaps a domestic structure which replaced the roundhouses. This is possibly supported by the presence in one of the terminals of a few elements of human bone, probably representing the disturbed partial remains of a neonatal individual. As neonates are often found in domestic settings (Rohnbogner 2018, 328), this may confirm that this structure was a house, although these burials also occur in buildings which seem to have a more agricultural use (e.g. Worth Matravers, Randall 2018, 225). It seems likely that if this was a domestic or other structure, it superceded the two roundhouses.

Subsequent to the creation of these structures and enclosures, a series of additions, amendments and replacements occurred, the suggested sequence provides the series of sub-phases which have been assigned. It is not possible to tell how long each of these lasted and in fact the degree to which any or all of the preceding features continued to play a role or for how long. However, it indicates a dynamic period of change in which activity appears to have increased from the simple beginnings described and was adapted to provide for new needs. During Period 5.2, for example, there were modifications to enclosure 1, creation of rectilinear enclosure 3 to the east and another possible enclosure, 2, to the south of a droveway which was created along the south-western aspect of enclosure 1. The latter broadly followed the space defined by the prehistoric pit alignments. Whilst this might be coincidence, it more probably reflects a natural or longstanding routeway between the vale to the north and the chalk escarpment. North-west of enclosure 1, the two side ditches of the droveway splay out, opening towards the slope down into the valley creating a funnel-shaped entrance into the droveway for livestock being driven up from possibly open grazing in the valley. This is a classic design for entrances into controlled and bounded landscape from open areas (Randall 2021, 57–8).

The droveway, once created, appears to have persisted throughout this period, at least into Period 5.3. Subsequent developments in Period 5.3 and 5.4 were relatively minor changes and additions, and probably represent limited re-arrangement, re-cutting and cleaning out of some ditches, but not a wholesale change. Deposits in the fills of features assigned to these last two episodes produced Colchester derivative brooches with a date range of AD 50–100/150 and glass dating to the 1st–2nd/early 3rd centuries AD, so it seems likely that the infilling was occurring by the 2nd century and the system probably fell into disuse around that time, given that there is no indication of later material. Another indicator that the use of space was changing in the in the later 1st or early 2nd century AD was the placement of the burial of a woman (SK 1076), within ditch 3, part of the droveway. This may also, however, have signified the marking of the space with this individual placed between the area used for dwellings and on the side of the routeway. Burial of individuals in this type of setting are well-attested for rural sites of this period (Smith *et al.* 2018, 231). An almost entire cattle skull in ditch 11 of enclosure 1 in Period 5.1 may have also been deliberately positioned to mark the boundary or may have represented the discard of primary butchery waste away from the dwellings. An almost complete Iron Age jar from one of the ditches, being deposited long after its manufacture, may have been an heirloom item placed as a special deposit. Lipid analysis indicated that it had been used for cooking dairy products and leafy plants (see Dunne *et al.*, Chapter 3).

In considering how this system of land division operated, there are some limited palaeoenvironmental remains which provide some elucidation, although it seems in the main that they are likely to have been derived from somewhere out-with the system, with the settlement represented by the roundhouses only perhaps contributing a portion of the material. The animal bones attributable to the Late Iron Age–Early Roman transition are mostly sheep/goat, followed by cattle although it is possible that the relative abundance has been affected by differential disposal, if much of it originated beyond the excavated area. Cereal remains from the site were limited to a single pit (2261), but which represents a late stage of processing of emmer and spelt grains. This most probably reflective of consumption of arable products in this area, and there is no evidence for production or storage. There is an indication from the lipid analysis that there was a reduction in the importance of dairy products from the preceding period (Dunne *et al.*, Chapter 3). However, the likelihood is that this landscape was used most for livestock farming. It has been suggested that sheep grazed on the chalk and cattle in the valleys (Allen 2017, 87, 91). At Cleevelands, Bishop's Cleeve, Gloucestershire, a Roman farmstead on the Severn valley clays, arable and pastoral farming was undertaken. Whilst isotope analysis indicated that most sheep/goat and cattle there had been reared on site, at least one may have come from the Cotswold uplands, either through trade or as a result of transhumance (Hart *et al.* 2021, 72). The regular or seasonal movement of animals between the valley and the enclosed and open grazing on the uplands is a possibility which must await future analysis.

Other aspects of the assemblage which date to this period indicate an origin in a modest settlement; the pottery comprises mainly local wares with a low proportion of regional imports, and only 20 sherds of samian (see Banks, Chapter 3). Much of what has been retrieved from the ditches may have originated in manuring with material which had been brought in from elsewhere. This is supported by the presence of a piece of window glass, and a few pieces of roof tile in Period 5.2 and 5.3 deposits, which suggest an origin in a well-appointed building, when no indication of such a building was evident within the confines of the excavation. The brooches are of a modest and frequently seen type in the Early Roman period.

Like the earlier settlement, there are generally only slight indications of other Roman period activity in the immediate environs of the site, consisting of individual finds or minor interventions. Of course, some of the crop marks of enclosures mentioned above may date to the transition and later Roman period. A 3rd-century barbarous radiate coin came from near Hackpen Farm; fragments of Romano-British pottery occurred on Uffcott Down to the south of the site; and the remains of walls associated with Roman pottery and a coin dating to the 1st century was found Barbury hillfort. Further evidence of buildings was also located at Basset Down, on the edge of the escarpment about 1.5km to the north-west (Walters 2001, cf fig. 7.1). Roman pottery, fired clay, and animal bone was recovered 760m to the north of the Collection Management Facility site during fieldwalking (CA 2017). It is difficult to speculate about how the enclosed land around Wroughton articulated with the surrounding landscape; land division is better understood to the north on the Thames valley gravels, and the Collection Management Facility site is located in an area where fewer contemporary sites are known than elsewhere in Wiltshire (Corney 2001, 7–8, cf. fig. 2.1). However, significant settlement of the Romano-British and early medieval period has been recently identified at Marlborough Road, Wroughton, about 1.7km to the north-east at the base of the scarp (AC Archaeology 2023).

The Roman town at Wanborough (*Durocornovium*), is located 7.5km to the north-east and the Collection Management Facility enclosures (Fig. 6.2) and any associated settlement may have fitted within its broader hinterland as that urban centre emerged. The pottery from the Collection Management Facility includes sherds of North Wiltshire colour-coated ware which were probably manufactured in the vicinity of *Durocornovium*. Wanborough is situated on the closest Roman road, Ermin Street (or Way) (Margary 41), which runs on a south-east to north-west orientation through the town and to the north-east of Swindon before heading to Cirencester. The earliest evidence for the construction of Wanborough is a building probably contemporary, and adjacent to, Ermine

Street, which dates to the Neronian period. To date there is little evidence of Late Iron Age settlement in the vicinity (Anderson *et al.* 2001; Corney 2001, 10–11). The broadly dated material from Collection Management Facility does not help unfortunately with refining an understanding of the date of change in the countryside and its relationship to the emergence of the town. The local distribution of villas and possible villas or Roman buildings has been discussed in the work on the villa at Groundwell Ridge (English Heritage 2006) and includes sites at Badbury (Walters 1981) and Lydiard Park (Wessex Archaeology nd); they are largely situated close to the Roman roads, which in this case, means some distance to the east. The distribution of villas on the Marlborough Downs is one of the densest in southern Britain (Walters 2001, 128), but this appears to contrast with the dispersed and modest nature of Roman buildings known around Wroughton.

The use of the Late Roman landscape

The enclosures and settlement appear to have fallen into disuse by AD 200. There seems to have been a lengthy hiatus, and it is possible that the area was used for unenclosed grazing during this period. A pit (1645), located on the line of the north side of the Period 5 droveway contained partial but articulated cattle remains radiocarbon dated to the second half of the 2nd century to first part of the 4th century AD. It may therefore have been contemporary with the latter part of the use of the Period 5 droveway and enclosures, post-dated it, or been contemporary with other activity which can be assigned to the Late Roman period. A date in the earlier part of this range is perhaps to be preferred at a point when the Period 5 features were still visible, and perhaps there was still a substantial use of the area for livestock grazing. The burial may represent the disposal of fallen stock, or something intended to mark the space, in a similar way to the human burial located to the north-west.

During the later 3rd or 4th century an oven was constructed within the circuit of the C-shaped enclosure, the ditch of which clearly was still visible, having accumulated more material during Period 5. Oven 2827 was substantial, being nearly 5m long, including the square chamber and flue, and constructed from chalk blocks. A radiocarbon date on a spelt wheat grain from the oven base indicates that it was in use during the second half of the 3rd century AD or first quarter of the 4th century. The crop remains recovered were those of spelt, with smaller amounts of emmer and barley. This is similar to assemblages from the nearby site at Ridgeway Farm, Purton (Wyles 2017a).

Whilst most recorded Roman ovens lie within contemporary settlements (Lodwick 2017, 60), seemingly isolated examples are known, including an example at Marlborough Road, Swindon, which was later than a small roundhouse settlement in the same location (Hood 2019, 116, 119) or at Hullavington where a crop-processing oven was found, and was about 1km from any other known

Roman settlement (Hart forthcoming). However, the distance from settlement is not clear. Much of the material from the oven was chaff, which occurred with fuel wood and rather than representing a crop being dried was rather more related to tinder used in the firing. It does, however, imply that cleaning of the crop may have taken place reasonably close by. This either implies that there was a settlement in the relatively close vicinity, or that crop processing was taking place in the fields, which suggests that the area was being used for arable cultivation at this time. In the latter case, this seems to have taken place in unenclosed spaces, unless they are preserved beyond the area of the excavation reported here. It is possible, however, that this relates to other settlement structures which are nearby elsewhere on the airfield.

The large size of the Collection Management Facility oven is significant. Its overall length was 4.85m which compares to other examples recently surveyed (ranging from 1.5m–3.2m long for T-shaped ovens, 1m–3.4m for figure-of-eight-shaped ovens and 2m–9m for keyhole-shaped ovens (Comeau and Burrow 2021, table 2)). The Collection Management Facility oven is T-shaped (for example Lodwick 2017, fig. 2.42) and lies at the larger end of the size range for such ovens. T-shaped ovens of comparable size are known, as at Manor Farm, Monk Sherborne, Hampshire; this form is the most common type on the Wessex Downs (Lodwick 2017, 60). In a recent review of such ovens in Wales, it was suggested that they signal production beyond the domestic consumption level, thus reflecting, for the Roman period, the demands of consumption centres such as towns and the military (Comeau and Burrow 2021, 114) and their association with surplus production was also suggested in a national survey of such features as part of the *Roman Rural Settlement Project* (Lodwick 2017, 55).

The scale of this oven therefore suggests that it provided part of the infrastructure of an estate involved in larger scale arable production. The evidence reflects the intensification of arable farming known to have been a feature of later Roman Britain, fueled by the demands of growing urban populations and, in southern Britain, supplied by the network of villas (Lodwick 2017, 61). There are no known villas in the vicinity, but there are indications of a high-status settlement at Burderop Down which is located on the plateau, just below the Marlborough Downs, 3km southeast of the Collection Management Facility site (HER ref. MWI15115). There, finds including stone and ceramic roofing tiles, bricks and Roman pottery have been noted along with traces of a hypocaust, suggesting either a villa or a substantial farm. A second rural Roman settlement may lie 4km east of the site near Buff Farm (HER ref. MWI15118) where later Roman pottery, roof tile fragments and quernstone fragments have been found. Earthworks forming a rectangular enclosure some 100m across and located immediately north of Barbury Castle, were partially excavated in 1886 at which time a wall was recorded along with Roman pottery (HER ref. MWI15221). However, none of these sites have been systematically investigated using modern techniques.

Late Roman burial – dispersed graves and the cemetery

During the Late Roman period, the use of the plateau for burial was expanded with the creation of a small cemetery, which included a few dispersed graves. Grave 2389 was also located within the area enclosed by the C-shaped enclosure. The radiocarbon date provided a range from the end of the 1st century AD to the first quarter of the 4th century, and it therefore may have belonged to either Period 5 or 6, given that there was other activity of both periods in this area of the excavation. An older woman had been buried probably within a wooden coffin as there were some structural nails in the grave. If dating towards the end of this span, her placement alongside the oven is perhaps puzzling, so it may be that the interment occurred before its construction. Burial within the enclosure earthworks may, however, suggest that she had a different status in life also suggested by the probable coffin.

Another burial, which sits more clearly within the Late Roman period is that of an older adult male SK 12053 buried in a north–south oriented grave 20m east of the C-shaped enclosure having been radiocarbon dated to the second half of the 3rd or 4th century AD. This seems to be clearly associated with the C-shaped enclosure but was probably contemporary with the Period 6 cemetery. In the latter case, this individual had isotopic values different from the other individuals which suggest that their dietary protein probably was derived primarily from grains and terrestrial herbivores. In contrast, the woman buried within the C-shaped enclosure (SK 2446) had elevated $\delta^{15}N$ values which might be associated with a diet richer in pig meat or freshwater fish (see Hamilton, Chapter 5). These apparently contrasting diets attest to variation amongst the local population, and possibly a chronological factor, but given the differences in both cases from individuals in the cemetery, and in the differing locations of the burials, one with a richer diet within an area that might be interpreted as more prestigious, one with a possibly more plant-based diet in an isolated location beyond it, there may be an indication here of status or role in the community which was burying their dead here during the Roman period.

The small cemetery was located in the centre of the excavated area, and as such, its full extent is known. It lay in a place which would have been outside of the areas enclosed in Period 5, and the remnants of those boundaries may have still been visible and the enclosures avoided. The cemetery contained 17 graves, each of which contained the remains of a single individual. The graves were in a reasonably tight group, but there is no indication of even an ephemeral enclosure around them. The burials were split into a northern and southern group, with the orientation of the graves apparently less uniform in the northern group, whilst there are some indications of rows in the southern group and a lack of intercutting which suggests that the graves remained visible or were marked. There seems to have been no preference for the orientation of the body within the grave. There was, however, in the northern group a tree-throw hole around which some of the graves appeared to cluster. These graves do not appear to have a common orientation or rows, and if contemporary they may have been aligned on the tree. If it was in place at the time of the burials, the overhang of the tree canopy may have covered graves 2338, 2863, 2878, 2329, 2326 and 2320. Of these, all but 2320 had their feet toward the probable location of the tree trunk.

The dating of the burials is, however, broad, and it is not possible to postulate clearly how the cemetery developed over time. It may be that a natural feature within the unbounded landscape was the initial focus, and the burials spread out from that point, but it is not possible to elucidate this. Hobnails were present in nine graves and tend to be a feature of Late Roman burial practice. Where there was cultural material present it dated to the later 3rd and 4th centuries AD, and a single radiocarbon date from SK 2314 spanned the same period.

With the exception of one child (SK 2879), all of those buried in this plot were adults, comprising seven males and nine females, mostly aged over 45 at death. Whilst the numbers are small this does not seem to reflect the profile of a normal population. Whilst adolescents are frequently the least represented, and there are more females than males, a greater number of young adult women might be expected as elsewhere (Rohnbogner 2018, 339) given the effects of child bearing, and perhaps more younger children due to infant mortality which is likely to have been high (Brothwell 1972; Lewis and Gowland 2007) in all settings during this period. Neonates may have been buried elsewhere, as is often the case; a few neonatal bones came from contexts in the enclosures dated to the preceding period.

The health status of the individuals in the cemetery included a range of conditions, often related to the age of individuals and a degree of manual labour. The pattern of degenerative disease and traumatic injury is not unusual in rural Roman contexts. Two males had indications of traumatic injury, including fractures and this is similar to that seen across all regions in Roman Britain and more commonly in males than females (Rohnbogner 2018, 338). Coupled with the demographic indicated here, it may be that this burial area was used largely for those labouring on an estate, rather than representing broader family groups. One older male, however, presented an example of DISH, a condition connected with a richer diet. Only a couple of examples of DISH were identified by Rohnbogner (2018, 337) in rural sites, whilst the prevalence in the urban cemetery at Lankhills, Winchester was 1.4%. This therefore provides an unusual example of the condition from a rural location, and perhaps suggests that this individual had some greater status or access to resources than his neighbours in the cemetery.

The form of the graves, cut into the substrate, was similar in all cases, and there was little to differentiate between individuals with respect to status or treatment. A few graves may have had planked linings, indicated by the presence of some carpentry nails. A couple of flints (a flake and a Neolithic arrowhead) may have been deliberately curated and placed as grave goods, although this is less certain for the flake. Hobnails and shoe cleats in nine of the graves, often clustered at the feet, suggests that these individuals were buried wearing boots or shoes and possibly clothed. The body position was generally extended, in all but two cases supine, sometimes slightly flexed.

Three burials had evidence for different treatment. The only child in the cemetery (aged 6–8 years) was located on the periphery of the group at the north-western edge. They had been buried prone, and there were chalk slabs lying above the body, although it is not clear whether these had been directly placed on the body or had been used to cap the grave. Lesions on the ribs and skull suggest that this child had suffered from a systemic infection which may have been active at the time of death. They also exhibited indicators of longer-term metabolic distress.

A mature female, SK 2314, was also buried in the southern cluster of graves, lying in an extended prone position with her arms flexed at the elbows. No pathological changes were noted other than indicators of poor oral health. This grave included a thick layer of chalk above the body. SK 2865, in the northern cluster on the north-west side of the tree-throw hole, was also buried in a prone position, but there were no finds or unusual grave fill. This woman had some indications of metabolic disease. Prone burials are generally uncommon (Philpott 1991, 71), and for there to be three examples within this small cemetery is of some interest.

The majority of burials in the region are single examples or one or two individuals in close proximity. There are a few larger groupings of burials such as Winterbourne and Boscombe Down Sports Field which include both inhumations and cremations, whilst it seems frequent that where there are multiple burials, these generally include fewer than ten individuals. Extended supine burial is most common but there are a number of different forms of grave including coffined examples known from Wiltshire (Foster 2001, 165–6), so this cemetery is perhaps on the larger side, but the rites practiced are not out of the ordinary. The presence of hobnails may mainly be a function of the Late Roman date of the interments (Philpott 1991) but are also the most common items in graves in the area, associated with both males and females (Foster 2001, 168), and this was the case at the Collection Management Facility (see Table 2.2). The inclusion of children (other than perinates) in formal burial also occurs elsewhere in the county (Foster 2001, 170).

The historic landscape: medieval, post-medieval and modern

As in the Mid to Late Roman period, the plateau was used for arable cultivation during the medieval and post-medieval periods, as indicated by a series of furrows across the site. These lacked dating evidence but pre-dated ditches shown on the 1886 1st Edition Ordnance Survey map which were identified within the excavation. Wroughton itself has early medieval origins (HER ref. MWI16512) and Saxon finds have been recovered from the surrounding area. The 1796 Wroughton Enclosure map shows that the site lay within a large open field following enclosure. This is shown on the map as Glebe land, indicating that it formed part of an ecclesiastical holding although the identity of the occupier has not been found. This land would have been used for sheep farming, although corn may still have been grown. The land had other uses too, as indicated by a series of small chalk quarries excavated up against one of the later boundaries depicted on the 1886 1st Edition Ordnance Survey map.

Later remains relate to the site's use as part of RAF Wroughton. Construction of the airfield began in 1939 and the first runway, built using concrete, was ready by 1941. The airfield housed No. 15 Maintenance Unit (15MU) which undertook service, modification and repair of a variety of aircraft whilst a second Maintenance Unit, No. 76, packed aircraft into crates for overseas shipment (Gibbs 1992; HE 2020). There was also the RAF General Hospital (known from 1967 as Princess Alexandra's Hospital) on the airfield. The airfield remained in use following the war until its closure in 1978.

Recording elements of the airfield did not fall within the project remit. However, eight slit trenches were found, all 7m to 10m long and up to 1.6m deep (Fig. 2.42). These were on a single north-west/south-east alignment, parallel to one of the runways. Their purpose is uncertain: they may have been designed to provide emergency air raid cover or dug as practice trenches for the Home Guard or US Army personnel stationed at RAF Wroughton during the Second World War. Slit trenches dug by the Home Guard and US Army are recorded within Barbury Castle (HER ref. MWI72691). These features represented the latest activity on site.

Conclusion

The excavations at the Collection Management Facility, Science and Innovation Park, Swindon have provided a relatively rare glimpse of later prehistoric settlement activity on the edge of the escarpment of the Wiltshire Downs as they overlook the intensively settled valley to the north. A rare example of a pair of double pit alignments probably dating to the end of the Late Bronze Age or Early Iron Age appears to define a route between the escarpment and the vale. It must extend to the south; how far is a matter of interest but can only be speculated upon at this point. A dispersed and shifting settlement of roundhouses and pits spread across the edge of the scarp from the Early Iron Age onwards, lasting perhaps into the earlier part of the Late Iron Age. It does not appear to have extended beyond the line of the pit alignments on its western side, although further settlement could lie in this direction. More clearly, it does appear to spread to the east, with several buildings and pits clearly extending beyond the limits of excavation. The scattered nature of the layout provides no hints as to the true extent of the settlement, which may be present across the edge of the escarpment. The pits in particular show complex patterns of deposition which are familiar from Iron Age contexts, but with some local twists, such as the inclusion of the sarsen stones available around the site. Burials contemporary with the settlement perhaps suggest some complex practices, with members of the community buried in and around the homes of the living. However, whilst the burials occurred within a relatively confined part of the excavated area, the outlying example seen in an evaluation trench to the north suggests that burial may also have been a widespread practice in the surrounding landscape.

The establishment of fields during the Late Iron Age/ Early Roman period and the development and change which these underwent over a couple of centuries appears to attest to changing agricultural priorities. Their presence, and the existence of the later Roman oven and the small, and apparently isolated, cemetery currently lacks context. They all attest to a landscape which has been apportioned for agricultural tasks, but throughout the Roman centuries the location of settlement in relation to the fields and crop processing is unclear. One can surmise that there is some nearby or adjacent building or buildings; the scale of crop processing undertaken might imply something substantial, and probably not too far away. The cemetery may have been in a peripheral location but is unlikely to be too remote from the homes of those interred within it. The excavations have provided tantalising snapshots of a busy landscape which await future elucidation.

Bibliography

AC Archaeology 2023 *Land off Marlborough Road, Wroughton, Wiltshire Archaeological post-excavation assessment report*, Report No. ACW1224/5/0

Aitken, E. and Wyles S.F. 2020 'Palaeoenvironmental assessment', in CA 2020, 98–115

Allen, L. and Wallis, J. 2011 'Worked bone and antler', in Hey *et al.* 2011a, 431–39

Allen, M., Lodwick, L., Brindle, T., Fulford, M. and Smith, A. 2017 *New visions of the countryside of Roman Britain, Vol. 2: The rural economy of Roman Britain*, Britannia Monogr. Ser. **30** London, Society for the Promotion of Roman Studies

Allen, T. and Cramp, K. and Lamdin-Whymark, H. and Webley, L. 2010 *Castle Hill and its landscape; archaeological investigations at the Wittenhams, Oxfordshire*, Oxford Archaeology monograph **9**

Allen, T.G. 1990a 'The Iron Age pottery', in Allen 1990c, 32–46

Allen, T.G. 1990b 'Fired clay', in Allen 1990c, 53

Allen, T.G. 1990c *An Iron Age and Romano-British settlement at Watkins Farm, Northmoor, Oxon*, Thames Valley Landscapes: the Windrush Valley **1**, Oxford, Oxford University Committee for Archaeology

Allen, T.G. and Robinson, M.A. 1993 *The prehistoric landscape and Iron Age enclosed settlement at Mingies Ditch, Hardwick-with-Yelford, Oxon*, Thames Valley Landscapes: the Windrush Valley **2**, Oxford, Oxford University Committee for Archaeology

Allen, T.G., Darvill, T., Green, L.S. and Jones M. 1993 *Excavations at Roughground Farm, Lechlade, Gloucestershire: a prehistoric and Roman landscape*, Thames Valley Landscapes: the Cotswold Water Park. Volume **1**, Oxford, Oxford Archaeological Unit and Oxford University Committee for Archaeology

Alonso, N. 2019 'A first approach to women, tools and operational sequences in traditional manual cereal grinding', *Archaeol. and Anthropol. Sci.* **11**(8), 4307–4324

AlQahtani, S.J., Hector, M.P. and Liversidge, H.M. 2010 'Brief communication: the London atlas of human tooth development and eruption', *Amer. J. Phys. Anthropol.* **142**, 481–90

Anderson, A.S. 1978 'Wiltshire fine wares', in Arthur and Marsh 1978, 373–392

Anderson, A.S. 1979 *The Roman pottery industry in North Wiltshire Swindon*, Swindon Archaeol. Soc. Rep. **2**

Anderson, A.S., Wacher, J.S. and Fitzpatrick, A.P. 2001 *The Roman 'small town' at Wanborough, Wiltshire*, Britannia Monogr. Ser. **19**

Anderson, R. 2005 'An annotated list of the non-marine mollusca of Britain and Ireland', *J. Conchology* **38**, 607–637

Anon. 2007 'Excavation and fieldwork in Wiltshire 2005', *Wilts Archaeol. Natur. Hist. Mag.* **100**, 232–38

Arnoldussen, S., Johnston, R., Løvschal M. (eds) 2021 *Europe's early fieldscapes. Archaeologies of prehistoric land allotment*, Switzerland, Springer

Arthur, P. and Marsh, G. 1978 *Early Roman finewares in Roman Britain*, Oxford, BAR Brit. Ser. **57**

AS (Archaeological Surveys) 2017 *Building One, Science Museum Group, Wroughton: Magnetometer Survey Report*, Job Ref: **736**

Associazione Italiana di Metallurgia (ed.) 2003 *Archaeometallurgy in Europe international conference: 24-25-26 September 2003, Milan, Italy* Milano, Associazione Italiana di Metallurgia

Aufderheide, A.C. and Rodriguez-Martin, C. 1998 *The Cambridge encyclopaedia of human paleopathology*, Cambridge, Cambridge University Press

Baker, P., Forcey, C., Jundi, S. and Witcher, R. (eds) 1998 *Proceedings of the Eighth Annual Theoretical Roman Archaeology Conference*, Oxford, Oxbow

Baldwin, A. and Joy, J. 2017 *A celtic feast: the Iron Age cauldrons from Chiseldon, Wiltshire*, Brit. Mus. Res. Pub. **203** London, British Museum

Barber, J. 1985 'The pit alignment at Eskbank Nurseries' *Proc. Prehist. Soc.* **51**(1), 149–166

Barclay, A.J. 2024 'Between Essex and Wessex: a review of Grooved Ware from the Upper and Middle Thames Valley', in Copper *et al.* 2024, 191–207

Barclay, A., Booth, P., Knight, D., Evans, J., Brown, D.H. and Wood, I., 2016 *A standard for pottery studies in archaeology*, Swindon, Historic England

Barclay, A. and Bradley, P. 2017 'The significance of quernstones – defining Bell Beaker 'domestic burials' at Amesbury Down, Wilshire', in Shaffrey 2017b, 148–165

Barclay, A., Cromarty, A.M., Gosden, C., Lock, G., Miles, D., Palmer, S. and Robinson M. 2003 'The White Horse and its landscape', in Miles *et al.* 2003, 243–268

Barclay A. and Glass, H. 1995 'Excavations on Neolithic and Bronze Age ring ditches, Shorncote Quarry, Somerford Keynes, Gloucestershire', *Trans. Bristol Gloucestershire Archaeol. Soc.* **113**, 21–60

Barclay, A., Gray, M. and Lambrick, G. 1995 *Excavation at the Devil's Quoits, Stanton Harcourt, Oxfordshire 1972–3 and 1988*, Thames Valley Landscapes: the Windrush Valley, Volume **3**, Oxford, Oxford Archaeological Unit

Barton, R.N.E., Berridge, P.J., Walker, M.J.C. and Bevins, R.E. 1995 'Persistent places in the Mesolithic landscape: an example from the Black Mountain uplands of South Wales', *Proc. Prehist. Soc.* **61**, 81–116

Bass, W.M. 1987 *Human osteology: a laboratory and field manual of human skeleton*, 3rd edition Springfield, MO, Missouri Archaeological Society

Bell, C., Stansbie, D. and Hey, G. 2011 'The Middle Iron Age' in Hey *et al.* 2011, 141–188

Berry, R. and Berry, A. 1967 'Epigenetic variation in human cranium', *J. Anatomy* **101**, 361–379

Berstan, R., Stott, A. W., Minnitt, S., Ramsey, C.B., Hedges, R.E.M. and Evershed, R.P. 2008 'Direct dating of pottery from its organic residues: new precision using compound-specific carbon isotopes', *Antiquity* **82**(317), 702–713

Bersu, G. 1940 'Excavations at Little Woodbury, Wiltshire', *Proc. Prehist. Soc.* **6**, 30–111

Best, J., Doherty, S., Armit, I., Boev, Z., Büster, L., Cunliffe, B., Foster, A., Frimet, B., Hamilton-Dyer, S., Higham, T., Lebrasseur, O., Miller, H., Peters, J., Seigle, M., Skelton, C., Symmons, R., Thomas, R., Trentacoste, A., Maltby, M., Larson, G. and Sykes, N. 2022 'Redefining the timing and circumstances of the chicken's introduction to European and north-west Africa', *Antiquity* **96**(388), 868–882

BGS (British Geological Society) 2020 Geology of Britain viewer http://mapapps.bgs.ac.uk/geologyofbritain/home.html? (accessed 5 February 2020)

Bianchi, G. 1995 'Plant waxes', in Hamilton 1995, 176–222

Birbeck, V. 2001 'Excavations at Watchfield, Shrivenham, Oxfordshire, 1998' *Oxoniensia*, **66**, 221–88

Booth, P. and Biddulph, E. 2011 'Iron Age pottery', in Hey *et.al.* 2011a, 348–362

Bowman, A. and Thomas, J. 1994 *The Vindolanda tablets*, London, British Museum Press

Bradley, P. and Lambrick, G. 2004 'Pits and possible postholes' in Lambrick and Allen 2004, 35–45

Bradley, R. 2002 *The past in prehistoric societies*, London and New York, Routledge

Brain, C. 1981 *The hunters or the hunted? An introduction to African cave taphonomy*, Chicago, University of Chicago Press

Brett, M. and McSloy, E.R. 2011 'Prehistoric pits and Roman enclosures on the A419 Blunsdon Bypass, Blunsdon St Andrew: excavations 2006–7', *Wilts Archaeol. Natur. Hist. Mag.* **104**, 95–114

Brickley, M. and McKinley, J. (eds) 2004 *Guidelines to the standards for recording of human remains*, IFA Paper No **7**, Reading, BABAO & Institute of Field Archaeologists

Bronk Ramsey, C. 2009 'Bayesian analysis of radiocarbon dates', *Radiocarbon* **51** (1), 337–360

Bronk Ramsey, C. 2020 *University of Oxford Radiocarbon Accelerator Unit calibration programme OxCal v4.4.2*, https://c14.arch.ox.ac.uk/oxcal.html

Brooks, S. and Suchey, J.M. 1990 'Skeletal age determination based on the os pubis: a comparison of the Acsádi-Nemeskéri and Suchey-Brooks method', *Human Evolution* **5**, 227–238

Brothwell, D., 1972 'Palaeodemography and earlier British populations', *World Archaeology* **4**(1), 75–87

Brothwell, D.R., 1981 *Digging up bones*, Oxford, Oxford University Press

Brown, G., Field, D. and McOmish, D. (eds) 2005 *The Avebury landscape: aspects of the field archaeology of the Marlborough Downs*, Oxford, Oxbow Books

Brown, L. 1984 'Objects of stone', in Cunliffe 1984, 407–456

Brück, J. and Booth, T.J. 2022a 'The ambivalent dead: curation, excarnation and complex post-mortem trajectories in Middle and Late Bronze Age Britain', *Proc. Prehist. Soc.* **88**, 193–220

Brück, J. and Booth, T.J. 2022b 'The power of relics: the curation of human bone in British Bronze Age burials', *European J. of Archaeol* **25**(4), 440–462

Bulleid, A. and Gray, H. S. 1911 *Glastonbury lake village volume I*, Glastonbury, Glastonbury Antiquarian Society

Bush, H and Zvelebil, M (eds) 1991 *Health in past societies: biocultural interpretations of human skeletal remains in archaeological contexts*, Oxford, BAR Int. Ser. **567**

Buteux, S. and Chapman, H. 2009 *Where rivers meet. The archaeology of Catholme and the Trent-Tame confluence*, **161**, York, CBA Research Report

Butler, C. 2005 *Prehistoric flintwork*, Stroud, Tempus

CA (Cotswold Archaeology) 2017 *Building One, Wroughton, Wiltshire: Heritage Assessment*, CA report **09158**

CA (Cotswold Archaeology) 2018a *Building One, Science Museum, Wroughton, Wiltshire: Written Scheme of Investigation for a programme of archaeological mitigation*

CA (Cotswold Archaeology) 2018b *Building One, Science Museum, Wroughton, Wiltshire: archaeological watching brief*, CA report **09158**

CA (Cotswold Archaeology) 2018c *Building One, Science Museum, Wroughton, Wiltshire: archaeological evaluation*, CA report **09158**

CA (Cotswold Archaeology) 2020 *Building One, Science Museum, Wroughton, Swindon: post-excavation assessment and updated project design*, CA report **9293_1**

Cappers, R.T.J., Bekker, R.M. and Jans, J.E.A. 2006 *Digital seed atlas of the Netherlands*, Groningen, Barkhuis Publishing and Groningen University Library

Case, H. 2003 'Beaker presence at Wilsford 7' *Wiltshire Archaeol. Natur. Hist. Mag.* **96**, 161–194

Cave-Browne, P. 1992 'The use of iron pyrites for the creation of fire', *Lithics* **13**, 52–60

Cerling, T.E. (ed.) 2013 *Treatise on geochemistry: archaeology and anthropology*, Oxford, Elsevier

Chadron-Picault, P. and Pernot, M. 1999 *Un quartier antique d'artisanat métallurgique à autun*, Paris, Editions de La Maison Des Sciences de L'Homme

Chadwick, A.M and Gibson, C.D. 2013 *Memory, myth and long-term landscape inhabitation*, Oxford, Oxbow Books

Chaffey, G. and Barclay A. 2013 'The MTV generations: remixing the past in prehistory – or forgetting to change old habits', in Chadwick and Gibson 2013, 208–225

Challinor, D. 2010 'Charcoal', in Powell *et al.* 2010, 184

Challinor, D. 2018a 'Wood charcoal', in Powell 2018, 225–228

Challinor, D. 2018b 'Wood charcoal', in Mason 2018, 88–91

Charrié-Duhaut, A., Connan, J., Rouquette, N., Adam, P., Barbotin, C., de Rozières, M.F., Tchapla, A. and Albrecht, P. 2007 'The canopic jars of Rameses II: real use revealed by molecular study of organic residues', *J. Archaeol. Sci.* **34**(6), 957–967

Charters, S., Evershed, R.P., Goad, L.J., Heron, C. and Blinkhorn, P. 1993 'Identification of an adhesive used to repair a Roman jar', *Archaeometry* **35**, 91–101

Clarke, A., Fulford, M.G., Rains, M. and Tootell, K. 2007 'Silchester Roman town insula IX: The development of an urban property c. AD 40–50 to c. AD 250', *Internet Archaeol.* **21**. https://intarch.ac.uk/journal/issue21/4/finds_pottery.htm (accessed 13 July 2021)

Clarke, D.L. 1970 *Beaker pottery of Great Britain and Ireland, Cambridge*, Cambridge University Press

Cleal, R. 1992 'The Neolithic and Beaker pottery' in Gingell, 61–111

Clough, S. 2023 'Human remains', in P. Guarino and A. Barclay, *In the shadow of Segsbury The archaeology of the H380 Childrey Waren Water Pipeline Oxfordshire, 2018–2020* Cotswold Archaeology Monograph No **16** Cirencester, 53–79

Coles, J.M. 1987 *Meare Village East: the Excavations of A. Bulleid and H St George Gray* Exeter, Somerset Levels Papers **13**

Colledge, S. and Conolly, J. 2007 *The origin and spread of domestic plants in Southwest Asia and Europe*, Walnut Creek, Left Coast Press

Cooper, A. Garrow, D. Gibson, C. and Giles, M. 2019 'Covering the dead in later prehistoric Britain: elusive objects and powerful technologies of funerary performance', *Proc. Prehist. Soc.* **85**, 223–50

Cootes, K., Axworthy, J., Jordan, D., Thomas, M. and Carlin, R. 2021 'Poulton, Cheshire: the excavation of a lowland Iron Age settlement', *J. Chester Archaeol. Soc.* **91**, 103–178

Comeau, R. and Burrow, S. 2021 'Corn-drying kilns in Wales: a review of the evidence', *Archaeologia Cambrensis* **170**, 111–149

Coplen, T.B., Kendall, C. and Hopple, J. 1983 'Comparison of stable isotope reference samples', *Nature* **302**, 236–238

Copley, M.S., Berstan, R., Dudd, S.N., Docherty, G., Mukherjee, A.J., Straker, V., Payne, S. and Evershed, R.P. 2003 'Direct chemical evidence for widespread dairying in Prehistoric Britain', *Proc. National Academy Sci. United States of America* **100**(4), 1524–1529

Copley, M.S., Berstan, R., Dudd, S.N., Straker, V., Payne, S. and Evershed, R.P. 2005 'Dairying in antiquity. I. Evidence from absorbed lipid residues dating to the British Iron Age', *J. Archaeol. Sci.* **32**(4), 485–503

Copley, M.S., Hansel, F.A., Sadr, K. and Evershed, R.P. 2004 'Organic residue evidence for the processing of marine animal products in pottery vessels from the pre-colonial archaeological site of Kasteelberg D east, South Africa', *South African J. Sci.* **100**(5–6), 279–283

Copper, M., Whittle, A. and Sheridan, A. 2024 *Revisiting Grooved Ware. Understanding ceramic trajectories in Britain and Ireland, 3200–2400 cal BC*, Neolithic Studies Seminar papers **20**

Corney, M. 2001 'The Romano-British nucleated settlements of Wiltshire', in Ellis 2001, 5–38

Correa-Ascencio, M. and Evershed, R.P. 2014 'High throughput screening of organic residues in archaeological potsherds using direct acidified methanol extraction', *Analytical Methods* **6**(5), 1330–1340

Cox, M. 2000 'Aging adults from the skeleton', in Cox and Mays 2000, 61–82

Cox, M. and Mays, S. 2000 *Human osteology in archaeology and forensic science*, London, Greenwich medical media

Craig, O.E., Forster, M., Andersen, S.H., Koch, E., Crombe, P., Milner, N.J., Stern, B., Bailey, G.N. and Heron, C.P. 2007 'Molecular and isotopic demonstration of the processing of aquatic products in northern European prehistoric pottery', *Archaeometry* **49**, 135–152

Cramp, L.J.E. and Evershed, R.P. 2013 'Reconstructing aquatic resource exploitation in human prehistory using lipid biomarkers and stable isotopes', in Cerling 2013, 319–339

Cramp, L.J.E., Evershed, R.P. and Eckardt, H. 2011 'What was a mortarium used for? Organic residues and cultural change in Iron Age and Roman Britain', *Antiquity* **85**, 1339–1352

Cramp, L.J.E., Evershed, R.P. and Eckardt, H. 2012 'Are you what you grind? A comparison of organic residues from ceramics at two Roman British sites', in Schruefer-Kolb 2012, 93–110

Cramp, L.J.E., Jones, J., Sheridan, A., Smyth, J., Whelton, H., Mulville, J., Sharples, N. and Evershed, R.P. 2014 'Immediate replacement of fishing with dairying by the earliest farmers of the northeast Atlantic archipelagos', *Proc. Royal Soc. Biolog. Sci.* **281**(1780), 1–8

Crummy, N. 1983 *The Roman small finds from excavations in Colchester, 1971–9*, Colchester Archaeological Report **2**, Colchester, Colchester Archaeological Trust Ltd.

Cunliffe, B. 1975 *Excavations at Portchester Castle, Volume I: Roman*, London, Society of Antiquaries

Cunliffe, B. 1984 *Danebury: an Iron Age hillfort in Hampshire, Volume 2 The Excavations, 1969–1978: the finds*, York, Counc. Brit. Archaeol. Res. Rep. **52**

Cunliffe, B. 1991 *Iron Age communities in Britain. An account of England, Scotland and Wales from the seventh century BC until the Roman conquest*, 3rd edition, London, Routledge

Cunliffe, B. 1992 'Pits, preconceptions and propitiation in the British Iron Age', *Oxford J. Archaeol.* **11**(1), 69–83

Cunliffe, B. 1995 *Danebury an Iron Age hillfort in Hampshire, Volume 6: A hillfort community in perspective,* Council for British Archaeology Research Report **102**

Cunliffe, B. 2000 *The Danebury Environs Programme. The prehistory of a Wessex landscape Volume 1 Introduction* Oxford, English Heritage and Oxford University Committee for Archaeology Monogr. **48**

Cunliffe, B. 2005 *Iron Age communities in Britain. An account of England, Scotland and Wales from the seventh century BC until the Roman conquest*, 4th edition London, Routledge

Cunliffe, B. 2009 *Iron Age communities in Britain: an account of England, Scotland and Wales from the seventh century BC until the Roman conquest*, 4th edition (reprinted), London, Routledge

Cunliffe, B. and Miles, D. (eds) 1984 *Aspects of the Iron Age in central southern Britain*, University of Oxford Committee for Archaeology Monograph **2**, Oxford, OUCE

Cunliffe, B. and Poole, C. (eds) 1991a *Danebury. An Iron Age Hillfort in Hampshire. Volume 4. The excavations 1979–1988: the site,* York, Council for British Archaeol. Res. Rep. **73**

Cunliffe, B. and Poole, C. (eds) 1991b *Danebury. An Iron Age Hillfort in Hampshire. Volume 5. The excavations 1979–1988: the finds*, York, Council for British Archaeol. Res. Rep. **73**

Cunliffe, B. and Poole, C. (eds) 2000 *The Danebury environs programme: the prehistory of a Wessex landscape. Vol. 2, Part 3: Suddern Farm, Middle Wallop, Hants, 1991 and 1996*, Oxford University Committee for Archaeology Monogr. **49**, Oxford, OUCE

Davies, A. 2018 *Creating society and constructing the past. Social change in the Thames Valley from the Late Bronze Age to the Middle Iron Age*, Oxford, BAR Brit. Ser. **637**

Davies, P. 2008 *Snails archaeology and landscape change*, Oxford, Oxbow Books

Davies, S. 1981 'Excavations at Old Down Farm, Andover, Part II: Prehistoric and Roman' *Proc. Hampshire Fld Club Archaeol. Soc.* **37**, 81–163

Davis, O., Waddington, K. and Sharples, N. (eds) 2008 *Changing perspectives on the first millennium B.C.,* Oxford, Oxbow

Davis, S. 2000 'The effect of castration and age on the development of the Shetland sheep skeleton and a metric comparison between bones', *J. Archaeol. Sci.* **27**(5), 373–390

Davis, S., Gonçalves, M. and Gabriel, S. 2008 'Animal remains from a Moslem period (12th/13th century AD) lixeira (garbage dump) in Silves, Algarve, Portugal', *Revista Portuguesa de Arqueologia* **11**(1), 183–258

Dias, G. and Tayles, N. 1997 "Abscess cavity'– a misnomer', *Int. J. Osteoarchaeol.* **7**, 548–554

Dobney, K.M., Jaques, S.D. and Irving, B.G. 1995 Of butchers and breeds: Report on vertebrate remains from various sites in the city of Lincoln, Lincoln, Lincoln Archaeological Studies **5**

Dore, J.N. and Wilkes, J.J. 1999 'Excavations directed by J.D. Leach and J.J. Wilkes on the site of a Roman fortress at Carpow, Perthshire, 1964–79', *Proc. Soc. Antiq. Scot.* **129**, 481–575

Driesch, A. von den 1976 *A guide to the measurement of animal bones from archaeological sites*, Cambridge, Massachusetts, Harvard University Press

Dudd, S.N. and Evershed, R.P. 1998 'Direct demonstration of milk as an element of archaeological economies', *Science* **282**(5393), 1478–1481

Dunbar, E., Cook, G.T., Naysmith, P., Tripney, B.G. and Xu, S. 2016 'AMS ^{14}C dating at the Scottish Universities Environmental Research Centre (SUERC) Radiocarbon Dating Laboratory', *Radiocarbon* **58**, 9–23

Dungworth, D. 2016 *Stanwick, Northamptonshire: assessment of industrial debris,* Research Report **10/2016**, Portsmouth, Historic England

Dungworth, D. with additions by Brooks, I. 2021 'Industrial remains', in Cootes *et al.* 2021, 143–147

Dunne, J., Evershed, R.P., Salque, M., Cramp, L., Bruni, S., Ryan, K., Biagetti, S. and di Lernia, S. 2012 'First dairying in green Saharan Africa in the fifth millennium BC', *Nature* **486**(7403), 390–394

Edlin, H.L. *1949 Woodland crafts in Britain: an account of the traditional uses of trees and timbers in the British countryside*, London, Batsford

Edwards, E. 2009 'Prehistoric pottery', in Powell *et. al.* 2009, 58–67

Egan, G. and Pritchard, P. *1991 Medieval finds from excavations in London: 3. Dress Accessories c. 1150–1450*, London, The Stationary Office

Eisenmann, V. 1986 'Comparative osteology of modern and fossil horses, half-asses, and asses', in Meadow and Uerpmann 1986, 67–116

Ellis, C., and Davies, A., 2024 *Early Thame. Archaeological investigations at Oxford Road, Thame, Oxfordshire 2015. Volume 2: the Roman and Saxon periods*, Oxford Cotswold Archaeology Monograph **2**

Ellis, C., and Powell, A.B. with Hawkes, J. 2008 *An Iron Age settlement outside Battlesbury hillfort, Warminster and sites along the Southern Range Road*, Salisbury, Wessex Archaeology report **22**

Ellis, P. 2001 *Roman Wiltshire and after*, Devizes, Wiltshire Archaeological and Natural History Society

Erkelens, C.J. 2017 *The question of cribra femora – examining the cause of cribra femora in a Dutch archaeological and medical skeletal collection*, Masters Thesis University of Leiden

Evans, D. and Alexander, M. 2009 'A Late Iron Age and Romano-British field system at site 10A, South Marston Park, Wiltshire', *Wilts Archaeol. Natur. Hist. Mag.* **102**, 114–128

Evershed, R.P. 1993 'Biomolecular archaeology and lipids', *World Archaeol.* **25**(1), 74–93

Evershed, R.P. 2008 'Organic residue analysis in archaeology: the archaeological biomarker revolution', *Archaeometry* **50**(6), 895–924

Evershed, R.P., Arnot, K.I., Collister, J., Eglinton, G. and Charters, S. 1994 'Application of isotope ratio monitoring gas chromatography–mass spectrometry to the analysis of organic residues of archaeological origin', *The Analyst* **119**, 909–914

Evershed, R.P., Copley, M.S., Dickson, L. and Hansel, F.A. 2008 'Experimental evidence for the processing of marine animal products and other commodities containing polyunsaturated fatty acids in pottery vessels', *Archaeometry* **50**(1), 101–113

Evershed, R.P., Heron, C. and Goad, L.J. 1991 'Epicuticular wax components preserved in potsherds as chemical indicators of leafy vegetables in ancient diets', *Antiquity* **65**(248), 540–544

Evershed, R.P., Mottram, H.R., Dudd, S.N., Charters, S., Stott, A. W., Lawrence, G.J., Gibson, A.M., Conner, A., Blinkhorn, P.W. and Reeves, V. 1997a 'New criteria for the identification of animal fats preserved in archaeological pottery', *Naturwissenschaften* **84**(9), 402–406

Evershed, R.P., Vaughan, S.J., Dudd, S.N. and Soles, J.S. 1997b 'Fuel for thought? Beeswax in lamps and conical cups from late Minoan Crete', *Antiquity* **71**(274), 979–985

Fairbairn, A.S. 2000 *Plants in Neolithic Britain and beyond.* Neolithic Studies Seminar Paper **5**, Oxford, Oxbow Books

Fasham, P. 1985 *Prehistoric settlement at Winnall Down, Winchester, and excavations of MARC 3 Site R17 in 1976 and 1977*, Hampshire Fld Club Monogr. **2**

Feiller, N., Gilbertson, D. and NGA, R. (eds) 1985 *Palaeobiological Investigations*, Oxford, BAR Int. Ser. **266**

Ferembach, D., Schwidetzky, I. and Stloukal, M. 1980 'Recommendations for age and sex diagnoses of skeletons', *J. Human Evolution* **9**, 517–549

Feugère, M. and Gŭstin, M. (eds) 2000 *Iron, blacksmiths and tools: ancient European crafts,* Montagnac, Mergoil

Finnegan, M. 1978 'Non-metric variation of the infracranial skeleton', *J. Anatomy* **125**, 23–37

Fitzpatrick, A.P. 1997 'Everyday life in Iron Age Wessex' in Gwilt and Haselgrove (eds) 1997, 73–86

Fitzpatrick, A.P. 2011 *The Amesbury Archer and the Boscombe Bowmen: Bell Beaker burials at Boscombe Down, Amesbury, Wiltshire*, Wessex Archaeology report **27**, Salisbury

Foster, A. 2001 'Romano-British burials in Wiltshire', in Ellis 2001, 165–177

Fulford, M., Rippon, S., Ford, S., Timby, J., Williams, B., Allen, D., Allen, J., Allen, S., Boon, G. and Durden, T. 1997 'Silchester: Excavations at the North Gate, on the North Walls, and in the Northern Suburbs 1988 and 1991–3', *Britannia* **28**, 87–168

Gale, R. and Cutler, D. 2000 *Plants in archaeology: identification manual of vegetative plant materials used in Europe and the southern Mediterranean to* c. *1500*, Westbury and Kew

Gibbs, J. 1982 'Wroughton Airfield', *Wroughton History Society*, 73–74

Gilchrist, R. 2008 'Magic for the dead? The archaeology of magic in later medieval burials', *Medieval Archaeol.* **52**, 119–59

Giles, E. 1970 'Discriminant function sexing of the human skeleton', in Stewart 1970, 99–107

Gingell, C. 1986 'Excavation of an Iron Age enclosure at Groundwell Farm, Blunsdon St. Andrew, 1976–7', *Wilts Archaeol. Natur. Hist. Mag.* **76**, 33–75

Gingell, G. 1992 *The Marlborough Downs: a later Bronze Age landscape and its origin*, Wiltshire Archaeol. and Natur. Hist. Soc. Monogr. **1**

Gosden, C. and Lock, G. 2003 'Becoming Roman on the Berkshire Downs: the evidence from Alfred's Castle', *Britannia*, 34, 65–80

Gosden, C. and Lock, G. 2013 *Histories in the making. Excavations at Alfred's Castle 1998–2000*, Oxford University School of Archaeology Monograph **79**, Oxford, OUCE

Gowland, R. and Chamberlain, A. 2002 'A Bayesian approach to aging perinatal skeletal material from archaeological sites: implications for the evidence for infanticide in Roman Britain', *J. Archaeol. Sci.* **29:6**, 677–685

Grant, A. 1975 'The animal bones', in Cunliffe 1975, 378–408

Grant, A. 1982 'The use of toothwear as a guide to the age of domestic ungulates', in Wilson *et al.* 1982, 91–108

Grant, A. 1984 'The animal husbandry', in Cunliffe 1984, 496–548

Grant, A. 1991 'The animal husbandry', in Cunliffe and Poole 1991, 447–87

Green, H.S. 1980 *The flint arrowheads of the British Isles: a detailed study of materials from England and Wales with comparanda from Scotland and Ireland. Part 1*, Oxford, BAR Brit. Ser. **75**(1)

Green, S., Booth, P. and Allen, T. 2004 'Late Iron Age and Roman pottery', in Lambrick and Allen 2004, 303–328

Greenfield, H. 2006 'Sexing fragmentary ungulate acetabulae', in Ruscillo 2006, 68–86

Gregg, M.W., Banning, E.B., Gibbs, K. and Slater, G. F. 2009 'Subsistence practices and pottery use in Neolithic Jordan: molecular and isotopic evidence', *J. Archaeol. Sci.* **36**(4), 937–946

Greig, J. 1991 'The British Isles', in van Zeist *et al.* 1991, 229–334

Griffiths, S. 2009 'Charred and waterlogged plant remains', in Powell *et al.* 2009, 86–89

Guarino, P. and Barclay, A.J. 2023 *In the shadow of Segsbury: the archaeology of the H380 Childrey Warren Water Pipeline, Oxfordshire, 2018–2020*, Cotswold Archaeology Monogr. **16**, Cirencester, Cotswold Archaeology

Gunstone, F.D. 2004 *The chemistry of oils and fats*, Oxford, Blackwell Publishing

Gwilt, A. 1997 'Popular practices from material culture: a case study of the Iron Age settlement at Wakerly', in Gwilt and Haselgrove (eds) 1997, 153–66

Gwilt, A. and Haselgrove, C. (eds) 1997 *Reconstructing Iron Age societies*, Oxbow Monograph **71**, Oxford

Halmemies-Beauchet-Filleau, A., Vanhatalo, A., Toivonen, V., Heikkilä, T., Lee, M. and Shingfield, K. 2013 'Effect of replacing grass silage with red clover silage on ruminal lipid metabolism in lactating cows. Fed diets containing a 60:40 forage-to-concentrate ratio', *J. Dairy Sci.* **96**(9), 5882–5900

Halmemies-Beauchet-Filleau, A., Vanhatalo, A., Toivonen, V., Heikkilä, T., Lee, M. and Shingfield, K. 2014 'Effect of replacing grass silage with red clover silage on nutrient digestion, nitrogen metabolism, and milk fat composition in lactating cows fed diets containing a 60:40 forage-to-concentrate ratio', *J. Dairy Sci.* **97**(6), 3761–3776

Hambleton, E. 1999 *Animal husbandry regimes in Iron Age Britain*, Oxford, BAR Brit. Ser. **282**

Hambleton, E. 2008 *Review of middle Bronze Age – late Iron Age faunal assemblages from Southern Britain*, English Heritage Res. Dept. Rep. Ser. **71-2008**, Portsmouth, English Heritage

Hambleton, E. and Maltby, M. 2008 'Faunal remains', in Ellis and Powell with Hawkes, 84–93

Hamilton, R.J. 1995 *Waxes: chemistry, molecular biology and functions*, Dundee, The Oily Press Ltd

Hamilton, J. 2000 'The animal bones', in Cunliffe and Poole 2000, 175–193

Hart, J., Havard, T., and Guarino, P. 2021 'Middle Bronze Age to Roman settlement, agriculture and burial in the Severn Vale: excavations at Cleevelands, Bishop's Cleeve, 2014–2016', *Trans. Bristol Gloucestershire Archaeol. Soc.* **139**, 53–76

Hart, J. forthcoming 'A Romano-British crop-processing oven at The Street, Hullavington: excavation 2024', *Wilts. Archaeol. Natur. Hist. Mag.*

Harwood, J.L. and Bowyer, J.R. (eds) 1990 *Methods in plant biochemistry, vol. 4: lipids, membranes and aspects of photobiology*, London, Academic Press

Haselgrove C. and Moore, T. (eds) 2007 *The later Iron Age in Britain and beyond*, Oxford, Oxbow Books

Haselgrove, C. and Pope, R. (eds) 2007 *The earlier Iron Age in Britain and the near continent*, Oxford, Oxbow Books

Hather, J.G. 2000 *The identification of Northern European woods: a guide for archaeologists and conservators*, London, Archetype Publications

Havard, T., Darvill, T. and Alexander, M. 2017 'A Bronze Age round barrow cemetery, pit alignments, Iron Age burials, Iron Age copper working, and later activity at Four Crosses, Llandysilio, Powys', *Archaeol. J.* **174**, 1–67

HE (Historic England) 2015 *Archaeometallurgy. Guidelines for best practice*, London, Historic England

HE (Historic England) 2020 'PastScape' https://www.pastscape.org.uk/hob.aspx-?hob_id=1432155&sort=4&search=all&criteria=hangar&rational=q&records perpage=10&p=&move=&nor=31&recfc=0 accessed 30 January 2020

Hearne, C.M. and Adam, N. 1999 'Excavation of an extensive Late Bronze Age settlement at Shorncote Quarry, near Cirencester, 1995–6', *Trans. Bristol Gloucestershire Archaeol. Soc.* **117**, 35–73

Hearne, C.M. and Heaton, M.J. 1994 'Excavations at a late Bronze Age settlement in the Upper Thames Valley at Shorncote Quarry near Cirencester, 1995–6', *Trans. Bristol Gloucestershire Archaeol. Soc.* **112**, 17–57

Heaton, T., Köhler, P., Butzin, M., Bard, E., Reimer, R., Auston, W., Bronk Ramsey, C., Grootes, P., Hughen, K, Kromer, B., Reimer, P., Adkins, J., Burke, A., Cook, M, Olsen, J. and Skinner, L. 2020 'Marine20 – the marine radiocarbon age calibration curve (0–55,000 cal. BP)', *Radiocarbon* **62**, 779–820

Hershkovitz, I., Greenwald, C., Rothschild, B.M., Latimer, B., Dutour, O., Jellema, L.M. and Wish-Baratz, S. 1999 'Hyperostosis frontalis interna: an anthropological perspective.' *American J. Phys Anthropol.* **109**(3), 303–25

Hey, G. 2007 'Unravelling the Iron Age landscape of the Upper Thames valley' in Haselgrove and Moore (eds) 2007, 156–172

Hey, G. with Robinson, M. 2011 'Domesticating the landscape: settlement and agriculture in the early Bronze Age' in Hey *et al.* 2011b, 311–330

Hey, G., Booth, P. and Timby, J., 2011a *Yarnton: Iron Age and Romano-British settlement and landscape*, Thames Valley Landscape **35**, Oxford, Oxford Archaeology

Hey G., Garwood, P., Robinson, M., Barclay, A., and Bradley, P. 2011b *The Thames through time. The Archaeology of the gravel terraces of the Upper and Middle Thames, early prehistory: to 1500 BC Vol. 2 The Mesolithic, Neolithic and early Bronze Age and the establishment of permanent human occupation in the valley* Oxford, Thames Valley Landscapes **32**, Oxford, Oxford Archaeology

Hey, G., Bell, C., Dennis, C. and Robinson, M. 2016 *Yarnton. Neolithic and Bronze Age settlement and landscape,* Thames Valley Landscapes **39**, Oxford, Oxford Archaeology

Higbee, L. and Mepham, L. *2017 Living on the edge. Archaeological investigations at Steart Point, Somerset,* Salisbury, Wessex Archaeology Occasional Paper

Hill, J.D. 1995 *Ritual and rubbish in the Iron Age of Wessex. A study on the formation of a specific archaeological record,* Oxford, BAR Brit. Ser. **242**

Hill, R.A., Lacey, J. and Reynolds P.J. 1983 'Storage of barley grain in Iron Age type underground pits', *J. Stored Products Research* **19**(4), 163–171

Hillman, G.C. 1981 'Reconstructing crop husbandry practices from charred remains of crops', in Mercer 1981, 123–162

Hillman, G.C. 1984 'Interpretation of archaeological plant remains: the application of ethnographic models from Turkey', in van Zeist and Casparie 1984, 1–41

Hillson, S. 1996 *Dental anthropology,* Cambridge, Cambridge University Press

Hingley, R. 1984 'Towards social analysis in archaeology: Celtic society in the Iron Age in the Upper Thames Valley', in Cunliffe and Miles (eds) 1984, 52–88

Hingley, R. 1989 *Rural settlement in Roman Britain* Seaby, London

Hoffman, M. 1974 *The warp-weighted Loom,* Oslo

Holbrook, N. and Bidwell, P. 1991 *Roman finds from Exeter,* Exeter, Exeter Archaeological Reports **4**

Holbrook, N., Wright, J., McSloy, E.R. and Geber, J. 2017 *The Western cemetery of Roman Cirencester: Excavations at the former Bridges Garage, Tetbury Road, Cirencester, 2011–2015.* Cirencester, Cotswold Archaeology

Hood, R. 2019 'Land at 364 Marlborough Road, Swindon: summary report on archaeological investigations', *Wilts Archaeol. Natur. Hist. Mag.* **112**, 111–120

Humphrey, J. 2003 (ed.) *Re-searching the Iron Age,* Leicester Archaeology Monograph **11** Leicester, University of Leicester

İşcan, M.Y. and Kennedy, K.A.R. (eds) 1989 *Reconstruction of life from the skeleton,* New York, Alan R. Liss Inc.

İşcan, M.Y. and Loth, S.R. 1984 'Determination of age from the sternal rib in white males', *J. Forensic Sci.* **31**, 122–132

İşcan, M.Y., Loth, S.R. and Scheuerman, E.H. 1985 'Determination of age from the sternal rib in white females', *J. Forensic Sci.* **31**, 990–999

Jennings, D., Muir, J., Palmer, S. and Smith, A. 2004 *Thornhill Farm, Fairford Gloucestershire. An Iron Age and Roman pastoral site in the Upper Thames Valley,* Thames Valley Landscapes **23**, Oxford, Oxford Archaeology

Johnstone, C. 2006 'Those elusive mules: investigating osteometric methods for their identification', in Mashkour 2006, 183–191

Jones, A.M. 2014 'Hay Close, St Newlyn East: excavations by Cornwall Archaeological Society, 2007,' *Cornish Archaeology* **53**, 115–55

Jones, A.M. and Taylor, S. 2008. 'Camelford school excavations, summer 2008, Iron Age activity revealed', *CBA Southwest Journal* **22**, 29–32

Jones, A.M., Gossip, J. and Quinnell, H. 2015 *Settlement and metalworking in the Middle Bronze Age and beyond. New evidence from Tremough, Cornwall,* Leiden, Netherlands

Jones, G.G. 2006 'Tooth eruption and wear observed in live sheep from Butser Hill, the Cotswold Farm Park and five farms in the Pentland Hills, UK', in Ruscillo 2006, 155–178

Jones, G.G. and Sadler, P. 2012 'Age at death in cattle: methods, older cattle and known-age reference material', *Envir. Archaeol.* **17**, 11–28

Jones, J. 2000 'Plant Macrofossils', in Rippon 2000, 122–156

Jones, M.K. 1978 'The plant remains', in Parrington 1978, 93–110

Katzenberg, M.A. and Saunders, S.R. *Biological anthropology of the human skeleton,* New York, Wiley-Liss

Kennedy K.A.R. 1989 'Skeletal markers of occupational stress', in İşcan and Kennedy 1989, 129–161

Kerney, M.P. 1999 *Atlas of the land and freshwater molluscs of Britain and Ireland,* Colchester, Harley Books

King, A. 1999 'Diet in the Roman world: a regional inter-site comparison of the mammal bones', *J. Roman Archaeol.* **12**, 168–202

Kolattukudy, P.E. (ed.) 1976 *Chemistry and biochemistry of natural waxes,* Amsterdam, Elsevier

Kolattukudy, P.E. 1980 'Biopolyester membranes of plants: cutin and suberin', *Science* **208**(4447), 990–1000

Kolattukudy, P.E. 1981 'Structure, biosynthesis, and biodegradation of cutin and suberin', *Annu. Rev. Plant Physiology and Plant Molecular Biology* **32**, 539–567

Kolattukudy, P.E., Croteau, R. and Buckner, J.S. 1976 'Biochemistry of plant waxes', in Kolattukudy 1976, 289–347

Kunst, L. and Samuels, A.L. 2003 'Biosynthesis and secretion of plant cuticular wax', *Progress in Lipid Research* **42**(1), 51–80

Ladle, L. 2018 *Multi-period occupation at Football Field, Worth Matravers, Dorset. Excavations 2006–2011,* Oxford, BAR Brit. Ser. **643**

Lambrick, G. and Allen, T.G. 2004 *Gravelly Guy, Stanton Harcourt Oxfordshire: the development of a prehistoric and Romano-British community,* Thames Valley Landscapes **21**, Oxford, Oxford Archaeology

Lambrick, G. with Robinson, M. 2009 *The Thames through time: the archaeology of the grave terraces of the Upper and Middle Thames: the Thames Valley in late prehistory, 1500 BC–AD 50,* Thames Valley Landscapes **29**, Oxford, Oxford Archaeology

Lamdin-Whymark, H. 2006a 'Worked flint and burnt unworked flint and stone', in Tannahill and Pomeroy-Kellinger 2006, 23–6

Lamdin-Whymark, H. 2006b 'Lithics and burnt flint', in Tannahill and Pomeroy-Kellinger 2006, 29–35

Lauwerier, R. 1988 *Animals in Roman times in the Dutch Eastern River Area*, Nederlandse Oudheden 12 Amersfoort, ROB

Laws, K., 1991 'Objects of Kimmeridge shale', in Cunliffe and Poole 1991b, 368–369

Lawson, A.J. 2000 *Potterne 1982–5: Animal husbandry in later prehistoric Wiltshire*, Wessex Archaeology Report. **17**, Salisbury, Wessex Archaeology

Lettre, G. 2011 'Recent progress in the study of the genetics of height', *Hum Genet* **129**, 465–472

Levitan, B. 1985 'A methodology for recording the pathology and other anomalies of ungulate mandibles from archaeological sites', in Feiller *et al.* 1985, 41–54

Lewis, M. 2007 *The bioarchaeology of children: perspectives from biological and forensic anthropology*, Cambridge, Cambridge University Press

Lewis, M., and Gowland, R., 2007 'Brief and precarious lives: Infant mortality in contrasting sites from medieval and post-medieval England (AD 850–1859)', *American J. Physical Anthropol.* **134**, 117–129

Lodwick, L. 2017 'Arable farming, plant foods and resources', in Allen *et al.* 2017, 11–84

Lovejoy, C.O., Meindl, R.S., Pryzbeck, T.R. and Mensforth, R.P. 1985 'Chronological metamorphosis of the auricular surface of the illium: a new method for determination of adult skeletal age-at-death', *American J. Physical Anthropol.* **68**, 15–28

Lovell, J., Wakeham, G., Timby, J. and Allen, M.J. 2007 'Iron Age to Saxon farming settlement at Bishop's Cleeve, Gloucestershire: excavations south of Church Road, 1998 and 2004', *Trans. Bristol Gloucestershire Archaeol. Soc.* **125**, 95–129

Lyman, L. 1994 *Vertebrate taphonomy*, Cambridge, Cambridge University Press

McCammon, R.W. (ed.) 1970 *Human growth and development*, Springfield, IL, C.C. Thomas

McDevitte, W. and Bohn, W. 1869 *Caesar's Gallic War*, translated from *De Bello Gallico, Julius Caesar*, New York, Harper and Brothers

McDonnell, J.G. 1986 *Report on slag recovered from excavations at Beckford, Worcestershire*, Ancient Monuments Laboratory Report **64/1986**, London, English Heritage

McDonnell, J.G. 1991 'A model for the formation of smithing slag', *Materialy Archeologiczne* **26**, 23–26

McKern, T.W. and Stewart, T.D. 1957 *Skeletal age changes in young American males, analysed from the standpoint of identification*, Massachusetts Quartermaster Research and Development Command Technical Report **EP-45**

McKinley, J. 2004 'Compiling a skeletal inventory; disarticulated and co-mingled remains' in Brickley and McKinley 2004, 13–16

Mackreth, D.F. 2011 *Brooches in Late Iron Age and Roman Britain*, Oxford, Oxbow Books

McQueen, M. 2009 *Barbury Castle environs. Air photo survey and analysis,* Special Project Report, English Heritage Res. Dept. Rep. Ser. no **81-2009**

McSloy, E.R. 2009 'The pottery', in Evans and Alexander 2009, 119–122

McSloy, E.R. 2011 'Finds', in Brett and McSloy 2011, 104–109

Maltby, J.M. 1981 'The animal bones', in Davies, S. 1981, 147–153

Maltby, J.M. 1985 'The animal bones', in Fasham 1985, 97–112

Manning, W.H. 1985 *Catalogue of the Romano-British iron tools, fittings and weapons in the British Museum*, London, British Museum Publications Ltd

Maresh, M.M. 1970 'Measurements from Roentgenograms.' in McCammon 1970, 157–200

Mashkour, M. (ed.) 2006 *Equids in time and space*, Oxford, Oxbow

Mason, C. 2018 *A Romano-British roadside settlement at Beanacre, Wiltshire*, Salisbury, Wessex Archaeology Occasional Paper

Mays, S. 2016 'Estimation of stature in archaeological human skeletal remains from Britain', *American J. Physical Anthropol.* **161(4)**, 646–655

Mays, S., Brickley, M., Dodwell, N. and Sidell, J. 2018 *The role of the human osteologist in an archaeological fieldwork project*, Swindon, Historic England

Meadow, R. and Uerpmann, H.P. (eds) 1986 *Equids in the ancient world*, Naturwissenschaften **19** Reichert, University of Tübingen

Meindl, R.S. and Lovejoy, C.O. 1985 'Ectocranial suture closure: A revised method for the determination of skeletal age at death based on the lateral-anterior sutures', *American J. Physical Anthropol.* **68**, 29–45

Mercer, R. (ed.) 1981 *Farming practice in British prehistory*, Edinburgh, Edinburgh University Press

Miles, A. 1962 'Assessment of age of a population of Anglo-Saxons from their dentition', *Proc. Roy. Soc. Medicine* **55**, 881–886

Miles, D., Palmer, S., Lock, G., Gosden, C. and Cromarty, A.M. 2003 *Uffington White Horse and its landscape Investigations at White Horse Hill, Uffington 1989–95 and Tower Hill, Ashbury, 1993–4*, Thames Valley Landscapes **18** Oxford, Oxford Archaeology

Miller, M.J., Whelton, H.L., Swift, J.A., Maline, S., Hammann, S., Cramp, L.J.E., McCleary, A., Taylor, G., Vacca, K., Becks, F., Evershed R.P. and Hastorf, C.A. 2020 'Interpreting ancient food practices: stable isotope and molecular analyses of visible and absorbed residues from a year-long cooking experiment', *Scientific Reports* **10(1)**, 13704

Miller, W. (ed.) 2007 *Trace fossils: concepts, problems, prospects*, Oxford, Elsevier

Milles, A., Williams, D. and Gardner, N. 1989 *The beginnings of agriculture*, Oxford, BAR Int. Ser. **496**

Mills, J.S. and White, R. 1977 'Natural resins of art and archaeology: their sources, chemistry, and identification', *Stud. Conserv.* **22**(1), 12–31

Mitchell, P. and Brickley, M. (eds) 2017 *Updated guidelines to the standards for recording of human remains*, Reading, CIFA and BABAO

Moffett, L. 2004 'The evidence for crop-processing products from the Iron Age and Romano-British periods and some earlier prehistoric plant remains', in Lambrick and Allen 2004, 421–45

Moffett, L., Robinson, M.A. and Straker, S. 1989 'Cereals, fruit and nuts: charred plant remains from Neolithic sites in England and Wales and the Neolithic economy', in Milles *et al.* 1989, 243–61

Moore, A. 2009 'Hearth and home: the burial of infants within Romano-British domestic contexts', *Childhood in the Past* **2**, 33–54

Moore, J. and Montgomery, J. 2023 'Isotope analysis for burial SK1865', in Guarino and Barclay 2023, 92–95

Moore, T. 2006 *Iron Age societies in the Severn-Cotswolds. Developing narratives of social and landscape change*, Oxford, BAR Brit. Ser. **421**

Moorees, C.F.A., Fanning, E.A. and Hunt, E.E. 1963 'Age variation of formation stages for ten permanent teeth', *J. Dental Res.* **42**, 1490–1502

Morris, J. 2008 'Associated bone groups: one archaeologist's rubbish is another's ritual deposition', in Davis *et al.* 2008, 83–98

Morris, J. 2011 *Investigating animal burials: ritual, mundane and beyond*, Oxford, BAR Brit. Ser. **535**

Morris, J. and Maltby, M. (eds) 2010 *Integrating social and environmental archaeologies: reconsidering deposition*, Oxford, BAR Int. Ser. **2077**

Mottram, H.R., Dudd, S.N., Lawrence, G.J., Stott, A.W. and Evershed, R.P. 1999 'New chromatographic, mass spectrometric and stable isotope approaches to the classification of degraded animal fats preserved in archaeological pottery', *J. Chromatography A* **833**(2), 209–221

Mudd, A., Williams, R.J. and Lupton, A. 1999 *Excavations alongside Roman Ermine Street, Gloucestershire and Wiltshire. The archaeology of the A419/A417 Swindon to Gloucester Road Scheme*, Oxford, Oxford Archaeological Unit

Mukherjee, A.J. 2004 *The importance of pigs in the Later British Neolithic: integrating stable isotope evidence from lipid residues in archaeological potsherds, animal bone, and modern animal tissues*, Unpublished PhD Thesis, University of Bristol

Mukherjee, A.J., Copley, M.S., Berstan, R., Clark, K.A. and Evershed, R.P. 2005 'Interpretation of δ¹³C values of fatty acids in relation to animal husbandry, food processing and consumption in prehistory', in Mulville and Outram 2005, 77–93

Mulville, J. and Outram, A. (eds) 2005 *The zooarchaeology of milk and fats*, Oxford, Oxbow Books

Needham, S. 2005 'Transforming Beaker Culture in New Europe', *Proc. Prehist. Soc.* **71**, 171–217

Needham, S. and Spence, T. (eds) 1996 *Refuse and disposal at Area 16 East Runnymede: Runnymede Bridge Research Excavations Vol. 2*, London, British Museum Press

OA (Oxford Archaeology) 2005 *Wroughton, National Museum of Science & Industry: Archaeological Evaluation Report*, Oxford Archaeology report

OA (Oxford Archaeology) 2006 *Archaeological Evaluation Report for the National Museum of Science and Industry, Wroughton*, Oxford Archaeology report

O'Connor, T. 2003 *The analysis of urban animal bone assemblages: a handbook for archaeologists*, The Archaeology of York **19/20**, York, Council for British Archaeology

Ogden, A. 2008 'Advances in the palaeopathology of teeth and jaws', in Pinhasi and Mays 2008, 283–307

Orengo, L., Bonnon, J.M. and Bevilacqua, D. 2000 'L'emploi des blos-tuyères dans les forges antiques du centre de la Gaule (Auvergne, Lyonnais et Forez au deuxième âge du Fer et à l'époque romaine): découvertes archéologiques et expérimentation', in Feugère and Gŭstin 2000, 121–136

Ortner, D.J. and Putschar, W.D.J. 1981 *Identification of pathological conditions in human skeletal remains*, Washington, Smithsonian Institution Press

Outram, A.K., Stear, N.A., Bendrey, R., Olsen, S., Kasparov, A., Zaibert, V., Thorpe, N. and Evershed, R.P. 2009 'The earliest horse harnessing and milking', *Science* **323**(5919), 1332–1335

Parker Pearson, M., Chamberlain, A., Craig, O., Marshall, P., Mulville, J., Smith, H., Chenery, C., Collins, M., Cook, G., Craig, G. and Evans, J. 2005 'Evidence for mummification in Bronze Age Britain', *Antiquity* **79**(305), 529–546

Parrington, M. (ed.) 1978 *The excavation of an Iron age settlement, Bronze Age ring-ditches and Roman features at Ashville Trading Estate, Abingdon, Oxfordshire 1974–75*, CBA Res. Rep. **28**

Payne, S. 1973 'Kill-off patterns in sheep and goats: The mandibles from Asvan Kale', *Anatolian Stud.* **23**, 281–303

PCRG (Prehistoric Ceramics Research Group) 2010 *Prehistoric ceramics research group guidelines*, Occasional Papers 1 and 2

Peacock, D.P.S. 2013 *The stone of life, querns, mills and flour production in Europe up to c. AD 500*, Southampton, The Highfield Press

Pearce, J. 1999 'The dispersed dead: preliminary observations on burial and settlement space in rural Roman Britain', in Baker *et al.* 1998, 151–162

Pearce, J. 2011 'Representations and realities: cemeteries as evidence for women in Roman Britain', *Med Secoli.* **23**(1), 227–57

Philips, B. 2005 *Blackland, Calne Without*, Unpublished Report, Bernard Phillips

Philpott, R. 1991 *Burial practices in Roman Britain: a survey of grave treatment and furnishing, AD 43–410*, Oxford, BAR Brit. Ser. **219**

Pine, J. and Preston, S. 2004 *Iron Age and Roman settlement and landscape at Totterdown Lane, Horcott, near Fairford, Gloucestershire*, Reading, Thames Valley Archaeological Services Ltd

Pinhasi, R. and Mays, S. (eds) 2008 *Advances in human palaeopathology*, Chichester, Wiley

Pollard, J. 1996 'Iron Age riverside pit alignments at St. Ives, Cambridgeshire', *Proc. Prehist. Soc.* **62**, 93–115

Pollard, M., Beisson, F., Li, Y. and Ohlrogge, J. B. 2008 'Building lipid barriers: biosynthesis of cutin and suberin', *Trends in Plant Sci.* **13**(5), 236–246

Poole, C. 1984 'Objects of Baked Clay' in Cunliffe 1984, 398–407

Poole, C. 1995 'Pits and propitiation' in Cunliffe 1995, 249–275

Poore, D., Thomason, D. and Brossler, A. 2002 'Iron Age and Roman activity at Brickley Lane, Devizes, Wiltshire 1999', *Wilts Archaeol. Natur. Hist. Mag.* **95**, 214–239

Powell, A.B. 2015 'Bronze Age and Early Iron Age burial grounds and later landscape development outside Little Woodbury, Salisbury, Wiltshire', *Wilts Archaeol. Natur. Hist. Mag.* **108**, 44–78

Powell, A.B. 2017 'An Early Bronze Age Burial, Early to Middle Iron Age settlement and Romano-British activity at Ridgeway Farm, Purton, Wiltshire', *Wilts Archaeol. Natur. Hist. Mag.* **110**, 17–55

Powell, A.B. 2018 'Romano-British edge-of-settlement activity and landscape organisation, north of Bath Road, Melksham', *Wilts Archaeol. Natur. Hist. Mag.* **111**, 211–229

Powell, A.B. and Barclay, A.J. forthcoming *Between and beyond the monuments: investigations in south-east Amesbury*, Wessex Archaeology Monogr. **36**, Salisbury, Wessex Archaeology

Powell, K., Laws, G. and Brown, L. 2009 'A late Neolithic/Early Bronze Age Enclosure and Iron Age and Romano-British settlement at Latton Lands, Wiltshire', *Wilts Archaeol. Natur. Hist. Mag.* **102**, 22–113

Powell, K., Smith, A. and Laws, G. 2010 *Evolution of a farming community in the Upper Thames Valley; excavation of a prehistoric, Roman and post-Roman landscape at Cotswold Community, Gloucestershire and Wiltshire. Volume 1: site narrative and overview*, Thames Valley Landscapes **31**, Oxford, Oxford Archaeology

Ramsey, C.B. 2009 'Bayesian analysis of radiocarbon dates', *Radiocarbon* **51**, 337–360

Randall, C. 2010a *Livestock and landscape: the exploitation of animals in the south west of Britain in later prehistory*, Unpublished PhD Thesis, Bournemouth University

Randall, C. 2010b 'More ritual rubbish? Exploring the taphonomic history, context formation processes and 'specialness' of deposits including human and animal bone in Iron Age pits', in Morris and Maltby 2010, 83–102

Randall, C. 2018 'The human remains', in Ladle, 221–234

Randall C. 2021 'A sheep's eye view: land division, livestock and people in later prehistoric Somerset, UK', in Arnoldussen *et al.* 2021, 53–70

Randall C., Green, C. and McConnell, R. 2016 'On the edge of the chalk: An Iron Age settlement at Grimstone Reservoir, Dorchester, Dorset', *Proc. Dorset Natural Hist. Archaeol. Soc.* **137**, 232–263

Ratjen, H. and Heinrich, D. 1978 'Vergleichende untersuchungen an den metapodien von fuchsen und hunden', *Archaeologisch-Zoologischen Arbeitsgruppe Schleswig-Kiel*

Ratnikov, V. 2001 'Osteology of Russian toads and frogs for paleontological researches', *Acta Zoologica Cracovensia* **44**(1), 1–23

Raven, S. 1990 'The Romano-British pottery', in Allen 1990c, 46–51

Redfern, R.C. 2016 *Injury and trauma in bioarchaeology: interpreting violence in past lives,* Cambridge, Cambridge University Press

Redfern, R.C. 2020 'Iron Age 'predatory landscapes': a bioarchaeological and funerary exploration of captivity and enslavement in Britain', *Cambridge Archaeol. J.* **30**(4), 531–554

Rees, S.E. 1979 *Agricultural implements in prehistory and in Roman Britain Oxford*, BAR Brit. Ser. **69**

Reimer, P., Austin, W., Bard, E., Bayliss, A., Blackwell, P., Bronk Ramsey, C., Butzin, M. Cheng, H., Edwards, R., Freidrich, M., Grootes, P., Guilderson, T., Hajdas, I., Heaton, T., Hogg, A., Hughen, K., Kromer, B., Manning, S., Muschleler, R., Palmer, J., Pearson, C., Plicht, J. van der, Reimer, R., Richards, D., Scott, E., Southon, J., Turney, C., Wacker, L., Adolphi, f., Büntgen, U., Capano, M., Fahrni, S., Fogtmann-Schulz, A., Friedrich, R., Köhler, P., Kudsk, S., Miyake, F., Olsen, J., Reinig, F., Sakamoto, M., Sookdeo, A. and Talamo, S. 2020 'The IntCal20 Northern Hemisphere radiocarbon ago calibration curve (0–55 cal, kBP)', *Radiocarbon* **62 (4)**, 725–57

Resnick, D. 1995 *Diagnosis of bone and joint disorders*, London, W.B. Saunders Company

Reynolds, P. 1974 'Experimental Iron Age storage pits: an interim report', *Proc. Prehist. Soc.* **40**, 118–131

Reynolds, P.J. 1987 *Ancient farming*, Aylesbury, Shire Archaeology

Richards, J.C. 1976 'Three Romano-British inhumations at Upper Lambourn', *Berkshire Archaeol. J.* **68**, 21–27

Rippon, S. 2000 'The Romano-British exploitation of the coastal wetlands: survey and excavation on the North Somerset Levels 1993–7', *Britannia* **31**, 69–200

Rivet, A.L.F. and Smith, C. 1979 *The place names of Roman Britain*, London, Book Club Associates

Roberts, C. and Cox, M. 2003 *Health and disease in Britain*, Sutton Publishing UK

Robinson, M.A., 2000 'Further considerations of Neolithic charred cereals, fruits, and nuts', in Fairbairn 2000, 85–90

Rogers, J. and Waldron, T. 1995 *A field guide to joint disease in archaeology*, Wiley

Rohnbogner, A. 2018 'The rural population' in Smith, Allen, Brindle, Fulford, Lodwick, and Rohnbogner, 281–345

Roth, N. 2016 *Regional patterns and the implications of Late Bronze Age and Iron Age burial practices in Britain*, Oxford, BAR Brit. Ser. **627**

Ruscillo, D. (ed.) 2006 *Recent advances in ageing and sexing animal bones*, Oxford, Oxbow Books

Russel, A.D. 1990 'Two burials from Chilbolton, Hampshire', *Proc. Prehist. Soc.* **56**, 153–172

Rylatt, J. and Bevan, B. 2007 'Realigning the world: pit alignments and their landscape context', in Haselgrove and Moore 2007, 217–234

Salque, M. 2012 *Regional and chronological trends in milk use in prehistoric Europe traced through molecular and stable isotope signatures of fatty acyl lipids preserved in pottery vessels*, PhD Thesis, University of Bristol

Saunders, S. and Herring, A. (eds) 1995 *Grave reflections, portraying the past through cemetery studies*, Toronto, Canadian Scholars' Press

Saunders, S.R. 1989 'Nonmetric skeletal variation', in İşcan and Kennedy 1989, 95–108

Saunders, S.R. 2008 'Juvenile skeletons and growth-related studies', in Katzenberg and Saunders 2008, 117–147

Sayle, K.L., Brodie, C.R., Cook, G.T. and Hamilton, W.D. 2019 'Sequential measurement of $\delta^{15}N$, $\delta^{13}C$ and $\delta^{34}S$ values in archaeological bone collagen at the Scottish Universities Environmental Research Centre (SUERC): a new analytical frontier', *Rapid Communications in Mass Spectrometry* **33**(15), 1258–1266

Scheuer, L. and Black, S. 2000 *Developmental juvenile osteology*, London, Elsevier Academic Press

Schmid, E. 1972 *Atlas of animal bones*, London, Elsevier Science Publishers

Schruefer-Kolb, I. (ed.) 2012 *More than just numbers? The role of science in Roman Archaeology*, Portsmouth, Rhode Island, Journal of Roman Archaeology

Schwartz, J.H. 1995 *Skeleton keys: an introduction to human skeletal morphology, development and analysis*, Oxford, Oxford University Press

Schweingruber, F.H. 1990 *Microscopic wood anatomy*, 3rd Edition. Swiss Federal Institute for Forest, Snow and Landscape Research

Seager Smith, R. 2000 'Worked bone and antler', in Lawson 2000, 222–39

Seager Smith, R. 2001 'The coarse pottery', in Anderson *et al.* 2001, 232–300

Sellwood, L. 1984a 'Objects of bone and antler', in Cunliffe 1984, 371–95

Sellwood, L. 1984b 'Objects of iron', in Cunliffe 1984, 346–370

Serjeantson, D. 1996 'The animal bones', in Needham and Spence 1996, 194–223

Serjeantson, D. 2011 *Review of animal remains from the Neolithic and Early Bronze Age of southern Britain (4000 BC – 1500 BC)*, English Heritage Research Department Report Series **29-2011**

Serneels, V. and Perret, S. 2003 'Quantification of smithing activities based on the investigation of slag and other material remains', *Associazione Italiana di Metallurgia* **1**, 469–478

Shaffrey, R. 2017a 'A re-investigation of British stone loomweights', in Shaffrey 2017b, 229–248

Shaffrey, R. (ed.) 2017b *Written in stone: papers on the function, form, and provenancing of prehistoric stone objects in memory of Fiona Roe*, St Andrews, Highfield Press

Shaffrey, R. and Roe, F. 2022 'Querns from the Bronze Age to the eleventh century AD: making use of local resources in the 'Oxfordshire grits', *Oxoniensia* **87**, 1–16

Sharples, N. 2010 *Social relations in later prehistory: Wessex in the first millennium BC*, Oxford, Oxford University Press

Shepherd, W. 1972 *Flint: its origin, properties and uses*, London, Faber and Faber

Simmonds, A. 2011 'Prehistoric, Roman and Anglo-Saxon activity at the Willow Brook Centre, Bradley Stoke, South Gloucestershire', *Trans. Bristol Gloucestershire Archaeol. Soc.* **129**, 11–35

Slota, P.J., Jull, A.T., Linick, T.W. and Toolin, L.J. 1987 'Preparation of small samples for ^{14}C accelerator targets by catalytic reduction of CO', *Radiocarbon* **29**(2), 303–306

Smith, A., Allen, M., Brindle, T., Fulford, M., Lodwick, L. and Rohnbogner, A. 2018 *Life and death in the countryside of Roman Britain*, London, Britannia Monograph Series **31**

Smith, M.J., Allen, M.J., Delbarre, G., Booth, T., Cheetham, P., Bailey, L., O'Malley, F., Parker Pearson, M. and Green, M. 2016 'Holding on to the past: Southern British evidence for mummification and retention of the dead in the Chalcolithic and Bronze Age' *J. Archaeol. Sci. Rep.* **10**, 744–756

Smith Thomas, H., 2005 *Getting started with beef and dairy cattle*, North Adams, MS, Story Publishing

Spangenberg, J.E., Jacomet, S. and Schibler, J. 2006 'Chemical analyses of organic residues in archaeological pottery from Arbon Bleiche 3, Switzerland – evidence for dairying in the late Neolithic', *J. Archaeol. Sci.* **33**(1), 1–13

Stace, C. 1997 *New flora of the British Isles,* 2nd edition. Cambridge, Cambridge University Press

Stace, C. 2019 *New flora of the British Isles*, 4th Edition. Cambridge, Cambridge University Press

Stansbie, D. 2009 'The Late Iron Age and Roman pottery', in Powell *et al.* 2009, 69–75

Stansbie, D., Allen, L., Boyle, A., Roe, F., Timby, J. and Hayden, C. 2011 'Iron Age and Roman society at Yarnton' in Hey *et al.* 2011a, 47–69

Stevens, C.J. 2007 'New flora of the British Isles. Reconsidering the evidence: towards an understanding of the social contexts of subsistence production in Neolithic Britain', in Colledge and Conolly 2007, 375–389

Stevens, C.J. 2011 'Crop-husbandry as seen from the charred botanical samples from Yarnton', in Hey *et al.* 2011a, 534–568

Stevens, C.J. and Wilkinson, K. 2001 'Economy and environment', in Walker *et al.* 2001, 33–42

Stewart, R.J. 2012 'The role of chert in later prehistoric lithic industries with specific reference to South-West England', *Geoscience in South-West England* **13**(1), 123–30

Stewart, T.D. (ed.) 1970 *Personal identification in mass disasters,* Washington, Smithsonian Institution Press

Stirland, A. 1996 'Patterns of trauma in a unique medieval parish cemetery' *Int. J. Osteoarchaeol.* **6**, 92–100

Stuart-Macadam, P.L. 1991 'Anaemia in Roman Britain: Poundbury Camp', in Bush and Zvelebil 1991, 101–113

Stuiver, M. and Polach, H.A. 1977 'Discussion reporting of ^{14}C data', *Radiocarbon* **19**(3), 355–363

Sykes, N. 2012 'A social perspective on the introduction of exotic animals: the case of the chicken', *World Archaeol.* **44**(1), 158–169

Sykes, N. 2014 *Beastly questions: animal answers to archaeological issues*, London, Bloomsbury

Tabor, R. 2008 *Cadbury Castle: the hillfort and landscapes*, Stroud, The History Press

Tannahill, R. and Pomeroy-Kellinger, M. 2006 *Swindon Gateway, Coate, Swindon, Wiltshire: Archaeological Evaluation and Fieldwalking Survey Report*, Unpublished report 2961

Thomas, J. 2003 'Prehistoric pit alignments and their significance in the archaeological landscape' in Humphrey 2003, 79–86

Thompson I. 1982 *Grog-tempered 'Belgic' pottery of South Eastern England*, Oxford, BAR Brit. Ser. **108**

Timby, J. 2001 'The pottery', in Walker *et. al.* 2001, 19–26

Timby, J. 2002 'The pottery', in Poore *et. al.* 2002, 220–226

Timby, J. 2004 'The pottery', in Jennings *et al.* 2004, 90–108

Timby, J. 2007 'The pottery', in Clarke *et al.* 2007

Tite, M.S. 2008 'Ceramic production, provenance and use – a review', *Archaeometry* **50**(2), 216–231

Tjelldén, A.K.E., Kristiansen, S.M., Matthiesen, H. and Pedersen, O. 2015 'Impact of roots and rhizomes on wetland archaeology: a review', *Conservation and management of Archaeol. Sites* **17**(4), 370–391

Tomber, R. and Dore, J. 1998 *The National Roman Fabric Reference Collection: a handbook*, London, Museum of London Archaeological Service

Trotter, M. 1970 'Estimation of stature from intact limb bones', in Stewart 1970, 71–83

Tulloch, A.P. 1976 'Chemistry of waxes of higher plants', in Kolattukudy 1976, 235–287

Tylecote, R.F. 1986 *The prehistory of metallurgy in the British Isles*, London, The Institute of Metals

Tylecote, R.F. 1999 'Ironworking' in Dore and Wilkes 1999, 569–71

Urem-Kotsou, D., Stern, B., Heron, C. and Kotsakis, K. 2002 'Birch-bark tar at Neolithic Makriyalos, Greece', *Antiquity* **76**(294), 962–967

Vandeputte, K., Moens, L. and Dams, R. 1996 'Improved sealed-tube combustion of organic samples to CO_2 for stable isotope analysis, radiocarbon dating and percent carbon determinations', *Analytical Letters* **29**(15), 2761–2773

Veen, M. van der 1989 'Charred grain assemblages from Roman-period corn driers in Britain', *Archaeol. J.* **146**, 302–319

Waddington, C. 1997 'A review of 'pit alignments' and a tentative interpretation of the Milfield complex', *Durham Archaeol. J.* **13**, 21–33

Wait, G. 1985 *Ritual and religion in Iron Age Britain*, Oxford, BAR Brit. Ser **149**

Wait, G. 2004 'Burial rites and ritual practices', in Lambrick and Allen 2004, 248–9

Waldron, T. 2009 *Palaeopathology, Cambridge Manuals in Archaeology*, Cambridge, Cambridge University Press

Walker, G., Langton, B. and Oakley, N. 2001 *An Iron Age site at Groundwell West, Blunsdon St. Andrew, Wiltshire: excavations in 1996*, Kemble, Cotswold Archaeological Trust

Walker P.L. 1995 'Problems of preservation and sexism in sexing: Some lessons from historical collections for palaeo-demographers', in Saunders and Herring 1995, 31–47

Walters, B. 2001 'A perspective on the social order of Roman villas in Wiltshire', in Ellis 2001, 127–146

Walton, T.J. 1990 'Waxes, cutin and suberin', in Harwood and Bowyer 1990, 105–158

Warren, P. 2006 *British native trees: their past and present uses, including a guide to burning wood in the home*, Wildeye

Watts, S. 2014 *The life and death of querns. The deposition and use-contexts of querns in south-western England from the Neolithic to the Iron Age*, Southampton, Highfield Press

Webb, P.A. and Suchey, J.M. 1985 'Epiphyseal union of the anterior iliac crest and medial clavicle in a modern multiracial sample of American males and females', *American J. Physical Anthropol.* **68**(4), 457–466

Webster, P. 1996 *Roman samian pottery in Britain*, CBA Practical Handbook in Archaeol. **13**, York, Council for British Archaeology

Wessex Archaeology nd *Investigations at Lydiard Park*, unpubl. Rep.

Wessex Archaeology 2013 *Land at Old Sarum, Salisbury, Wiltshire: post-excavation assessment and updated project design*, Salisbury, Wessex Archaeology unpubl. rep. **61682.03**

Wessex Archaeology 2016 *Greentrees School, Bishopdown, Salisbury, Wiltshire, Post-excavation assessment and updated project design*, Salisbury, Wessex Archaeology unpubl. rep. **105121.02**

West, D.L. and Hasiotis, S.T. 2007 'Trace fossils in an archaeological context: examples from bison skeletons, Texas, USA', in Miller 2007, 545–561

Whimster, R, 1981 *Burial practices in Iron Age Britain*, Oxford, BAR Brit. Ser. **90**

Whitehead, R. 1994 *Buckles 1250–1800*, Chelmsford, Greenlight Publishing

Whittaker, K. 2019 *The sarsen stones in Wessex project archive* Unpublished report, University of Reading

Whyte, T.R. 1988 *An experimental study of small animal remains in archaeological pit features*, PhD dissertation Knoxville, University of Texas

Wigley, A. 2007 'Pitted histories: early first millennium BC pit alignments in the central Welsh Marches', in Haselgrove and Pope (eds) 2007, 119–134

Wilson, B. 1992 'Considerations for the identification of ritual deposits of animal bones in Iron Age pits', *Int. J. Osteoarchaeol.* **2**, 341–349

Wilson, B., Grigson, C. and Payne, S. (eds) 1982 *Ageing and sexing animal bones from archaeological sites*, Oxford, BAR Brit. Ser. **109**

Wilson, D. 1993 'The Iron Age pottery', in Allen and Robinson 1993, 70–75

Woodward, P.J., Davies, S.M. and Graham, A.H. 1993 *Excavations at the Old Methodist Chapel and Greyhound Yard, Dorchester, 1981–1984*, Dorchester, Dorset Nat. Hist. and Archaeol. Soc. Monogr. Ser. **12**

Wroughton History Group (ed.) 1982 *Wroughton History Society: Part 1 – Studies in the History of Wroughton Parish*, Wroughton History Group

WYAS (West Yorkshire Archaeological Services) 2013 *Wroughton Airfield Solar Park, Swindon, Wiltshire: Geophysical Survey*, Unpublished Report no. **2553**

Wyles, S.F. 2017a 'Environmental evidence', in Powell 2017, 46–48

Wyles, S.F. 2017b 'Charred plant remains', in Higbee and Mepham 2017, 59–67

Wyles, S.F. and Stevens, C.J. forthcoming 'Charred plant remains', in Powell and Barclay, forthcoming

Zeder, M. and Lapham, H. 2010 'Assessing the reliability of criteria used to identify post-cranial bones in sheep, *Ovis*, and goats, *Capra*', *J. Archaeol. Sci.* **37**, 2887–2905

Zeder, M. and Pilaar, S. 2010 'Assessing the reliability of criteria used to identify mandibles and mandibular teeth in sheep, *Ovis* and goats, *Capra*', *J. Archaeol. Sci.* **37** (2), 225–242

Zeist, W. van and Casparie, W.A. (ed.) 1984 *Plants and ancient man: studies in palaeoethnobotany*, Rotterdam, Balkema

Zeist, W. van, Wasylikowa, K. and Behre, K.E. (eds) 1991 *Progress in Old World palaeoethnobotany*, Rotterdam, Balkema

Zohary, D., Hopf, M. and Weiss, E. 2012 *Domestication of plants in the Old World: the origin and spread of cultivated plants in West Asia, Europe, and the Nile Valley*, 4th edition, Oxford, Clarendon Press

Appendix 1
Iron Age pits

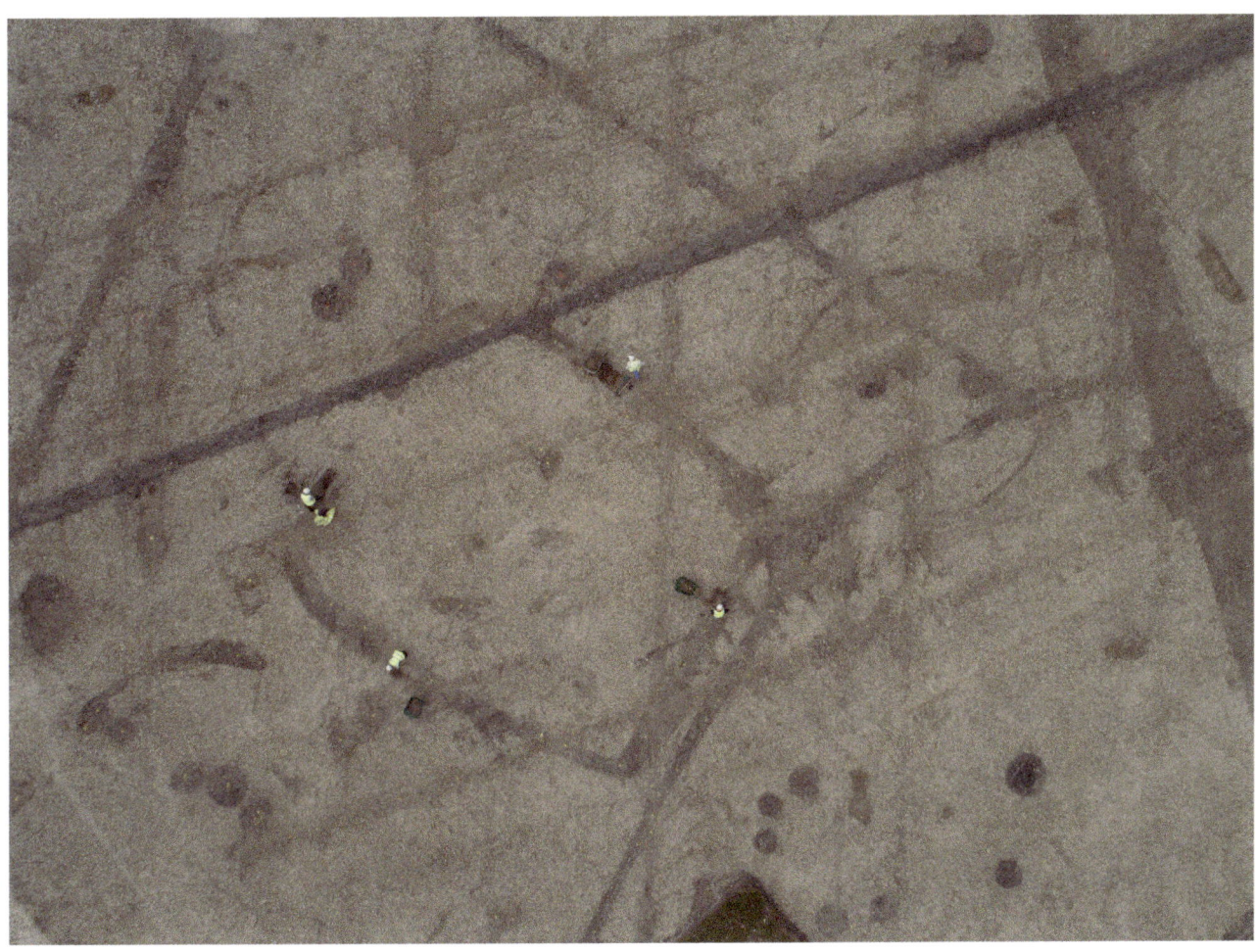

Aerial photograph showing pits amongst archaeological features

Feature Number	Length	Width	Depth	Plan shape	Profile shape	No of fills	Stone dumps	Pottery	Animal bone and ABGs	Human remains	Charcoal	Metal	Other	Comment
1048	1.34	0.68	0.84	Circular	Vertical/concave with flat base	5					A lot of charcoal in initial fill 1051		Shale bracelet fragment (Ra. 1002) in fill 1049	
1057	1.2	1.1	0.2	Sub-circular	Vertical sides and uneven base	1	A fragment of sarsen, possibly used as a quern (Ra. 1001)						Flint	
1068	1.6	1.6	1.14	Circular	Vertical sides	3			ABG in fill 1066, dog skeleton in fill 1067				Flint core and flakes in fill 1065	
1069	1.04	1.03	0.72	Circular	Vertical sides and flat base	3	Chalk pieces up to 300m in middle fill				Initial fill 1072 charcoal rich		Flint flake in fill 1070	
1073	1.22	1.11	0.56	Sub-circular	Steep concave sides and a flat base	1							Flint	
1222	2.45	2.3	0.29	Sub-circular	Steep concave sides and a flat/irregular base	2					SK 1206			
1225	1.25	1.25	0.42	Sub-circular	Vertical/concave with flat base	2							Flint flake from fill 1226	
1260	0.86	0.86	0.97	Circular	Vertical sides and flat base	4								
1276	1.42	1.28	0.49	sub-circular	Vertical sides and uneven base	2								
1279	1.35	1.26	0.46	Circular	Vertical sides and flat base	2							Slag, fired burnt clay from fill 1280	
1344	1.27	1.2	0.4	sub-circular	Steep concave sides and a flat/irregular base	5							Fired/burnt clay plate from fill 1345	
1358	1.16	1.1	1.07	Circular	Vertical/concave (undercut) with flat base	2								
1381	1.35	1.35	0.82	Circular	Vertical sides and flat base	4			Large part of neonatal sheep/goat in fill 1353 (ABG)		Layer of charcoal in base fill 1380	Iron nail from fill 1353	Flint core and flakes from fill 1352	
1384	1.4	1.35	1.6	Circular	Vertical sides (slightly undercut) and flat base	8		Early Iron Age sherd		SK 1489 in grave cut into top	In base 1934	Iron object in fill 1386	Fired/blunt clay plate in fill 1384, industrial waste in 1411 and 1933	
1389	1.47	1.4	0.41	sub-circular	Vertical sides and flat base	4	Large sarsen blocks through several fills						Fired/burnt clay plate	
1390	1.6	1.42	1.08	Sub-circular	Steep concave sides and a flat base	4							Flint	

Feature Number	Length	Width	Depth	Plan shape	Profile shape	No of fills	Stone dumps	Pottery	Animal bone and ABGs	Human remains	Charcoal	Metal	Other	Comment
1426	1.5	1.45	1.55	Circular	Vertical sides (undercut) and flat base	7	Dump of sarsens up to 560mm over burial, and similar sizes in later fill	Early Iron Age sherd		SK 1845 within pit	In 1631, over burial	Iron strip in 1428	Burnt daub with wattle-impressions in second fill 1632; industrial waste, bone point of possible pin, needle or textile awl (Ra. 1017) and saddle quern (Ra. 1014) in third fill 1631	
1430	1.86	1.82	0.65	Circular	Vertical sides and flat base	7			Cattle skull in initial fill 1435				Fired/burnt clay in 1433	
1450	1.14	1.12	0.24	Circular	Vertical sides and flat base	2							Flint	
1454	1.3	0.9	0.61	Oval	Vertical sides (undercut) and flat base	3		Decorated late Middle to Late Iron Age sherd Late Iron Age sherds	Initial fill 1455 – contained three perinatal sheep/goat ABGs				Flint cores, and scraper in 1457	
1470	1.3	1.25	0.55	Circular	Vertical sides and flat/irregular base	3								
1504	0.84	0.82	0.17	Circular	Vertical sides and sloping base	1								
1585	0.87		0.43	Circular	Concave sides and flat base	5					1587 second fill		Bone tool in upper fill 1590	
1591	1.41		0.47	Circular	Concave sides and concave base	3								
1600	1.38		0.5	Circular	Vertical sides; base not seen	1								
1643	0.65	0.65	0.24	Circular	Sloping irregular sides to an irregular base	2								
1663	0.7	0.68	0.26	Circular	Straight/sloping sides and flat base	2								
1669	1.28	1.14	0.59	Circular	Vertical sides, overcut towards base, and flat base	4	Large stones		Mandible lying on base under dump of initial fill 1670; 1671 partial dog and neonatal sheep/goat on north side of pit				Flint	
1681	1.25	1.16	0.54	sub-circular	Steep or uneven sides and uneven base	4							Flint	
1706	0.52	0.42	0.19	Sub-circular	Sloping sides and irregular base – described as pit or posthole	1								

Feature Number	Length	Width	Depth	Plan shape	Profile shape	No of fills	Stone dumps	Pottery	Animal bone and ABGs	Human remains	Charcoal	Metal	Other	Comment
1709	1.4	1.4	0.2	Circular	Vertical sides and flat base	2								
1716	1.41		0.23	Circular	Vertical sides and flat base	1								
1724	1.46	1.38	0.24	Circular	Vertical sides and flat base	2		Early Iron Age sherd	Several cattle horn cores				Industrial waste in 1725	
1743	1.5		0.47	Circular	Vertical sides (slightly undercut) and flat base	4		Early Iron Age sherds Late Iron Age sherds					Flint flake in 1739 and 1740	
1757	1.3	1.28	0.61	Circular	Vertical sides (slightly undercut) and flat base	2		Decorated late Middle to Late Iron Age sherd Late Iron Age sherds				Iron ploughshare tip from fill 1755 (Ra. 1010)	Flint flake in 1756	
1764	1.54	1.1	0.56	Oval	Vertical sides and flat base	3								
1770	1.07		0.84	Circular	Vertical sides (slightly undercut on one side) and flat base	4			Sheep/goat skull in lower fill					
1781	1.4	1.22	0.62	Circular	Vertical sides and concave base	3				SK 1778 in grave dug into top				
1784	1.34	1.21	0.49	sub-circular	Sloping concave sides to a concave base	4								
1802	1.1	1.16	0.56	Circular	Vertical sides (slightly undercut) and irregular base	2							Weaving comb fragments recovered from 1801 and 1802	
1803	0.61	0.5	0.28	Oval	Sloping concave sides to a concave base	2								
1806	1.47	1.4	0.72	Circular	Steep slightly concave sides and flat base	1								
1808	1.32	1.19	0.43	Sub-circular	Vertical sides and flat base	2								
1819	1.44	1.37	0.78	Circular	Vertical sides (slightly undercut) and irregular base	3								
1827	1.91	1.7	>1.07	Circular	Vertical sides - not fully excavated to base	6		Substantially complete vessel from fill 1833 – Middle Iron Age jar			1833 initial fill			
1834	1.12	1.12	0.39	Circular	Vertical sides and flat base	2								
1837	1.27	1	0.92	Sub-circular	Vertical sides and flat base	4						Iron knife fragment, iron sheet, and iron strip from fill 1838; fired/burnt clay in 1839		
1847	1.1	1	0.32	Sub-circular	Concave sides and flat base	2								
1851	2.11	2.06	1.22	Circular	Steep irregular sides and flat base	10			Two horse and two cattle skulls					

Feature Number	Length	Width	Depth	Plan shape	Profile shape	No of fills	Stone dumps	Pottery	Animal bone and ABGs	Human remains	Charcoal	Metal	Other	Comment
1865	1	1	0.24	Sub-circular	Steep sides and rounded base	1								Recut of 1851
1869	1.08	1	0.63	Sub-circular	Steep concave and a rounded base	1								Recut of 1851
1871	1.48	1.48	0.86	Circular	Vertical sides and flat base	4							Fired clay objects Ras 1018 and 1019 in upper fill 1874	
1884	0.89	0.88	0.22	Circular	Steep sides and uneven base	2							Flint flake and flint core in 1885	
1913	2.4	1.92	0.8	Sub-circular	Vertical sides and concave base	3								Recut of 1984
1914	1.64	1.6	0.67	Circular	Vertical sides and flat base	3								
1917	1.3	1.26	0.58	Sub-circular	Vertical sides (slightly undercut) and flat base	3					Initial fill 1642 and covering fill 1918			
1925	1.34	1.23	0.71	Sub-circular	Vertical sides (slightly undercut) and flat base	4				SK 1926 neonate				
1947	1.82	1.63	1	Circular	Vertical sides (slightly undercut near bottom) and flat base	4		Large pottery assemblage, with 30 sherds from fill 1951	ABG in fill 1951	SK 3235 within pit	Charcoal rich layer on base with no context number			
1965	1.71		0.66	Irregular	Irregular sides and base	3					1966 on base			
1971	1.5	1.4	0.16	Oval	Vertical sides (slightly undercut) and flat base	1							Slag	
1977	1.33		0.89	Circular	Vertical sides and flat base	4					1978 lens of charcoal third fill			
1984	2.4	1.85	0.7	Circular	Vertical sides and flat base	4		Late Iron Age sherds	Dog in 1962		Initial fill 1982			
2003	1.63	1.68	0.98	Circular	Vertical sides (slightly undercut) and flat base	8								
2012	1.55	1.42	0.7	Circular	Vertical sides and flat base	4			Domestic fowl in 2014					
2015	1.63	1.52	0.72	Circular	Vertical sides and flat base	6					2030 initial fill			
2032	1.37		0.53	Circular	Vertical sides (undercut) and flat base	4								
2043	1.64	>1	0.77	Oval	Vertical sides (undercut) and flat base	7		Early Iron Age sherd			2068 initial fill		Triangular fired clay loomweight (Ra. 1020) from fill 2041	
2044	1.25		0.97	sub-circular	Vertical sides and flat base	3					2047 initial fill			

Feature Number	Length	Width	Depth	Plan shape	Profile shape	No of fills	Stone dumps	Pottery	Animal bone and ABGs	Human remains	Charcoal	Metal	Other	Comment
2048	1.12		0.84	sub-circular	Vertical sides (slightly undercut) and flat base	6					2154 initial fill			
2056	2.5	2.4	1.19	Circular	Vertical sides and flat base	10					2290 charcoal lens third fill		Smithing hearth cake	
2070	1.5	0.6	0.25	Oval	Concave sides and rounded base	2								
2073	2	1.7	0.68	sub-circular	Vertical sides (undercut on SW side) and flat base	3								
2077	1	0.7	0.24	Oval	Concave sides and flat base	1								
2079	0.9	0.85	0.55	sub-circular	Concave sides and base	2								
2082	1.62	1.6	1.22	Circular	Vertical sides (undercut) and flat base	8		Early Iron Age sherd						
2084	1.4	1.31	0.7	sub-circular	Vertical sides and flat base	3		Middle Iron Age sherds			2085 initial fill		Exceptionally large volume of cereal remains	
2134	1.84	1.45	0.78	Oval	Vertical sides and flat base	3								
2138	1.45	1.35	0.78	sub-circular	Vertical sides (undercut) and flat base	3	Large sarsen stone in 2135	Sherds of late Middle or Late Iron Age date Decorated late Middle to Late Iron Age sherd Late Iron Age sherds				Narrow-bladed implement (Ra. 1022) from fill 2135	Flint	
2167	1.8	1.7	0.58	sub-circular	Vertical sides and flat base	4							Smithing hearth cake	
2171	2.4	1.5	0.4	Circular	Vertical sides and flat base	3		Early Iron Age sherd						
2172	2	2.5	0.65	Oval	Concave sides to flat base	3								
2178	1.41	1.26	0.61	Oval	Concave sides to flat base	2								
2203	3	1.65	0.92	Oval	Vertical sides (undercut) and flat base	6			Large amounts of animal bone lying on the base of fill 2205. ABG skull in 2206 on base				Flint	
2210	1.55	1.46	0.75	sub-circular	Vertical sides and flat base	3		Early Iron Age sherd				In second fill	Flint	
2216	3.32	1.07	0.76	Oval	Vertical sides and flat base	2								
2219	1.58	1.05	0.28	Oval	Vertical sides and uneven base	1								
2223	1.23	1.14	0.64	sub-circular	Vertical sides (undercut) and flat base	3		Middle Iron Age sherds	Sheep/goat skull in initial fill				Flint	
2231	1.57	1.44	0.44	sub-circular	Vertical sides and flat base	3								

Feature Number	Length	Width	Depth	Plan shape	Profile shape	No of fills	Stone dumps	Pottery	Animal bone and ABGs	Human remains	Charcoal	Metal	Other	Comment
2235	2.1	1.11	0.28	Oval	Steep concave sides and flat base	3					Notable charred material in several contexts			
2258	1.47	1.44	0.7	Circular	Vertical sides (undercut) and flat base	4	Three large (<40cm) sarsens on top of initial fill in the centre	Middle Iron Age sherds	Horse skull over sarsen blocks, polished canine tooth from fill 2260, fragment of horse tibia from fill 2260.		In fill 2260 over sarsens	Small waste lump (Ra. 1027) and droplet (Ra. 1029) of copper alloy.	Several fragments of a block tuyere from fill 2260	
2265	1.3		0.88	Circular	Vertical sides (undercut) and flat base	4					Middle fill	An iron strip with a rivet hole (Ra. 1026	Smithing hearth cakes	
2280	1.61	1.3	1.06	Sub-circular	Vertical sides (undercut) and flat base	6		Middle Iron Age sherd	Several Sheep/goat horn cores		In fill 2270		Large weight (Ra. 1021) from fill 2054	
2281	1.26	1.22	0.51	Circular	Vertical sides and flat base	1								
2283	1.19		0.41	Circular	Vertical sides (undercut) and flat base	2								
2298	1.49	1.45	1.1	Circular	Vertical sides (undercut) and flat base	6							Worked bone awl from fill 2301, smithing hearth cake	
2305	1.18	1.01	0.65	sub-circular	Vertical sides and flat base	3								
2483	1.49	1.47	1.14	Circular	Vertical sides and flat base	3								
2507	1.53	1.24	0.82	Sub-circular	Vertical sides (undercut) and flat base	6							Flint	
2521	1.08		0.24	Sub-circular	Vertical side, base not reached	1								
2536	>1.0	0.95	0.15	Irregular	Sloping sides and irregular base	1								
2545	1.4	>1.0	0.91	sub-circular	Irregular sides, base not seen	5							Flint	
2567	1.06		0.68	Circular	Vertical sides (undercut towards base) and flat base	4			Partial cattle (calf) hind legs in initial fill2569		Burnt flint and charcoal rich initial fill			
2578	1.42	1.4	0.82	Circular	Vertical sides and flat base	4							Bone bead or toggle (Ra. 1106) from fill 2580	
2583	2.43	2.2	1.24	sub-circular	Vertical sides (undercut towards base) and flat base	8								
2592	1.31	1.18	>1.0	sub-circular	Vertical sides (undercut) base not seen	3							Flint; worked bone tool from fill 2594	

Feature Number	Length	Width	Depth	Plan shape	Profile shape	No of fills	Stone dumps	Pottery	Animal bone and ABGs	Human remains	Charcoal	Metal	Other	Comment
2600	1.04	0.98	0.29	sub-circular	Vertical sides (undercut) and flat base	1								
2630	1.46	1.18	0.34	Sub-circular	Vertical sides (undercut) and flat base	2								
2669	1.16	1.12	0.46	Circular	Vertical sides (undercut) and uneven base	4		Near complete saucepan pot (Ra. 1077) from fill 2627 Middle Iron Age						
2674	1.68	1.63	0.53	Circular	Vertical sides and flat base	3								
2682	1.51		0.42	Circular	Vertical sides and flat base	1								
2689	1.9		1.1	Circular	Vertical sides (undercut) base unseen	5	Chalk and sarsens up to 450mm on base of pit, similar in a later fill							
2693	1.72		>1.0	Circular	Vertical sides (undercut) base unseen	3								
2697	1.2	1.18	0.5	Circular	Vertical sides (undercut) and flat base	5								
2737	1.54	1.4	1.08	sub-circular	Vertical/stepped sides and flat base	6					Several fills with frequent charcoal		Flint	
2738					Combined with 2737									
2748	1.11		0.67	Circular	Vertical sides and flat base	5	Burnt chalk deposit on pit base							
2763	0.9		0.28	Circular	Vertical sides and flat base	3								
2775	0.98		0.53	Circular	Vertical sides (undercut) and uneven base	5		Middle Iron Age sherds						
2783	1.64		0.45	Circular	Vertical sides (undercut) and uneven base	3								
2790	1.14		0.85	Circular	Vertical sides and flat base	3							Flint	
2799	1	0.93	0.52	sub-circular	Vertical sides (undercut) and uneven base	3							Flint	
2809	1.4	>1.15	0.48	sub-circular	Vertical sides (undercut) and flat base	4								

Feature Number	Length	Width	Depth	Plan shape	Profile shape	No of fills	Stone dumps	Pottery	Animal bone and ABGs	Human remains	Charcoal	Metal	Other	Comment
2831	0.88		0.23	Circular	Vertical sides (undercut) and flat base	1							Flint	
2835	1.37		0.75	Circular	Vertical sides (undercut) and flat base	3								
2838	1.4		0.77	Circular	Vertical sides and concave base	4								
2844	2.5	2.5	1.04	Circular	Vertical sides base not seen	7			2845 initial deposit, articulated cattle foot ABG					
2852	1.48	1.3	0.82	sub-circular	Vertical sides (undercut) and flat base	5	Initial fill chalk rubble and sarsens up to 450mm							
2882	1.15	1.09	0.49	sub-circular	Vertical sides (undercut) and flat base	5								
2890	1.38		0.84	Circular	Vertical sides (undercut) and flat base	3	Chalk blocks in all fills							
2896	0.8	0.78	0.6	Circular	Vertical sides (undercut) and flat base	2								
2900	1.57	1.48	1.13	sub-circular	Vertical sides and flat base	4								
2908	1.54		1.11	Circular	Vertical sides and flat base	7								
2928	1.5	1.45	0.55	Circular	Vertical sides and flat base	7								
2938	1.35	1.33	0.73	Circular	Vertical sides (undercut) and flat base	4	Chalk blocks in 2940				In fill 2940		Flint, griding stone in fill 2940	
2951	1.44	1.3	0.68	sub-circular	Vertical sides and flat base	5								
2991	1.44	1.38	0.5	Circular	Vertical sides and flat base	5		Middle to Late Iron Age sherds			Charcoal lens initial fill3006			
2999	1.12		0.3	Circular	Vertical sides and flat base	2							Flint	
3002	0.4	0.4	0.14	Circular	Not fully excavated	1								
3017	1.2	1.03	0.62	Sub-circular	Vertical sides (undercut) and flat base	3					Two charcoal rich fills initial and second fills 3018 and 3019			
3028	1.57	1.42	0.62	Sub-circular	Vertical sides and flat base	4								
3048	1.77	1.5	0.78	Sub-circular	Vertical sides and flat base	3		Decorated late Middle to Late Iron Age sherd						

Feature Number	Length	Width	Depth	Plan shape	Profile shape	No of fills	Stone dumps	Pottery	Animal bone and ABGs	Human remains	Charcoal	Metal	Other	Comment
3052	1.06	0.88	0.98	Sub-circular	Vertical sides and flat base	4	Chalk blocks in second fill on one side of pit							
3061	1.18	0.96	0.28	sub-circular	Concave sides to flat base	1								
3068	1.51	1.2	0.97	sub-circular	Vertical sides (undercut) and flat base	6			Cattle skull				Bone awl from fill 3062, a manuport of marcasite from fill 3064	
3080	1.29	1.23	0.5	Circular	Vertical sides (undercut) and flat base	2								
3083	1.38	0.99	0.58	sub-circular	Vertical sides (undercut) and flat base	4						In second fill 3086	Fired clay spindlewhorl (Ra. 1096) from fill 3086	
3088	1.27	0.78	0.63	Oval	Vertical sides (undercut) and flat base	1								
3101	1.4	1.26	0.5	Sub-circular	Vertical sides and flat base	3								
3113	1.05	0.47	0.36	Oval	Vertical sides and flat base	3			Dog skull in upper fill					
3141	0.9	0.89	0.27	Circular	Vertical sides and uneven base	1								
3143	1.36	1.35	0.41	Circular	Vertical sides and uneven base	1								
3145	1.8	1.5	0.48	sub-circular	Irregular sides to flat base	4		Late Iron Age sherds						
3150	0.93	0.89	0.62	Circular	Concave sides and uneven base	2			Horse hind limb ABG in 3151					
3164	0.83		0.7	Circular	Vertical sides (undercut) and flat base	3								
3198	1	0.6	0.5	Oval	Vertical sides and flat base	4								
3220	1.4	1.3	0.45	sub-circular	Vertical sides and flat base	2								
3228	1		0.51		Vertical sides (undercut) and flat base	1							Flint	
3230	0.9		0.58	Circular	Vertical sides and flat base	4								
3263	1	0.9	0.34	sub-circular	Vertical sides and flat base	1								
6005	1.05	0.88	0.25	Sub-Oval	Moderately sloping/concave sides and uneven base	1								
6015	1.25	1.10	0.53	Sub-Circular	Moderately sloping/concave sides and flat base	4								

Feature Number	Length	Width	Depth	Plan shape	Profile shape	No of fills	Stone dumps	Pottery	Animal bone and ABGs	Human remains	Charcoal	Metal	Other	Comment
6018	1.31	1.10	0.53	Sub-Circular	Steeply sloping/concave sides and flat base	2								
6022	1.26	1.05	1.67	Sub-Circular	Steeply sloping/concave sides and flat base	3								
6024	1.53	0.76	0.10	Sub-Circular	Gently sloping/concave sides and uneven base	1								
6026	1.19	1.15	0.06	Sub-Circular	Gently sloping/concave sides and uneven base	1								
6030		1.45	0.61	Sub-Circular	Steeply sloping/concave sides and uneven base	3			Dog ABG in 6035			Bladed iron implement from fill 6028		
6032	>0.78	1.60	0.11	Sub-Circular	Moderately sloping/concave sides and uneven base	1								
6034	1.10	1.02	0.17	Sub-Circular	Moderately sloping/concave sides and uneven base	1								
6052	1.46	0.90	0.43	Rectangular	Steeply sloping/concave sides and uneven base	1								
6057	1.21	1.08	0.61	Circular	Steeply sloping/concave sides and uneven base	2								
7012	1.14	1.3	0.14	Circular	Straight sides and flat base	1		Decorated late Middle to Late Iron Age sherd Late Iron Age sherds						
8006	1.01	0.91	0.38	Oval	Steep sides and flat base	2								
8009	1.22	0.90	0.31	Oval	Steep sides and flat base	2								
8012	0.87	0.70	0.32	Oval	Near vertical sides and flat base	2								
8015	0.68	0.56	0.20	Oval	Moderately sloping sides and flat base	2								
8018	0.94	0.82	0.30	Sub-Circular	Steep straight sides and flat base	2								
8021	0.67	0.71	0.25	Sub-Circular	Straight sides and flat base	1								
8023	0.56	0.65	0.33	Sub-Circular	Straight sharp sides and flat base	2								
8026	0.69	0.70	0.51	Sub-Circular	Steeply sloping sides and rounded base	2								
8031	0.85	0.80	0.33	Sub-Circular	Gently sloping/convex sides and flat base	2								
8044	0.82	0.80	0.37	Sub-Circular	Steep straight sides and flat base	2								

Feature Number	Length	Width	Depth	Plan shape	Profile shape	No of fills	Stone dumps	Pottery	Animal bone and ABGs	Human remains	Charcoal	Metal	Other	Comment
8048	0.91	0.80	0.31	Sub-Circular	Steeply sloping/concave sides and flat base	2								
8063	0.90	0.84	0.31	Circular	Concave sides and flat base	2								
8068	2.00	1.60	1.10	Sub-Circular	Steep sides slightly undercut and flat base	6	Sarsen in fill 8069 capping SK 8071			SK 8071 within pit	In base 8098, and higher in pit		Bone pins (Ras.1204 and 1205) from fill 8070; disc-shaped weights (Ras. 1208 and 1209) and spindlewhorl-loomweight (Ra. 1225) from fill 8070 grain rubber (Ra. 1200)	
8083	0.60	0.59	0.20	Circular	Steep sides, flat base	3								
8087	0.60	0.60	0.59	Circular	Near vertical sides and flat base	2								
8090	0.96	0.96	0.31	Circular	Steep sides and flat base	1								
8092	0.70	0.69	0.31	Circular	Moderately steep sides and flat base	2								
8100	0.85	0.81	0.38	Sub-Circular	Straight sides and flat base	1								
8102	1.40	1.29	0.75	Sub-Circular	Straight very steep sides and flat base	6								
8113	1.07	1.11	0.32	Circular	Near vertical sides and flat base	1		Late Iron Age sherds	ABG in 8114					
8115	0.65	0.65	0.44	Circular	Near vertical sides and uneven base	2								
8118	1.90	1.72	1.25	Circular	Near vertical sides and flat base	4		Largely complete slack-shouldered jar (Ra. 1214)	ABG in 8122 Remains of 4 puppies, a cattle skeleton, and several disarticulated skeletons of micro-mammals and frogs/toads				Thumbnail scraper, nine weights from fill 8122, including Ras 1223, 1213, and 1222	

Feature Number	Length	Width	Depth	Plan shape	Profile shape	No of fills	Stone dumps	Pottery	Animal bone and ABGs	Human remains	Charcoal	Metal	Other	Comment
9009	1.53	0.57	0.59	Circular	Steep/concave sides and flat base	4		Early Iron Age sherd Middle Iron Age sherds Late Iron Age sherds			In second fil 9010		Disc-shaped weights (Ras. 1202 and 1203) from fill 9010 A clipped pottery base with single central perforation (Ra. 1206), adapted for use presumably as a spindlewhorl	
9013	0.90	0.71	0.46	Circular	Steep/straight sides and flat base	2								
9019	0.70	0.68	0.45	Circular	Concave sides and concave base	2								
9025	0.58	0.57	0.30	Circular	Steep/concave sides and flat base	2								
9029	2.50	1.38	0.31	Oval	Steep sides and uneven base	1								
9066	1.00	0.5 to 1.0E	0.43	Sub-Circular	Straight sides and flat base	3								
9070	0.50	0.76	0.14	Sub-Circular	Moderate/concave sides and rounded base	1								
9072	0.49	0.84	0.24	Sub-Circular	Straight/undercut sides and flat base	1								
9074	1.22	1.10	0.57	Sub-Circular		3								
9078		1.75	0.60	Sub-Circular	Concave sides and flat base	2								
9124	0.92	1.02	0.21	Sub-Oval	Concave sides and flat base	1								
9150	0.93	0.99	0.24	Circular	Near vertical sides and uneven base	1								

Index

by Nicola King

Numbers in *italic* denote pages with figures, those in **bold** denote pages with tables

www.ingramcontent.com/pod-product-compliance
Ingram Content Group UK Ltd.
Pitfield, Milton Keynes, MK11 3LW, UK
UKHW061330260426
470335UK00008B/47